Personal Selling in a Modern Perspective

MARKETING SCIENCE INSTITUTE
SERIES OF BOOKS

PUBLISHED WITH ALLYN AND BACON, INC.

Brand Policy Determination (1967)
Comparative Analysis for International Marketing (1967)
Experiments on the Value of Information in Simulated Marketing
    Environments (1967)
Industrial Buying and Creative Marketing (1967)
Personal Selling in a Modern Perspective (1967)
Promotional Decisions Using Mathematical Models (1967)

OTHER PUBLICATIONS

Marketing Development in the European Economic Community (1964)
Promotional Decision Making: Practice and Theory (1964)
The Meaning and Sources of Marketing Theory (1965)
Marketing Education in the United States (1964)

MARKETING SCIENCE INSTITUTE

3401 Market Street

Philadelphia, Pa.   19104

THE MARKETING SCIENCE INSTITUTE was established in 1962 in Philadelphia for the purpose of conducting the kinds of basic research that would serve to advance the productivity and efficiency of marketing. The Institute's research and educational activity is designed to (1) contribute to the emergence of a science of marketing, and (2) stimulate increased application of scientific techniques to the understanding and solving of marketing problems.

Financial support for MSI is provided by leading business firms. In addition, the personnel of these firms contribute generously of their time and ability as members of MSI committees and study groups, and as advisors and consultants on MSI research projects and reports.

All research reports and findings of the Marketing Science Institute are made generally available through publication. In compliance with MSI policy, publication of this report has been approved by a majority of the Board of Trustees.

MARKETING SCIENCE INSTITUTE

PERSONAL SELLING
IN A MODERN PERSPECTIVE

PATRICK J. ROBINSON
Director of Management Studies
Marketing Science Institute

BENT STIDSEN
Senior Research Assistant
Marketing Science Institute

Allyn and Bacon, Inc.
Boston

Preface

MOST WRITERS on personal selling are in one of two groups. In the first group are advocates of "how-to-sell" principles. In the second group are those concerned with "making salesmen sell" or "how to manage salesmen."

Very few writers take an overview of the *total* organizational process of selling. To many writers and speakers, salesmen are robots who can be "selected," "screened," "motivated," and "fired up," while customers are enemy forces facing the "firing line" waiting to be "knocked dead" or to meet some other violent end.

SCOPE OF THE PERSONAL SELLING FUNCTION

The word "salesman" usually is reserved for individuals engaged in *direct* negotiations or transactions with buyers, whether the salesman visits the buyer (industrial and door to door salesman) or the buyer seeks out the salesman (retail salesman). Salesmen are the people whose sole job it is to deal directly with the customers for various products and services.

But what about other occupational categories? Is the waiter in a restaurant a salesman? Is the bus-driver a salesman? What about the airline stewardess? The train conductor? The office receptionist? Is the behavior of the floor salesman in a department store more important to the store's image than that of the delivery-man?

The point is that personal selling does not begin and end with the sales or marketing department. Personal selling is not a limited set of specifiable activities, but is *the entire set of personal contacts made by individuals on behalf of a selling organization.* In its broadest sense, personal selling is *interpersonal communication* (intended or unintended) that influences (positively or negatively) the economic performance of an enterprise.

Is it possible to choose from the population a certain segment which by definition makes good public contacts? The answer is not as clearcut as might appear from the literature on selection techniques. Obviously it is possible to set up certain screens to eliminate the more glaring instances of physical and psychological incapacity. But beyond this, it is by no means clear that available selection techniques provide much more than an illusion of "objectivity."

Imposition of rules and regulations may well be necessary for purposes of coordination, *but never for the purposes of "making" people behave in some specified situation.* That is not, of course, to say that everyone "knows" how to sell; but the remedy is training and not authoritarianism.

Some of the broad conclusions with reference to personal selling that might be derived from the modern behavioral sciences are:

1. The highly competent salesman does *not necessarily have a specifiable set of personality traits* in some regular fashion.
2. The salesman's perception and feeling of function and status are *closely related to the perceived rewards and constraints imposed by his firm.*
3. *A salesman's behavior evolves over time,* in keeping with perceived requirements of his environment.
4. It is his *motivation and competence which "make" an individual salesman behave in certain ways,* more than externally imposed rules and regulations.
5. The role of managerial and supervisory functions is to *facilitate individual performance,* and not to dictate or determine it.

ACKNOWLEDGMENTS

Acknowledgments are due a number of individuals who contributed substantially to the concepts and evolution of this study.

Dr. Russell L. Ackoff, Director of the Management Science Center, Dr. Paul E. Green, Professor of Marketing, and Dr. Peter T. FitzRoy, Assistant Professor of Marketing—all of the University of Pennsylvania—collaborated in a penetrating review of Operations Research studies, discussed in Chapters III and IV.

Mr. J. Shaffer, Consulting Market Analyst, New York, contributed significantly to the development of the COMPACT system of action and competence contained in Part Three.

Thanks are also due several men whose counsel was helpful at various stages of the present project: Dr. Lee Thayer, Professor and Director of the Center for the Advanced Study of

Communication, University of Missouri at Kansas City; Dr. William S. Peters, Professor of Business Administration, Arizona State University; Dr. J. Sayer Minas, Dean of Graduate Studies, Professor of Psychology and Management Science, and Chairman of the Department of Philosophy at the University of Waterloo, Waterloo, Ontario; and Dr. Charles L. Hinkle, Professor of Business Administration, University of Colorado, Colorado Springs.

In addition, each of the following reviewed the final manuscript in detail: Dr. W. J. E. Crissy, Associate Dean of the Graduate School of Business Administration at Michigan State University; Franklin J. Cornwell, Vice President of Monsanto Company; Dr. Charles S. Goodman, Professor of Marketing, University of Pennsylvania; and Herbert H. McDade, Director of Planning and Promotion of The Upjohn Company.

The authors' appreciation is extended also to the participants in the two executive seminars held at Princeton in early 1965; to the sponsor and member company executives who made themselves available for extensive telephone interviewing; and to the members of the Research Policy Committee who helped to improve the present manuscript.

Finally, recognition is due Mrs. Elaine Free and Mrs. Patricia Coffey, who collaborated in editing the final material for publication.

PATRICK J. ROBINSON
BENT STIDSEN

Contents

PART FIVE: IN SUMMARY

Highlights
of This Book

THIS BOOK is aimed at "putting the sales manager back into business." As opposed to restricting, mechanizing, or removing his responsibilities and "expertise," the emphasis here is on reinforcing and amplifying his seasoned judgments and relevant experiences through fresh perspectives.

The authors of this book deal in a serious but readable fashion with some of the important problems of personal selling. They view the persuasion process, between salesman and prospect, from the vantage point of modern communication theory; and some of the tools of the behavioral sciences are utilized.

Cases on the impact and the role of personal selling are analyzed in terms of operations research. Although mathematical models are developed, the management and research problems are presented without equations and elaborate charts.

For the prospective reader who might ask, "What's in it for me?" here are some highlights of the book:

1. *Personal Selling differs from nonpersonal selling in both obvious and subtle ways.*
   Recognition of personal selling's unique potential can help in promoting sales.
2. *Mathematical models of personal-selling expenditures versus results can be constructed, but still have limitations.*
   Their chief drawback centers on the critical assumptions which sales management must make (or at least be prepared to live with), in order for these models to provide practical guides to improved efficiency.
3. *Selling competence is an attribute frequently viewed as a vague term or an elusive goal.*
   The concept of selling competence can be used to focus judgment and experience on observed performance.
4. *A set of guidelines has been assembled in a conceptual*

model of sales competence and activities—the word is COMPACT, from competence and activities.

Any thoughtful businessman who has experienced the rewards and frustrations involved in the process of personal selling, will be intrigued with the discussion of this concept.

5. *The sales manager who understands the COMPACT model probably will make use of this when thinking of seller behavior or buyer behavior.*

COMPACT can be a compelling and flexible tool in the hands of a resourceful administrator or consultant.

6. *The COMPACT reference framework or matrix provides a standardized format for classifying and comparing observed activities of sales people.*

It is *not* a computer model or an accounting model. COMPACT is simply a methodical approach, taking into account the kinds of activities people perform and the relative dexterity and level of competence which they bring to bear in performing their tasks.

7. *The diagnostic value of COMPACT is a guide to improving selling operations.*

Everyone is familiar with such common expressions as "talking over someone's head," "talking down to someone," "insulting a person's intelligence," or "being on a different wave length," and thus being unable to achieve a "meeting of minds." These expressions describe situations that can be identified, diagnosed, and corrected using the COMPACT method of analysis.

8. *The analysis of selling tasks, selling behavior and the basic process of persuasion between sellers and buyers is a first step to more effective selection, training, organization, and compensation of a salesman.*

This in turn helps to identify those tasks for which nonpersonal selling can prove more efficient than at present, with COMPACT the key to this analysis.

The book is organized into five parts.

Part One presents the highlights of an extensive search and evaluation of the literature on personal selling. It becomes obvious that personal selling has been and is being considered from an almost *infinite* variety of viewpoints.

Part Two deals with some approaches to quantitative analysis of personal-selling operations. The concept of marginal analysis—of relationships of input (cost) and of output (revenue) is examined and applied. Three examples of studies of personal selling operations are described in some detail. The conclusions of the authors are also presented, derived from interviews conducted with sponsor and member companies.

Part Three is devoted to a presentation and explanation of the

Competence-Activity (COMPACT) Model. The role of personal selling in marketing is clarified.

The purpose of Part Four is to explore some of the implications of the previous concepts. Thus, the process of selling—as well as the process of selection, training, compensation, information requirements, and organizational control—are discussed, and with numerous insights and suggestions.

Part Five summarizes the essential aspects of the book, and relates these to a prospectus for future development.

STEUART HENDERSON BRITT
Editorial Director,
Marketing Science Institute

PART ONE

The New Role
of Personal Selling

I

The Objectives

ONE OF THE OUTCOMES of an earlier MSI study published under the title: *Promotional Decision Making: Practice and Theory*[1] was a list of possible areas for further research. The item on tnat list to which the present study traces its origin suggested a need "to establish guidelines for sales force allocation, with special emphasis on fitting men to markets, and gearing performance to tasks as part of the promotional mix."[2] In keeping with this statement the purpose of this book is to report on the results of a study of the personal selling function and it thus represents a further step by the Marketing Science Institute toward the development of a coherent scientific approach to the allocation and management of the various elements of the marketing mix.

OBJECTIVES

In a broad sense, this is a book about communication in marketing with specific reference to personal selling. It is an attempt to provide a concept of communication which is instrumental to the furthering of an understanding of the problems of personal selling from the point of view of marketing and sales *managers.* More specifically the objectives of the book may be outlined as follows:

1. To provide an indication of the state of the art in personal selling "literature" as well as to identify possible sources of a theory of personal selling.
2. To report on the methods and results of a number of experimental studies of the effectiveness of the personal selling functions.
3. To report on the development of a functional model of the marketing and personal selling environment.
4. To provide a contribution to the development of a theory of

marketing communication with specific reference to personal selling.
5. To explore some of the implications of such a theory for the management and execution of personal selling efforts.

The analysis draws upon a selection of the theories and research findings which the authors consider relevant to the development of a marketing oriented concept of personal selling. Attempts have thus been made to combine empirical observations and theoretical frameworks for the purpose of identifying and describing some fundamental aspects, processes, and activities inherent in, and peculiar to, marketing and personal selling.

PROSPECTIVE AUDIENCE

Salesmanship, or more generally interpersonal communication is an all pervasive requirement in human affairs, and it is of crucial importance that the student of business (and any other student for that matter) be given an opportunity to examine some of the problems involved. It is hoped that some of the ideas presented here will prove challenging to both teachers and students of salesmanship in the widest possible sense.

The report is recommended to the experienced marketing manager, sales manager, sales trainer, or salesman who is concerned with the problem of selling and communication, and who is prepared to seek new perspectives or reasoned support for his own insights. Even disagreement with the tenets of the book may help the reader develop a clearer formulation of his own notions. The sales trainer may find it helpful in the design of training programs since it provides some organization of the myriad of concepts, theories, and observational data surrounding the personal selling function. However, few definitive answers are provided in this volume *primarily because interpersonal communication is an intensely individual activity which is not necessarily facilitated by memorizing a few rules.* Even if the book only results in a clarification of this last point it will have served a useful purpose.

BACKGROUND OF THE STUDY

At the outset of the study a number of executive seminars were held with participants from both the business and academic world to obtain some understanding of the nature of the subject. In addition to struggling for a clearcut definition of personal selling, the participants had some difficulty determining what salesmen do, or to put it differently, what difference the efforts of a salesman make. As it turned out, these definitional problems were not limited to the participants of the seminars, but were encountered in later interviews with sales and marketing executives. To give an impression of the scope of the activity as perceived by the seminar participants a few excerpts from the discussion follow. These excerpts are edited for the sake of brevity but otherwise reflect the opinion of the speakers.

Personal selling has as its purpose communications. Whether it is communicating about a service or about a product, personal selling activity results from a need to communicate something which can be communicated. One just cannot sit down and write out something and anticipate every question that somebody is going to ask. Somebody must be there to feel the thing. . . .

There are three categories of marketing activities: advertising, sales promotion and personal selling. One could interpret this classification as all encompassing, and that somewhere within those three elements fall all the activities involved in marketing. This seems to omit product however, as a very important element of marketing, that is, the product qualities and the status of the product with respect to whatever it is competing with can have a very profound influence on all these other things. . . .

Personal selling is at least two things. 1. The word "selling" means the ultimate exchange of the merchandise for a cash consideration. It does not mean persuasion; it does not mean advertising. Selling is the end product of the whole business, because if that is not carried out, the business shuts up. "Personal Selling" must be an assignment which, by its very nature, is different from "Selling" as such, because that is the main objective of the entire business. 2. Personal selling is never automatic. In the case of consumer goods, few people buy these from a salesman. So, obviously, he does not sell it. Mostly a consumer good is not sold, it is bought. But it cannot be bought if it is not available in distribution; and if it is not given a reasonable degree of promotion. But none of the specific activities involved can be accurately described by the word selling. What about personal persuasion? The word selling does not mean persuasion. Personal persuasion may play a very important part in the activity of the sales department, but it is the technique or part of the technique by which the sales department accomplishes its specific objective, which is to get the merchandise out. In the case of consumer goods, it starts with getting it out where people can buy it; and half-dozen more related objectives can be added to that in order to establish a complex, but highly specific, assignment that the sales department must execute as a primary contribution to the end product which is selling. . . .

What about servicing? The work of the field force is, in large part, devoted to servicing customers. How could that be excluded from the term, personal selling? And yet, it is strictly a service function, that is, the means by which the assignment by keeping products in distribution effectively is carried out.

It is evident from these excerpts that a good deal of conceptual confusion exists about personal selling. E.B. Weiss further pursues this point in his book *The Vanishing Salesman* where he draws the following general conclusions:

1. Personal selling of presold mass-consumed lines and industrial goods is partly "traditional" selling and partly a newer function.
2. The newer functions are becoming more important and the traditional selling functions are shrinking.

3. Buying committees of giant distributors have altered traditional communication patterns between buyers and sellers.
4. Salesman selection, training and compensation is too often
   based on a wrong conception of the selling function.
5. Direct account relationships with giant buyers account for
   an increasing share of volume, and the regular salesman is
   seldom involved in direct account negotiations.

Interpretations of these conclusions have ranged widely depending upon the emotional involvement of the interpreter. From a research point of view, however, the conclusions suggest the following question: What are the significant strengths and weaknesses of
personal selling which differentiate it from other types of marketing activities? An answer to this question, developed in terms of
a concept of the marketing environment, should provide a much
needed basis for a more exact determination of the role of personal
selling in the marketing mix.

APPROACHES TO THE STUDY

The initial approach to this study of the role of personal selling
in the marketing mix comprised a search of the relevant "literature." While a great deal of writing has been done on the subject,
there are few concepts available which appear relevant to the
question of what role or function personal selling and the salesman play vis-à-vis the marketing environment. Consequently the
seminars, mentioned previously, were supplemented by individual
interviews of sales and marketing executives.

Concurrently, a second approach was initiated for the Marketing Science Institute by a team of researchers under the direction
of Dr. Russell L. Ackoff (Director of the Management Science
Center, University of Pennsylvania). This team conducted a
search of some seven years of accumulated operations research
studies from their previous experience at the Case Institute of
Technology, as well as an extensive search of the professional
literature. Some interesting experiments were unearthed, which
illustrate the usefulness of experimentation as a means of establishing some measure of the effectiveness of personal selling.

A third approach centered on an extended search and discussion
of available concepts and research evidence in the behavioral
sciences and economics. These efforts led to the evolution of the
"system of action" or COMPACT model which is explained in
greater detail in subsequent chapters. Developments in the field
of communications research also produced a useful contribution
to the study.

Material from all four approaches is included in this book. The
primary emphasis, however, is on the development of behavioral

framework which, while yet wanting in empirical verification, provides a step in the direction of a development of a theory of personal selling as an element of marketing, and, ultimately, as an element of all business activities.

ORGANIZATION OF THE BOOK

The report is divided into five parts, each of which differs from the other either in the method or conceptual level of the analysis presented. *Part One* constitutes an introduction to the subject of personal selling. *Part Two* consists of a description of the methods and results of three experimental studies of the personal selling function. *Part Three* presents a general structural-functional model which is developed and applied to both the selling and the corresponding buying functions. The presentation of the structural model is interwoven with a discussion of the nature and problems of interpersonal communications. *Part Four* presents a discussion of the application of the model described in Part Three, with reference to both the management and execution of the personal selling effort. *Part Five* contains a summary and a prospectus for future research as well as a glossary of terms and a selected bibliography.

Naturally, different readers will find different parts of the report more interesting or pertinent than others. Part Two, for example, dealing with quantitative methods and experimentation, can be read and studied separately without too much difficulty. The reader who has little interest in the quantitatively oriented operations research approach to problem solving may find a more natural connection between Parts One and Three. The busy sales manager, may find it desirable to concentrate on Part Four although most of the concepts applied therein are explained at greater length in Part Three. Summaries have been placed at the end of each chapter to facilitate the study of areas of particular interest to individual readers.

An Up-to-date View
of Personal Selling

SALES OCCUR for many and diverse reasons, not all of which are traceable to the efforts of marketers. Certainly marketing activities are instrumental in facilitating economic exchange, but the final outcome – sales – are necessarily codetermined by the objectives and activities of both buyers and marketers. Thus the first problem to be addressed is that of conceptualizing the relationship between buyers and sellers from an intercommunication point of view. At the base of the ability of these two groups to communicate with each other are the commonalities of concepts, objectives and language which arise from their common membership in the same or similar social groups. It follows that the process of communication between buyers and sellers must be analyzed within the context of these commonalities. The specific problem here is not to determine who causes whom to do what, but rather to determine the role to be played by personal selling in furthering the common objectives of sellers and buyers.

Quite apart from the problems involved in managing and performing the personal selling function, it is necessary to develop some understanding of the unique characteristics of face-to-face interaction versus those of mass communication. Clearly, the effectiveness of personal selling is at least partly a function of the degree to which the potential capacities of individual salesmen are employed. This brings up the problem of determining the extent of the potential capacities of individual salesmen and relating these to the overall objectives of the company by means of organizational control and effective management.

The essential perspectives explored in this study are thus:

1. The general nature of the relationship between buyers and sellers within the context of the social and economic environment.
2. The role of marketing and marketing management in the

context of the information requirements of both buyers and sellers.

3. The nature of personal selling and the differentiating characteristics of personal and nonpersonal selling.

4. The organization and management of personal selling in the context of its role in creating a relationship between buyers and sellers.

5. The nature and role of individual competence in the context of the nature of the potential relationship between buyers and sellers.

Each of these perspectives constitutes a level of analysis distinguishable from each of the others on the basis of the scope and content of the variables involved in the analysis. The basic assumption underlying and common to all of these perspectives is that the purpose of marketing is essentially that of establishing and maintaining a communicative relationship between buyers and sellers. Consequently, the roles of marketing and personal selling must be related to—among other things—the nature of the social and economic environment in which buyers and sellers exist and interact.

The reasons for adopting perspectives as broad as those outlined above are:

1. to avoid emphasizing any one aspect of the marketing and personal selling function at the cost of neglecting other important aspects; and

2. to facilitate the development of a conceptual model capable of discriminating between problem areas involving individual competence and effectiveness versus problem areas involving organizational effectiveness.

For example, the manufacturer who finds himself unable to sell an obsolete product is not likely to be able to solve his problem by means of new and better training techniques aimed at improving his salesmen's performance. The most important step toward the solution of a given problem is an identification of the level at which the problem exists, followed by an application of remedial action relevant at that level.

A more specific definition of what constitutes personal selling must necessarily be related to a definition of a larger and more inclusive marketing function. While it appears to be generally accepted that personal selling is an integral part of marketing, few attempts have been made to develop and operationalize a concept of the significant variables in this interrelationship. In the following pages a broad definition of marketing and the marketing mix will be presented and in subsequent sections the available literature on personal selling will be classified and examined briefly in the light of these definitions.

A DEFINITION OF MARKETING

The popularity of the marketing concept would seem to indicate that it is generally accepted that a business organization should maintain a market orientation in all its activities. That in itself is not, however, a very profound or revolutionary development. There is a tacit assumption in much of the marketing literature that the influence process involved is a one-way phenomenon initiated by the marketer. Such an assumption is based on an insufficient concept of the marketing environment. With or without a marketing concept, there is no necessary reason why marketers should be assumed to influence buyers more than buyers influence marketers.

Marketing *has* been defined by several writers as a two-way process; even so, it is often represented as a process of information search and information dissemination *by marketers.* If, in contrast, one were to imagine a theory of marketing developed by customers, the exact opposite concept would presumably result. Since both buyers and sellers are engaged in active search for information and contacts, a concept of marketing pertaining to the activities of either sellers or buyers, but not both, would be a highly unsatisfactory base upon which to develop a theory of marketing, and, more specifically, a theory of personal selling. Without a concept of marketing which is broad enough to include the activities of both buyers and sellers, a distorted view of the importance of any given activity is likely to obtain.

In the context of the present study, marketing is considered from the point of view of a process designed *to create, modify, exploit or maintain a communicative relationship between utility producing and utility consuming entities (individuals or organizations) of a social system.*[1]

This definition does not label any specific activity as a necessary aspect of marketing. It is limited neither to any specific set of theories, be they economic, or behavioral, nor to any specific type of analysis such as functional, institutional, or geographical.

The essential elements of the above definition may be represented schematically as follows:

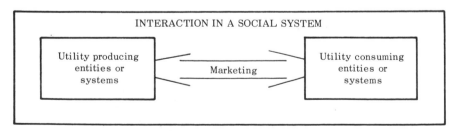

Utility producing entities include both manufacturers and middlemen, while utility consuming entities include both intermediate and final customers. This formulation puts middlemen, such as the secondary manufacturer, the wholesaler and the retailer, in both camps. In reality, the middleman is well aware of his dual commitment, as indicated by the many attempts to integrate vertically by both manufacturers and middlemen.

The link or relationship between producing and consuming entities constitutes marketing. In this sense marketing is not limited to activities performed by the producing entities, but includes also the search or shopping behavior of consuming entities. The perspective adopted here is somewhat different from and perhaps broader than that generally encountered in marketing literature. The essential point is that while *buying behavior* and *selling behavior* are necessary fundamentals for a theory of marketing, it is the understanding and improvement of the *relationship*—whether short run or continuing—between the two groups which is crucial to such a theory.

While marketing efforts of both producers and users are aimed at bridging the *differences* in their intentions and goals, there are also important *similarities* of intuitions and goals, or commonalities, between them resulting from the process of socialization of individuals. Because of these similarities and differences in individuals within a society the general market for economic products is neither completely homogeneous, in the sense that it is devoid of individualistic behavior, nor is it completely heterogeneous, in the sense that all buying and selling behavior is idiosyncratic.[2] Even within the context of the same product, such as vacuum cleaners or cosmetics, marketers' activities based on both homogeneity (preferential use of mass communication) and heterogeneity (preferential use of personal selling) have led to apparently successful results.

Each of the various groups of individuals within a social system has its own particular concept or general set of concepts of a given product, both as an object by itself and with reference to its use. The nature of these varying concepts and the number and characteristics of individuals in each of the different groups is of crucial importance to the development of an effective and efficient marketing mix.

THE CONCEPT OF A MARKETING MIX

The concept of a marketing or promotional mix is derived from the economic notion of using alternative combinations of variable productive factors to produce a specified output at some optimum level of cost. The output or product can result, for example, from a combination of high labor and low capital inputs, or from a combination of low labor and high capital inputs. Similarly, promotional expenditures (inputs) have been divided alternatively between personal and nonpersonal media according to a variety of pre-determined ratios. In the context of the total marketing concept, the marketing mix has, of course, been expanded to include such elements as product development, market research, merchandising, point of purchase promotion and other marketing-related activities.

The traditional concept of the marketing mix thus, in accordance with its economic antecedent, the production function, tends to emphasize the more readily measurable input elements (dollars) rather than the more qualitative outputs (usefulness of the data or messages to the buyer). The important question, however, to be faced in the selection of a given marketing mix is not only *how much* for advertising or personal selling (although that is ultimately a necessary concern) but also what are the relevant messages and which media can best deliver them. The immediate problem becomes one of what has to be accomplished rather than how to do it.

A given marketing mix, then, is a set of activities, chosen from many such available sets, designed to establish, modify, exploit or maintain existing or implicit commonalities between a *producing entity and one or more consuming entities or systems, with reference to a given product or product class.*

Clearly the number of alternative mixes is enormous, and it is at present impossible to handle the allocation problem quantitatively, mainly because of inadequate measurements and insufficient methodology. In many respects the concept of a marketing mix is similar to that represented in a chemical formula. Changes within, additions to, and subtractions from a given chemical formula can produce widely varying effects, a phenomenon known as interaction or "synergism" in the jargon of both the chemist and the biologist. In the context of marketing, the effect of a change in the level of personal selling expenditures (inputs) itself depends on the existing level of nonpersonal selling effort. The problem of optimizing over the entire range of possible levels of all elements in the mix is exceedingly difficult without some prior assumptions about the dynamics of the relationship between producer and consumers. These assumptions are not a part of the economist's productive factor allocation model and must, therefore, be derived from an understanding of the dynamics of the relationship between producers and consumers. More specifically, a better understanding must be developed with respect to the processes involved in "communicating," "persuading," "influencing" and "selling."

PERSONAL SELLING–A DEFINITION

The increasing importance of nonpersonal promotional tools has contributed to a curious neglect of personal selling in modern marketing. In both practice and theory, advertising or mass communication has received far more attention than personal selling or interpersonal communication.

Traditionally, personal selling has not been regarded as a part of a broader marketing concept. For example, in 1925 Harry R. Tosdal defined salesmanship as follows:

Salesmanship is the art exercised by the seller of effecting economic exchanges.[3]

At a somewhat later date Paul W. Ivey defines salesmanship this way:

Salesmanship is producing values in people's minds, persuading customers to see your viewpoint, appreciating merchandise so much yourself that you can make other people appreciate it.[4]

By contrast, the following definition of personal selling, contributed by the American Marketing Association in its 1965 edition of the *Marketing Handbook,* does indeed differentiate clearly between interpersonal and mass communication:

Personal selling is oral presentation in a conversation with one or more prospective purchasers for the purpose of making sales.[5]

The implicit limitations, however, connoted by the words "oral" and "conversation" as well as the phrase "making sales" seriously restricts the usefulness of this description. If the meaning of these words is not to be stretched beyond recognition, a somewhat more realistic definition would be helpful.

More recently F.B. Evans[6] has initiated a new approach to the study of salesmanship, defining it, at least by implication, as interpersonal interaction. Work by C. I. Hovland,[7] Raymond A. Bauer,[8] and Theodore Levitt[9] suggests a broader communication model which takes into account the influences of the buyers on the salesman in addition to the usual assumption of salesmen influencing buyers. Much of this work is still incomplete, but it appears to be promising and some useful concepts can be derived from it. Similarly, the "soft sell" versus "hard sell" distinction made by Professor Edward C. Bursk[10] has contributed to the study of personal selling by bringing into focus the role of management in personal selling.

One often encounters the argument that the role of the personal salesman is to "make sales." Besides the somewhat circular reasoning involved in this argument one may also ask what roles advertising, branding, and packaging are to play whenever these are combined with personal selling. Granted that the objective of the *total* marketing mix is sales, profit, or some related objective, an optimal combination of promotional activities still requires an understanding of the individual activity's specific or incremental contribution to the achievement of a given overall objective.

The definition adopted here, for the purpose of exploring the role of personal selling in the marketing mix is closely related to the earlier definition of marketing:

Personal selling is interpersonal, face to face, interaction for the purpose of creating, modifying, exploiting or maintaining a communicative relationship between utility producing and utility consuming entities or systems.

This definition, while distinguishing clearly between personal and nonpersonal communication, enables one to take into account the several levels of communication occurring in interpersonal interaction. The definition also allows for the many types of personal contacts utilized in marketing, ranging from the door-to-door salesman to the industrial sales representative. In many respects, personal selling resembles the majority of situations involving interaction among people, and it is possible to bring much of the existing body of communication theory to bear on the problems of personal selling.

THE STATE OF THE ART IN PERSONAL SELLING

The conclusions derived from any study of personal selling and salesmanship depend to a large extent on the perspective adopted by the researcher and the range of resources which this perspective or framework allows him to consider as variables. The lack of a generally accepted concept of personal selling contributes greatly to the confusion of viewpoints presented by authors of books and articles on personal selling. Nevertheless, an attempt will be made in the following sections to provide a summary of the present state of the art.

The Importance of Personal Selling

Based on limited surveys, it has been estimated *that approximately 55 percent of total sales expenses of United States industry have involved personal selling,* with the remainder allocated to nonpersonal means (36 percent for advertising and nine percent for point of purchase and all other). A survey reported by Sawyer[11] indicated:

1. In 1954 the average cost of an industrial salesman's call was $20.00 (a later survey conducted in 1966 indicated that this figure had risen to $35.55 in 1965, with a range from $4.75 to $819,000).[12]

2. The average cost of industrial direct mail pieces was $1.00 per contact.
3. The average cost of a trade paper advertisement was less than one cent.

With cost differences of this magnitude it is clearly imperative that some means of establishing the comparative effectiveness of alternative marketing tactics be developed, so as to enable the marketing manager to assemble a mix of ingredients which balances communication effectiveness and economic efficiency.

Deane H. Wolf and Gerald Albaum report the results of a survey conducted among 80 companies listed in the American Institute of Management's "Manual of Excellent Managements, 1957." They found that about one-third of the products, orders, customers, salesmen and sales territories respectively generated from 70 to 75 percent of sales and profits. This conclusion applied to all companies, regardless of size and type of product sold.[13] While this phenomenon has been identified by most experienced marketers, its implications for policy decisions have not always been recognized.

The "Characteristics of Goods" Theory

The *actual* mix of personal versus nonpersonal selling effort varies substantially across product classes. For example, in the cases of such products as candy bars and razor blades, virtually all promotional expenditures involve nonpersonal selling means such as advertising, displays, and vending machines. In other product categories, such as machine tools and heavy electrical machinery, practically all sales effort involves personal selling contacts, plus moderate amounts of sales promotion support.

To explain why these large differences exist across product classes as well as in channels of distribution and pricing policies marketing theorists have long been interested in what has come to be called the "Characteristics of Goods" theory. The objective of this theory is to explain differences in promotional mix, channels, and pricing in terms of differences in product and market variables across various product classes.[14]

It seems fair to say, however, that the "Characteristics of Goods" theory, as presently formulated, is of limited operational use to marketers. The theory states, that if such characteristics of the product-market situation as unit price, time and effort spent in purchasing the product, and technical complexity of the product are "low," then the sales effort will tend to "favor" nonpersonal, as opposed to personal, selling means. No attempt has been made to develop a functional relationship or explain why certain characteristics of a good appear to be related to variations in the mix of personal versus nonpersonal selling effort across product classes.

A large part of the problem, however, concerns the lack of data on industry mix differences among various product classes. Nor can these data be developed easily, inasmuch as no standard nomenclature exists among firms with regard to classes of selling effort. Moreover, many firms do not maintain detailed allocations of sales effort expenditures by product class.

One attempt to assemble data on promotional mix differences, by product class, has been reported. E.H. Lewis[15] surveyed 38 manufacturing firms, including some 22 product classes, and found the following average ratios (in many instances, based on a sample of a single respondent firm) of advertising outlays to personal selling outlays:

Ratio of Advertising Outlays to Personal Selling Outlays

Product Class	Ratio	Product Class	Ratio
Food Products	12:1	Bulk Seed	1:3
Lawn Seed	4:1	Women's Apparel	1:3
Grocery Products	2:1	Paint	1:3
Malt Beverages	2:1	Insulation	1:3.5
Lawn Mowers	1:1	Kitchenware	1:4
Cellulose Tape	1:1	Auto Equipment	1:5
Furnaces	1:1.5	Control Devices	1:6
Feed	1:1.5	Farm Machinery	1:6
Roofing	1:2	Bakery Flour	1:7
Electrical Supplies	1:2	Industrial Equipment	1:11
Bedding	1:3	Paper Specialties	1:11

A major problem in determining the significance of the above averages is that *intra-product* variation can be extreme. For example, Lewis found that the *range* of the ratio varied between 1:1 and 1:5 for firms in the product class, "women's apparel." This range reflects, of course, both the heterogeneity of the product class itself and the differing practices of firms nominally classed as manufacturers of women's apparel. Possibly, useful distinctions within the class would reconcile these *intra-product* differences, and so strengthen the ratio analysis.

Efforts were made in the interviews conducted by the Marketing Science Institute to test the empirical usefulness of the "Characteristics of Goods" theory. It seems evident, on the basis of a qualitative analysis of the data derived from these interviews that any given marketing manager's *perception* of the economic and behavioral characteristics of his relevant market is as important, if not a more important factor, in the determination of promotional allocations, than the economic and technological characteristics of the specific product involved.

The Integration of Personal Selling

It is also apparent from the literature that a problem exists concerning the optimum utilization of salesmen with regard to product. A well-known management consultant and teacher of management concludes that in many companies:

The largest group of salesmen (and the most effective ones) are usually put on the products that are hard to sell either because they are yesterday's products or because they are also-rans which managerial vanity desperately is trying to make into winners. Tomorrow's important products rarely get the sales effort required. And the product that has sensational success in the market, and which therefore ought to be pushed all out, tends to be slighted.[16]

It is important to note the difference, however, between products or services which are hard to sell because they are "also-rans" and products or services that are hard to sell because they are either technically complicated or require substantial changes in the user's present procedures before they can be accepted and utilized.

In a wider sense there is also a problem of integrating personal selling efforts with the buyers' information and product acquisition and consumption process. As one buyer said:

It's been gradually gotten across to them (suppliers) that they won't be left out in the cold if they don't make routine calls as often as they used to; they'll be considered. But we also get across the point that our buyers are in the business of buying—they're not in the business of being sold.[17]

Purchasers are beginning to concern themselves with what has been termed "supplier development" thus indicating that the existing means of maintaining relationships between buyers and sellers is somewhat less than satisfactory from a buyer point of view.

The basic concept of supplier development. . .is relatively simple. Supplier development is the creation of a new source of supply by the purchaser. A company can through its marketing efforts develop new customers. Exactly the same parallel exists on the procurement side. A company can through its procurement efforts develop new suppliers. . . . Thus the initiative in developing new sources of supply lies, not with the supplier, but with the purchaser.[18]

The increasing attention to the purchasing function as a profit producing activity could result in radical changes in the functions of the salesman. Introduction of modern electronic communication links, such as intercompany computer and telecommunication networks, presents a wholly new situation for which the present level of understanding of personal selling appears to be seriously inadequate. Selling teams, systems selling and buying committees which are becoming increasingly prevalent, represent a new area of planning and management which cannot easily be accommodated within the present concept of personal selling.

The Management of Personal Selling

The problems of the sales manager are discussed at length in sales management literature. The independent variable here, of course, is the sales manager, while the salesman is sometimes regarded almost as a robot capable of being "carefully screened," "properly trained" and "appropriately stimulated."

If the salesman is faced with difficult communication problems, to which there are no general solutions, the sales manager is, by comparison, faced with even more difficult tasks. In a series of ten articles one sales trainer concludes that in general, sales managers' ten biggest mistakes are:

1. Flubbing the communications task.
2. Hiring by hunch.
3. Spending meeting dollars to create big yawns.
4. Pushing the trainee in over his head.
5. Ignoring what motivates salesmen.
6. Developing others but not himself.
7. Playing the one-man fire department.
8. Failing to show sales leadership.
9. Slighting the planning task.
10. Guessing at territory potential.[19]

In addition to managerial problems such as those indicated above, the sales manager is also normally faced with considerable administrative duties. Consequently, it is no great surprise that one researcher was able to conclude that "most practicing managers have relatively little time to study managing."[20]

The problems involved in managing people have received extensive treatment by numerous writers and will be further explored in Part Four. Suffice it to say at this point that the managerial task is one of coordinating and combining individual efforts into a total organizational effort to achieve some overall goal or a set of goals. It is possible, of course, to develop systems which relate the efforts of people to an overall goal and indeed, system engineers have gone a long way toward achieving this. In any specific organization, however, managerial problems center not on "people" in general, but on specific individuals. This distinction is seldom made explicitly in managerial literature and it is not to be found in formal organization charts, yet it is at the heart of the managerial task.

Selecting and Training Salesmen

Several writers have suggested that recruitment, selection and training of salesmen remain serious problem areas. A survey published in *Sales Management,* for example, concluded that:[21]

1. Many students, usually the vast majority, do not or would not want to become salesmen.
2. Many of these same students have some very uncomplimentary things to say about the occupation of personal selling.

With regard to selection of prospective salemen one writer concludes among other things "that outstanding salesmen are often introverted, not person-oriented, sensitive to rejection by others, and often a study in tension."[22] These conclusions appear to run counter to the usual list of personality traits advocated for selection purposes. Perhaps the "wrong" people are being hired quite systematically. A strong possibility also exists that success in selling is only marginally related to the personality traits of the salesman.

Training of salesmen has long been a controversial issue with reference to both content and amount of training required by salesmen. *Sales Management* reports:

The consensus [from interviews with six sales managers] seems to be: There would be more good men in sales if companies took their training job seriously and knew better what they were doing; there would be fewer failures among the men who are put to work if there were better leadership among sales managers.[23]

Content and quantity of training should clearly be geared to an understanding of the salesman's function. From a marketing standpoint the salesman may be engaged in a variety of activities, none of which can be defined as selling, although they may bear an indirect relationship to sales. The following excerpt should bear out this point:

In the course of a day, a P & G salesman may be called upon by his various customers to be a business advisor, advertising counselor, accountant, or economist, and, at the same time, he must keep abreast of each customer's interests and requirements.[24]

Possibly even more important, then, than the salesman's technical qualifications is the fact that the salesman continually engages in interpersonal relationships. All too often training programs prepare him insufficiently for this or they do not prepare him at all. One author writing about human relations in selling has this to say:

There may be specific infallible rules that guarantee customer acceptance of your sales presentation. In fact, many authors have recorded these approaches or formulas as guides to sales success. Following these rules makes selling a *science* and results in a fair measure of accomplishment. However, a salesman who uses an *individual* approach to each customer—based on his individual personality pattern—is practicing an *art*. [25]

Even though the author of the above excerpt has become entangled in the art-versus-science issue, his point is otherwise well taken. The problem facing the modern salesman, training director, and sales manager is far too complex to be treated in a "how to sell" manner. Here the researcher can hope to unravel some of the complexity inherent in human relationships by providing simplifying concepts which will pinpoint the important relationships and provide hypotheses for testing in specific situations.

The Selling Job

One frequently encountered approach in selling literature stresses the "how to sell" rules and techniques for "handling customers." Typical titles are: *How to Overcome Objections in Selling, How to Sell Intangibles, and Tested Ways to Close the Sale.* [26] Generally these books narrate the hard-earned experiences of very successful salesmen and primarily because these "super" salesmen are often exceptionally eloquent, some of the books make both interesting and fascinating reading. From the standpoint of teaching, however, the "how to sell" approach appears to be ineffective primarily because the reader is so far removed from the writer in time, space, and perception that the chances of successful communication, let alone a useful learning experience, are remote. This problem is further aggravated when the "expert" engages in semantic games such as the following:

[The salesman should] 1. tune in on the buyer's wave length, 2. head right; see things as the buyer does, [and] 3. avoid "interference" by staying tuned in. [27]

Despite the apparent interest in the customer, the general perspective encountered in most selling literature is centered on, and limited to the salesman. He is considered the sole independent variable acting upon an apparently passive or at least pliable subject:

The salesman's empathy, coupled with his intense ego drive, enables him to home in on the target effectively and make the sale. He has the drive, the need to make the sale, and his empathy gives him the connecting tool with which to do it. [28]

The classification of personality characteristics of salesmen and buyers shown below further indicates the assumption of initiative on the part of the salesman, and the notion of an essentially passive buyer.[29]

Salesmen	Buyers
Self-confident	Impulsive
Earnest	Talkative
Persistent	Deliberate
Enthusiastic	Indecisive
Imaginative	Timid
Original	Suspicious
Determined	Stubborn

With such characteristics it is perhaps surprising that a group of college students, surveyed in 1962, should categorize salesmen as, among other things, "psychologically maladjusted!"[30] Be that as it may, there is no inherent and necessary reason that there should be either more or less psychological differences between a salesman and a buyer than there are between two salesmen. By its very nature, selling, or communicative interaction between individuals, is a learned ability or competence which is far more complex and dynamic than any list of personality traits is capable of conveying.

Trends Found in the Literature

While there exists a considerable volume of literature on personal selling, it generally reflects a highly mechanistic interpretation of human behavior and interpersonal influence. The bulk of the literature concentrates on establishing some patterns or rules for behavior. This simplistic, nonintegrated approach to personal selling is not only deficient from a conceptual point of view but also leads to some operationally adverse results:

1. The concern with the development of specific "rules" to govern behavior in particular situations negates the basic advantage of the salesman as a promotional medium. Such rules tend to hamper him as a flexible and dynamic communicative link between selling and buying systems.
2. The emphasis upon psychological characteristics to the virtual exclusion of other elements of interpersonal competence

represents a failure to take into account and turn to full advantage the basic nature of human learning and concept formation.

3. The emphasis upon control in personal selling tends to minimize the basic complexity and motivational significance of individual goals and standards. This results in both misleading and inadequate guidelines for the management and performance of the personal selling function.

4. The frequent failure of sales organizations and literature to take into account and encourage full individual participation in the selling process reflects a relatively superficial understanding of the roles of selling and salesmen. This, in turn, has hampered many companies in their efforts to recruit competent sales people.

5. The literature exhibits little understanding concerning the interdependence of individual performance and organizational structures. Though much remains to be learned in this area, there is evidence, based on work in organizational theory and behavior, that the quality of individual motivation and performance is at least partly dependent upon the nature of the organizational framework within which the individual performs.

PERSONAL SELLING AND THE
BEHAVIORAL SCIENCES

The major contribution of the behavioral sciences to personal selling, and more specifically to the management of personal selling, has been the development of psychological selection techniques of which personality inventories and aptitude tests are examples. The main purpose of these tests is ostensibly to enable the sales manager to distinguish between *potentially* good salesmen and *potentially* bad salesmen. Whether or not such tests do in fact constitute effective screens depends not only on the actual existence of the variables the tests purport to measure and the relationship of these variables to actual behavior, but also on the underlying concept of a "good" sales performance. Social scientists have more recently reached the following major conclusions with respect to the social and psychological characteristics of salesmen:

1. There is no significant relationship between intelligence test scores and sales success....

2. No significant relationship has been found between independent measures of personality traits and sales success ....

3. No correlation exists between age and sales success. . . .

4. There is no correlation between measurable character traits and sales success. . . .
5. There is no significant correlation between level of education and sales success. . . .
6. No significant correlation exists between level of sales activity and sales success among individual salesmen. . . . [That is,] attempts to increase the level of sales activity [have been less successful in increasing] sales volume than an equal amount of attention directed toward improving the selling method.
7. Each of the above factors has significance when studied in relation to all of the others in individual salesmen. . . . [31]

Undoubtedly, tests can be used to select individuals who are likely to excel at a job in which manual dexterity is important. This does not imply, however, that those with low test scores cannot be trained to do the work, but that those with high test scores can, on the average, be trained more easily, at less cost, and perhaps can continue in the job longer, with more satisfaction to themselves. There is still considerable doubt, however, whether selection tests can be designed to predict an individual's potential ability to conceptualize and communicate. Some of the reasons for this doubt are discussed in Chapter XIII.

The postwar period witnessed a significant growth in the field of communications research. Drawing on developments in probability sampling, attitude scaling, and factor analysis, researchers [32] attempted to measure the attitude changes induced by large scale propaganda and advertising campaigns conducted through mass media. The apparent analytical tractability of uniform messages delivered by a medium whose coverage could be measured, to an audience whose "attitudes" could be gauged, made the study of mass communication an attractive field for researchers. These developments could not fail to influence and stimulate those concerned with the measurement of the effectiveness of personal selling and of sales management. Yet, direct application of behavioral research to the analysis of selling activities has been limited and sporadic in character. [33] Nevertheless, as will be seen in later chapters, the behavioral sciences afford potentially important contributions to the study of selling activities. At a broader level, applications of psychological, sociological, and anthropological theory have already been instrumental in the introduction of many new concepts into the discussion of marketing.

MACROECONOMICS AND PERSONAL SELLING

Traditionally personal selling has been ascribed a major economic role by most of its advocates. One author and salesman writes:

You read and hear about the 175 million Americans who have raised their national standards of living to fantastic heights.

They have raised them? No, not 175 million people. Most of them resisted.

A million salesmen are the real raisers! Or two million, or ten million? Whatever the number, there is room for more, for the American salesman is the real cause of America's economic superiority. [34]

Even though the salesman, at least in his own estimation, may have been a major factor in economic development, economists have almost totally ignored the selling function. While the economist, John Maynard Keynes, recognized the influence of psychological factors on the propensity to consume, he did not accord them particular significance. Nor did he suggest that the propensity to consume could be influenced through a process of persuasion brought to bear on these psychological factors. In all fairness to Keynes, there was little substantial proof during the depression of the dynamic influence of the selling function. Consequently, Keynes seems to define the psychological factors influencing the propensity to consume as mere habit:

The fundamental psychological law, upon which we are entitled to depend with great confidence both *a priori* from our knowledge of human nature and from the detailed facts of experience, is that men are disposed, as a rule and on the average, to increase their consumption as their income increases, but not by as much as the increase in their income. . . .For a man's habitual standard of life usually has the first claim on his income, and he is apt to save the difference which discovers itself between his actual income and the expense of his habitual standard. [35]

It was not Keynes' intention to develop a theory of marketing, much less of personal selling, nor is macroeconomic theory particularly well-suited as the sole base for a marketing theory, primarily because of the tendency of some economists to rely on static models. Yet, much of the terminology, and many of the concepts presently existing in marketing are derived from economics and further theoretical developments in marketing must necessarily take into account the relevant aspects of economic theory. One conceptual hurdle which must be overcome before full use can be made of economic theory in the development of a distinct marketing theory is outlined by Sydney Weintraub:

In an economy where advertising flourishes, we cannot be unmindful of the fact that these outlays fit rather awkwardly into the concept of a social order in which productive resources are deployed strictly according to consumer desires; advertising operates to reshape desires, even after we concede that some advertising campaigns are notoriously unsuccessful. The traditional portrayal of the economic process, of producers acknowledging the inviolateness of consumer tastes and adapting to them, is not wholly accurate. Resources are not merely adapted to given consumer ends; instead, tastes are partially shaped to producer ends, depending on consumer receptiveness to sales appeals, and entrepreneurial ingenuity, initiative, and imagination in creating them. Although sales pressures modify our views on the motivating forces of economic activity, it is by no means tantamount to the conclusion that all sales techniques are inexorably iniquitous. . . . Sometimes the precise line of demarcation between selling and production costs is difficult to draw; still, the idea of producing to fill an existing scale of preferences, and of activities devoted to changing the preference structure, is clear in principle and acted on in practice.[36]

Significant efforts have recently been devoted to the problem of relating macroeconomic theory to sociological theory.[37] Undoubtedly further efforts in this direction will be of basic importance to the development of a marketing theory.

MICROECONOMICS AND PERSONAL SELLING

Microeconomic theory has been conspicuous by its absence in more recent marketing literature. The primary reason for this dearth of contributions from microeconomics is the "perfect knowledge" assumption underlying much of this theory. This does not mean that microeconomic theory is inapplicable to marketing and selling, but it does mean that it must be supplemented with contributions from other fields, notably organization and communication theory.

The adequacy of the economist's frame of reference in dealing with the wide variety of behavior problems which do not involve conscious interdependence among the acting agents cannot be seriously subjected to question. As soon as we leave the realm of unconscious interdependence, however, an attempt to deal with problems of deliberate cooperation we find ourselves increasingly falling back on concepts and generalizations whose relationship with the main body of thought is more or less tenuous. The duopoly or oligopoly problem is a case in point. Although interesting work . . . had been done on the "small numbers" case within the basic conceptional frame of reference employed by the economist, effective incorporation of these issues into the main body of thought did not seem feasible until the advent of the theory of games.[38]

Certain contributions from economics and behavioral sciences have been brought together under one roof by operations research and the management sciences. Some examples of attempts made by management scientists to explore experimentally the existing assumptions underlying the practice of personal selling are discussed in some detail in Chapters III and IV. However, operations research has produced little in the way of a theory of marketing or personal selling, nor has it been widely applied for the purpose of experimentation in the field of personal selling.

These, then, are the general sources from which concepts relevant to personal selling must be drawn. The combined literature constitutes an overwhelming collection and much of it is so widely divergent in concepts and evidence that it is difficult if not impossible to combine into one coherent theory. Moreover, concepts

and working hypotheses are being continually changed and dis-
carded in favor of others. Clearly, not all available concepts and
evidence can be included in one book, and the material on the
following pages is consequently the result of a choice of what has
been considered by the authors as the most important contributions from several very dynamic scientific fields of inquiry.

SUMMARY

With very few exceptions,[39] writers in the field of marketing and
personal selling have failed to develop a unified and coherent set
of perspectives which: (1) accommodates personal selling within
the framework of a concept of marketing, and (2) provides a means
of logically relating the several aspects and levels of problems
involved in managing and performing personal selling activities.

In this chapter an attempt has been made to develop and inter-
relate a set of definitions of marketing, the marketing mix, and
personal selling. Although a set of definitions does not solve any
problems, it does, if logically related, provide a conceptual base
from which to undertake further explorations.

The definition and perspective of personal selling adopted here
is different from that normally encountered in the existing personal
selling literature. In this book, the customer or buyer is considered as an integral and active part of all marketing and selling
activities insofar as a continual interaction between buyers and
sellers is occurring. Any attempt to develop a theory of marketing
and selling must consequently be aimed at the relationship between
buyers and sellers and not merely at one of these entities or systems to the exclusion of, or at the expense of, the other.

A great deal of confusion of concepts and viewpoints is evident
in the personal selling literature. Too many "easy" techniques
and "solutions" are being offered as if they were the long-sought-
after answer to the sales manager's or salesman's problems. The
very advantage of personal selling as a promotional tool is the
dynamic flexibility of communicative competence of the salesman.
Consequently, there is no one way to sell, nor is there only one
way to manage, and skepticism must be the wages of he who claims
otherwise.

As already shown in an earlier MSI publication[40] a theory of
marketing and more specifically, a theory of personal selling must
derive from several sources. In the following pages will be found
concepts and research findings from cultural anthropology, sociology, social psychology, psychology and communications research.
Also, the theories of economics (particularly microeconomics) and
the experience of operations researchers are relevant additions to
what, hopefully, is a contribution to a theory of personal selling.

The operations researcher's viewpoint is presented in the

form of four experimental cases in Part Two of this volume. The assumption structures and methodologies underlying these experiments are of primary interest, and both the strengths and weaknesses of operations research (O.R.) in a personal selling context are illustrated in these two chapters.

Should the reader have no immediate interest in the quantitative techniques of operations research, Part Two may be omitted. Part Three (beginning with Chapter V) takes up the analysis of personal selling from the behavioral and communicative perspectives. While this analysis may be slightly more meaningful when related to the case material in Part Two, the omission need not be a serious one.

PART TWO

Quantitative Analysis
of Personal Selling

PART IV

III

Analysis of Selling Costs
and Returns

MARKETING IS NOT the only endeavor in which development of intuitively based art and skill has preceded scientifically based knowledge and understanding. For example, engineers have built machines that worked before theories explaining them were developed. Similarly, marketing managers have frequently been in the position of trying to find a policy that works without having a theory that explains the phenomena involved. The work of analysis has frequently proceeded on the basis of tentative hypotheses, modified by successes and failures in application. In some cases, operations research has resorted to experimentation and analysis without having a theory to work with before the fact and often without generating any theories afterward. Nevertheless, the underlying drive of these quantitative approaches is to "explain" as well as to describe the phenomena studied. Data on application of operations research to marketing problems have not been as plentiful as one might desire, though many applications undoubtedly are unavailable for publication because of their competitive value. Within the field of marketing, personal selling in particular appears to have received less attention from operations researchers than some other elements of the marketing mix. In time, however, both the number of applications made and the percentage of these published will undoubtedly increase, making it possible to accumulate more systematically the knowledge gained from these applications.

THE PURPOSE OF PART TWO

The purpose of Chapters III and IV is to report on the method and results of three experimental studies of personal selling conducted under the supervision of Dr. Russell L. Ackoff. Chapter III contains a brief discussion of quantitative analysis and the role of experimentation in selling, as well as a detailed description of an experimental study of an existing personal selling operation. Chapter IV is devoted to the description of three additional studies, one of which is an example of an application of time and duty measurements and methods to a personal selling operation. In addition, Chapter IV contains a brief discussion of the results of a series of interviews with a number of marketing executives.

QUANTITATIVE ANALYSIS IN SELLING

It is not always clear what is meant by "quantitative analysis." It is certainly something more than collections of numbers about selling operations since selling, in this sense, has long been a quantitative field. Indeed, if any company with a sizable marketing and personal selling operation were to collect all the operational and accounting data pertaining to these activities, a considerable pile of data would result.

Why is it, then, that one so frequently encounters the phrases "information scarcity" and "lack of knowledge" in connection with both marketing and personal selling? The answer lies in the differences between "data," "information," and "knowledge." There is clearly no scarcity of data since any good accountant, in combination with a marketing researcher, can inundate the best of marketing managers with data. Yet, this same marketing manager may still maintain that there is a scarcity of information about his operation. He may even, in the face of an enormous data flow, maintain that his accountants and marketing researchers "fail to communicate."

There is a crucial difference here between data and information which cannot be bridged by mere good will. Information to the marketing manager, or to any individual for that matter, is data to which he can attribute some "meaning." Knowledge, on the other hand, is internalized information and encompasses the individual's "ordering of the world," which in turn accounts for his ability, or inability, to attribute meaning to incoming data.

Since much of a marketing manager's knowledge is intuitive, it is evident that conflict easily arises between him and the researcher, who is attempting to verbalize that which the marketing manager knows intuitively. By the same token, conflict may also arise as a result of the marketing manager's verbalization of that which any good researcher knows intuitively. The "problems of communication" which arise in this connection will be discussed in some detail in Chapter X. Suffice it here to suggest that scarcity of information is not so much a function of a shortage of data about marketing and selling operations as it is a function of inability to render meaningful the data that already are available. As will be shown later, to "render meaningful" is to "organize" observational data. The methods of quantitative or mathematical analysis constitute one way of organizing data, although by no means the only one. The advantage of using available quantitative or mathematical techniques as means of organizing data pertaining to a given operation is that these techniques, in most cases, provide a well-defined set of computational procedures once a given problem has been defined to satisfy any specific technique.

In discussing applications of mathematics in psychology, one writer makes a threefold distinction among the uses of mathematics in that field.[1] The distinction is made between *discursive, deterministic,* and *statistical* applications of the quantitative approach.

Since the discursive or explanatory statement does not provide a specified set of computational procedures by which to determine the "value" of any given variable, it is no more than a convenient shorthand in which to express a specific relationship. Yet it may often be the starting point for an organized approach to a given problem area.[2]

In the case of the deterministic approach to quantitative analysis, the variables are more completely specified and postulates made about their interactions. A deterministic analysis of a given marketing problem is based on the assumption that the values of the dependent variable, the output, can be influenced by precisely (i.e., not subject to random variations) by changing the levels of the independent variables, the inputs. Clearly, such an assumption may not necessarily hold in the "real" world.

A third use of quantitative methodology in organizing data is in its statistical form. Models are built, based upon certain assumptions, of a process that generates observable data. Data are collected, processed through the model, and judgments are made about the values of the parameters which are assumed to govern the process subject to specific probabilities or "odds."[3]

The procedures involved in each of these three applications of mathematical techniques are covered in any good text on statistical methodology.[4] Suffice it to say that *if* appropriate market and promotional variables can be specified, then experiments can be conducted to show their effects; and this process may be deliberately altered in desired directions in either small scale tests or full scale operations.

The difficulties involved in applying quantitative or mathematical techniques to a given problem area are not confined to those of determining significant variables. A. M. Weitzenhoffer observes, for example, that:

Failure to recognize the fact that psychological magnitudes rarely have all the properties of numbers has led to the formation of mathematical equations which have a superficial appearance of validity but are unsound and misleading.[5]

In other words, mathematical techniques have limitations of their own which occasionally render them invalid as "organizers" of data. This does not mean, of course, that many useful applications of mathematical techniques cannot and have not been made to marketing and selling problems. Yet it does call attention to the fact that the researcher must join the marketing manager in continually questioning some of his own dearest assumptions if significant progress is to be made in organizing and verbalizing marketing knowledge.

MARGINAL ANALYSIS AND OPTIMUM ALLOCATION

The key problem facing the marketing manager is that of allocating resources to the various elements of the marketing mix within the constraints of his total promotional budget. The establishment of the promotional budget itself constitutes what the economist would call a "scale" problem, as opposed to the problem of allocating elements of the budget. Similarly, of course, the determination of the total marketing budget is an allocation problem for the top managers.

Economic theory provides a simple statement of the problem of "optimum" allocation of resources to several alternative input elements in the form of marginal analysis. Basically, the theory underlying marginal analysis provides the rule that expenditures on *total* promotion should be kept at a point where marginal revenue equals or exceeds marginal cost. With reference to the allocation problem, marginal analysis stipulates that funds should be allocated among activities to levels where the marginal gain per dollar cost among all activities is equal.

The economic problem of allocating personal selling effort among territories is similar to that of allocating elements of the marketing mix. The rule for an "optimum" allocation among several territories is "that the level of selling expenditure in each territory should be such that the incremental receipts per dollar of selling effort should be equal among all territories."[6] Allocation of efforts within a given territory should follow the rule that marginal gain, or revenue, should be equal to or greater than marginal cost. These economic rules depict "ideal" situations, and application of the rules in practice requires that a great deal be known about the relationship between promotional dollar inputs and sales revenue outputs. Yet the economic theory of marginal analysis at least provides a set of parameters for the problem of allocating selling effort.

THE ROLE OF EXPERIMENTATION IN PERSONAL SELLING

Experiments may be conducted for several purposes. Paul E. Green and Donald S. Tull[7] distinguish between three uses of the term. In some cases, the term experimentation is used synonymously with *measurement* in which case the experimental objective generally is to provide numerical values for predetermined parameters of a model. In other cases, experiments are conducted to determine the *relationship* between some input variables and one or more output variables. Finally, experimentation may be conducted to *identify* the relevant variables of a given activity, as well as to determine the functional or "causal" relationships among these variables.[8]

The experiments which are described in this and the following chapter are of the latter type, insofar as attempts are made at identifying the significant variables influencing the relationship between inputs and outputs with reference to personal selling. Attempts are simultaneously made to determine the type and degree of relationship linking input variables with the dependent variable (sales).

STUDY 1: THE RELATIONSHIP
BETWEEN NUMBER OF CALLS AND SALES

The following operations research study on selling effectiveness was conducted for the Lamp Division of the General Electric Company. In planning for the number of salesmen required over a five-year period during which considerable total expansion of the market was anticipated, it had been necessary to assume (for lack of any definitive data) that the average number of accounts covered in the past by a salesman was optimum (i.e., forecasts of manpower requirements were based on past budgeted loads per man without raising the question whether these loads were "optimal"). It was subsequently suggested that a project be initiated to investigate the validity of the assumptions made regarding the average number of accounts that should be assigned to salesmen. The work of the project is described in detail here as an early example of the operations research to a specific problem in personal selling. The compromises that had to be made in carrying out the assigned task vividly illustrate the gap between optimization as a problem in economic theory and its attainment in fact.

Background

In the summer of 1953, a Task Force was created by the General Manager of the Lamp Division of the General Electric Company to prepare a "Five-Year Plan" for the Division. The resulting plan contained five elements:

1. Objectives for each of the five years for each class of product.

2. Operating procedures by which those objectives should be attained.
3. Determination of resources required to attain the objectives using these procedures.
4. Specification of a new organizational structure for the Division.
5. Assignment of authority and responsibility for various types of decisions and actions required of management. [9]

As part of the study of resource requirements, it was necessary to determine how many additional salesmen would be required in each of the next five years. The anticipated need for additional salesmen was partly a result of an expected market expansion and partly a result of the recommended organizational structure. In this new structure, three finished-product departments, each with its own marketing organization, were created; and where there had previously been only one sales department with each salesman offering all products, the creation of the three new departments resulted in the splitting of many accounts so that, in the future, salesmen from two or three of the product departments would have to call on the same account.

To estimate the number of additional salesmen required in view of these recommended changes, the Task Force had assumed that the average number of accounts previously covered by a salesman was "optimum," and the shortage of time available to the Task Force in which to prepare the five-year plan had not permitted this assumption to be investigated. The Task Force felt sufficiently insecure, however, about the stipulated requirements for additional salesmen to suggest, on completion of its work, that a project be initiated to determine the average number of accounts that should be assigned to salesmen; and this recommendation was accepted.

Formulation of the Problem

The simplifying assumptions underlying the study are that a salesman's effectiveness depends on the following:

1. The way he allocates his time among his existing and prospective accounts.
2. The types and number of accounts assigned to him.
3. The personal characteristics of the salesman.

Optimization of sales effort would, it was therefore assumed, involve consideration of at least these three factors. Limitations of time and funds, however, made it impractical to attack the problem on three fronts at once. Consequently, attention was directed initially to the problem of allocating the salesman's time to a specified set of accounts. Under the circumstances, any findings in such a study would be easier to implement than findings relative to the other two factors. Once the study was begun, however, it was possible to obtain important information about the types and number of accounts that should be assigned to a salesman. The salesman's personal characteristics were studied in a second experiment which is outlined in Chapter IV.

The Measure of Effectiveness

Ideally, the research team would have preferred to use the profit obtained from a salesman's efforts as a measure of his effectiveness. However, since approximately 15,000 different products were involved, it was decided to use "dollar volume of sales per year" (hereafter referred to as dollar volume) as the measure of effectiveness. It was realized, of course, that an increase in a particular salesman's dollar volume might decrease profit, if the product mix were to change simultaneously in certain ways. It was assumed, however, that if average dollar volume of sales per salesman were to increase, total profit would increase as well.

The decision to use sales volume as a measure of effectiveness was also influenced by the fact that the manufacturing and distribution costs of an item and hence the profit derived from its sale, depend on the volume and mix of products sold in any particular period of time. Therefore, even if it were possible to extract from accounting records some profit figure for one time period, such a figure would not necessarily be applicable to another time period.

The Model

Once the problem had been formulated and the measure of effectiveness specified, the team began to search for a mathematical model which would provide an ideal solution.

The first step would be to obtain a curve or corresponding mathematical equation that would express the sales volume per customer as a function of sales time spent with that customer. It appeared reasonable to expect that such curves would be close to the "S" shape of a learning curve. The plateau of these sales-response curves would represent the saturation of the account with sales time. Indeed, if sales time were increased beyond some "supersaturation point," it seemed likely that sales volume would decrease. The customer might, for example, be antagonized by excessive demands on his time by the salesman. In subsequent studies of the effect of advertising expenditures on sales such supersaturation was indeed found and it was possible to increase sales by reducing promotional expenditures.

Since each salesman has only a fixed amount of time available the problem becomes one of allocating that time to the available accounts (each of which is represented by a sales-response function) in such a way as to maximize his total sales volume. It was evident that such curves could not be obtained practicably for *individual* accounts since the computation would require data on both sales and salesmen's calls over a period of several years (seasonal and irregular variations made a period of less than one year unreliable). Futhermore, it would be impracticable to apply a set of thousands of individual curves, even if these were accessible.

Consequently, a "practical" revision of the model was made. It was assumed that those accounts which react to sales time in the same way can be identified and classified as a group. Sales volume for each individual account, within any given group, then may be plotted against total sales time spent with a customer during a specified year. A curve may be fitted to these points to describe the responsiveness of the group of accounts. The nature of the curve that was anticipated is shown in Figure 1. Such a curve, if obtainable, could be used to represent each account in that class for the purpose of optimum allocation of time for each salesman.

FIGURE 1

Ideal Volume-Time Curve for One Class of Accounts

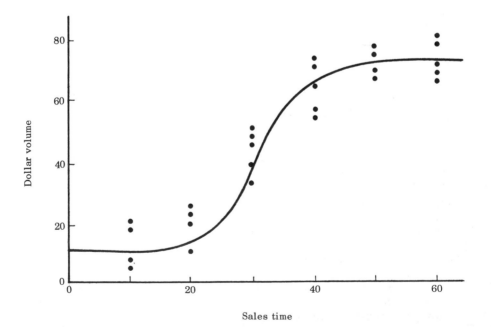

Sales time

Moreover, if the slope of the sales-response curves were found to be consistently decreasing within that range lying between "reasonable" time per account, on the one hand, and supersaturation, on the other, then it would be possible to employ a very simple computational procedure to determine how a salesman's time should be allocated to his accounts so as to maximize the expected sales volume.

To classify accounts, a listing had to be made of account characteristics that might affect their responsiveness to sales time. Discussion with management and sales personnel yielded a list of nine apparently pertinent characteristics:

For All Accounts

1. Classes of product handled by the customer.
2. Number of customer's employees.
3. Customer's total net sales.
4. Distance of customer from salesman's office.
5. The population of the community in which the account is located.

For Distributors

6. The number and mix of distributors in the community.
7. Number of distributor's salesmen.
8. Nature of distributor's business (e.g., electrical, hardware, etc.).
9. Percentage of distributor's sales made to retailers.

The district with the best available sales-call data (Sales District A) was selected for a trial of the model. To obtain the required data on each characteristic of each of several hundred accounts in the district, it was necessary to go beyond company records. Salesmen in the district were given a set of questions concerning their accounts to which they were to get answers by interviewing these accounts.

The sales-call reports which were available did not report the time spent on calls or in preparation, travel, or waiting, and data available from a study done in 1942 made it clear that different types of accounts required different amounts of time. It was necessary, therefore, to design and conduct a time study of a sample of salesmen. This time study, while it ultimately did not contribute substantially to the principal results of the main study, yielded some important side results that will be discussed below.

Data Analysis

Once all the required data on each account were obtained, they were coded and put on an IBM card. It took more than a month, however, to get all the information on each account. In the meantime, what data were available were used in a series of preliminary analyses directed toward obtaining a useful classification of accounts. These analyses may be summarized as follows:

1. First, with the most obvious classification of accounts (by type of business and product involved), annual dollar volumes were plotted against number of calls. The results were very disappointing, as is shown in Figure 2, which is typical of the plots obtained. More sophisticated classification by use of combinations of characteristics yielded no better results.

2. Sales-response curves were drawn arbitrarily through subsets of points on the plots obtained in 1. However, analysis of the characteristics of accounts falling about these curves failed to reveal any significant differences among these arbitrary subclasses of accounts.

3. A grid was superimposed on the plots, and averages were determined for columns and rows, separately and in combination, with the hope that these "average" points would yield sales-response curves. But none did.

FIGURE 2

Example of Actual Plot of Dollar Volume Versus Number of Calls Per Account

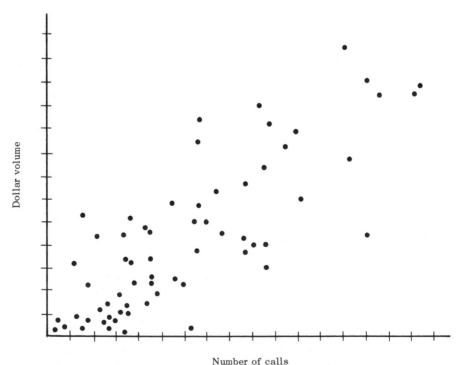

Number of calls

In all, more than a hundred different plots were made while the complete data were being collected, but the effort was fruitless. Once all the data were in and on cards, multiple linear and curvilinear regression analyses were run with dollar volume treated as the dependent variable. The only independent variable with which dollar volume was significantly correlated was number of sales calls. Not a single account characteristic turned out to be statistically significant. It should be noted *that this result did not even prove that increased numbers of calls cause increased dollar volume:* it might have been that salesmen simply were calling more often on their larger accounts, whether necessary or not!

At first these results seemed to constitute an impasse. Initially only two explanations for the failure to obtain sales-response curves seemed possible:

1. Dollar volume is not affected by the number of calls.
2. The wrong account characteristics had been used.

FIGURE 3

Example of Plot of Dollar Volume Change
Versus Change in Number of Calls

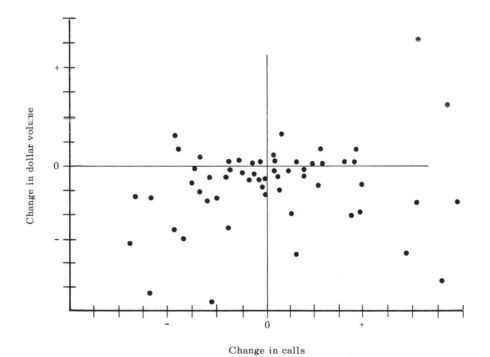

Change in calls

During this vain effort to "save" the study, another possible explanation of the results obtained was found: perhaps accounts were being saturated with sales calls and consequently the data obtained represented random fluctuations about the plateau of sales-response curves. If this were so, it would follow that changes in numbers of calls per year (in the saturation region) should not be accompanied by changes in dollar volume.

The team set about at once to check this new inference. Changes in dollar volume from 1953 to 1954 were plotted against changes in number of calls for the same years. One of the typical plots obtained is shown in Figure 3. All of the plots appeared equally random. The following hypothesis was then tested: There is no difference in average change in annual dollar volume between accounts that received an increased number of calls in 1954 and those which received a decreased number. Using appropriate tests, this hypothesis was confirmed for every class of accounts.

The same data were then converted into percentage change in dollar volume and number of calls, separately and in combination, and similarly inconclusive results were obtained. A study of changes in dollar volume between 1952 and 1953 also met with failure. In the case of distributors (on whose accounts G.E. salesmen also made calls), the analyses were made on direct and indirect calls separately, but again with the same negative results.

Two types of analyses were made to determine if the quadrant location of an account (in plots such as that shown in Figure 3) could be explained by the characteristics of the accounts as follows:

1. The average and range of the values of each characteristic for each account in each quadrant were computed. Statistical analyses revealed no significant differences among quadrants with respect to any one or any combination of characteristics.
2. A small sample of salesmen, not aware of the basis of the grouping, was given a list of their accounts grouped by quadrants. They were asked to determine whether or not they could find any way of distinguishing among the groups. Such additional characteristics as the following were suggested by the salesmen:
   a. Percentage (salesman's estimate) of customer's potential realized.
   b. Attitude of account's management toward him (rated on a five-point scale).
   c. Attitude of account's salesmen toward him (similarly rated).
   d. Knowledge of account's salesmen of G.E. lamps (also rated on a five-point scale).

Despite this "reaching" for characteristics none could be found that would distinguish among the four groups of accounts.

It appeared that the hypothesis of saturation had been confirmed. Probability and credibility, however, are not always in agreement and in this case they were not. When plots such as the one shown in Figure 3 were shown to salesmen, they refused to accept the conclusion that changes in number of calls over the years shown had not affected dollar volume. Indeed they suggested several reasons why this could not be so for a number of specific accounts and hence would not accept the conclusion even though it derived from the "average."

A more credible proof had to be, and was, found. It went as follows: first, accounts were classified by whether they had an increase or decrease in number of calls in 1953 as compared with 1952. They were then subclassified in terms of increases or decreases in number of calls in 1954. This yielded four classes of accounts:

FIGURE 4

Account Classification

		Changes in sales calls 1953-54	
		Increase	Decrease
	Increase	1	2
Changes in sales calls 1952-53	Decrease	3	4

A statistical analysis was performed to determine whether or not there had been a significant change in average dollar volume between classes (1) and (2) and classes (3) and (4) (Figure 4), but none was found. The distribution of changes in dollar volume for each of the four classes of accounts is shown in Figure 5. Accounts that received an increase (or decrease) in calls in one year were unaffected on the average by whether or not they received an increase (or decrease) in the succeeding years.

While in the main, this result tended to be accepted, it was valid for only one sales district. To remedy this situation, corresponding analyses were performed for the other two sales districts for which data were available, and similar results were obtained.

FIGURE 5

Distribution of Dollar Volume Change by Class of Account
(District A)

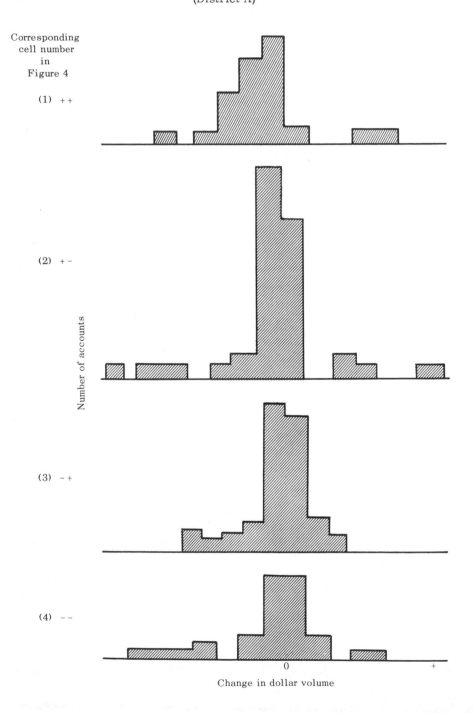

Conclusions Drawn

What use could be made of these results? The problem of allocation of sales effort among accounts had not been and could not be
solved with the available data, and time did not permit the generation of the required data. These results, however, could be used
to make a more basic revision of allocation of sales effort than
had been expected.

For the three-year period studied, the data indicated that,
within the range of change in number of calls on accounts, there
was no effect on the average dollar return from the accounts included. This suggested that some reduction in number of calls
could have been made without reducing sales. The question was:
How much of a decrease in sales time could have been made without reducing the sales made to these accounts?

The maximum amount of reduction in calls that could be immediately justified by the available data would result from cutting
back to the smallest yearly number of calls that each account had
received in the three-year period. If, for example, an account
received 60 calls in 1952, 40 in 1953, and 50 in 1954, the number
of calls could apparently have been cut to 40 in 1954 for this account. It was assumed that any further cutback in calls would move
the account off the sales-response-curve plateau and begin to
decrease the dollar return from that account. *In the absence of
knowledge* about the shape of the curve for any account, this assumption was a conservative one, since a further reduction than
this could probably have been made for many accounts without
decreasing their dollar volume. The available data supported the
hypothesis that the accounts were saturated with calls, but it did
not indicate the extent of that saturation beyond the range of
number of calls made in the 1952-54 period.

For the three districts a computation was made of the reduction in calls that would have occurred in 1954 had this procedure
been followed. The average percentage reduction thus revealed is,
unfortunately, a "classified" figure. It was, however, considerably
larger than anyone had expected. From this reduction in number
of calls per account it was easy to determine how many additional
accounts on the average a salesman could handle. Indeed, it was
shown by generalization from the three sales districts that the
existing sales force was adequate to handle the increased number
of accounts resulting from the reorganization of the Division and
the anticipated increase in business for the first year of the Five-
Year Plan.

The question of whether or not heavier assignments to salesmen would affect total dollar return because of sales performance
was also raised. Of the twelve salesmen in Sales District A, three
were already carrying a larger number of accounts than the recommended average. These three were compared with the others
with respect to total dollar volume and dollars of sale per call.

As can be seen from Figures 6 and 7 they not only obtained a higher return per call on the average than the other nine salesmen, but also a higher total dollar volume. If, however, these two groups of salesmen are considered to be random samples from the population of salesmen, these differences were not statistically significant. Analysis of the mix of accounts of the three salesmen as compared with the others did not reveal any significant differences.

FIGURE 6

Dollar Return Per Call Versus Number of Contracts

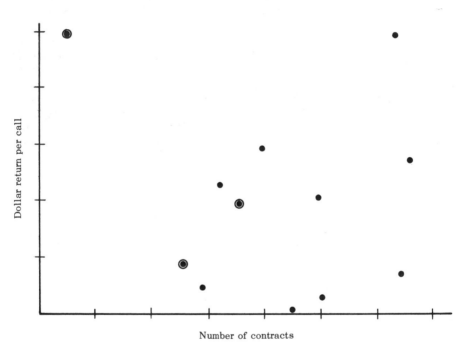

Number of contracts

Controlling the Situation

A final approach to the problem was made by examining the relation between changes in number of calls over the three-year period (1952–54) and changes in dollar volume. In this analysis the team concerned itself only with the *net* changes between 1952 and 1954. Although no statistically significant relation was found, there was some indication that there might, over a longer time period, be a lag in the response of dollar volume to changes in number of calls. Consequently, if the recommended reduction in average number of calls per account were to be adopted, some control or checking procedure was required.

FIGURE 7

Total List Sales Versus Number of Contracts

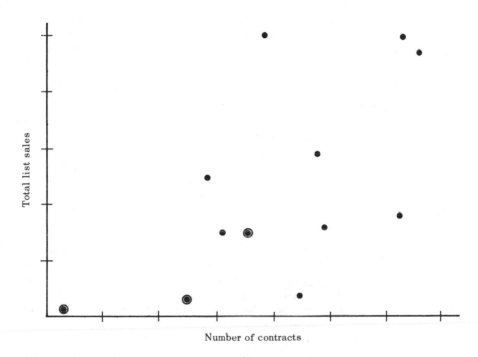

Note: The three dots furthest to the right (Figures 6 and 7) represent the performance of salesmen with greater than the recommended average number of accounts. The encircled dots represent the performances of personnel who have other responsibilities in addition to selling and have no particular significance here.

The procedure developed was a simple one, but it required the systematic maintenance of sales-call reports. It consisted of an annual multiple correlation analysis of changes in dollar volume that year with changes in number of calls for each of the preceding ten years. A routine prescription for this control was prepared for company personnel. If a significant correlation were found between dollar volume and separate or combined annual changes in calls, it would reveal any lag in response and, hence, start to give data of use in constructing sales-response curves.

In subsequent years the number of sales calls per account was systematically further reduced by small increments. In the third year the saturation point apparently was reached in several areas and sales-call frequency was stabilized there. This process was continued until a similar state was reached in other areas.

Related Research Findings

The data collected made it possible to perform several important analyses on related aspects of sales effort. These are summarized here.

With the cooperation of salesmen in District A, a time study was made of one month's operations. In addition to the regular call report form, the salesmen filled out additional information for each call during the month of June, 1954. For each call the mileage, travel time, waiting time, and interview time were recorded. In addition the amount of "administrative time" in the office was recorded.

The sample thus obtained consisted of only nine out of more than 300 salesmen, and the data were derived for only one month of performance (perhaps not even a typical one). Consequently no far-reaching conclusions could be drawn, but some of the patterns and relations were consistent enough in the sample to indicate the probability that they applied rather generally. Some of the more interesting results were as follows:

1. Travel time was related to distance traveled only within wide limits, and a more important factor was apparently the type of territory in which the salesmen operated. Calls in metropolitan areas consumed much more travel time than might be anticipated; those in "country" territories, much less. The time per call in the two areas was almost identical, although the distance traveled per call was twice as great, and the most stable estimate of travel time seemed to be a percentage of the total available time of the salesman and not the distance traveled. The range of sample used was limited, with only a few individual calls representing more than 60 miles traveled. A test of a district involving greater distances between accounts would be needed to confirm this result since it was obtained for a predominantly metropolitan district.

2. Waiting time was apparently an insignificant proportion of the total time involved: namely, about six minutes on the average and the same regardless of the type of call being made.

3. Interview time showed a rather stable relation to the type of account called upon. The average times of four major classes of accounts were tested for significance, and the differences were found to be significantly greater among the groups than within them. Differences in salesmen, in location of accounts, or in other characteristics tested did not seem to affect the average call time. These results would also require examination by a further sample, and if similar results are found, they could be sufficient to sup-

port differences in direct-selling expense among these types of accounts.

4. "Administrative time" was a higher proportion of the total time than expected. However, this was the least reliable of the estimates, since it resulted from a sample of only nine fulltime salesmen, whereas the call data came from a sample of over 1,000 calls.

The cooperation of the salesmen in the collecting and processing of the data was elicited by means of a complete explanation of the basic purpose of the analysis. It was emphasized that the study was not a review of their own efficiency. The salesmen completed a daily call report form indicating each call (including office time spent), the time spent on each interview, and the mileage. The net mileage and time for each call were computed by subtraction and punched on IBM cards.

Return Per Sales Call by Type of Account

It was possible to estimate the sales and cost per call for each type of account thus enabling the research team to estimate the cost of sales by type of account. These data, which had not previously been available to division management, together with an estimate of the profit derived from a class of accounts provided an estimate of net return per sales dollar by type of account. Differences in "dollars per call" were as great as eight to one among major account classes, and several hundred to one among minor account classes. These results indicated *that the practice of allocating sales cost proportionately to sales (dollar) volume can lead to serious errors.* Modification of this accounting procedure was suggested and steps were taken in this direction.

The analysis was extended to include calls on prospects that were converted into accounts. These "realized" prospects were classified in the same way as the existing accounts, and return per call was determined for both the sum of "before conversion" and "after conversion" calls per year, and "after conversion" calls alone. Two important results were obtained:

1. On the average, new accounts yielded considerably less return per call (in the first year) than old accounts.
2. Certain classes of new accounts, however, yielded more return per call in the first year than certain classes of old accounts.

This indicated that a reallocation of calls from certain types of established accounts to other classes of prospects could be expected to increase the productivity of sales effort.

Optimum Number of Calls on Prospects

The analysis described in the previous section suggested the following operation. A table was prepared listing the number of prospects and the number of calls made on them over the two-year period, 1952-53 (Table 1). It is apparent from these data that three calls per prospect yields the maximum return in number of accounts per call on the average. If, in fact, only three calls had been made on accounts on which four or more calls were actually made, and on the assumption that additional prospects of the same type could have been found, 248 calls (1148-900) would have been made on approximately 82 additional prospects with the same number of salesmen. These calls could have yielded (248/13.8) or 18 accounts while the data in the table indicate that these calls actually yielded only eight (73-65) accounts. The policy of a maximum of three calls per prospect, could then, on the basis of this analysis, yield a 14 percent increase in number of new accounts (from 73 to 83) with the same number of calls. The actual data indicated a possible increase of 11 percent.

TABLE 1

Direct Prospect Analysis [a.]

No. of Calls	Cumulative No. of Accounts Obtained [b.]	Cumulative No. of Prospects Dropped	Cumulative Totals, No. of Calls	No. of Calls per Conversion
1	30	220	500	16.7
2	50	300	750	15.0
3	65	325	900	13.8
4	70	350	1,010	14.4
5	72	370	1,090	15.1
6	73	380	1,148	15.7

a. Total number of prospects called on (1952-53) = 500
b. Numbers slightly disguised.

Division of Time Between Sales and
Service

On the call reports maintained in one sales district, several of the salesmen described their activity during the call. These activities were classified as sales (e.g., arranging sales meetings, writing orders, instructing customer's salesmen) or service (e.g., checking billings, taking inventory, changing source of supply). The data were incomplete and could not be assumed to be representative,

but they nevertheless indicated about an even division of the salesman's time between sales and service.

The appearance of this large percentage of time spent in
servicing customers suggested the need for the systematic accum-
ulation of more representative data to substantiate the possibility
of having agents less expensive than salesmen perform at least
some of the service functions—possibly service representatives
working out of the district sales offices.

Recommendations and Action Taken

The recommendations submitted on the basis of this study were
the following (as quoted from the final report):

Analyses of data on sales calls and sales volume from a sample of three
sales districts showed that within the range of the number of calls currently
being made on accounts, variations in the number of calls have no effect
on sales volume. Specifically, the study indicated that (assuming the same
mixture of sales and service calls) the number of calls required, on the
average, to obtain 1954's volume of business could have been reduced by
X percent. Put another way, the average salesman could have carried $X/$
$(100-X)$ percent more accounts in 1954 (an average of Y) without having
affected the sales volume obtained per account.

This conclusion suggests that the estimates for additional sales force
requirements made by the Task Force be revised down. The present sales
force is more than adequate to handle the increased number of accounts
created by the reorganization of the Division into three lamp departments
with separate sales forces.

In addition to this main result, several subordinate conclusions
and recommendations were reached:

A study of the way salesmen spend their time indicates that a significant
portion while on duty is not spent with customers. This suggests that additional time can be made available for sales both by decreasing time
spent in the office and by more efficient use of this office time in planning
sales activity. This study made only on one sales district should be extended to other districts before general conclusions are drawn.

A study of the responsiveness of prospects to calls in one sales district
shows that by restricting the number of calls that are made on a prospect
to Z, an 11 percent increase in the number of new accounts per year can
be obtained (on the assumption that additional and equally good prospects
are available).

A study of remarks made concerning the nature of calls made on accounts
on a restricted sample of call reports shows that time is about equally divided between sales and service functions. Therefore, it may be possible
to separate these functions so that highly skilled salesmen can be used to
better advantage. *Before such conclusions could be drawn, a more systematic study would be required.*

On the basis of these recommendations several actions were
taken. The plan to add to the sales force the number of salesmen

recommended by the Task Force was curtailed. Also, District Sales Managers were urged to initiate salesmen-call reports on a regular basis, and one of the new finished-product departments instituted call reports as a standard part of the salesman's operations. Finally, a new report form was designed by the research team, using the knowledge it had gained during the study and the District Sales Managers were encouraged to take the initiative in carrying out self-analysis along the lines indicated by the study.

At the end of the first year under the five-year plan, sales-volume objectives were met. *The annual saving* realized by *not* acquiring the additional number of salesmen originally recommended was approximately *25 times the cost of the study.*

IV

Measuring Effectiveness
and Developing Incentive Plans

IN THIS CHAPTER four extensions of the analysis begun in Chapter III are presented. First, the problems of measuring effectiveness are discussed in light of information obtained in a number of interviews with marketing executives. Next, a second operations research study is presented, in which the differences in sales volume among several territories are examined with regard to some combination of differences in territorial characteristics, personal characteristics of the salesman and the nature of the salesman's activities. Then, the third operations research study is described, in which an experimental design was utilized to determine the effects of changed expenditures for advertising, point-of-purchase materials, and personal selling effort upon sales volume. Finally, an application of the methods of time and duty study, together with a comparison of the results of several such studies, is outlined.

As already indicated, the purpose of presenting these experimental studies is *partly to demonstrate the method of experimentation and partly to provide a base from which to develop a more generalized theory of personal selling.* The critical reader will have little difficulty in questioning the relatively crude assumption structure underlying these experiments. Indeed, the remainder of this volume will be devoted to the search for an improvement of the assumptions made here about human behavior. Yet, it is by means of experimental efforts such as these that the demand for new and improved concepts is given impetus and direction.

AN INPUT-OUTPUT VIEW OF THE PROMOTIONAL TASK

To illustrate the problem of promotional effectiveness in terms that relate to the concept of a marketing mix, the language of input-output analysis provides a useful expository device. The objectives of a given promotional effort, by which is meant some set of data delivered by specified media, are often difficult to specify; however, one may, for example, seek only to inform a given set of buyers, or one may seek to modify the attitudes or predispositions of a set of buyers toward a product or a seller. These undefined, but nevertheless differentiated, psychological responses can be considered as outputs that are sought through promotion. The general relationship involved may be illustrated as shown.

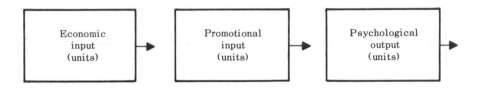

On the assumption that the achievement of a particular marketing goal requires certain intermediate psychological outputs, the implication is that these outputs require different input mixes. The problem of promotional allocation, therefore, becomes one of *segmenting markets in such a manner that a given set of psychological outputs are achieved at the lowest possible economic cost.* The units of promotional input in this context, represent some measure of effectiveness in terms of psychological outputs. Some of them might, for example, represent the effectiveness of personal selling efforts in informing, influencing, and persuading.

The psychological outputs essentially constitute informational or data inputs to the buying situation which, in turn, produces an economic output as shown below:

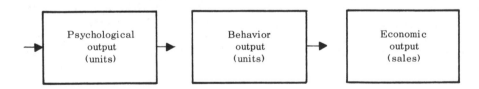

For example, a minimum sales goal in a specific market might be developed. In this context, the total market may be segmented with reference to different classes of customers, or with reference to different time periods projected into the future. The problem here is one of finding the levels of psychological inputs that will minimize economic costs and, at the same time, satisfy the specified sales objectives. The "behavior outputs" thus represent the economic response of the buyer to functionally differentiated psychological inputs and their "values" may consequently change as a result of changes in the buyer himself apart from the effects of promotion.[1]

From this simplified version of the input-output model it is evident that the *effectiveness* of a promotional mix or any one promotional medium must be some function of the psychological variables entering into a buying situation regardless of their source. The *efficiency* of any one promotional medium constitutes a relative measure of a given medium's "ability" to achieve a specified level of effectiveness at a minimum cost.

THE EFFECTIVENESS, EFFICIENCY CONUNDRUM

Perhaps one of the most difficult problems in the management and operation of personal selling is that of measuring and influencing both effectiveness and efficiency of the selling function without unduly sacrificing significant elements of either of these two qualities. In the context of economic theory the problem appears deceptively simple since effectiveness is equated with efficiency in the concept of "maximum" or "optimum" return. While this simplicity is philosophically satisfying, it hardly constitutes an operational definition of either effectiveness of efficiency or both. To clarify the issue, the relationship between efficiency and effectiveness may be stated as follows:

$$\text{Efficiency} = \frac{\text{Effectiveness}}{\text{Cost}}$$

It is immediately evident that the efficiency of performance of a given task or function may be influenced either by decreasing the cost or increasing the effectiveness of the performance. In the experiment described previously the primary emphasis was placed on influencing the cost of the personal selling function for a given and predicted level of effectiveness. The usual measure of effectiveness of marketing and selling operations is sales revenue or occasionally profits. Upon further examination of the personal selling function it is evident, however, that it is possible to divide the problem of measuring selling effectiveness into several subproblems each of which can be distinguished in terms of the entities, or systems, and the relevant standards of measurement involved:

1. The strengths and weaknesses of the personal selling function (total sales force) *in a given marketing environment.*
2. The effectiveness and efficiency of a given salesman in a *specific territory.*
3. The effectiveness and efficiency of a given salesman vis-à-vis a *specific buyer.*

All too often selling effectiveness is discussed with reference to only one of these levels without due recognition of the importance

and interrelatedness of *all* the levels. With reference to the first
level, the important point, in addition to the problems involved in
establishing the "optimum" size of a given sales force, is the
more fundamental question of determining the applicability of
personal selling in a given marketing environment. Ideally, one
would require some explicit concept of the strengths and weaknesses of personal selling as a promotional tool to make generalized statements about the utility of a sales force in a specific
environment. No such concept exists, however, and since the
problem does not admit of a "maximum" solution within the state-
of-the-art of economic and quantitative theory and methodology
some alternative approach had to be found. To secure some initial
indication of the views held by marketing executives on this problem, the Marketing Science Institute conducted a survey among
twelve sponsor and member companies, none of which can be
identified here, but all of which have had a great deal of experience in the use of personal selling. The data derived from that
survey are not sufficiently specific to be subjected to statistical
analysis, but some results of a clinical analysis of the data are
summarized below.

SOME EMPIRICAL OBSERVATIONS
ABOUT THE ROLE OF PERSONAL SELLING

One of the conclusions developed in the earlier promotional
decision making study,[2] in connection with the examination of
decisions involving trade-offs, among personal selling, sales
promotion, and advertising efforts, was that consumer goods
companies tended primarily to focus most attention on advertising
as a means of promoting their products, while, in contrast, indus-
trially oriented companies appeared to focus more on the personal
selling function. This tendency toward a "typical" promotional mix
is outlined diagrammatically in Figure 8.

The survey completed in connection with the present study
revealed a number of possible reasons for this difference in degree
of utilization of personal selling between consumer and industrial
marketing organizations. The cost of customer contacts was found
to vary markedly between personal and nonpersonal means, and
markets for frequently purchased consumer products were found
generally to be broadly dispersed, reasonably homogeneous with
respect to information requirements, and generally producing a
relatively low return per sale. Consequently, nonpersonal means
would be expected to predominate in the consumer market because
of the relatively low cost per contact of this type of promotion.

On the other hand, it is characteristic of industrial markets
and selected luxury consumer goods (power boats, swimming
pools, vacation homes) that the number of potential customers is

FIGURE 8

Promotional Mixes for Consumer and Industrial Goods

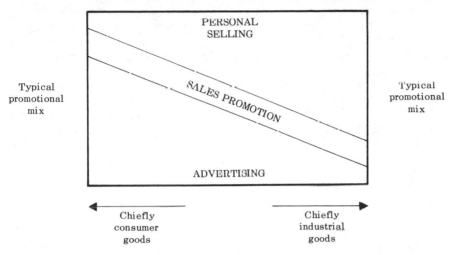

relatively small, the value systems of potential buyers are more disparate, and the expected revenue per customer "conversion" is high. *Not only is there greater requirement for personal selling, but the market characteristics are such as to permit higher cost contacts.*

The differences in utilization of personal selling between consumer goods and industrial goods producers and middlemen do no more than indicate that there are some economic constraints on the uses of personal selling in certain large markets. Within these broad constraints, however. a number of different situations prevail. As an illustration, a firm selling a packaged food product may utilize salesmen only for trade contacts with supermarket chain buyers or individual store owners. All promotion directed at the ultimate consumer may involve nonpersonal means such as broadcast advertising, point-of-purchase displays, and direct mail. The firm, however, may view the salesman's task as involving display arrangement, advice to the store owner on inventory policy, and taking care of store owner complaints on return items. In this situation the functions which personal versus nonpersonal sales effort serve are quite different and, in effect, complementary. Another firm selling the same product class may elect to utilize food brokers rather than employ its own salesman. While the same general function is being performed, this latter firm's sales effort mix would differ markedly from that of the firm which employed its own salesmen.

Even though most of the companies interviewed by the Institute employed some combination of personal and nonpersonal promo-

tional means in their marketing efforts, all the respondents tended
to view personal selling as distinct in *purpose* from nonpersonal
sales efforts whether or not a consumer item was involved. On the
whole, salesmen were viewed as "problem solvers," giving advice
to buyers on such matters as product functions, inventory policy,
and display setups. In other words, respondents *did not view
personal and nonpersonal selling as interchangeable* even within
the limits established by economic constraints.

It was indicated in Chapter II that the so-called Characteristics
of Goods theory has so far failed to explain the emphasis on personal selling in certain markets. Even if a theory of personal
selling based on product differences were developed, however, it
would still be highly unsatisfactory from a planning point of view
primarily because products, and people's perceptions of products,
change continually. If a theory of personal selling is to be developed
which will provide some guidelines for examining the feasibility
and applicability of personal selling in a given market on the basis
of the broad economic parameters mentioned above, a more comprehensive approach to the establishment of the strengths and
weaknesses of personal selling as a unique promotional tool is
required.

EFFECTIVENESS OF THE SALESMAN IN A
GIVEN TERRITORY

It was evident from the Institute's interviews that the concept of
engineering salesmen or technical representatives is spreading to
consumer goods companies in the form of specialized and "pro-
fessionalized" salesmen. Less emphasis is being placed on order
taking, in line with greater centralized buying operations on the
part of supermarket chains and large wholesalers and more attention is being given to technical and marketing services both in
consumer and industrial selling. In light of such changes the
system of developing quotas on the basis of forecasts of the
"potential" of a given territory is of questionable value and so,
perhaps, is the usefulness of the territory as an entity of the market
area, at least in certain markets.

In any case, as was emphasized in the previous chapter, the
efficiency with which a salesman covers a given territory is not
necessarily, if at all, related to his effectiveness as measured in
sales. The following experimental study constitutes a specific
attempt to develop a satisfactory measure of, as well as a method
of influencing, the effectiveness of any given salesman's efforts
with reference to a specific territory. In this case the research
team recognized that several variables were influential in producing sales, and consequently attempted to separate the effects
of three broad classes of variables—namely territorial character-

istics, personality characteristics of salesmen, and the activities of salesmen—to arrive at some measure of what difference the salesman's efforts made in a given territory.

STUDY NUMBER 2:   DEVELOPING A MEASURE OF EFFECTIVENESS

As already indicated, the nature of the company involved in this study cannot be revealed but it has many characteristics in common with a publisher of college textbooks. It introduces a relatively large number of "new products" each year. Its representatives call on college instructors who specify books to be purchased by their students but do not make the purchases themselves. In fact, instructors usually receive copies of the books they want without cost. Although the representatives occasionally call on textbook stores, this is usually not to obtain orders.

The question asked in this study was how to measure a salesman's performance so that an effective system of rewards could be developed and so that a determination could be made of the appropriate size of territories. The assumptions underlying the approach that was developed were as follows: The difference in sales volume between different territories is due to some combinations of differences in (1) territorial characteristics, (2) what the salesman is (i.e., his personal characteristics), and (3) what the salesman does.

Since all the competitors distribute their product nationally, the composition of competition in each territory was essentially similar. Of course, a competitor's effectiveness in any specific territory might be due to the effectiveness of his salesmen, but since information relevant to this possibility was not available, it had to be "overlooked" in this situation.

It was also assumed that other types of marketing effort were evenly distributed over sales territories, an assumption that appeared quite reasonable in this case. Understanding the method used in this study requires an explanation of the concept of *variance* of territorial sales. If for each time period (e.g., month or year) the average amount sold per territory is calculated from total sales, then the difference (deviation) of each territory's actual sales from the average can be determined. It is now possible to square these deviations, thus making them all positive (since the square of negative numbers is a positive number), and to calculate the average of these squared values. This average is the statistical *variance* of the sales, and measures the spread or dispersion of actual territorial sales around the average. If average territorial sales are used to *forecast* each territory's sales, this variance can be used to measure the reliability or precision of such a forecast.

Now suppose another forecast is prepared using information about the *potential* of each territory—for example, its size (population), median income, number of retail outlets, and so on. The average deviation of each territory's actual sales from this forecast constitutes the variance of the forecast. If, for example, the variance of actual sales around the *forecast* is only half as large as that around the average of actual *territorial sales,* then the territorial characteristics employed in the forecast are said "to account for" 50 percent of the variance reduction. Clearly, a perfect forecasting technique would produce a variance equal to zero.

The study began by preparing a forecast based on territorial characteristics, and was developed of all territorial characteristics that informed persons believed were relevant. Those characteristics for which current or accurate measures could not be obtained had to be dropped, although with some reluctance. The final forecasting procedure did not contain measures of all the remaining variables tested, since, as is often the case, many of these turned out to show no relationship to sales.[4]

Such a forecasting procedure "accounts for" a determinable amount of the variance of territorial sales. In the case involved here, 30 percent of the variance was accounted for by territorial variables. (In other studies larger and smaller percentage reductions have been attained.)

The next step was to determine how much of the variance around the forecast could be accounted for by the personal characteristics of the salesman assigned to each territory. The company involved uses a personnel selection procedure which includes extensive psychological testing of candidates for selling jobs and scores on these tests were examined to determine how much of the "residual" or remaining variance (70 percent) they could account for.

In this case seven psychological variables accounted for 52 percent of the residual variance. Included among these variables were (1) persuasive ability, (2) mental adaptability, and (3) steadiness.

A combination of these two analyses shows the amount of variance of territorial sales accounted for to be:

$$30 + .52 \,(.70) = .66 \quad \text{or} \quad 66\%$$

Further efforts were then made to account for the remaining 34 percent of the variance, but with little success. Some of it can be due to variables not considered or to characteristics of the statistical analysis, but at least some portion of it is due to what the salesman does, and this is the important point. What the salesman *does,* in contrast to personality and territorial characteristics would appear to account for no more than 34 percent of the variance around average territorial sales. Hence, the salesman's *performance* should be evaluated only with reference to this "residual" variance, and this can be done in the following way.

Each territory's sales are predicted, using the territorial and salesman characteristics. The difference of actual sales from the forecast is determined *and it is this difference which should be used in evaluating the salesman's performance.* Normally this can be done by converting the difference into a percentage of the forecast:

$$100 \left[\frac{\text{Actual Sales - Forecast Sales}}{\text{Forecast Sales}} \right]$$

If this percentage is positive, the salesman's performance is better than expected; if it is negative, his performance is below expectations. Clearly, then, a more equitable basis is provided for incentive and bonus payments than that supplied by actual sales alone.

The information obtained from an analysis such as the above may also be useful in evaluating personnel selection procedures. Furthermore, the analysis itself can be refined continuously as better information becomes available and time permits the use of more sophisticated, although also more time consuming, statistical techniques. In any case, the key problem addressed here is that of matching rewards with a measure of productivity which more nearly indicates the "effect" of the salesman's performance. In Chapter XIV this same problem will be considered more generally and in a qualitative fashion with reference to the relevance of any given salesman's activities against certain general buyer characteristics. It will be shown then that the nature of the relationship between buyers and sellers is such that the relevance and quality of a salesman's efforts are not measurable entirely, if at all, in terms of sales.

In the following study, attempts were made at developing a reward scheme which would provide an equitable and continually increasing incentive for sales made above a given forecast. The study was also designed to investigate the combined and individual "effects" of the different elements of the company's marketing mix. Even though the experiment thus covers several aspects of marketing and does not completely isolate personal selling effort as the sole dependent variable, it does provide an interesting example of a highly developed incentive plan.

STUDY NUMBER 3:
INFLUENCING THE SALESMAN'S EFFECTIVENESS

This study involves a major producer of a widely sold packaged food. Marketing management wanted to know how much to spend annually on (1) advertising, (2) salesmen, and (3) point-of-sales displays and materials. Since available data did not permit direct analyses to be made, an experiment was designed. The experiment was somewhat constrained as a result of management's being initially reluctant to allow more than a handful of the company's approximately 250 territories to be experimentally manipulated. The design involved the determination of three levels of each variable, on the basis of "last year's budgeted territorial expenditure" for each of the three promotional methods:

Advertising
1. 25% reduction
2. 0%—no change
3. 50% increase

Sales Effort
1. 50% reduction
2. No change
3. 50% increase

Point-of-Sale
1. 50% reduction
2. No change
3. 25% increase

These levels yield 27 (3 × 3 × 3) possible combinations and, hence, the minimal number of territories, 27, was used in the initial experiment. This experimental design made it possible not only to measure the effect of changes in levels of each of the three controlled variables, but also to determine if sales were influenced by interaction between effects of simultaneous changes in more than one factor.

First it was necessary to determine what measure of performance was to be used. Monthly sales to retailers by territory in dollars was one possibility, but it was unsatisfactory for several reasons. These sales volumes are obviously affected by factors other than the three controlled in the experiment, such as territorial characteristics, competitive characteristics (which varied by territory in this case), and buying behavior. Therefore, a forecast was developed based on territorial and competitive characteristics and on seasonal patterns of consumption and sales of the two product classes involved. The forecast thus developed accounted for a substantial percentage of the variance of monthly territorial sales around their average. The measure of performance used, then, was the percentage deviation of actual monthly sales from that forecasted for the territory.

The results of this experiment on the principal class of products yielded a different result for each of the three promotional methods as shown in Table 2.

It will be observed, first, that sales were more sensitive to changes in advertising and point-of-sale promotion than to changes in personal selling, which apparently was at approximately the optimum level before change. In particular, the effect of

TABLE 2

Effects of Changes of Expenditures on Sales
in Percent Error of Forecasts
Product Class I

Variable	Percentage Change				
	−50%	−25%	0%	+25%	+50%
Sales Effort	−1.9		0		−0.1
Advertising		+5.0	0		+5.1
Point-of-Sales	−6.3		0	−10.6	

advertising could apparently be improved by either increasing or decreasing expenditures. The reason for this will be considered in a moment.

The corresponding effect on sales of the second product class is shown in Table 3.

TABLE 3

Effects of Changes of Expenditures on Sales
in Percent Error of Forecasts
Product Class II

Variable	Percentage Change				
	−50%	−25%	0%	+25%	+50%
Sales Effort	+3.5		0		+29.1
Advertising		+20.0	0		+17.2
Point-of-Sales	+19.0		0	−22.6	

For this product class personal selling efforts were too low and point-of-sale appeared to be much too high. The effect of advertising was similar to that found in the case of the first product class.

Since the smaller of these differences could be due to variables not controlled in the experiment or "cancelled out" by the forecasts, the conclusions drawn had to be appropriately tempered. Point-of-sale efforts were reduced for product class II and advertising was reduced for both product classes. Sales effort was kept at the same level even for product class II because the cost of increasing the effort 50 percent could not be justified by the amount of profit which would be realized from the increased sales. The forecasted results of these changes were obtained subsequently, thus confirming the experimental predictions. Since there apparently were no significant interactions between changes in different modes, the results could be and were treated independently.

The curious effects of changes obtained with reference to advertising were investigated and found to be due primarily to the fact that the response of high income groups was different from that of other groups. Decreases in expenditures on advertising produced increases in purchases by high income consumers and decreases in purchases by others while increases produced the converse effect.

The relative insensitivity of sales to expenditures on personal selling appeared to indicate that the salesmen were not using their time effectively. This led to two actions: first, the development of an incentive plan that would make them "try harder;" and second, a study of how they spend their time.

The field selling force was organized in divisions and the divisions were grouped in regions. Hence there were essentially four levels of sales effort:

1. Salesmen
2. Division Sales Managers
3. Regional Sales Managers
4. Corporate Sales Managers

Specific incentive schemes were developed to cover each of these levels. The scheme developed for salesmen was a volume-based incentive plan rather than a profit-based plan since the salesmen have no control over price and, hence, cannot affect profitability of sales. In addition, it was considered risky to provide salesmen with detailed profit information since movement of these men to employment by competitors was not uncommon.

The basic characteristics of the incentive plans were set down in meetings between top management and the researchers:

1. A maximum total payment was established as a function of gross annual sales volume.
2. Forecasts prepared by the researchers were to be used to establish the base (i.e., expected sales) for each salesman rather than budgets set by negotiation and other "mysterious" processes.
3. Total payments to the salesmen under the new plan should be approximately the same as the total bonuses which were actually paid by the company during the previous three years.
4. No person should receive an incentive payment in excess of a specified percentage of his salary (which percentage cannot be revealed here). In addition, it was agreed that,
   a. The difficulty of actually obtaining a given percentage increase over forecasted sales increased with the size of the volume forecasted. That is, it was harder to increase sales by copy

expected sales were $1,000,000 than one in which it was $100,000.

b. It was more difficult to get the second percentage increase in sales than the first, still more difficult for the third, and so on.

c. The plan should take account of seniority or rank (grade) of the salesman.

d. Since, on the average, 50 percent of the salesmen would not meet forecasted sales, incentive payments should begin at a figure less than the forecasted amount but should be small until the forecast had been exceeded. This was to keep them "trying" rather than have them "give up" during a bad year.

e. The method of computing incentives must be simple enough so that each salesman can compute it himself.

The form of the incentive equation which satisfies these conditions is:

$$A \left(\frac{\text{Actual Sales}}{\text{Forecast Sales}} - B \right)^C \times \sqrt{\text{Forecast Sales}} \times \text{Grade}$$

Various combinations of the values of A, B, and C were tried in a simulation from which estimates of individual and total payments could be calculated. These constants were varied until the results of the simulation satisfied conditions 1, 2, and 3 above. A plan developed in this manner was installed after being unanimously approved by the field selling force as well as by management.

Since the plan was installed at the time the previously mentioned changes were made in expenditures in advertising and point-of-sale, it was not possible to measure its effect separately. The combined effect, however, was to produce a rate of increase in sales over that of the industry as a whole greater than ever had occurred before. This indicated strongly that, in the case of this company, *the individual salesman's activities are probably more important, within certain limits, than the number of salesmen employed by the company.*

A detailed study was subsequently conducted on how salesmen actually used their time. Data were collected for a period of twelve months, and managers and researchers who saw the preliminary data were convinced of the study's potential usefulness as an aid in modifying salesmen's activities in the direction of greater productivity.

Although it would be premature to discuss results, the methods used in the study may be of interest. Each of the several hundred salesmen kept a complete record of his time for one out of every four months over a year. These records were so arranged that analyses could be made by week, month, quarter season, district, and region. Daily records were kept on a 3 1/2 x 9 inch card for all seven days of the week. The period between 6:30 a.m. and

11:00 p.m. was broken down into 15-minute intervals and the salesman accounted for his time by inserting a code number to designate
his activity during each interval. These were as follows:

1. Travel (local and not-local differentiated)
2. Selling a customer
3. Service to a customer
4. Routine checking
5. Checking competition
6. Training
7. Entertaining
8. Waiting
9. Attending meeting
10. Preparing routine report
11. Preparing special report
12. Giving an oral report
13. Personal
14. Other

For each activity other than "Personal" the salesman also
was required to indicate where it took place:

1. At a company office
2. At home
3. At a wholesaler's place
4. Other

If the salesman was calling on a retailer he indicated the
product class involved and the type of retailer, specified by a
preestablished classification. He also indicated whether or not a
wholesaler's representative was present with him.

The data collection procedure was thoroughly discussed with
the salesmen before the process was initiated. They were assured
that only gross statistics, and no individual analyses, would be
submitted to the company. Careful examination of the records
turned in indicated that these were kept honestly. For example, the
average number of hours worked was very close to expectations
and apparently was not inflated. Variations from day to day, week
to week, and month to month indicated that insertions on the forms
were not made in any systematic way. Even so, some effects
attributable to the research procedure itself cannot be completely
discounted.

As indicated above, the analysis of these data is still in process.
But already some important results have been obtained. Relationships have been found between "the amount of time spent in certain
activities involving certain products and types of retailers" and
"sales of these products to these retailers." Gross differences in
performance with certain types of accounts in different regions also

seem to be explained. It is also clear that the salesmen had to do too much record keeping. Consequently, a follow-up study directed toward simplifying their record keeping was projected.

Discussion of the Experiments

Even on the basis of the limited experience briefly reviewed in these two cases, it is apparent that significant improvements in the effectiveness and efficiency of personal selling operations can be attained by "custom-made" studies of the problems at hand. It is equally apparent, however, that a more general concept of the role of personal selling is required before the full force of experimentation can be brought to bear on, and combined into, a theory of personal selling.

Perhaps the single most serious criticism which can be leveled at the above experimental cases is the dependency upon "countable" data necessitated by the quantitative methodology. Most marketers are well aware of the serious limitations of sales volume and profit as measures of selling and effectiveness. Indeed, the total business organization depends for its survival and growth upon the realization of a certain level of sales and profit, but it is not entirely clear how the salesman can be held responsible for the overall results of the organization's activities. The research team, of course, realized this problem and decided to use a measure of statistical variance of actual sales around a forecast as a measure of selling effectiveness.

Yet, if the problems of determining the effectiveness of the sales force and a given salesman in a specific territory were merely a function of a manager's or a researcher's forecasting ability, these problems might be alleviated relatively easily by the use of some participative method which enabled the salesman to influence the process, thereby at least maintaining agreement if not achieving accuracy. It appears, however, that the problem of establishing measures of effectiveness, relevant to all or even one of the three levels outlined earlier in this chapter, is conceptually more complex than it was possible to show in these experiments because of the simplifying assumptions which had to be made. This relative lack of conceptual complexity is particularly evident in view of the current discussion of the changing role of the salesman.

In a recent book, Professor Joseph W. Thompson[5] elaborates on a concept of the salesman as a "manager" of a given territory and as a member of the marketing management "team." He provides the following example:

In the following example the interaction of the market manager, the sales manager, and the salesman's job is seen. This company, a nationally known manufacturer of sterling silver tableware, visualizes market management (vice-president of marketing), sales management, and the salesman as a vertically and horizontally integrated marketing team. Management, confronted in 1964 with a booming economy but almost static sales in sterling tableware, implemented a decision to investigate the possibility of manufacturing stainless steel tableware, a product which apparently was enjoying greatly increased consumer acceptance.

The market manager, through his sales managers and the sales force, researched the marketplace to discover what types, patterns, and price range of stainless steel tableware were being purchased as well as who were purchasing and where. Based on this research, market management in cooperation with production designed and produced a number of possible patterns of stainless steel tableware. Market management then in cooperation with sales management had the new patterns of stainless steel tableware market tested by the sales force. Results of these tests were reported to sales management. Reports were then made by sales management to market management. A decision was then made by the market manager in cooperation with finance and production (obviously the president made the final decision, however) to produce an extensive line of stainless steel tableware in a specific price range. Market management directed the advertising department to prepare an advertising and sales promotional program. Meanwhile each salesman selected in his territory retail outlets for the sale of the company's new line. Finally market management meshed the activities of the advertising department, sales management, and the sales force into one smoothly functioning selling team.

A major point being made in the case above is this: Sales management in this company still retained many of its functions of recruiting, selecting, compensating, etc., but the more the company utilized its sales force as market managers of a territory, the more the sales manager's role was involved with controlling and directing the market activities of the sales organization rather than supervising, stimulating, and motivation. Psychological fact suggests that when the salesman is viewed as a manager, less personal or sales-management-to-salesman supervision, stimulation, and motivation is needed.[6]

The essence of this example is that the potential role of the salesman is not limited to selling in the usual sense of that word, but that it constitutes a broad set of managerial activities. Clearly, the utilization of these *potential* capacities of the personal selling function requires more than a mere change in terminology; it requires a major shift in the philosophy of management and control of the function, as well as a more dynamic concept of effectiveness than that provided by economic theory.

EFFECTIVENESS OF THE SALESMAN VIS-À-VIS A BUYER

It was concluded in the first experiment that too much effort on the part of a salesman can be detrimental to sales. It is relatively easy to explain in economic terms the limitation on the amount of purchases that are going to be made by a given buyer. It is much more difficult to explain in operational terms why a certain excessive number of calls should influence the sales of a given product. The research team suggested that a buyer might become annoyed by an "unreasonable" call frequency. If this reasoning is acceptable, then it would seem that a salesman must somehow be able to distinguish between situations where selling is "unreasonable" and situations where selling is "reasonable," particularly if he operates under a compensation scheme which rewards only selling and does not provide any incentive in cases where "not selling" may increase sales.

One of the basic advantages of personal selling as an element of marketing is the salesman's potential ability to provide a dynamic link between the producer and one or more users of a given product or product class. Yet the problem of establishing some measures and standard of effectiveness of individual salesmen is quite frequently treated as if the activities and qualities of the salesmen were fully predictable. The most extreme example of this assumption of predictability is, of course, the "canned" sales presentation which essentially reduces the salesman to a wandering loudspeaker. The point to be made is that the majority of salesmen are potentially capable of doing far more than repeating a prerecorded message and the potential effectiveness of salesmen is therefore, in such cases, not being utilized, with resultant adverse effects upon the efficiency of the marketing mix.

By way of analogy, one would not expect a production manager to advocate the building of a plant with several hundred percent over-capacity, but that is in fact what occurs in many marketing operations. The reasons for this are many and involved and will be discussed in more detail in later chapters. Suffice it here to say that the effectiveness of a salesman is partly a function of his own competence with regard to a set of buyers, and partly a function of the degree to which the marketing manager is capable of facilitating the utilization of the salesman's potential ability.

CONTROLLING EFFECTIVENESS

Countless techniques have been proposed, and many of them used, to control the effectiveness and efficiency of the individual salesman. The time and duty study developed in the production plant has been applied to the salesman in the field. Here, as in the case of many other techniques the emphasis is on the "countable" data involving little reflection upon the actual meaning of such data as number of arguments presented, number of products mentioned, and time spent between calls. Indeed, the concept of control as applied to personal selling has, in many cases, not moved appreciably beyond the accounting notion of eliminating fraudulent behavior. Indeed, time and duty studies can be used to make certain that a salesman stays on the job, but they can give little if any indication of the *quality* of his performance. That is, they are effective primarily in calling attention to inefficiencies in performance, but the results of a time and duty study do not in and of themselves suggest remedial action, nor do they aid in determining whether such action is likely to have adverse effects on the *effectiveness* of the salesman's performance.

Observation is another technique which has been and is used to assess the effectiveness of salesmen in the presence of a buyer. Quite apart from the inevitable biases of the observer, which may be further aggravated by the expectations of biases on the part of the interpreter assessing the observer's report, no concepts have been advanced in personal selling literature which purports to explain what difference observation makes in the performance of a given salesman. It seems evident that observation, which does not lead to training, constitutes a futile exercise since the observer clearly sees what he wants to see, and not necessarily what he in some ideal sense should see.

One of the key problems underlying the effectiveness of observation as a control technique is the lack of a generalized concept of what constitutes "good" performance. A performance which differs from the observer's expectations is not necessarily bad; it may indeed be "better" than that which the observer is capable of expecting. Ultimately, observation constitutes a process of communication in which the observer attempts to interpret or "organize" the cues he perceives in his environment. In this sense, all measures of effectiveness, whether used for control purposes or not, are attempts at organizing the data deriving from events in the environment.

EXAMPLE OF A COMBINED OBSERVATION, TIME AND DUTY STUDY

As an example of the type of data typically derived from an observationally based time and duty study, a report resulting from such a study is summarized below. The summary includes comparisons with data gathered from similar studies such as a report published by Mr. Noble Hall of the Atlantic Refining Company [7] and a published study of the effectiveness of wholesale drug salesmen. [8] Unfortunately the names and products of the other five companies represented below have had to be disguised, but both the product differentiations and the selling situations are sufficiently similar among all six companies to warrant comparison.

The company originating the time and duty study (hereafter called Company X) was concerned about the relative selling effort devoted to its primary versus its specialty products as well as questions concerning time and cost allocations within the personal selling function. During the initial period of the study attempts were made to minimize possible mistrust or uncertainty on the part of the salesmen by guaranteeing anonymity, and by allowing salesmen and researchers a short time period to become acquainted. The researchers were subsequently required to maintain diaries of their observations while traveling with the salesmen for a period of one week. These diaries were later checked for validity against the salesmen's own records.

The purpose of the study was threefold:

1. To compare various time and duty studies which had been prepared by Company X and other companies.
2. To appraise the apparent performance of general salesmen on the basis of available information while pointing the way toward possible improvements or fields for further study.
3. To examine the selling function in relation to the total working time of a salesman as a basis for possible revisions of cost allocations and comparison with current accounting practices.

The data derived from the Company X study as well as similar data from selected other companies are shown in Table 4. The results and recommendations from the Company X study are summarized below:

1. The Company X salesmen appear to spend too much time in making a field call. In some instances the distances traveled may contribute to this. At times, inefficient routing of calls or calling during the buyer's absence may be factors. In any case, room for substantial time savings was indicated.
2. The time spent in credit and collections seemed excessive. If cut in half it would still leave above average time in which to do the work and so free some six percent of total field time for other duties. This suggested a need for re-examining divisional methods of billing. In addition, salesmen's tactics in handling these matters could be analyzed and perhaps modified.
3. Related Sales Activities was the largest item shown in the breakdown and so presents the greatest potential point of time saving. These activities arose chiefly from matters of company policy and necessary duties not actually constituting Direct Selling Effort. Over 45 percent of the salesman's time was taken up by Related Sales Activities, whereas the group average was only 37 percent of total field time.
4. Company X salesmen apparently spent less than one percent of their time on new business contacts whereas the group average was six percent. In view of the highly competitive climate that existed, it seems that soliciting new and competitive business should be allocated substantially more time, if only to retain a fair share of the market, and particularly so in regions where an increased market share was being sought.

SUMMARY TABLE OF SUPPORTING DATA

	Company X Percent	Company A Percent	Company B City Percent
FIELD TIME			
Promotional Selling	18.8	22.1	7.4
Buyer Assistance	14.3	11.3	15.4
Total Dir. Selling Effort	33.1	33.4	22.8
Related Sales Activities	45.7	44.1	52.0
New Business Contacts	0.8	1.6	5.8
Waiting and Misc.	9.6	6.5	10.9
Nondirect Conversation	10.8	14.4	8.5
Total Field Time			
(Excl. Trav. & Personal)	100.0	100.0	100.0
SPECIFIC FACTORS			
Credit & Collections			
(Incl. in Related			
Selling Activities)	11.8	4.1	0.9
Housekeeping	2.8	0.1	2.2
Av. Calls/Man Per Day	6	8	9
Av. Work. Day (Hrs.)			
(Excl. Meals & Personal)	7.9	7.8	8.8
Av. Time (Min.) Per Call			
(Incl. Travel Time)	78	59	60
Net Time (Min.) Call	48	32	36
(Excl. Travel)			
Av. Travel Time (Min.)	30	27	24
Between Calls			
SPECIALTY PRODUCTS ANALYSIS			
Percent of Dir. Sell. Effort on			
Spec. Products	76.1	56.8	
Percent of Field Time on Spec.			
Prod.	21.8	14.6	
Percent of Salesmen's Time Now			
Allocated to Spec. Products	9.1	13.6	

FOR COMPARATIVE TIME AND DUTY STUDY

Company B Other Percent	Company C Percent	Company D Percent	Company X Industrial Average Percent	Wholesale Drug Average Percent	Atlantic Refining Company Percent
11.3	14.6	14.9	15	25.4	10.4
12.6	17.0	17.7	15	23.9	17.9
23.9	31.6	32.5	30	49.3	37.3
42.0	18.2	18.8	37	13.4	38.5
5.7	11.6	8.8	6	—	3.0
8.5	16.1	16.8	11	28.3	11.9
19.9	22.5	23.1	16	9.0	9.0
100.0	100.0	100.0	100	100.0	100.0
0.5	6.4	6.5	5.0	—	2.7
2.2	2.4	2.5	2.0	—	2.4
8	11	12	9	9	12
8.8	8.4	8.4	8.3	7.7	8.0
66	47	43	59	49	41
39	25	25	34	36	30
27	22	18	25	13	11
68.2	56.0	48.9	61.2	—	—
8.7	17.8	15.9	15.8	—	—
9.3	4.8	—	9.2	—	—

5. It was concluded that Company X did not spend sufficient time on Buyer Assistance as a whole, and that Display Assistance, Managerial Advice and Sales Technique training were lacking. This presented a rather fundamental problem since few, if any, of the salesmen were equipped for giving adequate guidance in these matters. Salesmen training and refresher schools could be helpful in offsetting these apparent shortcomings. (It is doubtful that printed sales promotion aids would solve this lack of buyer knowledge.)

6. In view of the large amount of time spent on specialty products, there was left only about 25 percent of direct selling time for Company X's salesmen to promote the sale of primary products. Apparently these items required very little selling. If this were the case and additional time did not have to be spent on these primary lines, then any reduction in time spent on specialty selling should give added time for more customers per man, a higher call frequency or reduced sales force.

Discussion of the Time and Duty Study

It is evident from the original Company X report that care was taken in the design and execution of the above summarized study and that comparisons were made with companies which could reasonably be assumed to possess characteristics and selling problems similar to those of Company X. Yet it is worth noting that the summarized conclusions do not necessarily follow from the figures nor do these figures in and of themselves suggest any specific or even general remedial action. The key question with reference to the effectiveness and the efficiency of the personal selling function is what the salesman does and *why* he does it, rather than *how much* he does.

Ideally, of course, the data collected, with reference to a given activity, should be pertinent to some decision making process which in turn should be relevant to some "significant structure" in the environment, and not solely be determined by the requirements of a specific problem solving technique. An approach to this ideal would seem to require some concept of selling performance which not only identifies the level at which ineffectiveness and inefficiency occur in any specific situation, but also aids in determining the relevant operational characteristics of a management or decision and control system. It is this basic problem which will be addressed in the following chapters, beginning with a structuring of the relationships involved in selling and followed by the development of a concept or theory of the interactive process, or interpersonal communication process, which characterizes the personal selling function.

SUMMARY OF PART TWO

The primary purpose of Chapters III and IV is to report on the method and results of three studies of personal selling activities conducted under the supervision of Dr. Russell L. Ackoff. The first study undertaken was designed to determine the relationship between actual sales and number of calls made by salesmen. It was found, in this specific case, that salesmen were actually making too many calls and that sales volume was unaffected when the number of sales calls was drastically reduced. On the basis of this finding the researchers suggested a reassignment of salesmen and a reallocation of effort so that the same number of salesmen could cover more customers.

The problem addressed in the second study was one of establishing a measure of a salesman's performance so that an effective system of rewards and a measure of some appropriate size of territories could be developed. The method involved the measurement of how well the salesmen did as compared with a forecast based on a combination of territorial characteristics (size, median income, number of retail outlets, and others) and personal characteristics of the salesman (including persuasive ability, mental adaptability and steadiness). The researchers concluded that the quality of the salesman's performance accounted for approximately 34 percent of the variance of actual sales around the forecast, and on this basis an incentive plan was developed designed to reward only that part of the variance attributable to the factors isolated as controllable by the salesman.

The third case involves the design of an experiment to determine how much to spend annually on advertising, salesmen, and point-of-sale displays and materials respectively. It was observed, first, that sales for this specific company apparently were more sensitive to changes in advertising and point-of-sale than to personal selling effort. Both personal selling and point-of-sale were thought to be at approximately an "optimum" level, whereas improvements in the effect of advertising could be achieved by appropriate changes.

Each of the three studies or experiments was successful in the sense that significant gains were made in performance as a result of the changes suggested by the research team. Furthermore, even though the results of the studies do not in themselves constitute a theory of personal selling, they do provide fresh insights and some starting points for the development of more general concepts.

In addition to the experimental studies, attempts are made in the two chapters to outline some implications of economic theory for the problems of personal selling. It is concluded from this latter discussion that while economic theory provides a comprehensive method of describing the relationships between such relatively complex concepts as effectiveness and efficiency, it does not by itself provide an operationally relevant definition of the complex relationships involved in personal selling activity.

The discussion contained in the following chapters is designed to improve this economic framework by introducing appropriate concepts from the various behavioral sciences with the ultimate aim of contributing to the development of an operationally viable theory of personal selling.

PART THREE

The Competence-Activity (COMPACT) Model

V

Systems, Communication, and Motivation

IT IS EVIDENT from the experimental cases in Part Two that the relationship between selling effort and actual sales is more involved than might have been anticipated. Difficulties in producing generalizable results through experimentation arise primarily from the complexity of the behavioral aspects of the buyer-seller relationship.

While it seemed clear in the study described in Chapter III that sales were unaffected by reductions in the number of calls made by the company's salesmen, it does not necessarily follow that such extra calls did not serve some useful function. Similarly, an incentive plan based on a variance around a forecast depends for its relevance—from a performance point of view—almost entirely upon the quality of the forecast. Indeed, application of quantitative techniques to personal selling situations in the manner suggested in Part Two can be carried out only by assuming away most of the behavioral and communicative aspects of selling. But it is precisely these essentially human aspects which are central to an effective use of personal selling as a marketing tool. These considerations as well as the understandable reluctance of marketers to experiment with their sales forces, provide an incentive to search for and utilize available theory and research findings from the behavioral sciences relevant to the problem areas of personal selling.

Thus it is the purpose of the following chapters to develop and present a foundation for an application of qualitative, dynamic concepts of behavior and communication relevant to marketing and, more specifically, to personal selling. The present chapter is devoted to the introduction of a number of modern concepts from the behavioral sciences and communication theory which are basic to the material developed in subsequent chapters. Although efforts are made in the following to avoid excessive use of technical jargon, certain terms and concepts peculiar to the behavioral sciences are sufficiently important to be unavoidable.

Attempts will be made, however, to clarify these in the course of the discussion.

THE NATURE OF MARKET RELATIONSHIP

It was noted earlier that there is an apparent tendency, in marketing literature and practice, to assume a one-way relationship between buyers and sellers. This simplistic view of market relationships undoubtedly derives from the influence of economic theory. The classical economists postulate the concept of the entrepreneur who essentially becomes the dynamic cause of economic change and economic development. Despite the development of the marketing concept this view of a one-way cause and effect relationship still exerts an important influence on existing marketing theory. Thus application of theory and research findings from the behavioral sciences appears to have been guided largely by the implicit assumption that "marketing is what marketers do." This assumption is logically insufficient and moreover stands in the way of the development of a viable concept of marketing:

Neither the consumer-oriented view nor the vendor-oriented view of marketing is complete. Each assumes a tidy universe applicable to consumer or to vendor, yet each is as influential a force in marketing arrangements as the other. Given consumers with needs and vendors with goods or services to sell, we must suggest a relationship between the two which may be regarded as inherent and not as instituted by either party to the transaction. [1]

A concept of personal selling as an element of marketing must consequently be based on a concept of market relationships which takes into account the transactive nature of marketing. As the experiments described earlier suggest, the assumption that the salesman's efforts are somehow causal in obtaining sales may easily lead to an increase in selling effort where too much effort is already being expended. While it is occasionally useful to search for underlying causes of observed events, care must be exercised in assigning such causes. Few marketers would maintain that all buyers buy because salesmen sell. There are clearly any number of possible reasons why buyers purchase some products and not others.

Market relationships, then, are not solely a reflection of the activities engaged in by marketers. To achieve some understanding of the behavioral processes involved in market relationships, it is necessary to develop a conceptual framework which incorporates the totality of the process and which at the same time enables the researcher and practitioner to study any one aspect of the process in relation to the whole. Too much emphasis on personal selling as *selling* without due regard for the buying process can easily cloud proper recognition of the importance and nature of the interactive processes involved.

SOME BASIC ELEMENTS
OF A THEORY OF PERSONAL SELLING

A theoretical framework and method of analysis known as *functionalism*[2] (derived primarily from anthropology[3] and sociology[4]) is particularly well-suited as a facilitator in analyzing a system of interpersonal interaction. This method of analysis not only provides a basis for a better understanding of the relationships between a social system (such as a society or an organization) and the parts composing it (institutions and individuals). It also aids in positioning the significant elements of interaction in relation to other, larger systems. An important element of functional analysis is the scientific construct of a *system* which may be defined as a set of *interacting elements* possessing certain *properties*, at least some of which are unique to any system.

The relation of system to property is an intimate one. Properties are essentially the observable aspects or characteristics of the empirical world. Whenever we define or denote a property, it always seems to be a property *of* something. For this something we use the term *system*. Thus, properties, where they occur, occur as aspects or characteristics of systems. To make the circle complete, we might define a particular system as roughly that which possesses such and so properties.[5]

Salesmen, buyers, products and organizations can all be considered as systems with observable properties all of which can be qualitatively described, and some of which can be quantitatively measured. The main objective of a theory of personal selling is to define the participating systems in terms of those properties or characteristics which are operationally meaningful to personal selling as an element of the marketing system. Consider, for example, the interaction between a salesman and a buyer. This interaction may be analyzed as a system possessing certain quantitative or countable properties, such as height, weight, and age of participants, length of time they spend together, number of words spoken, and magnitude of exchange achieved (in dollars), if any. In addition to these measurable properties, however, the system also possesses a number of qualitative ones: that is, properties which cannot be counted but which, nevertheless, have operational relevance and meaning, and therefore, "count." These include ability of the participants to communicate with each other, the motives and goals of each member, the meanings or images they assign to each other, and such ascriptive qualities as neatness of dress and quality of verbal acumen. (It should be noted here that verbal acumen does not constitute ability to communicate.)

The distinction made here between quantitative and qualitative properties is fine but nevertheless important. While one might, for example, measure the outcome of selling interactions in terms of dollars, this dollar measure essentially represents the value or utility of the product or service exchanged. If this measure is taken as an indication of the salesman's ability to communicate – regardless of the buyer's corresponding ability and predilection to buy – then a qualitative conclusion has been drawn from a quantitative measure. Such a conclusion is useful only if it can be shown, and the experiment in Chapter III indicates that it cannot, that sales as measured in dollars are entirely a function of the salesman's activities.

Thus a theory of personal selling should incorporate some rules or guidelines for indentifying *relevant operational properties* of the participating systems. An operational property in this respect is one which can be manipulated and demonstrated as related to the function or operation of the system. The time a salesman spends with a buyer, for example, is *manipulatively related* to the interactive system consisting of the buyer-salesman, but general indications are that it is not a relevant property with respect to the effectiveness of the interaction. By the same token, the socioeconomic status of a buyer may be a *relevant* property of the interaction system; but it cannot readily, if at all, be *manipulated.*

Since interpersonal interaction is essentially a process of communication the relevant properties of the participating systems – organizations, salesmen, and buyers – are those which govern the ability of these systems to influence and to be influenced. The following analysis of the relationships between systems is therefore designed to develop concepts of the properties of communication systems and of the nature of communicative influences.

A concept of individual motivation is also an essential element of a theory of personal selling. The notion that salesmen cause sales was questioned earlier and consequently an alternative explanation must be sought to account for a buyer's activity independent of marketers' and salesmen's efforts. Since, on the other hand, it is empirically evident that salesmen *do* influence sales, this proposed concept of individual motivation must allow for such influences. In other words, neither forces within the individual nor outside influences, such as attempts to "motivate," are by themselves responsible for individual behavior, whether involving salesmen or buyers. A set of concepts is therefore required which will account for the mutual efforts of buyers and sellers to search for and adapt to each other. *The total efficiency of a firm's marketing efforts is achieved not only through the efficiency of the marketer's information dissemination efforts but also through the efficiency of the information acquisition efforts of buyers.*

The Concept of Functionalism

The functional approach to the analysis of marketing behavior, which was initiated by Wroe Alderson[6] constitutes a useful foundation for the assembly of various contributions from the social and behavioral sciences. Alderson described the functionalist viewpoint as follows:

Functionalism asks two characteristic questions about any set of phenomena which can be regarded as a system: "How does the system work?" and "How can it be made to work better?"

Functionalism implies a commitment to what is coming to be known as the total systems approach. To ask how marketing works is to ask how all its component parts and constituent activities work together to produce an end result. Fortunately it is possible to put the same question meaningfully about a subsystem such as a household or a firm. Any behavior system or [social system] can be regarded as having an internal pattern of activities and external relations to the rest of the environment. However the behavior system is defined, the subject for study is the behavior of the system as a whole.[7]

Functional analysis, then, begins with the proposition that all behavior is related; it examines relationships rather than looks for causes and effects among individuals and organizations.

An accepted premise of the functionalist position is that no human custom, institution, or set of behaviors exists *in vacuo;* there must always be an interplay between the component elements of a social system and a continuing interdependence between them is created on many different levels.[8]

The basic element of functional analysis is the social system as a system of action.[9] The concept of a social system is an analytical device designed to separate, without isolating, significant internal variables from the external influences upon a given interaction. Thus the concept of a social system is a specific case of the scientific system construct discussed earlier.

Social systems or systems of action have subsystems which relate to the larger system in terms of functional requirements. For example, a producing organization must attempt to inform prospective buyers of the availability of its products. Information dissemination, thus, is a functional requirement of the economic organization and this requirement gives rise to the subsystem—marketing. Within marketing, planning and allocation of marketing activities, for example, constitutes in turn a behavior system or functional requirement. Any system or subsystem of action can be analyzed in terms of the quality and quantity of *interaction* internal to the system. In addition, the required inputs to and outputs from a given system or subsystem can be determined and analyzed on the basis of the value of the *function* served by the system.

Functionalism thus provides a means of structuring and organizing the analysis of purposeful human behavior and interaction both in its totality and with reference to specific orientations of the interaction. In this respect economic and behavioral analysis can be rendered complementary rather than competing *orientations* in the analysis of human behavior. Moreover, the functional framework provides a basis for maintaining consistency of performance with reference to the purposes and objectives of a given organization thus minimizing the danger of suboptimization of the efforts of specific elements of that organization.

The functional framework will be explained further in the following chapter. It is sufficient for the moment to keep in mind that functional analysis provides a means for structuring, and relating the activities (properties) of social systems with respect to the function served by these systems. It remains to examine the process by which the given systems interact and influence each other.

A Concept of Communication

There are basically two ways in which individuals can influence each other: namely, through physical force or through communicative influence. It is clearly the latter which is of interest in the present context.

The term "communication" has been used to describe a number of different concepts and activities. Professor Raymond Bauer in a recent paper contrasted two theoretical models of communication:

1. The *social model* of communication is a model of one way influence in which the communicator presumably has power and "does something to the audience" with or without its consent. This model of communication emphasizes the exploitation of man by man. It is commonly held by the general public, and is thought to be the model generally used by those in advertising and public relations, and by those engaged in propaganda and the engineering of consent. The social model of the supposedly powerful communicator has been the target of social critics. In fact, however, the history of communications research seems to offer more support for a different model.
2. The *scientific model* of communication more accurately reflects what is known from communications research. It views communication as a two-way transaction between communicator and audience in which each party is engaged in problem solving, in which there is mutual influence, and in which each party both gives and gets something.[10]

The conceptual confusion in communication theory suggested by Professor Bauer is further aggravated by the semantic confusion of the term "communication" itself. Dr. Lee Thayer has commented upon the uses of this term as follows:

Even a cursory examination of the communication "literature" will reveal an almost infinite variety of problems and topics dealt with under the rubric of communication. Surely it must be obvious that a single concept cannot *usefully* cover a phenomenon of such diverse nature as "a communication" (some marks on a page), "a communication" (what goes on between the "black boxes" in a computer), "a communication" (what the female part-ridge does during mating season), "a communication" (an *attempt* to modify attitudes), "a communication" (the process of information storage and retrieval), and so on and on. These are but random, and are not extreme examples. In the last six years of the literature, I counted more than 25 conceptually different referents for this term.[11]

Confusion such as this may well explain why communication theory has contributed so little to personal selling. There is a tendency to define communication as something which can be studied apart from people and which has active effects on the receiver. In other words, communication is considered a tool which the sender (ad-vertiser or salesman) invokes to produce certain effects upon the receiver (buyer).

It is not at all clear, for example, what "persuasion" is in a model which separates communication from people. Even within the context of a two-way communication model one encounteres statements such as the following:

What happens in many cases is that people hear a persuasive communication, they understand it, and they accept it immediately. But then right afterwards, they say to themselves all the counter arguments that may dislodge the acceptance of the communication.[12]

The author of the above statement apparently ascribes persuasive-ness to the communication (the statement or the advertisement), but such an assumption, makes it extremely difficult to explain varying degrees of persuasiveness of a statement. Further, this assumption has led to a great deal of emphasis on developing the salesman's presentation to the neglect of developing the general communicative competence of the individual salesman.

Yet it is clear even to a casual observer that some individuals are more easily persuaded to behave in a certain fashion than others. It would appear, then, that persuasiveness varies with individuals for a particular statement. Indeed, *any specific state-ment can be persuasive only in the context of a given situation involving a specified set of individuals and actions.* Again, to ascribe persuasiveness to words and things outside and apart from people leads to the conclusion that people are essentially passive participants in the act of communication. It is empir-ically evident however, that people are *not* passive in communica-tive acts and that they are in fact capable of persuading or dissuad-ing *themselves* to act, in a given situation.

To gain some headway in the confusion of terms and concepts

evident in communication theory it is necessary to step back for a moment and reconsider the meaning of the term communication and with it such terms as information giving and persuasion.

Perhaps the most basic point which must be made is that *the "meaning" of words and gestures inhere in people and not in the words and gestures themselves.* Essentially words and gestures are tools, the meaning and uses of which people acquire or learn in the process of socialization. The word selling has no active meaning in and of itself apart from the people who use it. It is useful, therefore, to separate the tools of communication (words, gestures and pictures) from the "understanding" of these tools or cues. *In the following chapters the term communication will be taken to mean the psychological process of understanding or taking account of the cues or data originating in an individual's environment.*[13] That is, talking or "noisemaking" is not in and of itself communication, nor is writing or gesturing communication until someone takes account of the words and symbols and converts them into information.

The above remarks have several implications which will be further explored in subsequent chapters, but the most important implication, is that *the receiver (or buyer) becomes an integral part of the marketer's and salesman's attempts at influencing his behavior.* The emphasis in following chapters will be on the conceptualization of the various elements of the influence process, based upon a concept of communication as a dynamic process of information dissemination, acquisition, and consumption.

Motivation and Communication

The field of motivation theory is no less confused than that of communication, and it appears that the term motivation, similar to the term communication, has been liberally applied to too many different concepts. Two aspects of individual motivation have been particularly confused: (1) why does an individual act at all? and (2) why does the activity take a particular form? [14] The first question can be taken to refer to the basic *physiological* energizers of a living system while the second question refers to the psychological energizers of an individual. The physiological energizers are clearly of little interest to either the psychologist or the marketer, while the psychological energizers are of concern to the marketer to the extent that these are influenceable.

The fact that people do act and behave is not the primary problem for motivation as a psychological concept. Physical movement is an essential part of life. The corresponding basis for mental or psychological life is *awareness. Without awareness of self and environment there is no basis for communication, learning, and development.*

By way of illustration, the process of physiological energization might be compared with the psychological energization process. The physiological system (the human body) derives energy from certain foodstuffs through a process of metabolism. The body is capable of absorbing and processing only certain chemical substances and either rejects or fails to process others. The *psychological* energization process is communication as defined earlier. That is, it is an input of raw data to the psychological system of the individual who possesses a certain awareness (ability to take account of) which allows for the processing or the conversion of such raw data into information. Since the individual's awareness is finite, it facilitates the acceptance of certain data and results in the rejection of, or the failure to process, certain other data.

A connection can thus be shown between a theory of communication and theory of motivation with reference to the basic process of psychological energization. A question still remains, however, as to the particular form the behavior of an individual takes. A number of theories have been developed to account for the "why" of individual behavior. "Drives" and "needs" are perhaps the most familiar notions to marketers. Briefly, the theory holds that behavior results from a limited number of physiological and psychological drives and needs and that the nature of these energizers determine the direction of individual action. A more generalized version of the drive-reduction theory is a theory built on the concept of tension-reduction, which states that changes in the environment and in the internal state of the system (the individual) result in a disequilibrium, thus creating tension or conflict (anxiety) among the variables of the system. Behavior, then, is thought to be directed toward the reduction of such tensions.

While the tension-reduction theory has succeeded in "explaining" reactive behavior it is not well-suited as a basis for "explaining" purposeful behavior. As Abraham Maslow has convincingly shown,[15] deficit motives (needs and drives) must be supplemented with growth motives (desire to become) to provide a sufficiently dynamic theory of motivation to account for individual behavior. Similarly D.C. McClelland has written:

All motives are learned . . . . What has become of the traditional notion that all psychogenic motives are built on primary biological drives? Strictly speaking we should no longer think in this fashion. States of biological need have no unique function in producing motives; they are merely one of the conditions which dependably (in all individuals) give rise to motivational associations . . motives are individually acquired but certain situations will produce pleasure or pain with such regularity either through biological or cultural arrangements that the probability of certain common motives developing in all people is very high.[16]

The notion of needs and drives is not adequate as an explanation of the underlying "motivators" of buying and selling behavior. This does not mean that biological drives and needs are nonexistent; rather it means that biological drives are not motives as such *but conditions for interpreting environmental cues.* Indeed the individual system, physiological and psychological, can be conceived of as possessing a number of such conditions, or pre-dilections to behave in a certain fashion in a given situation at a given time.

The individual system of predilections (motivations) to act in a certain way essentially constitutes an *information and decision system* with reference to communicative or interactive relation-ships. This intrapersonal information processing system has two fundamental aspects: (1) the neurological system which provides the ultimate organization of human thinking and communication, and (2) the psychological system which provides the organization effecting the form or direction which an individual's behavior takes.[17]

The psychological organization of an individual, considered as an information processing and decision system, consists of "nodes" (concepts) and "links" (connections between the concepts). The motivation underlying an individual's behavior is dependent upon that part of his conceptual network containing his value concepts.

What is a value, or what are values, in terms of the present suggestions for an information processing model of motivation? The view taken here is that values are one kind of concept. There are, of course, many other kinds of concepts. What is a concept? In terms of an information processing model, a concept may be defined as a symbol which has associated with it a set of attributes or properties.

Values are concepts which include an attribute or attributes indicating that they are to be approached, to be desired, to be wanted, in short, to be posi-tively valued on the one hand, or on the other to be avoided, to be feared, to be negatively valued. Included also is information concerning the degree to which the concept in question is to be positively valued or negatively valued.[18]

The values involved here are not only moral values but include all the standards which an individual applies to his own behavior as well as to that of others. Thus, an individual's values constitute an exceedingly complex, but interrelated dynamic system:

In fact it appears highly likely that the values which an individual acquires form a hierarchy, not a fully logically consistent hierarchy, but one never-theless in which a limited number of values are basic in the sense that other values are derived from them and still other values derive from these in turn.[19]

The individual acquires this complex system of values through a process of learning. Learning is a form of communication which may be divided into two types with respect to the desired or actual effect of a given communicative situation: (1) communication which results in addition to, changes in, or deletions from the individ-ual's value system and (2) communication which results in action within the individual's value system and therefore, in some sense, reconfirms or reinforces his value system. The first type of communication is perhaps closest to that which is popularly called learning while the second type is more akin to habit formation.

In the following chapter an organizing grid or matrix is developed to show the relationships between these two types of communications. An attempt will also be made to show that this differentiation is precedent to understanding the potential communicative capacities of personal and nonpersonal media.

One basic premise underlying the subsequent chapters is that an individual, considered as a biological system, is disposed to action, that is, he will "do" something merely because he is alive. The form and orientation of his actions will be a function of his conceptual competence, both with reference to his values and to his general and specific concepts of himself and his environment. Individuals cannot be "motivated" as such (i.e., made to behave in a certain manner), but they can be influenced with respect to the direction their behavior takes if a communicative situation can be developed which relates to the individual's psychological organization or his information "inputability" as established by the quality of his conceptual network.

A Concept of Competence

If the "why" of human behavior is essentially a result of a psychological energization process analogous to the physiological process of metabolism, then an individual's *ability* to take account of data or cues in his environment is a central issue. As in the cases of both communication and motivation, ability to take account of one's environment has been studied from a number of angles. The concept of *thresholds,* for example, has been researched to determine the physiological limitations of the human being to *perceive* cues and changes in cues as well as to establish the psychological limitations of the individual's *ability* to "make sense" of his perceptions. In addition to the concept of thresholds, the concept of "selective perception" has achieved some popularity in marketing. Bernard Berelson and Gary A. Steiner describe this concept as follows:

Of all possible stimuli — i.e., all bits of energy actually capable of firing receptors at any given moment — only a small portion become part of actual experience; and that portion is not a random sample of what is objectively available. To begin with, the observer, of course, plays an active part in determining what will be allowed to stimulate the receptors at all: we look *at* some things, ignore others, and look *away* from still others ("selective exposure"). Beyond that, only a fraction of those stimuli that have gained effective entry to a receptor ever reach awareness ("selective awareness").[20]

It is possible to distinguish between at least two categories of selective perception: (1) selection on the basis of some deliberate or conscious process of choice and (2) selection on the basis of some nonconscious process. (It should be noted that this differentiation is not the equivalent of the widely used distinction between "rational" and "irrational" behavior.) The corollary to selective perception: namely selective communication, can be similarly differentiated. The process of conscious selection of cues is essentially the basis for the so-called problem-solving activities, or ability to take account of new cues representing events which have not previously been encountered by the individual. The process of nonconscious selection of environmental cues undoubtedly accounts for the greater part of an individual's behavior and is basically a learned ability which has become "internalized." In other words, it has become part of the individual's psychological makeup. This acquired ability to select cues, and in turn perceive and communicate selectively in given situations, has given rise to the concepts of "roles" and "expectations." Thus, the word salesman symbolizes a certain set or repertoire of behaviors which an individual buyer learns to expect a salesman to perform. The role concept, which will be given further attention in the following chapter, is prevalent as an analytical technique in sociology and social psychology and has also received recognition in personal selling literature and practice.

The interrelationships of communication, motivation and selective perception as outlined above can be analyzed within the concept of the individual as an information and decision system. This may be defined as a system oriented toward the conversion of data into information for the purpose of behaving according to and within the constraints of a set of values. Indeed, individuals differ with respect to their ability to take account of and to cope with a given situation. It will be shown in Chapter VIII that these individual variations in ability can be differentiated on a "competence scale" which expresses individual differences in terms of several dimensions of conceptual capacity to take account of and behave in specified situations.

The aims of the competence concept are very similar to those of psychological testing and other rating instruments. Even though the aims are similar, however, and even though competence is in many respects an extremely involved concept, it does have the advantage of rating individuals (as information and decision systems) in terms of operationally relevant properties. Personality characteristics, as defined by the various personality tests, may effectively differentiate individuals, but no remedial action, with reference to the individual rated, can be recommended on the basis of such characteristics. The concept of competence, which perhaps is no less difficult to apply, can nevertheless be linked to the available theories of learning and communication. Thus enabling the manager *and* the salesman to propose and implement remedial action—for example in the form of training or through modifications of the prevailing systems of rewards and penalties. In addition, an attempt is made to relate competence to individual performance so that an observer's intuitive abilities may be utilized in an assessment of this performance.

SUMMARY

The cases presented in Part Two of this book demonstrate the need for developing a theory of personal selling which can provide a coherent set of assumptions and hypotheses from which to plan and implement further experimentation. The elements of such a theory as outlined in this chapter are: (1) a model of *interpersonal interactions* designed to show the theoretical relationship among the multitude of activities which can be observed in personal selling situations, (2) a concept of *communication* which will provide a plausible explanation of the process of interpersonal and mass influence, (3) a concept of *motivation* which is operationally relevant to the process of interpersonal influence, while also providing a more generalized explanation of the "why" of individual behavior, and (4) a concept of *competence* involving a scale on which to differentiate individual conceptual ability as determined intercommunicatively and as it relates to the existing knowledge about training and learning processes.

The material of Part Three provides a broad foundation for an application of a communication-motivation model. Part Four of the book outlines some implications of the theory for personal selling with reference both to the management and the execution of the selling effort. For the convenience of readers, a glossary of terminology in this and subsequent chapters is provided at the end of the report.

VI

The System of Action

IT IS OFTEN said that both economic and behavioral theory have relevance to marketing. Even so, many attempts to create a theory in marketing all too clearly show the seams between behavioral and economic theory as well as between the psychological and sociological approaches to behavioral theory. John Howard in his *Marketing: Executive and Buyer Behavior* [1] uses the expression "the economic buyer," and "the social-psychological buyer," and the "psychological buyer." This approach seems inherently unsatisfactory, however, since it bends the object of analysis (i.e., the buyer) to the existing disciplinary division of theory. The buyer in all three instances is, of course, the same individual, but the separation of behavioral disciplines makes it difficult to develop a unified concept of buying and selling behavior.

Nevertheless, if the marketing theorist or researcher is to make more than sporadic use of the large volume of evidence from the behavioral sciences, in combination with available economic theory, he must provide, or be provided with, an over-all analytical perspective. It is the purpose of this chapter to outline such a perspective.

The function of an analytical perspective is similar to that of a road map. It must serve to highlight the significant variables encountered in the real world, while avoiding unnecessary detail. Also, it must enable the practitioner to formulate certain hypotheses about the likely outcomes of a set of alternative courses of action—just as the road map enables the traveler to hypothesize about the outcomes of each of his alternative routes. The analogy of the map can be easily carried too far, considering the state of the art in behavior research, but it might prove a useful indication of the level of achievement toward which the research should strive.

BEHAVIOR PROCESSES

The underlying philosophy of the functional model presented here is that *human behavior constitutes an integrated, continuously ongoing process.* Certain parts of this process are directly observable or overt, while other parts are not directly observable, but overt. Some of the more important implications of this view are:

1. An individual's behavior, whether as a manager, salesman, or a buyer, is not necessarily, if at all, explainable in small convenient "cause and effect" segments.
2. The "rationality" versus "irrationality" dichotomy, popularly made with reference to buyer behavior, becomes meaningless other than as an indicator of an outside observer's ability to identify an immediate "cause" or rationale for any other individual's observable behavior. *All behavior is, in some sense, rational;* so the problem facing *both* marketers and buyers becomes one of determining and influencing the rationale for the behavior each observes in the other.
3. An individual's behavior, for the most part, is based on concepts which are "out of consciousness." This does not necessarily imply that such behavior is either "emotional" or "irrational." It merely implies *that an individual internalizes certain behavior rules and acts upon them without necessarily reexamining them continuously.*
4. The marketer, or for that matter the salesman, cannot directly influence an individual buyer. *The sole means of influence lies in the changes which can be effected upon the individual's environment within the constraints of his ability to take account of such changes.*
5. Any individual, whether manager, salesman, or buyer, possesses an information and decision system which, by virtue of the value concepts contained in it, *develops a certain set of predilections to act in a more or less specific manner in any given situation.* The process of influence required to change such predilections is essentially different from, and more "intensive" than, one of information giving.

This concept of individual behavior *processes* represents what may be termed a "holistic" approach to the analysis of human behavior, and more specifically, selling and buying behavior, as opposed to the more atomistic cause-and-effect approaches. For example, to say that a given advertisement or sales pitch causes an individual to buy a certain product or service is essentially to take this instance of buying and selling action out of the context of the total behavior framework involved. Even though buying behavior is only a part of an individual's total behavior repertoire, it does not follow that a separate set of analytical rules and methods are required, or are even appropriate, for the problems of discovering the "why" behind this buying behavior.

A holistic concept of human behavior implies that the activities of an individual are related in terms of an ongoing purposeful process and also that an interdependent and co-determining relationship exists among the behavior processes of all individuals in a given society by virtue of their common membership in that society. *Consequently, the behavior of a sales manager cannot be considered entirely apart from the behavior of salesmen reporting to him, nor can the behavior of a salesman be considered entirely apart from the behavior of the sales manager to whom he reports and the buyers to whom he is selling.*

This interdependence of human behavior raises some serious problems for the observer, the researcher, and the manager of that behavior. Not only are the participants of a given interaction incapable of completely separating themselves and their own behavior from that of other individuals but they are capable of taking account of only a limited set of concepts at any given moment in time. Therefore, it is necessary to utilize some conceptual framework which facilitates the analysis of human behavior while compensating for man's inability to contemplate the entire world at once. The concept of systems of action, the basic characteristics of which were briefly outlined in the previous chapter, offers such a framework; and the properties of this construct will be discussed in some detail in the remainder of this chapter.

THE SYSTEM OF ACTION [2]

One of the most conspicuous features of modern societies is that of organization, and a considerable volume of literature and research has been devoted to analysis of organizational behavior and problems. The definition of the term organization provided by Professor Herbert A. Simon of Carnegie Institute of Technology is perhaps typical of the general orientation of organizational literature:

the term *organization* refers to the complex pattern of communications and other relations in a group of human beings. This pattern provides to each member of the group much of the information, assumptions, goals, and attitudes that enter into his decisions, and provides him also with a set of stable and comprehensible expectations as to what other members of the group are doing and how they will react to what he says and does. The sociologist calls this pattern a "role system"; to most of us it is more familiarly known as an "organization." [3]

An organization, then, is a specific of the system construct discussed earlier. Furthermore, it is possible to conceptualize a number of *levels* of systems within the organizational construct, distinguished from each other on the basis of the scope and orientation of the organizational planning and decision making. A business organization may thus be described as a system consisting of individuals as focal points or "nodes" with lines of communication and authority serving as "links." In a similar manner, it is possible to describe the individual, as was mentioned earlier, as a psychological system with concepts as nodes, the links being evidenced by the individual's ability to perceive (consciously or nonconsciously) various conceptual relationships.

The viability of an organization or a social system is some function of the "quality" or information processing ability of the nodes and of the information carrying capacity of the links. Essentially two approaches to organizational analysis are encountered in the literature; namely, the system of action approach and the goal model approach. The differences between these two approaches are cogently expressed by Amitai Etzioni in his *Modern Organizations:*

Using a system model we are able to see a basic distortion in the analysis of organizations that is not visible or explicable from the perspective of goal-model evaluation. The latter approach expects organizational effectiveness to increase with the assignment of more means to the organization's goals. In the perspective of the goal model, to suggest that an organization can become more effective by assigning fewer means to goal activities is a contradiction. The system model, however, leads one to conclude that just as there may be too little allocation of resources to meet the goals of the organization, so there may also be an over-allocation of the resources. The system model explicitly recognizes that the organization solves certain problems other than those directly involved in the achievement of the goal, and that excessive concern with the latter may result in insufficient attention to other necessary organizational activities, and to a lack of coordination between the inflated goal activities and the de-emphasized, non-goal activities.[4]

The system of action concept involves a set of functional requirements or phases which must be satisfied by any operating system if it is to maintain its viability. The implicit assumption here is that the primary objective of a system of action, whatever its scope, is to ensure its own perpetuity. It should be noted that this objective is not necessarily different from the economists' maximization of profit or utility postulates, if one is willing to concede that maximization of profit, in its narrower monetary sense, is both necessary and sufficient for the survival of an organization. If the profit maximization concept is taken in a broader context as including the maximization of the satisfaction of social value, then it becomes merely a specific formulation of the survival objective.

For the present purposes a system of action may be defined

as a process of interaction between an individual *(actor)* or a group of individuals (organization) and a *situation.* It is this process of interaction which gives rise to the concept of personality in the case of an individual and to the concept of organization in the case of a group of individuals. That is, a personality is the relational system (information processing and decision system) of a living organism enabling it to interact with an environmental situation. The system of action occurring at the interface of an individual and a problem situation (or at the interface of an organization and a problem situation) is analyzed below in terms of a set of five functional requirements (phases) each of which describes a necessary although not a sufficient condition for a successful actor-situation interaction. Success in this respect is dependent upon the degree to which the acting individual (or organization) can attain a self-approved goal or objective while maintaining himself (itself) as a viable system.

THE FUNCTIONAL PHASES OF A SYSTEM OF ACTION

The functional phases of a system of action provide a means of classifying the significant aspects of a given interaction (actor-situation) on the basis of the function served by any specific activity. A general outline illustrating the relationship between the five phases of an interaction, which taken together constitute the system of action, is shown in Figure 9.

Phase 1: Awareness, consciously or nonconsciously, of a problem situation and allocation of resources to the improvement of the perceived situation.

Phase 2: Acquisition of necessary resources from the environment for the purpose of facilitating the attainment of the established objective.

Phase 3: Goal seeking behavior by the actor in the context of the perceived situation.

Phase 4: Harmonization of the goal seeking activity with the existing internal "organization."

Phase 5: Commitment or internalization of the methods and results of the preceding actions.

There is a striking similarity between these phases and a logical decision making sequence, such as the Adaptive Planning and Control Sequence (APACS) developed in an earlier Marketing Science Institute study of promotional decision making.[5] Indeed, the functional phases of a system of action do have a dual nature. Not only do they represent guidelines for the planning-decision-making implementation sequence of instrumental action, but they also enable a delineation of problem areas with reference to the interaction between an individual or an organization and their

environmental situations. The system concept forces the identification of the relevant interaction variables and the phases themselves call attention to the dynamics of the interaction among
these variables. In addition, the system concept allows for identification of the "significant others" or relevant external variables
which interact with and influence the behavior of an individual or
an organization.

FIGURE 9

Functional Components or Phases of a System of Action *

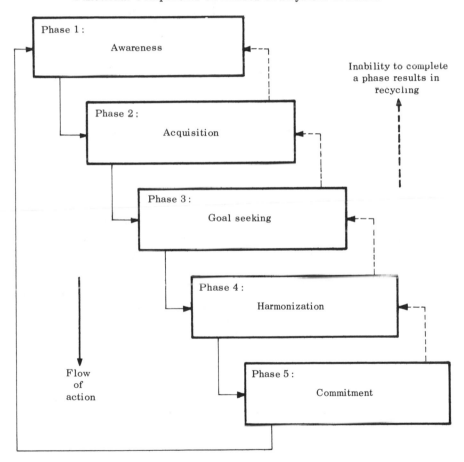

*The system used here is based on the four functional requisites of the
Parsonian System of Action, although Parsons *et al.* combine Phases 1
and 5 into one phase related to system value patterns. The authors are
indebted to Mr. J. Shaffer, Market Analyst, Sperry & Hutchinson, New
York, for the present formulation of the system of action.

In terms of the system of action, the participating individuals or groups of individuals may be conceived of as proceeding through the five phases from awareness or problem identification to commitment to the outcome of a given line of action. Since each of the five phases is equally important as a condition (requirement) for the successful operational performance of any given system, they can be used to isolate significant problem areas in a so-called "going concern," as well as serve as guidelines for problem solving.

This analytical framework will be used in the following chapters as a basis for a discussion of the significant aspects of the interactions between selling (utility producing) entities and buying (utility consuming) entities. Before actual application can be attempted, however, it is essential to achieve a basic understanding of the entire system of action framework. Hence, the nature and orientation of each of the five functional phases is elaborated below.

Phase 1: Awareness

The prerequisite for any instrumental action is the perception of a problem: that is, awareness of a discrepancy between an *apparent state* and a *desired state* of any given behavior system. Awareness in this sense is essentially the ability to take account of the circumstances of a given situation, and as mentioned in the previous chapter, awareness underlies the basic psychological energization of any information and decision system. Awareness of any given problem may follow from a purely routine scanning of the environment (i.e., a system may be "programmed" to perceive certain changes in the environment); or, it may follow from a deliberate and conscious effort to search for and solve significant problems.

In any case, both the problem perceived and the solution designated will depend upon the level of awareness of the systems involved in the interaction as well as upon the significance the systems ascribe to a problem in light of their respective goals and values. It should be noted here that differences in awareness among individuals or groups of individuals are not so much the result of the degree of "rationality" of each system involved as they are a result of differences in orientation and complexity of the models on the basis of which a system (individual or organization) organizes and defines the world around itself. It is clearly possible to perceive a great many problems or discrepancies between that which "is" and that which "could be" in the interactions of practically all living systems. Yet if the systems involved do not perceive such discrepancies, no problem exists for them and no remedial action is likely to follow.

The very core of the marketing task is to achieve a matching of the awareness and action between producers and users of economic goods and services. The difficulty of this matching process follows primarily from differing orientations and standards of sellers and buyers in combination with the fact that ability to perceive and take account of a given set of discrepancies or problems, precludes the ability to perceive and take account of other problems.

Phase 2: Acquisition

All living systems continually engage in an adaptive exchange of resources with the external world. A business organization acquires capital goods, manpower, and information pertaining to the requirements of product markets. At the level of the individual, the acquisition of resources involves the exchange of physical energy (work) for goods and services, information, and knowledge.

While the *awareness* phase of the system of action constitutes a condition or latent ability of the system to perceive or take account of its environment, resulting in a commitment to engage in action, the *acquisition* phase consists of search behavior. The level of awareness of a given system is not directly observable and must consequently be inferred from the type and amount of search behavior in which the system engages. One of the real problems encountered in the search for a theory of information acquisition and consumption (communication) is that of developing a set of rules on the basis of which inferences about existing levels of awareness may be made from data pertaining to observable behavior. For example, studies showing that some individuals will spend a comparatively small amount of time searching for and purchasing a house, have resulted in various incompatible conclusions. It is not clear at all whether the buyer who engages in the greatest amount of search behavior, measured on a purely quantitative basis, possesses a high concern for customers and/or a high level of awareness, nor is it clear whether little or no search indicates either a low concern for outcomes or a high level of awareness.

In a study of industrial purchasing behavior by the Marketing Science Institute,[6] a classification scheme was developed which relates the amount of search behavior exhibited by industrial purchasing agents to the comparative "newness," from the buyer's point of view, of the product or service involved. In later chapters of the present volume, attempts will be made to develop a generalized form of that classification scheme applicable to industrial as well as intermediate and final buyers.

Phase 3: Goal Seeking

While the acquisition phase is similar to the input function, the goal seeking phase is akin to the output function of the economic input–output model discussed in Chapter IV. In economic terms, the output of a given business organization is a product or a service. The physical products coming off the production line do not by themselves, however, constitute a meaningful output. Both a product and a service must be given conceptual "meaning" or utility by the user since mere physical availability does not provide it. It is here that marketing comes into the process as an instrumental activity designed to bridge the communication gap between the producer and the consumer. The nature of this communication gap will be the focal point of the discussion in later chapters.

Neither seller nor buyer exists in a vacuum, and the utility of a given product or service is partly a function of concepts held in common by both. Similarly, the effectiveness of a given marketing mix is partly a function of the degree to which it relates to these common or mutual concepts, while its efficiency is partly a function of the extent to which it succeeds in exploiting the mutual interests of sellers and buyers. The industrial marketing task is generally considered somewhat different from marketing to middlemen and final consumers. While certainly there are differences between these buying systems, an attempt will be made to show that the marketing task involved differs only in degree and not in kind.

Phase 4: Harmonization

The perpetuation of a system of action is dependent upon the successful integration or internal coordination of the various elements constituting the system. Herbert Simon provides an explanation of the nature of this functional requisite on the level of the organization as follows:

It is obvious that without communication, there can be no organization, for there is no possibility of the group influencing the behavior of the individual. Not only is communication absolutely essential to organization, but the availability of particular techniques of communication will in large part determine the way in which decision making functions can and should be distributed throughout the organization. [7]

It seems evident, for example, that many of the *informal* aspects of an organization are devoted to the harmonization, or maintenance of internal balance, of the relationships between individual members. While the formal or official system of communication generally is functionally or even hierarchically oriented, the informal system of communication is oriented toward the satisfaction of the informational requirements of the individuals involved and changes with their requirements. In general, the less the official, or artificial, system of communication and control takes into account and accommodates the informational needs of individuals, the more prevalent will be the informally or natural system of communication and the more individual energy will be expended upon its maintenance.

With reference to the individual in the context of a system of action, *experiences derived from a given activity must be harmonized with his previous and existing framework of experiences.* Just as the salesman must be able to harmonize his activities as a salesman with his self-image as an individual, so the buyer must be able to harmonize the consumption or use of a given product with *his* self-image.

At the interface of the individual and the organization, as in the case of a salesman or a purchasing agent, this requirement for harmony produces a series of latent conflicts or so-called "communication problems" to which a number of approaches have been applied, ranging from systems engineering to pure human relations approaches. Whichever approach is used to solve the problems of communication and control across the individual-organization interface, new problems are bound to arise because of the impossibility of predicting individual reaction to systems of control. This area of organizational control will be explored in more detail in Chapter XV.

Phase 5: Commitment

The fifth and last phase of a system of action refers to the value commitments of an individual to a system of action. In terms of an organization, Chester A. Barnard provides an explanation of the nature of this phase:

Every effort that is a constituent of organization, that is, every coordinated cooperative effort, may involve two acts of decision. The first is the decision. The first is the decision of the person affected as to whether or not he will contribute this effort as a matter of personal choice. It is a detail of the process of repeated personal decisions that determine whether or not the individual will be or will continue to be a contributor to the organization . . . . This act of decision is *outside* the system of efforts constituting the organization . . . although it is . . . a subject for organized attention. [8]

The second act of decision mentioned by Barnard refers to the *organizational* decision making function which, he suggests, is outside the personal domain and part of the organizational system of action. From the organization's viewpoint, individual loyalties may often be found to be either misdirected or misinterpreted. For example, a salesman, as a participant in the organizational system of action, may be loyal to the company he represents, to his supervisor the buyer, to the buyer's company, among several other possible objects of loyalty. Failure on the part of sales management to understand these diverse objects of loyalty may create serious communication blocks between the salesman and his company.

Commitment, or development of loyalty, is prevalent among

buyers, with reference to specific products, company images, individual salesmen, and other members of the selling organization. Commitment essentially follows from the successful completion of the four preceding phases of the system of action. It occurs at various levels of intensity ranging from mere preference to complete internalization of a given activity. The more intense the commitment, the less chance there is of producing a change in the individual's behavior.

LEVELS OF BEHAVIORAL ORIENTATION

The five phases of the system of action provide a framework for isolating and analyzing certain elements of the process of interaction between two or more living systems. While application of the phases to the analysis of a given interaction provides a means of determining the point at which an interaction breaks down, these phases do not in and of themselves assist in determining either the reason for the breakdown or the appropriate remedial action required. It is evident for example, that some degree of awareness is necessary for any communication to occur, but it is also evident that communication can occur at *different* levels of awareness with respect to any given subject. A similar hierarchy of levels is also applicable to the behavioral content of the other four phases.

The concept of levels of behavioral orientation is aimed at a general characterization of individual or organizational motivational orientation and abilities to interact (to influence and to be influenced) with significant others in their environment. The concept is based on the assumption that the activities of individuals and organizations are related to and affected by a complex hierarchy of orientations and standards, all or part of which will be relevant to the analysis of any given system of action.

Five suggested levels of behavior orientation are sketched below. Each of these levels denotes two distinct aspects of individual communicative (interaction) ability or competence: (1) a set of motivational enablers (goal structures) underlying an individual's behavior in a generalized situation such as a buying-selling situation, and (2) a set of communicative capacities which basically determine an individual's (or an organization's) ability to influence and to be influenced by a situation in the interest of achieving his (its) goals. While the assumption thus is that all behavior is goal-oriented, it is recognized that both the goals (motivational orientation) and the means (communicative capacities) may vary between actors (individual or organizations). Application of the five levels of behavioral orientation in subsequent chapters should assist in clarifying the scope and substance of the concepts involved.

Level 1: Physical Activity

This level of behavior orientation encompasses *motivational* conditions inherent in an actor as a *physiological* system. In the case of an individual a certain amount of behavior is directed toward the satisfaction of bodily requirements for food, water, air, etc. Similarly, a certain amount of organizational behavior derives from and is strongly influenced by the physical configuration of an organization (i.e., machinery, plant layout, office locations, etc.). These physiological (or physical) systems are necessary conditions for instrumental or productive behavior but they are not sufficient conditions. Indeed, while the biological system is the basic source of energy for the individual, it also serves to limit his behavior by virtue of its structure and consequent requirements.

From the point of view of relational *competence* this level of behavior orientation denotes basic communicative ability, demonstrated by such physiologically-determined attributes as memory, speech, and sensory perception. These attributes comprise the raw material of communication, and represent fundamental facilitators (and constraints) of human behavior at all levels of competence activity.

An individual performing only at this level (i.e., utilizing only these abilities) however, is behaving essentially mechanistically, or merely "going through the motions." While simple rote activity may be accomplished well and efficiently, conceptual abilities are not apparent or used to a minimum degree.

From the point of view of an organizational entity this level of relational competence denotes the channels of communication and data storage and retrieval facilities available to the organization. Again, it is important to note that these physical structures are necessary but *not* sufficient conditions for either internal or external organizational communication.

Level 2: Adaptive Behavior

This level denotes a set of motivational orientations based on the psychological characteristics or traits of an individual. The concept here is that an individual considered as an information and decision system possesses a certain psychological structure which influences the direction of that individual's behavior. Just as one can differentiate psychologically determined "types" of individuals so one can differentiate "types" of organizational frameworks. In the latter case one may differentiate authoritarian and democratic or participative and non-participative types of organizations thereby describing the conditions governing external and internal organizational communication.

From the point of view of relational or communicative competence this level denotes an individual's responsiveness and capacity to adaptively relate to the situation with which he is interacting. Similarly, the adaptiveness of an organization considered as an information and decision system is dependent upon some network of definitions of the relationships among the various entities of which the organization is composed.

Level 3:   Instrumental Performance

The ability to behave in any specific situation does not necessarily imply either the generalizability of this behavior to other dissimilar situations, or the personal involvement of the behaving individual. Both of these characteristics, generalizability of goal seeking behavior and personal involvement, are distinguishing qualities of the performance level. The motivational orientation underlying individual behavior at this level is conditioned by the individual's concepts or understanding of functional relationships between various interactional situations.

It may be helpful here to differentiate behavior as an end in itself and behavior as a means to the achievement of a goal. The salesman who is required to concern himself solely or primarily with the perfection of certain ways or manners of behaving will achieve any predetermined goal (i.e., functional relevance) only incidentally. On the other hand, the salesman who is aware of, and perceives a personal involvement in, the achievement of a specified goal or set of goals will tend to develop behavior repertoires conducive to the attainment of that goal. This means-end distinction as it relates to the problems of interpersonal communication will be explored further in Chapter X.

In the case of an organization considered as an information processing and decision system this level denotes the operational information flows instrumental to the attainment of organizational objectives. It is the "quality" of these flows which most decisively influences an organization's ability to maintain a sustained performance over time.

Level 4: System Integration

This level of behavior orientation denotes a set of motivational conditions inherent in an individual's concepts of his total and significant environment. The notion is that, given a set of concepts of himself in the context of his environment, an individual will be motivated to integrate his various performances or roles into a coherent, to him, system of behaviors which in turn expresses him to other individuals whose opinion he considers significant. In the case of an organization the requirement is for efforts to integrate the various operational functions so as to avoid suboptimization.

With reference to relational or communicative competence,

performance at this level of competence denotes the fact that the individual has successfully integrated his personal goals into the strategic or metagoals of the institution. Effective selling and buying behavior is dependent upon the individual's ability to integrate personal and institutional goals with a minimum of dissonance or conflict. At this level an individual exhibits not only a sense of personal purpose but also an ability to perform in a role reflecting responsibilities and tasks which goes beyond immediate self-interest. The relational competence of an organizational information and decision system pertains to a framework of control designed to relate internal (operational) and external (market) elements in the interest of the attainment of some *conceived* overall objective.

Level 5: Value Integration

The final level of behavioral orientation involves the overall value concepts governing the activities of an individual or an organization. The values which ultimately govern the direction of individual behavior are moral or ethical values. Individual competence at this level denotes an internally consistent set of moral standards and value commitments in terms of which the individual can appraise and make value judgments about any of his performances. Moral or ethical values have become institutionalized in various ways thus ensuring a certain degree of compliance by individual members of a group. Certain professional societies specify a moral code designed to govern the performance of their members. No doubt one of the basic factors in the apparent decline of the image of personal selling as an occupation is the lack of specified value concepts which can be associated readily with the personal selling function.

One criterion for assessing the overall performance of an economic organization is the functional relevance of its activites in terms of the value patterns of the overall society. In this context the strategic objectives and plans of an organization are fundamentally moral statements. On the whole, the literature on organizational theory is barren on this point and while the problems of strategic planning will not be of particular concern in the following chapters there is a serious need for efforts to formulate a philosophy of organizational behavior centering on the organization as a self-organizing system.

THE COMPETENCE-ACTIVITY (COMPACT) MODEL

The diagram in Figure 10 shows the general relationship between the phases of a system of action and the competence levels at which interactions may be analyzed. Each of the competence levels represents a "layer" of orientations of the acting system toward its situation and simultaneously represents a more or less explicit set of relational or communicative capacities. In the case of an organization, for example, the influence of control proceeds from top management's strategic decisions (i.e., the determination of the values for the organizational system) to the concrete activities at the operating levels. Similarly, the limitations on possible strategic moves inhere in the physical and communicative capacities of lower levels.

In terms of the individual, considered as a system of action, similar rules hold with reference to the behavior levels. In addition, as will be explained in greater detail later, the competence *levels provide a basis for taking into account the various orientations which may underlie the activities of a given individual.* Thus, the model offers a basis for sorting out some of the several

FIGURE 10

An Outline of the COMPACT Model

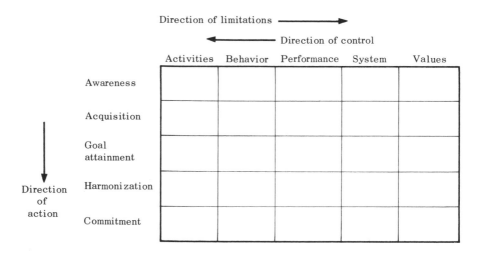

elements of a given interaction; for example, a salesman-buyer interaction, as well as for developing a competence"scale"against which to compare the required and the actual ability of a given individual with reference to a specified set of situations. For purposes of convenience, the competence-activity matrix shown in Figure 10 will be referred to as the COMPACT model.[9] Of course it does not eliminate the problems involved in inferring values and concepts from observable behavior, but it does aid in developing a consistent approach to such inferences. The

COMPACT model, moreover, provides a useful medium for facilitating the application of the various insights drawn from such divergent fields as cultural anthropology, sociology, and psychology.

ECONOMIC PRODUCTS AS OBJECTS OF ORIENTATION IN SOCIAL INTERACTION

The functional phases and levels of orientation sketched above relate to the interaction between individuals or groups of individuals. The behavioral disciplines provide a vocabulary with which to label these elements of behavior and social interaction. It remains to show the general relationship between communicative interaction and economic products and services within the framework of the system of action.

The economic distinction between goods and services provides the key to the relationship between social interaction and economic production. A *service* is thus a social interaction with an economic value attached to its *performance.* A physical *product* is an object with an economic value attached to its *quality.* While the service thus constitutes a direct performance, the product can be thought of as the *consequence* of a performance by the producer. The nature of both qualities and performances is that of *messages* which gain the quality of *information* only as a result of the *meaning* the buyer attaches to them.

The transformation of messages or data into information is the subject matter or communication, and it is also the subject matter of marketing. Distribution logistics (i.e., the movement of physical goods from producer to user) is to marketing as the Shannon and Weaver information theory, with its concepts of channel capacity and noise, is to communication; and as such it constitutes the physical boundaries of the feasible at least as far as marketing is concerned. In any case, physical distribution is the subject of technological innovation, while the strategic use of media and attachment of meaning to economic output are the subjects of social innovation. Successful social innovation proceeds from a clear understanding of the nature of the present conditions, and such understanding involves the comprehension of the interplay between technology and behavior facilitated by communication. Marshall McLuhan, in his *Understanding Media*, expresses it this way:

Energy and production now tend to fuse with information and learning. Marketing and consumption tend to become one with learning, enlightenment and the intake of information.[10]

. . . the peculiar and abstract manipulation of information as a means of creating wealth is no longer a monopoly of the stockbrokers. It is now shared by every engineer and by the entire communication industries. With

electricity as energizer and synchronizer, all aspects of production, consumption, and organization become incidental to communications.[11]

*The potential role of the personal salesman in this developing
network of instant electronic communication is greater than ever,
but it depends for its realization upon the development of a better
understanding of the nature and complexity of communicative interactions among individuals and organizations.*

SUMMARY

The COMPACT model represents a convenient tool for analysis
of communicative interaction. It enables the observer to focus
on the specific range of interactions which relate to his problems,
and it provides a set of functional phases for the purpose of classifying the elements of an action sequence. These functional phases
are:

1. Awareness
2. Acquisition
3. Goal Seeking
4. Harmonization
5. Commitment

Application of these five generalized requisites enables the
researcher to construct a system model for any specific system
of action for the purpose of detecting strengths and weaknesses
in the participating system.

An important condition for valid analysis is the explicit identification of the level at which the analysis is to be performed and
the consequent relevant variables of the specific system. Five
such levels were suggested each denoting a specifiable set of
motivational conditions and a set of relational or communicative
enablers. These five levels of behavioral orientation are:

1. Physical Activity
2. Adaptive Behavior
3. Instrumental Performance
4. System Integration
5. Value Integration

The goal should be to provide a unified framework for the
combination of psychological, social-psychological, economic,
sociological, and anthropological theory and research. Even without
such a global accomplishment, however, the system of action
framework provides a useful guideline for the design of market
research, advertising, and selling-effectiveness research, as

well as organizational analysis. In the following chapter the COMPACT model will be applied to an analysis of the marketing system as a means of bridging the communication gap between the utility producing organization and the utility consuming entity.

VII

Marketing and Communication

THE MODEL OUTLINED in the preceding chapter provides foundation for analysis of cooperative and competitive patterns of human behavior and interaction. The phases of a system of action can be described as modes of orientation of the acting unit toward its situation of environment. A given mode of orientation signifies direction of attention toward some object or some aspect of an object. It is the purpose of the present chapter to develop and examine the broad elements of a concept of marketing as a mode of orientation, or phase of activity, of the economic organization or the firm. Marketing has variously been defined as a set of activities, a set of performances (such as advertising, personal selling, and sales promotion), and as the subject matter of marketing management. The COMPACT model not only aids in explaining the relationship between these several definitions, but also facilitates examination of the controlling influences exerted by the organizational framework.

Most organizational marketing functions are overwhelmingly complex sets of interactions, as any marketing manager knows; and it is not the purpose here to present an exhaustive description of these interactions. The objective is to develop an outline of what are considered the more significant structural relationships which characterize the marketing function, both as an element of the larger system — the economic organization — and as a system of action in its own right.

THE FUNCTION AND SCOPE
OF AN ORGANIZATIONAL SYSTEM

The marketing function is generally performed in and circumscribed by an overall organizational framework variously labeled the firm, the company, or the economic enterprise. In other words, the

marketing organization can be considered as a functional subsystem of the company, and as such is subordinate to the objectives
and activities of the company as a whole. Some marketing texts
take account of this structural arrangement by stressing the
similarities between top management and marketing management
activities, and this is probably sufficient for some purposes. To
equate the scope of marketing with that of company management,
however, misses an essential element of organizational strategy
and structure.

The reference here is not necessarily to individuals, although
in some companies the top marketing executive may well be
considered a subordinate, hierarchically speaking, to other executive officers. The reference is rather to the *function* which
must of necessity be coordinated with other functional elements
of the organization such as production and finance. Figure 11

FIGURE 11

The Generalized Functional Phases of the Firm

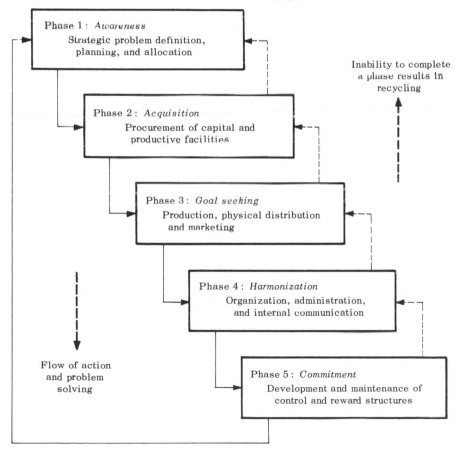

shows the generalized functional phases of activity of the business enterprise. *The strategic policies of a given company have the effect of establishing the boundaries of the marketing operation with respect to three general classes of selling situations:*

1. Situations which *necessarily* result in sales (i.e., sales which occur regardless of the quality and quantity of marketing efforts).
2. Situations which may *possibly* result in sales, given a certain degree of influence.
3. Situations which will not produce sales *regardless* of the amount and quality of effort expended by the marketer.

In addition to these three general classes of selling situations, the specific market situation established by any strategic policy may also result in certain serendipitous outcomes (i.e., outcomes which are neither expected nor sought).

The important point to be made here is that the effectiveness of a marketing operation must be understood in terms of the controlling factor imposed by the efficacy of the strategic policies of any given economic organization. The diagram in Figure 12 shows a three-dimensional model of a generalized marketing system in the context of the firm. These three dimensions and their relationships will be further clarified in the course of the following chapters, but briefly described, they are:

1. The planning-decision-making implementation sequence of phases which provides the analytical, and possibly normative, steps of any system of action.
2. The organizational hierarchy, the various levels of which are differentiated on the basis of scope and standards underlying each of the action orientations.
3. The individual competence scale which provides a crude and basically intuitive means of differentiating individual members of the organization on the basis of their conceptual capacities as information and decision systems with reference to the conceptual capacities required by any given task.

Each of the small cubes in the three-dimensional model thus represents an activity phase at a specific organizational level performed at some level of individual competence. Within the organizational framework an individual may serve part of, or more than, one of these functional elements. The organizational levels are differentiated on the basis of the scope and significance of the decision making:

The real distinction between policy-making and administration is not to be found in the formal separation of functions nor in the official titles of positions, but in the significance of decisions for organizational structure and functioning. The president of an organization may devote himself to routine administration while his administrative assistants make policy. Actually, of course, in most organizations, there is some correlation between policy-making and position in the hierarchy. The relationship is so imperfect, however, that some political scientists have tended to reject the distinction between policy-making and administration completely. [1]

FIGURE 12

A Three-Dimensional Model of the Marketing
System in the Context of the Firm

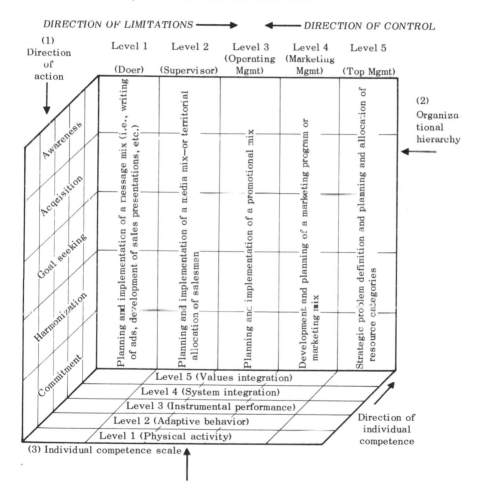

The three-dimensional COMPACT model thus represents a guide to the conceptualization and analysis of organizational relationships not indicated in formal organization charts. As will be shown in some detail in Part Four, the interrelationships

among organizational hierarchies and individual competence also
have important implications for the development and maintenance
of control and information systems in the marketing organization.
In addition, the model has descriptive, if not predictive, implications, primarily in industrial marketing, for the planning and
implementation of personal selling approaches to any given organizational buying situation.

Each of the levels of hierarchy and competence depicted in
the model must necessarily be defined in relation to all other
levels in the absence of any absolute standards. Certainly, the
literature abounds with normative definitions of organizational
relationships; but, as is gradually being discovered, particularly
in systems engineering, *the logically "best" organization is not
necessarily the most effective one.* Within the state of the art
of organizational theory it is therefore necessary to rely on
definitions which are descriptive of past organizational behavior.
In a study of the history of several large and successful business
organizations, Alfred D. Chandler, Jr. develops the following
description of the scope and nature of strategic policy making:

Strategy can be defined as the determination of the basic long-term goals
and objectives of an enterprise, and the adoption of courses of action and
the allocation of resources necessary for carrying out these goals. Decisions to expand the volume of activities, to set up distant plants and offices,
to move into new economic functions, or become diversified along many
lines of business involve the defining of new basic goals. New courses of
action must be devised and resources allocated and reallocated in order to
achieve these goals and to maintain and expand the firm's activities in the
new areas in response to shifting demands, changing sources of supply,
fluctuating economic conditions, new technological developments, and the
actions of competitors.[2]

The goal function of the economic enterprise is production
of goods and services, the utility of which is some function of the
value patterns of the society in which the organization operates.
The aim of strategic planning is thus to establish the economic
niche in which the organization will operate as well as to plan
and implement the overall allocation of organizational resources
to the various functional activities of the enterprise. Whereas
the marketing man must concern himself with the relationship
between *economic production* and the *individual user,* the strategic
decision maker, must concern himself with the relationship
between the *social system,* or society and *economic production.* It
is this latter activity which Peter Drucker terms entrepreneurship
for the purpose of "economic performance."[3] Unfortunately, the
problems of strategic decision making have been largely ignored
in management science and so the meaning of such terms as
entrepreneurship and economic performance remains fundamentally
intuitive.

In any case, the results of strategic decisions circumscribe the marketing efforts of the enterprise. The economic niche in which the company will operate has been defined, and this decision is often by necessity long-range. Similarly, functional resource allocations are made at the strategic decision making level. According to several writers, internal resource allocations have in recent decades been directed more toward marketing than any other functional element of the enterprise. If this increased emphasis on marketing results in improved communications between producers and users of economic goods and services, both are in a position to gain. *If, on the other hand, increased marketing effort is substituted for effective strategic decision making, then the meaning and capacity of marketing tools have been misconceived.* One of the strategic planning problems of the company is the allocation of internal resources such that each is utilized as fully as possible. Such allocation requires an understanding both of what marketing can and cannot do, and an understanding of the nature of the social and economic function the company or organization intends to serve.

THE FUNCTIONAL PHASES OF A MARKETING SYSTEM

In a broad sense, marketing encompasses all the activities and data flows which occur at the interface of producing and buying systems, regardless of the initiator of the relationship. It has become generally accepted, however, to speak of marketing in a somewhat narrower sense as the activities and data flows which originate on the producer's side, and of procurement, purchasing, or buying as the behavior occurring on the user side of the relationship.

While a similar division will be adopted in this and the following two chapters, it is important to keep in mind the fact that *all marketing activities, whatever the source, are ultimately co-determined by all participants in the marketing process by virtue of their abilities or inabilities to take account of their respective environments.*

The diagram shown in Figure 13 briefly summarizes the activity phases of the generalized marketing system of action. The implications of each of these phases and the relevant hierarchical levels will be discussed in some detail below. In the following chapter, attention will be turned to the area of buying behavior.

Phase 1: Definition and Planning of the Marketing Mix

Market relationships established as a result of strategic decisions made by the top management of a given enterprise may, according to one marketing theorist, be thought of as potential in nature:

In an exchange economy, the relationship of producer and consumer, i.e., the market, is a universal fact. The mere fact of relationship, however, is insufficient to generate an exchange. The existence of a market relation is the foundation for exchange, not a substitute for it . . . . From a marketing point of view, the market relation is both an obstacle and an opportunity. It is real enough and yet it is not fully realized. It is not actual but rather potential.[4]

FIGURE 13

The Basic Functional Phases of the Marketing System
from the Point of View of the Seller

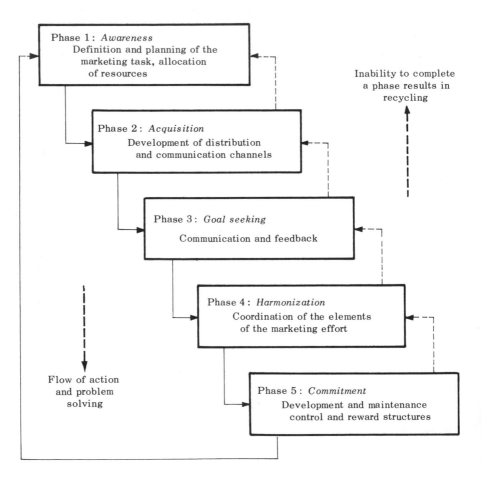

The area of problem definition and planning (awareness phase) in the marketing system should thus have as its main objective

the development of a communication plan designed to realize
this potential relationship. Two specific objects of orientation,
the product and the buyer, will be discussed briefly below. The
marketing-planning function as such has been described at some
length in an earlier study published by the Marketing Science
Institute. That study discusses:

. . . the allocation of funds and resources among the various promotional
methods available in marketing [and] . . . includes the process of identification and evaluation of the marketing administrator's alternatives, and
also an analysis of the methods and problems of selection from among these
alternative allocations.[5]

The planning activities may result in a formal plan, or may
be of a more informal nature, depending on the internal organizational requirements and the complexity of the external market.

Definition of relevant product qualities. Products have been classified in various ways: according to buyer (industrial versus
consumer goods); according to a notion of necessity (luxury versus
necessity products), and according to length of life of the product
(durable versus nondurable goods). None of these classifications
is satisfactory from other than a textbook point of view. Luxury
products are luxuries from the point of view of only the buyer who
can afford them; and it is not entirely clear how durability relates
to desirability and function.

A classification of goods or services for marketing purposes
must take into account the requirements of the buyer systems to
which the product relates.[6] Consequently a product must be classified in at least some, if not all of the following categories:

1. the product as a *concept* or *symbol*
2. the product as *merchandise*
3. the product as an object of *possession*
4. the product as an object of *identification*
5. the product as an object of *commitment*

The product or service considered as a *concept* relates to
its symbolic qualities perceived by the buyer. This is perhaps
one of the most important and also one of the most difficult
tasks facing the marketer, particularly because he is apt to describe the concept behind his product as "obvious." The concept
which a buyer holds of any given product essentially determines
the category into which he places it, and its attributes which he
will consider important. In its broader implications, this represents a problem of relating technological innovations to the
existing individual, social, and cultural frameworks of buyers.
In a somewhat narrower sense the problem is one of determining

"what to say" about any given product. The main thrust of so-called motivation research has a bearing on this problem and Ernest Dichter, in his *Handbook of Consumer Motivations* [7] provides numerous examples of misconceived products. There are as yet no general guidelines in this area of product concept definition, but some of the problems involved are discussed in Chapter X.

The product considered as *merchandise* constitutes classification of the physical qualities of an economic good or, alternatively, the physical performances of an economic service. The objective of merchandising activities is to present the product most advantageously from the point of view of packaging and physical appearance as in accordance with buyer expectations and in light of competitive offerings.

To the classical economist, *consumption* (i.e., the buyer's possession of the product) constitutes the end of the exchange process, and marketing theorists, drawing upon economic theory, have thus primarily concerned themselves with the activities and contingencies occurring *before* the purchase of a product. More recently, however, marketers have become aware of an apparent difference between a buyer or customer and a user or consumer. This difference is especially evident in industrial marketing but undoubtedly occurs in consumer marketing as well. The use or consumption phase constitutes perhaps the most crucial test of a product or service since it is here that product concepts and qualities are combined with perceived performance. That is, whatever the *user* thinks the product should be and do, regardless of the source of his expectations, is compared with what the *user* perceives the product as actually being and doing. The user may recognize utilities in the product which the marketer has never considered, but, on the other hand, he may be unable to perceive sufficient utility to justify both this and subsequent purchases.

The product considered as an object of *identification* involves a matching of product performance with the buyer's existing framework of experiences. Even a well-performing product or service may thus turn out to be unacceptable to the buyer for reasons which will be explored further in the following two chapters.

If a given product has successfully met the requirements of the buying system, the buyer may go to the point of developing a *commitment* to the extent of purchasing or not purchasing the same product when replacement is required. As already indicated, commitment may occur at various levels of intensity, but in general it signifies internalization of a given system of action. That is, the buyer may not only develop selective perception with reference to any given product, he may also be entirely unaware of the reasons underlying subsequent purchases. This purchasing consistency is often described as brand loyalty.

Definition of relevant buyers and buying performances. Ideally, a classification of buyers should identify the relevant participants in any given marketing system, on the basis of some property or set of properties which are susceptible to influence by the means and media controllable by the marketer. The industrial-middleman-final customer classification is generally known, and even though it does not provide a definition of the influenceable properties of each of these classes of buyers—as would be indicated by the growing recognition of similarities between industrial and consumer marketing—it does serve as a useful basis for describing the various assortments of products handled at each of the levels in the distribution channel:

Goods are associated in different patterns at various levels in the channel. The basis of this association is the difference in technologies which apply at successive levels. Goods are associated at the manufacturing level because they can be made on the same equipment or in the same plant. They are associated at the wholesale level because of similarities among trade customers and similar requirements for shipment and storage. They are associated at the retail level because of consumer purchasing habits and convenience. [7]

Determination of any given buyer's place in the distribution channel, however important, constitutes only the beginning of an operational classification of buying systems. In a study of industrial purchasing behavior completed recently by the Marketing Science Institute,[9] it was found that the complexity of organizational buying behavior was significantly related to the "newness" of the product to the buying company. Buying situations could thus be classified with reference to the information required in a rebuy, modified rebuy, and new purchase situation. For purposes of generalizing this classification scheme to all categories of buyers, each member of the distribution channel, as well as each final buyer can be considered as *buying systems,* each of which engages in a certain sequence of behaviors within the context of a given organizational level and at a specific level of competence. Insofar as these properties are defined by such characteristics as the buyer's place in the distribution channel, his social status, and other socioeconomic and demographic data, useful classifications may clearly be made on these bases. It should be noted here, however, that socioeconomic and demographic data are rough summations of results of past behavior and as such they may not be indicative of future behavior.

In the following two chapters attempts will be made to apply the COMPACT model to a generalized analysis of buying systems, the purpose being to reveal some significant structure on the basis of which the strengths and weaknesses of a given marketing mix may be analyzed.

Phase 2: Development of Distribution
and Communication Channels

This phase of the marketing system pertains to the necessity
of adapting marketing activities to the patterns of buying activities
in the environment. Wroe Alderson developed the concept of a
transvection to describe the entire set of transformations and
selections a product undergoes from raw material acquisition
to the final transaction prior to end use or consumption:

A transvection is the unit of action for the [marketing] system by which a
single end product such as a pair of shoes is placed in the hands of the
consumer after moving through all the intermediate sorts and transformations from the original raw materials in the state of nature . . . . A
transvection includes the complete sequence of exchanges, but it also
includes the various transformations which take place along the way.[10]

The concept of the transvection not only provides a basis
on which to analyze and "optimize" the number of transformations and sorts which a product undergoes between producer
and user, but also offers a useful basis on which to determine
the data requirements at each sorting point. The number of
different sorting points in any given distribution channel thus
determines the extent of the marketing task, while the analysis
of each of the sorting points as systems of action aids in determining the kind of data required and the medium necessary to
convey these data to each of the buying or "transformation"
systems in the channel.

Improvement of the channels of distribution and communication
will not solve the problems of marketing as such. The problem
of content still remains. One might surmise that with the development of instant electronic data transfer, more effort will be
applied to the discovery of rules for translating data into information (communication) and information into knowledge (learning).
Until these rules are discovered and operationalized, however,
the marketing man's job will remain as tough as ever.

Phase 3: Communication and Feedback

The basic function of the marketing system is communication,
by means of which the economic potential of the enterprise is
realized. The distance between the producer and the user of
goods and services has several dimensions. Alderson suggested
three dimensions [11] while McInnes suggests a five dimensional
relationship.[12] Table 5 shows these dimensions and compares
them with the classification of products outlined earlier in this
chapter.

Any physical object which man produces derives its existence,
form, and use from a concept. When Alexander Graham Bell

TABLE 5

The Dimensions of the Relationship Between the
Producer and User of Goods and Services

	Functional Classification	Dimensions Suggested by Alderson	Dimensions Suggested by McInnes
(1)	Concept	Form	Perception
(2)	Merchandise	Space & Time	Space & Time
(3)	Possession		Ownership
(4)	Identification		Valuation
(5)	Commitment		

invented the telephone it was not the machine he had to sell but the concept of long distance communication. Similarly, the manufacturers of computers are faced with the necessity of developing and marketing data processing and information systems quite apart from the computer itself which, although it generally becomes a more or less integral part of the data system developed, in and of itself has virtually no utility.

Even apart from these more complex product concepts the very name of a product implies a concept, however simple. The meaning of the word soap does not inhere in a square bar of a certain mass. It inheres in the meaning individuals attribute to such concepts as cleanliness and hygiene. Indeed, the *meaning or utility of all economic products and services inhere not in the products themselves but in the uses and values which they serve.*

It is the objective of marketing to relate inherently meaningless objects and performances to the use and value framework of the buyer. Industrial and consumer marketing differ not in the least in this respect, although they do vary with respect to the specific uses and values attached to physical objects. Consequently, it is necessary for the marketer to develop knowledge about the origin and nature of product concepts, the uses and values buyers attach to his products, and the requirements for transforming these use and value concepts into action.

The concept of utility as used here can be described in terms of the several levels of orientation suggested earlier. In general, utility may be defined as that value concept an individual is capable of attributing to any given product. In other words, the competence of an individual buyer or organizational buying system to conceive of uses for a product to determine the degree of utility which the buyer will be capable of deriving from that product or service. Clearly, the "newness" of a product has a bearing on buyers' ability to perceive its potential utility. In general, however, the ability of the marketer to relate any given product to the existing conceptual orientations of buyers will be basic to a determination of the required content and media of a marketing mix suitable for an effective promotion of that product.

The marketer's job does not end with the completion of a given purchase. There is still the problem of keeping the buyer or user satisfied, either by means of service or by means of reinforcing communication. The more the marketer can do to optimize the utility of the product *after* the purchase, the greater the chance that the buyer will buy the product again on the next purchase occasion. Empirical evidence derived in the study of industrial purchasing behavior, mentioned previously,[13] indicates that repeat purchases of a specific product over time, for whatever reason, results in what might be called "functional autonomy" of the buying behavior involved. That is, even though the buyer's original reason for choosing the product may have been forgotten, it is continually purchased "because it is purchased." Even without significantly different information (much of which might be ignored anyway because this specific purchase is not "a problem"), the buyer is likely to continue buying the specific product. Clearly, such functional autonomy of action may also develop with reference to a given supplier company or a given salesman.

Phase 4: Organization and Coordination
of the Elements of the Marketing System

The effectiveness and the efficiency of any given marketing system cannot be established purely with reference to the activities internal to the marketing organization. Since the goal of marketing efforts is that of giving meaning, or utility, to products or services, it is evident that effectiveness and efficiency must be appraised from the points of view of both seller and buyer. In other words, even though advertising may appear to be the most effective means of *disseminating* a given set of data, it may not be the most effective means of *receiving* data from the buyer's point of view.

The problem of coordinating and organizaing the marketing effort is thus one of establishing the most effective and efficient marketing mix, promotional mix, and message or data mix, within the context of the existing communication gap between marketer and buyer. This communication gap may have several dimensions, but can, in general, be attributed to differences in conceptual orientation and communicative capacity of the participants in the system.

As indicated above, the various elements of any given marketing effort, seen from the marketer's point of view, may be considered at several different but interrelated levels. Thus, the marketing mix refers to the total mix of marketing activities, the promotional mix refers to an array of communication channels available to and used by marketers and buyers (i.e., advertising, personal selling, and sales promotion), the media mix refers to the several media available for advertising purposes, and the message mix refers to the content of the various advertisements and sales appeals (Figure 12).

A decision to adopt any given marketing mix or implement a specific marketing plan clearly serves as a constraint or control on the alternatives available for a promotional mix. Similarly, the communicative abilities and inabilities inherent in the conceptual competence of buying systems establish the effective boundaries of *possible* influences.

Phase 5: Development of Controls and Reward Structures

The willingness of an individual to coordinate his behavior with other individuals in the pursuit of the same goal is not solely a function of the formal organization. Indeed, too much structuring of interpersonal relationships may have a strangling effect on individual motivation and initiative. Herbert Simon describes the problem of organizational integration in the following manner:

To understand the process of decision in an organization, it is necessary to go far beyond the on-the-spot orders that are given by superior to subordinate. It is necessary to discover how the subordinate is influenced by standing orders, by training, and by review of his actions. It is necessary to study the channels of communication in the organization in order to determine what information reaches him which may be relevant to his decisions. The broader the sphere of discretion left to the subordinate, the more important become those types of influence which do not depend upon the exercise of formal authority.[14]

The problem involved here has variously been described as one of "motivating" or one of "controlling" individuals in an organizational context. Peter Drucker, distinguishing between "controls" (collection of data) and "control" (giving direction), provides the following description of the relationship between data and action:

If we deal with a human being in a social institution, "controls" must become personal motivation to lead to "control." Instead of a mechanical system, the control system in a human-social situation is a volitional system. That we know very little about the will is not even the central point. A translation is required before the information by the "controls" can become ground of action — the translation of one kind of information into another which we call *perception*.[15]

If a given set of data deriving from some instrumental process does not in and of itself specify a course of action, let alone alternative courses of action, the same can be said of the majority of reward or incentive plans. A promise of a reward for achieving any specified result does not by itself define a path, let alone the most effective and efficient path, to that result. Whatever guidelines an individual derives from the data pertaining to his task will be some function of his conceptual capacity or competence, which also will influence his perception of the meaning of any given reward structure. As indicated in Chapter IV, a given reward or incentive scheme may result in individuals "trying harder," but it does not provide any guidelines with reference to *what* it is the individual should try harder to do.

The concern here is not so much with the development of a solution to the problem of relating the individual to an organization, since "solutions" already abound in literature and practice. The concern is primarily with the development of a set of concepts of motivation, communication, and competence which are logically and operationally related. Part Four of this volume is largely devoted to an examination of communicative links and influence processes with specific reference to the organization of the personal selling effort.

SUMMARY

The purpose of the present chapter has been to outline the broad elements of a concept of marketing as a function linking the economic enterprise with a given set of buyers. As an element of the firm, marketing is subordinated to the strategic decision making function which implicitly or explicitly defines the situation in which the marketing system must operate. On the other hand, marketing as an element of the buying environment provides a set of limiting conditions on the effectiveness of any strategic policy by virtue of the communicative constraints inherent in buying systems. In the following chapter a concept of a generalized buying system will be outlined and in later chapters attempts will be made to show in some detail the kinds of problems the system analysis will expose when applied to personal selling and the salesman. The brief demonstration of the functional tool of analysis in this chapter illustrates at least two important points.

The first is an attempt to understand any item as part of a larger whole, as the product of multiple, interacting forces, rather than the result of a single cause that can be ferreted out like a detective uncovering a murderer. The second is that these forces are regarded as natural rather than good or bad. One's own hopes, fears, and ideas of what *should* be, are set aside in favor of discovering what *is* . . . the policy maker, like most other people, has it ingrained in him from his early years to measure human affairs in terms of good and evil. Starkly simple explanations are sought to the neglect of deeper understanding and hence opportunity for control.[16]

Functional analysis is not a wonder tool producing an answer to all or any "how to" questions. It is rather a tool of analysis which, if applied carefully, will produce a number of questions, and that is, after all, the important thing: to set up the right problem before attempting to produce a solution.

VIII

A Concept of Buying Systems

IT IS UNDERSTANDABLE if marketers think of their own efforts as being the sole cause of buying behavior, particularly in view of the conspicuous nature of such marketing activities as advertising and personal selling. Not only has more effort been expended in describing the patterns of behavior exhibited by marketers, but a tacit assumption that the flow of influence is initiated by and proceeds from marketers to buyers appears to underlie much research and writing in this area.

The point was made earlier, however, that marketing in a broad sense encompasses the behavior of both producing and buying systems and therefore constitutes a *process of interaction,* the purpose of which is to bridge the gap between the two types of systems. In the previous chapter some consideration was given to the functional elements of the marketing system from the marketer's point of view. In this and the following chapter an attempt will be made to develop an analysis of buying systems, both organizational and individual. *A buying system is essentially an information and decision system engaging in a behavior process requiring certain data inputs and producing certain data outputs.* Buying behavior can be analyzed from a number of viewpoints, depending upon the orientations and standards employed by the observer-researcher. Specifically, the following analytical perspectives can be used:

1. Cultural commonalities: the motivational orientations and standards held in common by a majority of the members of a society.
2. Role commonalities: the behaviors and expectations held in common by individuals in similar roles.
3. Situation specific analysis: the motivational orientations and standards held in common by buyers in similar situations.
4. Buyer specific analysis: the psychological or personality approach to the analysis of behavior.

5. Object specific analysis: analysis of buyer behavior with reference to a given object (i.e., a product or a service).

Each of these approaches to the analysis of buyer behavior essentially represents the subject of different behavioral science disciplines. The purpose in discussing them here is to provide some input material for the development of a more comprehensive classification of buyer behavior, rather than to offer an exhaustive summary of each of the behavioral science disciplines involved.

CULTURAL COMMONALITIES

The cultural commonalities of buyers and sellers is probably among the most neglected areas in marketing literature and marketing research. Yet, one of the prerequisites for the effectiveness of an advertising program, for example, is the existence of certain mutual or common orientations among the individuals to whom the advertising is directed.

One of the diagnostic features of a culture is its selectivity. Most specific needs can be satisfied in a variety of ways, but the culture selects only one or a very few of the organically and physically possible modes. "The culture selects" is, to be sure, a metaphorical way of speaking. The *original* choice was necessarily made by one or more individuals, and then followed by other individuals (or it wouldn't have become culture). But from the angle of those individuals who later learn the culture the existence of this element in a design for living has the *effect* not of a selection made by these human beings as a reaction to their own particular situation but rather of a choice which still binds, though made by individuals long gone. [1]

Culture, in other words, represents a set of assumptions or decision premises which serve both to facilitate and limit the process of choice in decision making. In a broad sense culture represents the "things *people* take into account," as well as the general values people apply in interactions with other people. The point of view of the cultural anthropologist is thus to analyze the individual in terms of what he has in common with others. Edward T. Hall in *The Silent Language* [2] identifies three levels of culture from the point of view of the degree of awareness and the individual's process of socialization. These three levels he terms the formal, informal and technical modes of behavior. [3] The *formal* mode of behavior refers to the traditional rules and values of a culture. In the modern industrial organization one can, for example, find a great deal of formal awareness giving rise to ritualistic behavior along the lines of: "It has always been done this way here." According to Hall, "formally aware people are more likely to be influenced by the past than they are by the present or future." [4]

The *informal* mode of behavior refers to the internalized systems or repertoires of behavior shared by individual members of a culture. It was stated earlier that the greater part of human behavior, both in general and with respect to buying behavior, is "out of awareness" with regard to the reasons or motivations underlying it. The cultural anthropologist postulates that such internalized behavior has been learned by the individual through a process of imitation. Clearly, imitation is a form of communication which includes both the verbal and the nonverbal cues which are produced in social interactions. By way of computer analogy, the individual, through a process of imitation of other individuals coupled with a kind of trial and error experimentation, becomes "programmed" to behave in a certain fashion in any given situation. The "program" is continually changed by learning or unlearning, and it is this adaptive process that is important for the understanding of the process of communication since it serves to expand the time and space limitations often assumed to exist in interpersonal interaction.

Technical awareness and learning are fully conscious and verbalizable. While formal and informal behavior rules are essentially interactive in that they are apparently not directly transmittable by verbalization; technical behavior rules and guidelines can be recorded in manuals or handbooks. A job description, for example, is frequently an attempt to transfer formal and informal behavior guidelines on a technical level and therefore is often virtually useless to the individual for whom it is written.

The relationship between the concept of individual competence and the levels of culture suggested by Hall is outlined in Table 6. Since individual competence varies within groups, organizations and societies, the different levels of competence cannot be entirely explained in terms of cultural factors. On the contrary, it appears that culturally determined behavior patterns are essentially epiphenomena (i.e., by-products of other phenomena) with respect to the analysis of individual behavior. Nevertheless, the cultural approach to analysis of behavior is capable of producing

TABLE 6

The Concept of Competence and Levels of Culture

Competence Levels	Culture Levels
Level 1: Values	Formal
Level 2: System	
Level 3: Performance	Informal
Level 4: Behavior	
Level 5: Activity	Technical

a useful contribution to an understanding of the generally accepted standards and beliefs of individuals both as buyers and sellers.

ROLE COMMONALITIES

Essentially, an economic organization, or a household, is a socio-cultural institution pertaining to cooperation with, and concern and responsibility for "significant others." Sociologically speaking, each member of an organization takes it upon himself, or contracts, to perform a certain role vis-a-vis other members of an organization.

The role concept thus provides an analytical entity cross-cutting the analysis of individual behavior. It is, in one sense, a composite unit of behavior referring to the interaction of an individual with a given social institution. In another sense, the role concept takes into consideration only that part of individual behavior which relates to the specific social institution under analysis.

The role concept is abstracted from the concrete behavior of the people in particular points in the social system, and can be thought of in two ways. On the one hand we can think of the regularities in the behavior of, say, factory foremen and abstract out of the behavior of many foremen the particular manner of acting in this role. These regularities in behavior are also accompanied by regularities in the ways of thinking and feeling about other people as referring to the expectations other people have about the way a particular person should behave. [5]

The role is consequently a structural concept relating certain parts of individual behavior to a given social system framework. A word of caution is in order here. There is a tendency, both in theory and practice, to regard a specific role, say that of salesman, as being a *determinant* of individual behavior in that role; or, in other words, a salesman behaves the way he does *because* he has accepted the *role* of salesman.

As a structural concept the role, as distinct from function, is a relatively narrow unit of analysis. As Herbert Simon points out:

In its original connotation of a dramatic part, "role" implies too specific a pattern of behavior. A mother does not have set lines to speak; her role behavior is highly adaptive to and contingent upon the situation in which she finds herself. Moreover, there is room for all sorts of idiosyncratic variation in the enactment of a social role. [6]

The problem metioned above is primarily a conceptual one. Consider for a moment a situation of interaction between two individuals—a dyadic relationship. In this context, the role, insofar as it has meaning to both members of the dyad, is a *communicative device.* That is, the role is itself a cultural or social institution serving the purpose of facilitating social interaction. It is important to note here that *the role, when it is identified as a communicative device, becomes a facilitator and not a determinant of individual behavior and interaction.*

The meaning of roles and their relation to the total social system or society is part of the cultural framework of that society. "He is a salesman" or "she is a secretary" may *mean* one thing to a North American and something else to a European. Verbal descriptions of the meaning which an individual attributes to a role, however, often amounts to mere culture-bound language definition. A salesman is "someone who sells," or, as a number of college students put it when asked to comment on the meaning they attached to the role of salesman: "A salesman is someone who makes people do what they don't really want to do." The current discussion concerning the woman's "role" as housewife or career woman is built upon a similar language definition, level of understanding, and description.

The role concept considered from a communication point of view is thus essentially a definitive concept rooted in certain expectations common to a group or a society of individuals. The elements of role performance arise from expectations held by the individual with reference to the effect his own behavior has on others, as well as with reference to the willingness and ability of others to follow the rules and conventions invoked by the role performer. By saying and doing certain things, dressing in a specific fashion, or adopting a certain position in relation to another individual, the performer attempts to influence the interaction in a certain direction. The role performer may, of course, become so engrossed in his own performance that the objective behind the role playing gets lost in the attempt to perfect the dramatic effect. The classic example is the student who tries so hard to adopt the role of listener, vis-à-vis the lecturing professor, that he forgets to listen.

The primary limitation of role analysis as widely utilized is the tendency to construe the role as a standard from which individuals "deviate" or with which individuals are in "conflict." The very significance of the concept of communicative competence derives from the fact that individuals possess differing levels of capacity to use and interpret a variety of role conventions; and the competence which a given individual brings to a specific interaction is related to the degree to which he is capable of conforming to *as well as deviating* from any particular role.

It is perhaps possible for a salesman, a buyer, or any other individual to behave completely within a given and predictable role concept, resulting in ritualistic and noncommunicative behavior. But, in general, the ability of a given individual to perform in a specific situation (and therefore, his ability to communicate) cannot be explained solely within the concept of a role. The fact that he engages in a certain sequence of behavior with another individual implies little or nothing about his motives for doing so. It is consequently difficult for an observer to decide whether the individual is deviating from a role, or whether he is performing a role unknown to the observer. The events and outcomes peculiar to any given interaction are codetermined by the participants, and a good communicator is that individual who can lead, inspire, or incite some other individual, or group of individuals, to action. Such communicative behavior may well depend for its success upon a violation of the receiver's expectations (i.e., the sender's deviation from a generalized role). Interpersonal conflict is neither generally preferable, nor generally avoidable, but is incidental to a process of communicative interaction.

Expectations, it will be recalled, are internalized anticipations with respect to the results of an individual's behavior and the behavior of others. That an expectation is internalized means that it is not normally subject to deliberation. Moreover, it is not subject to change unless it be unlearned—that is, unless evidence becomes sufficiently impressive to make a specific expectation dysfunctional for the individual holding it. As long as the salesman behaves as the buyer expects him to behave, by virtue of his understanding of the salesman's role, little or no change is likely to occur in the behavior of the latter.

To sum up, from a sociological point of view, "role" is a structural concept relating individual behavior in terms of commonalities. From the point of view of communicative relationships, the role is a descriptive concept serving to define the *situation* in which the interaction occurs. When the sociologist speaks of role deviance and role conflict, he is essentially describing some incidental aspects of a communicative interaction. One is thus led to think of communication as partly representing *deviance* from mutual expectations, and this may be useful for some analytical purposes. In the present context, however, the concept of individual competence, which constitutes a more dynamic and less standardized unit of analysis, subsumes the sociologist's role concept.

SITUATION SPECIFIC ANALYSIS OF BUYER BEHAVIOR

The concept of individual competence essentially relates the capacity of an individual to a generalized behavior situation or interaction. The concept of a behavior situation comprises all possible elements of any given interaction, including the physical surroundings, which might influence the events and outcomes of a specific communicative encounter. Situation specific analysis thus differs from role analysis in that it stresses the individual's potential ability to take account of and adapt his performance, or alternatively adapt his environment, to suit his own purposes, rather than stressing his *ability to conform* to the expectations of others.

As the competence scale suggests, there is more to problem solving and decision making than meets the eye. Experimentation in learning processes and computer simulation of human thought processes is just beginning to bring to the point of verbalization the complexity of the individual's interaction with his environment. In later sections of this chapter an attempt will be made to outline the process of decision making from a buyer's standpoint, with reference to his social and organizational environment. The range of possible influences upon organizational buying behavior was the subject of an empirical study recently completed by the Marketing Science Institute [7] and is cited below wherever appropriate.

ACTOR SPECIFIC ANALYSIS OF BUYER BEHAVIOR

Actor specific analysis constitutes essentially a psychological approach to the study of buyer behavior. Several attempts have been made to relate personality traits to buyer behavior; but although the approach is theoretically sound, it is presently of questionable value to the marketer. Tucker and Painter provide the following explanation:

. . . The dearth of evidence on this point can be explained in part by supposition. First, the concept of personality itself has not been very clearly formulated. Second, the instruments available for the ready classification of personality types are few and generally suspect. Third, most self-respecting psychologists are apparently convinced that marketing behavior, pervasive as it may be, is of interest for commercial purposes only. Fourth, marketers probably have little understanding of the need for experimental evidence of their assumptions. [8]

The utilization of psychological research in marketing requires the identification of so-called personality traits. Even if one were able to establish with some degree of certainty a set of discriminating traits, it is difficult at present to see what one would do with such data. That is, if it were found that all buyers of a given brand of coffee were aggressive, dominant, and authoritarian types, it is not clear how a coffee distributor could capitalize on that knowledge.

OBJECT SPECIFIC ANALYSIS OF BUYER BEHAVIOR

The object specific approach to the analysis of buyer behavior is probably the most common in present commercial marketing research. Such research generally seeks to establish a set of buyer profiles for a given product. The data normally utilized are socioeconomic, such as income, family size, and ownership of residence. Even in its present, unsophisticated state, the object specific approach can reveal some useful information about the size and location of a product market, but it leaves much to be desired in terms of prescribing action.

Each of the approaches to the study of buying behavior outlined above provides some useful concepts and evidence which will be drawn upon in subsequent chapters. In general, it may be stated that a buyer *acts* within his capacity to acquire and consume information in relation to a set of *cultural, social, and physical objects.*

BUYER DECISION MAKING

Compared to the attention paid in marketing literature to the marketer's competitive problems, the decision making processes of buyers have received much less consideration. Marketers appear in many respects to have adopted the economist's oversimplified view of demand as a propensity to consume or alternatively as a process of maximization of satisfaction in some sense. Kenneth Boulding aptly describes this economic viewpoint:

Even as one states the operation of economic behavior, however, as the economist apparently conceives it, one is struck with the extraordinary assumption that it makes about the image. Alternatives do not usually have the courtesy to parade themselves in rank order on the drill ground of the imagination. Our relational image is faulty at the best. Our image of the consequences of our acts is suffused with uncertainty to the point where we are not even sure what we are uncertain about. The economists have tried to deal with the problem of uncertainty by supposing that each of the alternatives in our image presents itself to the mind not only with utility tags attached but also with whole probability distributions. Economic man, clever fellow that he is, now maximizes the expected value of his acts, a feat of mathematical agility which it would take centuries of experience and enormous electronic calculators to perfect. [9]

The process of decision making leading to purchase and use does not comprise of just one decision, but constitutes a sequence of information acquisition and decision making instances. The diagram in Figure 14 shows the general categories of a buying decision sequence. The parameters and variables of this sequence ultimately establish the relevance of the data distributed and paid for by marketers.

The match of required and supplied information may be represented by two overlapping circles. [10] The circle on the left, designated S, represents the information provided by suppliers. The circle on the right, designated B, represents the information desired by and acceptable to the buyer.

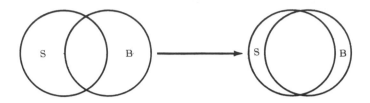

In general, the objective of the marketing system is to increase the overlap of the two circles. As Professor Wroe Alderson put it:

FIGURE 14

The General Categories of Buying Behavior

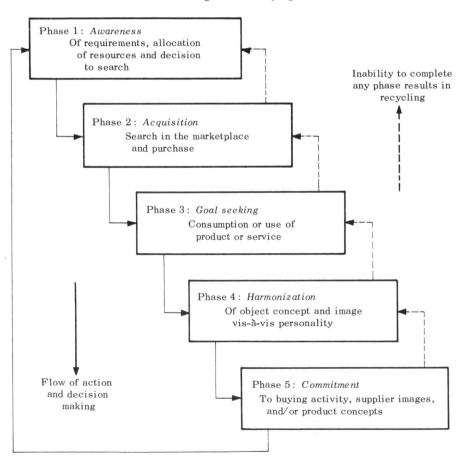

The minimum information which should appear in the overlap is [product] name, what it is claimed the product will do and usually the name of the maker or of the retailer who sells it. A product with this amount of information may be said to be barely identified. The consumer will need this data if he is to take any action at all after seeing an advertisement . . . . If the supplier has guessed right, the product may be said to be adequately identified for the purpose at hand. [11]

Within the context of the state of the art in marketing and communication, success in achieving the above objectives relates to the marketer's ability to understand intuitively the significant elements of the buyer's decision making framework as well as to the availability of the normally utilized demographic data.

THE CASE OF THE INDUSTRIAL BUYING SYSTEM

The Marketing Science Institute's study of industrial purchasing behavior provides some interesting insights into buyer decision making. The research team found it possible, for example, to distinguish between "hard" and "soft" purchasing companies. In the former group price appeared to prevail as the criterion of major importance in purchasing, with emphasis on delivered cost, value analysis, and negotiations with potential suppliers; and the purchasing department performed fairly routine functions. In the latter group, purchasing agents concentrate a great deal on supplier relations work:

In the case of a so-called "soft" purchasing company, the purchasing agent will probably spend a considerable part of his time nurturing supplier relations. The purchasing department in such cases will usually have less influence over the procurement process than its counterpart in the "hard" purchasing company. Major emphasis in the latter is on price reduction with consequent sustaining pressure on suppliers . . . .

The buying company's interest in being a good customer is based upon more than a spirit of altruism. As a purchasing agent expressed it, "In the long run, my job is a lot easier if my suppliers think of me as a good customer. I want them to want my business, because when they do they will hustle to get it and to keep it." The establishment, cultivation, and maintenance of good supplier relationships are considered to be intrinsically more important than the outcome of individual transactions. [12]

The industrial purchasing process is more complex in many respects than final or consumer purchasing, primarily because of the frequently complicated organizational relationships involved. For example, it was found in the cited study that salesmen frequently are mistaken in their judgments regarding the bounds of the purchasing agent's prerogatives:

While it is true that purchasing agents serve a screening function, attempts to avoid them frequently boomerang, since the purchasing agent may still exert a strong blocking influence even when he cannot influence the outcome of the buying situation positively . . . . A veto by top management is usually clear and direct. A veto by a buyer may be more subtle.[13]

Another buyer who was interviewed in connection with the study summarized his role as purchasing agent in the following statement:

I'm really a generalist among a group of specialists. Production people, designers, maintenance, accounting, marketing, and legal specialists are all involved in the procurement process, bringing their special training and viewpoints to bear. I'm the guy who has to integrate all of these separate entities into a workable scheme that will meet our needs.[14]

Since organizational buying systems thus divide the decision sequence required for a purchase to be made between various individuals, or functions, at different hierarchical levels, purchasing agents tend to take on the quality of middlemen between the marketer and the user of the products. This arrangement presents a complex communication problem for the marketer and for the salesman since *they must attempt to direct their messages at individuals in the organization who have both the competence to convert them into usable information and the authority to influence decision makers.*

In the following sections the COMPACT model will be applied to a generalized organizational purchasing situation in an attempt to outline the various analytical dimensions of the buying system's information acquisition and consumption problems.

The Activity Dimension of Buying Behavior

The industrial marketing study provides evidence in favor of the premise that a *sequence* of decisions underlies the majority of industrial purchases. Not all of these decisions are made on the same organizational level, but to simplify the following outline of the several phases of buying activity, the existence of organizational levels, as well as the existence of differences between individual decision makers, will, for the moment, be disregarded. These two dimensions will be added later to complete the buying behavior model. The diagram in Figure 15 outlines the categories of purchasing decisions with specific reference to the industrial situation.

Phase 1: The Buying System's Awareness

The information requirements of any given buying system will, to a large extent, depend upon the strategic policies, the structural relationships, and the competencies of the individuals participating in the purchasing process. Even though industrial purchases are perhaps subjected to more formal analysis than other kinds of purchases, there are inevitably some aspects of any product or supplier which are assumed to be known and consequently remain unexamined. One important analytical problem for the marketer is that of determining, if only in broad terms, a buying organization's ability to take account of the product concepts offered. Some of the basic questions arising in this connection are: How are problems perceived and defined in the buyer organization? Who is instrumental in defining these problems at the various levels? What information is utilized and by what means and methods is it processed? In what capacity does the purchasing agent function in this phase? What are the objectives of the purchasing function and how are they implemented?

FIGURE 15

Categories of Industrial Purchasing Decisions

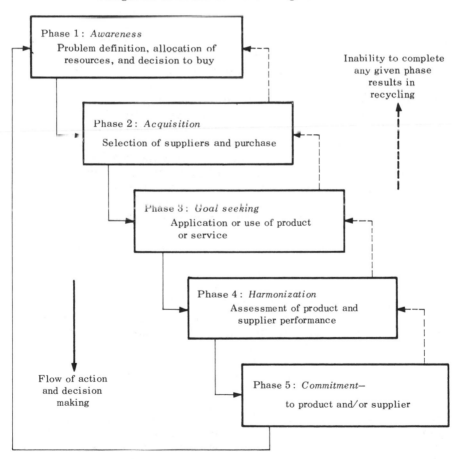

Phase 2: The Buying System's Acquisition Process

The procurement process itself includes the selection of suppliers, acquisition of relevant information (as defined by the buyer), and the actual purchase. In this connection, it was found in the study of industrial purchasing behavior cited earlier that a fundamental responsibility of the purchasing agent is *to protect the cost structure of his company so far as purchased items are concerned,* [15] through supplier discovery and development, systems analysis, and purchasing research. The buyer appears to be the only person influencing the procurement process who is evaluated primarily on the basis of cost savings. Some of the broad questions which should provide the basis for an analysis of a given buying system's supplier selection and purchasing procedures are: What procedures are apparent in supplier selection? Who recommends and who has the intermediate and final decision responsibility in supplier selection? How are selections assessed? Who are the present suppliers and why? What role do personal relationships play in supplier selection? Who writes the specifications for a given product?

Phase 3: The Buying System's Goal Seeking

In the majority of cases the selling-buying process is not concluded at the point where the sale is made. Since the buying system's satisfaction depends to a greater extent on the performance of the product or service with regard to expectations, the marketer cannot afford to be indifferent to either the expectations or the reasons the buying system had for purchasing the product (which may differ drastically from those perceived and intended by the marketer). Thus, depending upon the complexity of the product concepts involved, this phase may require not only a service effort but also an educational effort on the part of the marketer. Some of the questions arising in this connection are: What role does the product play in the buying system's production and marketing processes? On what basis does the buying system assess product performance? How well does the product fit the buying system's requirements? Could the buying system's uses of the product be improved or, alternatively, could the product be improved or changed to better serve the buying system's purposes?

Phase 4: The Buying System's Harmonization
or Control Procedures

According to the Marketing Science Institute's study of industrial purchasing behavior, the staff members of the buying organization become involved in buying situations either due to their responsibility for and authority over purchasing decisions, or due to their information position in the company decision making network. The number of these influences was said to vary from as many as 40 in a so-called "new task" situation to as few as two or three in the highly routinized "straight rebuy" situations.

In the context of complex organizational relationships it becomes important for the marketer not only to determine who the effective decision makers are, with reference to a given purchase, but also the basis on which these decision makers assess their own performance. Each decision maker is likely to have a set of criteria for assessing the acceptability of a given supplier and any specific product, and even a high quality product may be rejected for reasons which have little or nothing to do with its performance. The chief executive of a buying organization may, for example, be concerned with the influence that associations with a given supplier are likely to have on his own company's image, or he may be concerned with additional functions served by the supplier, such as financing or advertising. The production engineer, on the other hand, may be interested in the technical soundness of the product, while the purchasing agent is likely to be concerned with cost, delivery schedules, and availability. An analysis of the process through which these divergent views are harmonized should supply an answer to questions such as the following: What are the various information requirements of the buyer organization? What is its future and how does the supplier fit into that future? What commitments does the buyer organization require of the supplier? How does the buying system assess the purchased products with reference to price, quality, performance, delivery, or service? What service is required? What guarantees does the buying system require?

Phase 5: The Buying System's Commitments

One of the categories of buying situations differentiated in the Institute's study of industrial purchasing behavior was that of a "straight rebuy" situation. The "straight rebuy" is characteristically the most routine of buying situations in which the requirement has been previously established, information needs are minimal or nonexistent, and no alternative products or suppliers are considered. In other words, the buyer is not "in the market" for new suppliers.

The phenomenon of commitment arises partly from repeat performances of a similar line of activity which has resulted in satisfactory results. Initial purchases of a given product may be made for any number of reasons, including product quality and personal relationships. Repeat purchases, however, appear to have a tendency to attain a certain degree of functional autonomy which in turn tends to preclude the perception of adverse data

—particularly in situations where complex organizational decision making machinery must be set in motion to change traditional procedures.

Commitments may be of several types and may occur on several levels but fall primarily into three categories: (1) economic commitments (special distribution and communication facilities), (2) legal commitments (contracts and guarantees), and (3) psychological commitments. The third type of commitment is by far the most subtle and will be discussed in more detail in the following chapters. An analysis of the buying organization's commitments is primarily historical and may be based on questions such as the following: What commitments does the buyer's organization have? How are these likely to influence the supplier's efforts? What is the buyer's past experience with relevant suppliers and what influence is that likely to have on the present and future relationship? Are important and significant psychological or personal commitments involved? What influence do existing commitments tend to have on the buying organization's decision making sequence.

THE CASE OF THE WHOLESALE AND RETAIL BUYER

Both the wholesaling and retailing businesses have undergone drastic transformations from the specialty store to the integrated department store chain and from the independent grocery store served by wholesalers to the supermarket chain combining both the wholesaling and retailing operation in one organization. Moreover, the development of electronic communication media (telephone, teletype, and intercompany computer links) and their introduction into the communication channel between manufacturers and distributors is bound to produce even more changes in the so-called distribution channel.

Where does all this leave the personal selling function? E.B. Weiss makes the following suggestion:

The buying committee is destined to play a *dominant* role in the buying of those giant retailers (and wholesalers) that account for the lion's share of total volume for most presold brands. As a consequence, perhaps 80 per cent of manufacturer salesmen calling on *mass* retailers and wholesalers will be spending maybe 80 per cent of their time with buyers whose decision-making powers are being sharply curtailed.[16]

Apparently, some manufacturers, in the midst of the battle between their own and private brands have failed to exploit fully the changing conditions of distribution channels. The balance of power, as it were, appears to be passing to the retailers who are now integrating backward into manufacturing. Some manufacturer controlled retail outlets of prewar fame have had to capitulate in the face of the greater flexibility of the distribution chain. Marshall

McLuhan in a recent book suggests a possible reversal or perhaps a wholly new development unknown in today's marketing structure:

Automation was first felt and seen on a large scale in the chemical industries of gas, coal, oil and metallic ores. The large changes in these operations made possible by electric energy have now, by means of the computer, begun to invade every kind of white-collar and management area . . . . With electricity as energizer and synchronizer, all aspects of production, consumption and organization become incidental to communications.[17]

It is the framework itself that changes with new technology, and not just the picture within the frame. Instead of thinking of doing our shopping by television, we should become aware that TV intercom means the end of shopping itself, and the end of work as we know it at present.[18]

In any case, the personal selling function has still a potentially important role to perform in integrating the manufacturer and distributor operations. The chain operation, however large, is not all-knowing; indeed it requires a tremendous input of information only the more routine of which can at present be supplied by electronic devices. Application of the functional framework to the analysis of the distributor's buying function reveals a set of questions which when answered in terms of a specific buying situation will aid in allocating the various communication media of the marketing mix:

Phase 1: Awareness

What means does the retail or wholesale buyer have for communicating with individual stores? Who defines requirements? Are buying operations centralized or decentralized? How do buyers get information? Do they rely on salesmen or literature or have they other means of keeping informed?

Phase 2: Acquisition

On what basis are suppliers selected? Do buyers make deliberate comparisons by supplier or by product? What does the buyer consider important: price, quality, delivery, and/or service? Who is involved in the decision making: buying committee or store manager?

Phase 3: Goal Seeking

What image is the distributor organization attempting to build? How does it measure its accomplishments? How can the supplier aid in achieving the expressed or implicit goal? What services can be provided by the supplier?

Phase 4: Harmonization

How does the distributor assess the suppliers? Who is involved in the assessment? How does the chain control its stores? How can the control measures of the chain be integrated with those of the supplier?

Phase 5: Commitment

What commitments do the distributors have? How will they influence the present and future relationship with the supplier? What past experience has the distributor had with the supplier and what will that mean now and in the future? What is required to extract a commitment from the distributor?

Some attempt to answer the above questions is a prerequisite if the potential contributions of sales representatives are to be fully exploited. As in the case of the industrial buying system, the functional framework is descriptive; as such, it provides a means of isolating significant areas for further research and at the same time it helps to ensure that no significant problem areas have been left out of consideration.

THE ORGANIZATIONAL DIMENSION
OF THE PURCHASING FUNCTION

Figure 16 outlines five levels of individual motivational orientation (competence) and five levels of organizational scope of planning and decision making. Each of these two hierarchies represent the organized context of individual behavior. (For the complete framework, see Figure 17 on page 146.) An individual operating on behalf of himself will organize his behavior according to the concepts and conditions which make up his motivation, standards, and values. Within the context of the organizational framework, however, the individual's conceptual and motivational frameworks (by means of which he controls and directs behavior on his own behalf) are frequently superseded or displaced by policy and procedural plans and traditions. The industrial purchasing agent, acting on behalf of an organization, will be limited in his decision making power to the organizational level or levels within which his function has been defined. In addition, however, the methods and procedures in terms of which he performs his function are frequently defined organizationally.

While the possible overlap of an individual's ability to organize and control his behavior with reference to his perceived environment and the organizationally determined policy and control framework frequently gives rise to so-called organizational con-

FIGURE 16

The Elements of Organized Behavior

Individual		Level		Organization
Physiologically deter-mined motivations and abilities	Physical activity	1	Activity standards	Procedural or "how to do it" guidelines
Psychologically deter-mined motivations and abilities	Adaptive behavior	2	Supervisory	Rules for adaptation of procedures to local contingencies
Performance or goal oriented motivations and abilities	Instrumental performance	3	Operating management	Plans for implementation of organizational objec-tives
Systemic or integratively oriented motivations and abilities	Integration system	4	Integrative management	Plans for integration of organizational and en-vironmental resources
Value oriented or moral behavior	Integration value	5	Strategy	Determination of strate-gic objectives

flicts, it is sufficient, for the purposes here, to consider the implications of the organizational framework from the point of view of the marketer attempting to influence the industrial or the governmental procurement process. In the following sections the five levels of organizational behavior will be outlined and in the following chapter individual buying behavior will be discussed.

Level 1: Activity Standards

Ultimately all buying constitutes a set of more or less efficiently performed activities. In other words, the actual purchase consists of "doing" certain things, using certain forms and procedures, and keeping track of and filing certain data. From the buying system's point of view the available data inputs constitute an effective limitation upon the higher level planning performances, while the emergent plans constitute an effective control or para-meter upon the data collection procedures.

In the case of organizational or institutionalized purchasing behavior, the individual's behavior is frequently modified by the procedural rules and controls imposed by the organizational framework. It has been suggested, for example, that organizational buyers are being relegated more and more to the role of clerks with little or no decision making power.[19] To the extent that this is so, it would appear that personal influence is of little import as an element of promotion. That is, the relevant abilities of salesmen, for example, would be shifting from those related to interpersonal influence toward those related to sizing up and analyzing networks of organizational influence. The increasing use of computer tie-ins between supplier and buyer organizations is another procedural invention which presumably would tend to increase the efficiency of data transfer over a relatively narrow range.

While the organizational framework serves the individual as an enabler insofar as it defines for him the "acceptable" and the "unacceptable" activities by means of which he performs his task, this same framework also limits the behavior and decision making freedom of the individual. That is, any organizational framework implies certain modes of orientation and procedures which may or may not be commensurate with the modes of orientation and behavior which are "natural" to the individual member. The more specific aspects of this interrelation between the individual buyer and the organizational framework have yet to be established, but there is little doubt that the process by which any given organization gets influenced by and adapts to its environment is significantly related to the procedural flexibility or inflexibility of the organization.[20]

Level 2: Supervisory Level

Within the context of product performance, requirements, technical objectives such as delivery schedules, inventory requirements, and availability become the governing factors. It should be noted here that these distribution problems and considerations may be decisive in the case of routine buying situations without the requirement for renewed attention at higher decision levels. This does not, of course, mean that the supplier attempting to make inroads into a routine situation must rely on delivery and availability advantages to be successful. On the contrary, *the problem will primarily be one of getting the issue reopened at higher decision levels* (i.e., the new supplier must attempt to make the routine purchase situation a higher level "problem" for the buying organization or system).

The supervisory level, in the case of organizational buying behavior, accounts for the occasional procedural adaptations which are required in any complex behavior situation. Supervisory prerogative is not necessarily assigned to a separate individual, but may well be exercised by the doer, depending upon the size and division of labor characterizing the given organization. In addition to the problems of adaptation, the supervisory function is frequently taken to be that of a "watch dog" and an impressive volume of literature has developed around the conflicts and communication "problems" surrounding the supervisory function. The main point here, however, is that the supervisory function is both a source of flexibility (adaptation) and a source of constraints in the sense that the function transmits and enforces organizational plans for, and rules of, performance.

Level 3: Operating Management

The level of operating management encompasses the decision making and activities relevant to the general implementation of organizational objectives. Clearly, the scope of decision making involved at this level is greater than that at the two lower levels described previously, and influences taken into account are consequently broader. In general, the considerations at this level involve performance-cost relationships and the pursuit and maintenance of a functional goal with reference to the efficiency of some output producing process.

There is tendency in the literature on buying behavior to impute a higher degree of "rationality" to the industrial purchasing process than to that of the final buyer. One of the reasons for this may well be the more obvious requirement for the rationalization of some functional, or goal oriented, relationship among the various purchases of an industrial organization. Despite this apparent difference in the "rationality" underlying industrial and consumer purchasing, however, little or no empirical research has been conducted to establish the specific nature of the final consumer's purchasing system and the criteria which he applies to the development and maintenance of a suitable assortment of possessions. In this context, the assumption of consumer "irrationality" appears to have served as a barrier to theory development and research in consumer and buyer behavior.

Level 4: Integrative Level

The integrative level of the organization refers to the planning and decision making involved in the assignment and coordination of resources to functional or operative levels. In an industrial context the considerations surrounding make or buy decisions may serve as an example. The concern is primarily with the requirements of an integrated production process with a minimum of bottlenecks and excess capacity. The industrial organization is likely to subject integrative problems to a certain amount of technical analysis, whereas the final consumer and the trade buyer are more likely to consider these problems from a somewhat more informal point of view.

Level 5: Strategy Level (Top Management)

Strategic decision making, with reference to an organization, involves the establishment of the boundaries within which the procurement process operates. Even though little is as yet definitively known about the process of strategic decision making, thus making it difficult for a supplier to deliberately influence such decisions, the effects of strategic decisions are evident in the degree of centralization versus decentralization of decision making in the buying organization. The decision to buy certain products, specifically capital goods and equipment, may be directly related to the strategic policies of the buying organization. In addition such policies establish an explicit or implicit set of organizational goals which tend to serve as constraints upon lower level decision making as well as to establish, within broad boundaries, the considerations and environmental data which are "important" and "decisive" and those which are "unimportant" and "irrelevant."

FIGURE 17

A Three-Dimensional Model of the Buying System
in the Context of the Firm

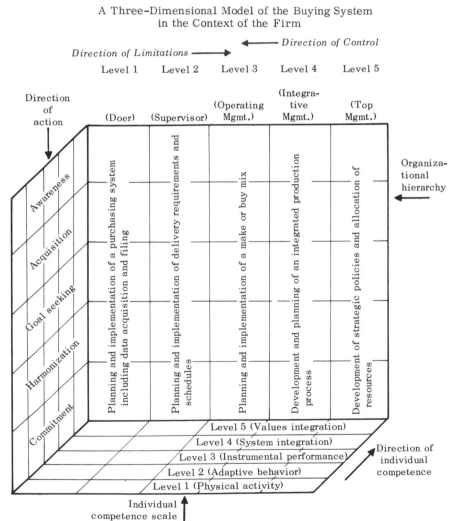

SUMMARY

The purpose of the present chapter has been to outline a number of possible approaches to the development of a concept of buying systems as well as to provide a descriptive framework for the analysis of organizational buying systems. Two of the three dimensions of the COMPACT model were briefly outlined with primary reference to industrial buying; namely, the organizational problem solving and action phases and the levels of organizational decision making (Figure 17). A more comprehensive analysis of such systems is provided in a recently completed study of the industrial purchasing process published by the Marketing Science Institute.

In the analysis provided here it was shown in a general form that application of the COMPACT model can lead to a systematic analysis of the sequence of decisions comprising a given purchase. At the same time, the model leads to a systematic analysis of the various organizational levels, and their relationships, which are potential influences in a given purchasing situation.

In the following chapter, an attempt will be made to develop an analysis of the individual as a buying system with special attention to the application of the third dimension of the COMPACT model; that is, the concept of individual communicative competence. Some of the implications of both this and the following chapter will be further discussed in Part Four.

IX

A Classification
of Individual Buying Behavior

THE ORGANIZATIONAL FRAMEWORK outlined in the preceding chapters basically represents the economic enterprise as a *structure of definitions* of organizational and interpersonal relationships.

The organization . . . takes from the individual some of his decisional autonomy, and substitutes for it an organization decision-making process. The decisions which the organization makes for the individual ordinarily (1) specify his function, that is, the general scope and nature of his duties; (2) allocate authority, that is, determine who in the organization is to have power to make further decisions for the individual; and (3) set such other limits to his choice as are needed to coordinate the activities of several individuals in the organization.[1]

The purpose of the present chapter is to develop the third dimension of the COMPACT model with specific reference to buying behavior. The major premise here is that the connecting link between organizations and individuals is *communication*, a premise which will be further examined in the following chapter. While the firm is generally considered to represent an embodiment of organized behavior, the basic sources of all organization are the organic or neurological and psychological systems of the individual, which enable him to attribute "meaningfulness" to objects and events in the environment. In this respect, it should be noted *that all buying behavior is organized behavior whatever the source of organization.* The very process of taking into account certain data while neglecting other data implies that the individual organizes his environment in a certain fashion. It is this process of taking into account, which ultimately governs the behavior of an individual regardless of whether or not the "something" taken into account is "intended" by someone else. In the following section, an attempt will be made to develop a general concept of individual personality systems, on the assumption that conceptual and interpersonal competence to take account of and act upon available data are significant properties of these systems. In Part Four, some of the implications of this concept for promotion and, more specifically, personal selling will be explored.

THE PROCESS OF SOCIALIZATION

An important point made earlier and often not clearly understood is that *the meaning and utility of economic products inhere in people and not in the things themselves.* Meanings and utilities are broadly prescribed by the society in which the individual lives and as such these meanings become internalized or "known" by the individual.

A person does not learn what a word "means." He learns to attach (if properly socialized) a socially acceptable meaning to it. A person does not learn what certain behaviors by other persons mean. He learns to attach meaning and/or significance to these behaviors. At first, another person's behavior has no meaning for the observer. But the observer *learns* to ascribe a meaning to the other person's behavior. Failure to comprehend and remain constantly sensitive to this fact is a direct and fundamental cause of miscommunication and interpersonal misunderstanding. It is a point which cannot be overemphasized.[2]

Through a process of socialization an individual acquires an ability to perceive and act in certain situations. The fact that a producer or marketer is at all capable of predicting utility and, therefore, demand is evidence that certain commonalities exist between the producer's and the user's socialized points of view. Thus, an individual not only develops an ability to take account of and act in certain situations, but he also develops a set of expectations which enables him to predict in general the behavior of others in similar situations. These commonalities of perceiving and acting, which are primarily a reflection of a similar culture, also enable an individual, such as a salesman, to influence the behavior of others; that is, they provide the common denominator for understanding *intentional* communication.[3] These commonalities clearly do not account for all individual behavior, but there is a tendency for the individual to organize conceptually the world around him as he perceives others organizing their world. This is evidenced by the fact that certain values and concepts become institutionalized as laws (written or unwritten), as organized ways of life (households and business organizations), and as customs and traditions.

Within the context of these socially institutionalized values an individual exhibits a certain level of competence in perceiving and behaving. That is, *he has a certain repertoire of behaviors which he can mobilize for the purpose of achieving a given goal.* The process of acquiring a repertoire of behaviors constitutes learning or acquisition of ability to conceptually "map" the environment. The main point here is that the social-institutional framework of occupational roles and general behavior "rules" do not directly *determine* the behavior of individuals; they serve to *facilitate* the individual's "organizing" or defining of his environment. The behavior of an individual is some function of his ability or competence to *actually* interpret or define this environment. The "interaction" here between competence and motivation may be explained as follows:

> Once a situation is institutionally defined and the definition upheld by an adequately integrated system of sanctions, action in conformity with the relevant expectations tends . . . to mobilize a wide variety of motivational elements in its service. Thus, to take one of the most famous examples, the "profit motive," which has played such a prominent part in economic discussion, is not a category of psychology at all. The correct view is rather that a system of "free enterprise" in a money and market economy so defines the situation for the conducting . . . of business enterprise, that [individuals] must seek profit as a condition of survival and as a measure of success of their activities. Hence, whatever interests the individual may have in achievement, self-respect, the admiration of others, etc., to say nothing of what money will buy, are channeled into profit-making activity. In a differently defined situation, the same fundamental motives would lead to a totally different kind of activity.[4]

In other words, the so-called profit motive, and with it a number of other economic incentives, is essentially an institutionalized standard which serves as a condition for performance in certain occupations. Such economic incentives subserve a certain degree of conceptual competence on the part of individuals who seek to achieve gratification of more fundamental psychological motives.

As indicated in Chapter V, the individual, whether buyer or salesman, can be thought of as an information and decision system engaging in certain systems of action. In the following section, the phases of such systems of action will be discussed with reference to individual buying behavior.

INDIVIDUAL BUYING BEHAVIOR
AND THE SYSTEM OF ACTION

The Marketing Science Institute's study of industrial purchasing behavior, previously cited, outlines a buying situation classification scheme emphasizing the nature of the customer's requirements as governing the planning of marketing effort. The study concentrates upon describing various types of buying situations and steps in the industrial procurement process as they are related to personal and organizational characteristics of the buying company, attributes of the supplying industry, and socioeconomic factors.[5] In the present study, the competence-activity framework is presented as a tool for studying *the behavior of both industrial and consumer buyers and sellers over time.* The COMPACT model is easily adaptable as a device for analyzing individual competence in any buying-selling situation in order to facilitate the adaptation of selling proficiency to buyer requirements.

As an information and decision system, the individual receives communicative "inputs" from the environment and provides communicative "outputs" to the environment. The personality may thus be thought of as *an open system engaged in purposeful interaction with physical, social and cultural objects* (as opposed to a closed system which is self-sufficient and generally not adaptive). The diagram in Figure 18 shows the phases of such interaction. These phases, which are the same as those applied in the organizational case, are basically categories for classifying the components of action,[6] and they can be considered roughly similar for all buyers be they industrial, trade, or final customers. The differences between these buyers are not so much a function of the structural requirements of the buying situation as they are a function of the interplay between organizational structure and values and individual values and competencies. It was found, for example, in the study of industrial purchasing behavior that the basic elements of the purchasing agent's or buyer's task could be characterized as follows:

1. Assuring long-range sources of supply and a continuing selection of qualified suppliers.
2. Generating alternative solutions to procurement problems.
3. Maintaining good relationships with suppliers.
4. Reconciling the internal requirements and personalities with the external environment.
5. Minimizing costs of purchases.
6. Assuming responsibility for the mechanics of the procurement process.[7]

The study also indicated that industrial buying is generally a highly personal and informal process, although the accompanying paper flow is often highly formal and rigid.

Phase 1: Awareness

The initial phase of the buying system of action is popularly known as the "need-arousal" stage, and there is no substantial reason to avoid this term if it is used in its broadest possible sense. The awareness phase constitutes a motivational orientation on the part of the buyer to search for and convert environmental data into information. The conceptual competence of the individual will determine his capacity to apply "meanings" to the full variety of data actually available.

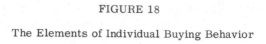

FIGURE 18

The Elements of Individual Buying Behavior

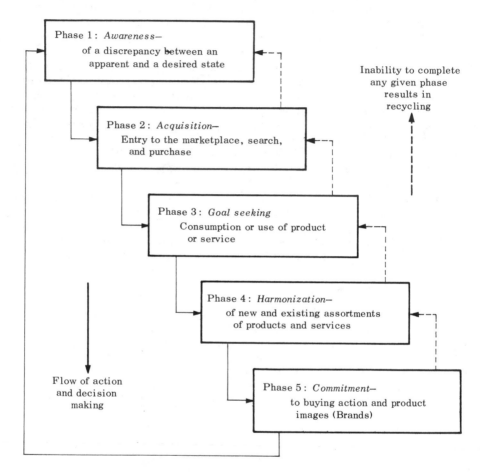

   The actual decision making process of the buyer in this phase
involves the following elements:

1. Understanding or "disambiguation" of the meanings attached
   to incoming data with reference to the buyer's goal requirement.
2. Allocation of available resources to alternative courses
   of action.
3. Decision to institute a search for suppliers and products
   in the marketplace.

While the occurrence of some outside event may be a necessary condition of the personality's communicative exchange with the environment, the conditions essential for both action and communication are ultimately determined by the personality system. That is, an advertisement or some other form of promotion may be a necessary condition for the individual's knowing about a given product; but unless he takes account of the message of the advertisement, no communication occurs and no action will follow. The principle involved here goes deeper than that suggested by the concept of "selective perception" and will be further explored in Chapter X.

It is important to note here *that the buyer's awareness is not limited to what is going on at any one moment, nor is it limited to objects and events in the immediate environment.* Not only does the buyer take into account his past experiences and commitments, consciously or nonconsciously, but he also takes into account the perceived abilities and constraints imposed upon him by virtue of his own socialized point of view. Consquently, the more complex a buyer's reference framework, the more difficult it is to determine exactly what it is he takes into account when he decides to select a given course of action.

All behavior involves conscious or unconscious selection of particular actions out of all those which are physically possible to the actor and to those persons over whom he exercises influence and authority. The term "selection" is used here without any implication of a conscious or deliberate process. It refers simply to the fact that, if the individual follows one particular course of action, there are other courses of action that he thereby forgoes. [8]

The problem facing the marketer here is aggravated by the fact that the buyer himself is unable to verbalize all his reasons for any given "selection" of a course of action. As will be seen later, it is possible to circumvent this problem, in the case of some products at least, by accepting the assumption that the utility which a buyer attributes to a specific product is "the same as" or "similar to" the utility attributed to the product by any or most other members of that culture. This theory of the representative nature of a small sample of depth interviews is used by motivational researchers, and it undoubtedly has some validity.

It should be noted here that awareness does not necessarily imply ability to recall or verbalize. Nonconscious awareness undoubtedly accounts for a large part of human behavior, a factor which has long plagued market researchers. On the other hand, the mere existence of awareness is a minimum and not a sufficient condition for action. While it is the nature of a living system to act, the direction this action will take is dependent upon the system's values and standards; and these ultimately determine the utility of any given line of action.

Phase 2: Acquisition

The second category of action components attributable to an individual in the context of a system of action refers to a set of instrumental exchanges with the environment for the purpose of facilitating goal attainment. As an open system, the personality engages in search for, or serendipitously acquires, certain informational or energy inputs in exchange for informational or energy outputs. An individual works, buys, goes to school, reads the newspaper, and performs a multitude of other activities which to him are logically related within the context of his values and standards. As a participant in an economic organization, for example, the individual performs a certain set of activities in return for certain rewards, the meaning or utility of which is some function of the individual's conceptual competence. The more keenly developed an individual's system of concepts or knowledge of the surrounding environment, the more fully he will be able to relate himself to any given social or physical object.

The buyer's ability to "sell himself" on a given course of action will determine his readiness to buy once he enters the marketplace. An individual may thus find himself in the marketplace either accidentally (he is not ready to buy and does not know what he wants), or purposely (he is ready to buy and knows what he wants). In addition, he may enter the market in search of alternatives (he is not ready to buy, but knows what he wants), or in search of specific information (he is ready to buy, but does not know what he wants).

The important point here is that *the prospective buyer is continually trying to sell himself during this phase,* particularly if he has a highly developed concern for the conceptual and expressive meanings of physical objects. This process of self-persuasion is the key reference point to the promotional task. *The process of selling is not centered* in the salesman or the ad, but in the buyer; and this interpretation, as will be shown in Chapter XI, is the key to the role of personal selling in the marketing mix.

Phase 3: Goal Seeking

The third phase of the buying system of action is initiated when the buyer has purchased an object and begins to use it. The important aspects of the product at this stage are its ability to fulfill the expectations attributed to it in the purchasing phase as well as the original intentions the buyer had in mind when he committed himself to the search for the product. Products have occasionally been bought and not consumed, a phenomenon which has led to a distinction between customer behavior and consumer behavior. The decision to consume is a "real" one made consciously or nonconsciously on the basis of the buyer's expected value of the product and his ability to conceptualize and derive that value. The degree of utility, so to speak, which an individual is capable of deriving from a product is thus some function of the meaning he attributes to the product with reference to his own goals and values. It is also important to note here *that the potential utility attributed to a product by the producer may be different from the utility the buyer actually derives from the product.* Indeed, the fact that a producer *may or may not* conceive of the potential utility of a given product in the same way as the user greatly complicates any attempts at quantitative measurement of marketing communication effectiveness.

As an organized information and decision system, the individual personality is oriented toward the achievement of a goal or set of goals. These goals are not necessarily very explicit or even conscious, nor are they always completely attained. The main point to be made is that the greater part of an individual's behavior proceeds *toward* a purpose or an end and not *from* a "cause."

Goal-seeking activities basically constitute consumption of information or physical goods; and, as a corollary, goal-seeking activities result in production of physical and psychological energy. The nature of the goal will be determined ultimately by the *values* of the personality, while the utilization of the resulting energy will be determined partly by the *state* of the personality system. The concept of entropy may have an interesting application here. Entropy is a thermodynamic concept and its precise definition involves sophisticated concepts of physics and mathematics. Basically, however, the concept may be described as follows:

In a descriptive sense, entropy is often referred to as a "measure of disorder" and the Second Law of thermodynamics as stating that "systems can only proceed to a state of increased disorder;" as times passes, "entropy can never decrease." [9]

The concept of entropy in thermodynamic theory refers to the energy contained in a completely *closed* system. However, even with reference to the personality system which is an *open* system, the concept has been used to separate informational (energy) inputs utilized to *maintain* the entropy, or "order" of the system (i.e., to produce so-called negative entropy) from energy inputs utilized to *increase* the level of "order" in the system. A psychological system experiencing a high level of entropy (disorder) thus will require a relatively high level of informational or energy input to *maintain* its existing order and an even greater input to *increase* its order. So far, the concept of entropy has been used in information theory only as an indicator of the *amount* of information required by a given system. The usefulness of the concept in the broader context of the personality system itself

has yet to be established. It would seem, however, that the differences between an outgoing and a withdrawn or passive personality can be usefully explored in terms of the energy required by
each of these two "types" of personality systems to maintain
their integrity or "wholeness" as systems.

Phase 4: Harmonization

Central to most individual behavior is a self-concept or image
of self in terms of which the individual conceives and justifies
his goal seeking activities.

Each of us, whether we realize it or not, has a self-image. We see ourselves
in some way — smart, slow, kindly, well-intentioned, lazy, misunderstood,
meticulous, or shrewd; we all can pick adjectives that describe ourselves.
This is the "I" behind the face in the mirror, the "I" that thinks, dreams,
talks, feels, and believes, the "I" that no one knows fully.[10]

The Harmonization category of action components is related
to the individual's efforts to integrate his self image with his
images of his environment. To facilitate this process of integration, the individual possesses certain mechanisms of defense
(internally integrative) and certain mechanisms of adjustment
(externally integrative).[11]   Briefly, defense mechanisms are
thought to enable the personality system to absorb conflicts in
perceived images, while adjustment mechanisms encompass the
individual's withdrawal from or identification with some perceived
external object or image. Beyond the "slack" provided by these
integrative mechanisms, however, the existence of conflict brings
pressure to bear directly on the individual's self-concept. For
example, a manager may be able to rationalize or "explain away,"
in terms of external factors, a certain amount of inefficiency
and ineffectiveness traceable to his department. Beyond a certain
acceptable level, however, these negative results become more
than just a vague threat to his self-concept; and therefore direct
changes in his behavior and perhaps in his self-concept, become
necessary if he is to preserve his integrity as a viable system.[12]
    The buyer's assessment of the product concept and image
with reference to his values and motivational standards largely
represents a theoretical distinction between the actual consumption phase and the integration of the individual personality elements. Once the distinction has been made, however, it is
empirically evident that buyers will actively search for information at this stage to reinforce their experiences with a product.
The relevant aspect of the product here is the compatibility of
its image with the individual's self-concept, often quite apart from
the technical qualities of the product in use. The concept of cognitive dissonance is applicable to this phase:

Dissonance is said to exist between some information and a given action if, considering this information all by itself, it would ordinarily lead a person not to engage in the given action. If this is true, it leads one to the idea that such dissonance must exist after a person has made a decision between two alternatives which are both rather attractive.[13]

The theory of cognitive dissonance states that individuals will engage in communicative interaction with their environment following an important decision. Consequently, it has been inferred from observable behavior that individuals are seeking to justify their decisions, presumably in relation to some concept of social reality. It may also be inferred from the same observable behavior that individuals are attempting to increase the utility or meaning attributed to the object or event to which the decision was related.

In any case, the outcome of this phase of the system of action is crucial for the future behavior of a buyer with reference to the specific product or service in question. If the buyer finds that he can "identify" with a product, he will enter the fifth and last phase of the system. If for some reason, however, the object does not provide the level of self-gratification which the buyer desires, he will either exit from the system at this stage or he will internalize a negative conclusion in the fifth phase of the system, the commitment phase.

The competence dimension gives a clue to the nature of the cognitive dissonance phenomenon. A perfectly good product, in terms of physical and functional attributes, may be either conceptually or socially unacceptable from the individual's point of view. Just which one or more of these standards is applicable in each case is clearly a subject for market research. It is generally not sufficient to ask the buyer, whether before or after the purchase, why he does or does not purchase a given product without carefully specifying the level of standards applied. It will be shown later that if steps are not taken to carefully define research questions in terms of levels of competence standards, the interviewer runs the risk of getting irrelevant and ambiguous answers to his questions.

Phase 5: Commitment

The various concepts, values, and relationships with which an individual interacts will, if they are viewed as beneficial by him, become objects of commitment. Psychological commitment is a complex process the nature of which may range from habit formation to moral commitment or obligation. Similarly, commitments may develop with respect to things, images, people, behaviors, organizations, and such vague concepts as "a way of life."

Commitment constitutes a stabilizing factor in the personality with reference to certain external physical, social and cultural objects. Consequently, commitments are instrumental in the individual's resistance to change. On the other hand, changes in the objects of commitment themselves are undoubtedly instrumental in producing change in individual behavior. This latter point will prove important in later discussions of the personal selling function.

Successful identification with a supplier or product image in general leads to buyer commitment. The result of this phase is thus essentially loyalty to a supplier or product concept. Alternatively, of course, unsuccessful identification may lead to the opposite outcome. The buyer develops an experience or habit which becomes internalized in the sense that it is not consciously recalled whenever a new decision on a similar purchase is required. A number of studies of brand purchases have been made to establish the strength of this loyalty. Generally, loyalty is considered to be measurable in terms of the number of purchases a buyer has made of a specific brand relative to another as well as the sequence of brands purchased over time. From this is calculated the probability that a specific brand will be purchased in the future. One limitation of this type of approach is that it reveals little or nothing about the *process* of brand loyalty development let alone the meaning a buyer will attach to a future brand. The development of product or brand loyalty depends not only on product quality but on the array of meanings which the buyer attributes to the object. Depending on the buyer's level of competence or concern with identification, these meanings may range from the object's conceived ability to satisfy the buyer's biological needs to its acceptability according to his moral standards, and include all the intervening levels of motivational standards.

THE COMPETENCE DIMENSION OF BUYING BEHAVIOR

Each of the categories of action components (phases of behavior) outlined above is applicable to all personality systems. That is, all living systems exhibit a certain level of awareness, a certain level of search behavior, and a certain hierarchy of goals. To account for and to provide an analytical basis for explaining the differences in the levels of awareness acquisition, goal seeking harmonization, and commitment between individuals, a concept of interpersonal competence is proposed. The diagram shown in Figure 19 illustrates the relationship between the phases of action and the levels of competence. The descriptions provided at each of the intersections of action and competence are designed to indicate the significance of each of these levels and should not be taken as exhaustive or even as adequate explanations of the complexity of individual behavior. The purpose here is primarily to indicate the nature of the individual competence-activity analysis.

The preceding analysis of the generalized buyer system is designed to identify the specific phases where the buyer actively seeks information, as well as to examine these elements of the buying process which are possible shoals on which it might become grounded. The actual communication process will be examined in Chapter X, but it is important to keep in mind that the buyer requires a constant stream of information at all stages of the buying process. Furthermore, the process may be stopped at any stage, thus nullifying or even creating a negative effect on all the efforts that went into the process before it was curtailed.

Level 1: Physical Activity

The first and lowest level of competence represents ability to recognize, interpret, and act upon biological needs and drives. Many psychologists recognize only this level of "motivation" and attempt to explain all behavior in these terms. However, as Gordon W. Allport has argued:

At low levels of behavior the familiar formula of drives and their conditioning appears to suffice. But as soon as the personality enters the stage of ego-extension, and develops a self-image with visions of self-perfection, we are, I think, forced to postulate motives of a different order, motives that reflect propriate striving. Within experimental psychology itself there is now plenty of evidence that conduct that is "ego involved" (propriate) differs markedly from behavior that is not. [14]

Even though biological needs and drives may be the first "motives" the individual learns to recognize, his psychological system is capable of developing awareness of and responsiveness to a far greater variety of cues than those emanating from his physiological system.

A buyer performing on the level of activity will, in general, attach a relatively narrow range of meanings to products. His buying behavior is comprised of a series of unconnected acts performed for the purpose of gaining immediate gratification. Since the buyer's points of reference are assumed to be primarily physiological needs and drives, there is reason to believe that the concept of brand loyalty is inapplicable at this level. There is as yet, however, no indication that this type of buying behavior is limited to any one social class or income group, although more research is required to establish the relationship between the levels of competence and socioeconomic data.

Evidently, some industrial purchasing agents are relegated to concerning themselves primarily with purchasing *activities* with little or no planning and decision making power, and so apparently are a significant number of salesmen. These problems

FIGURE 19

COMPACT Model of a Generalized Individual Buying System

Competence levels ———→

→ Direction of limitations

Direction of action	Level 1 Activity	Level 2 Behavior	Level 3 Performance	Level 4 System	Level 5 Values
Awareness	Concern with objects* as facilitators of biological gratification	Concern with objects* as concepts or qualities	Concern with objects* as possessions	Concern with objects* as affiliations	Concern with objects* as commitments
Acquisition	Selection on the basis of physical qualities	Selection on the basis of conceptual qualities	Selection on the basis of functional requirements	Selection on the basis of social requirements	Selection on the basis of moral standards
Goal seeking	Immediate satisfaction	Satisfaction of conceptual wants	Satisfaction of functional phases	Satisfaction of social requirements	Satisfaction of moral requirements
Harmonization	Assessment in terms of physical attributes standards	Assessment in terms of self-concept	Assessment in terms of functional performance standards	Assessment in terms of social standards	Assessment in terms of moral standards
Commitment	Internalization of object categories	Internalization of object concepts	Internalization of object performances	Internalization of social significance of objects	Internalization of moral significance of objects

*Economic products and services.

of organizational behavior will be further discussed in Part Four.

Level 2: Adaptive Behavior

While it is evident that certain activities of all individuals (and perhaps all or most of the activities of some individuals) can be explained in terms of the requirements of their *physiological* systems, it is also evident that certain behaviors of most individuals are related to their *psychological* system quite apart from the functional and social utility of such behaviors. In other words, an individual behaves in a certain fashion "because" of the kind of person he is. Psychologists have delineated numerous personality characteristics which they claim will determine an individual's ability to perform a given task. While there are undoubtedly certain traits peculiar to some groups of personality systems, it is not at all clear that such characteristics are *determinative* with reference to interpersonal or communicative competence. It is proposed here that the individual who is capable of behaving *only* in terms of and with reference to one peculiar set of related personality characteristics is highly incompetent as a communicator. Conversely, *the competent individual is capable of adapting his behavior* (and therefore his personality characteristics) *to the functional, social, and cultural requirements of a wide range of interaction.* For example, the best salesman is presumably he who can behave either aggressively or submissively on the basis of the requirements of any given situation, and not merely be aggressive regardless of the requirements of the situation. In the case of the individual who does operate at the adaptive level of competence, it is highly likely that *external* standards and commitments strongly influence his behavior. That is, the rewards and penalities controlled by some other individual or organization are likely to govern a large part of his behavior.[15]

At the behavior level physical objects take on conceptual significance for the buyer. In other words, physical objects take on communicative importance and besides being viewed as extensions of the body are also viewed as extensions of the mind. At this level, food becomes nutrition, gasoline becomes "tigers," and beer becomes "relaxation," at least for the producer. Much has been made in personal selling literature of describing "how to sell" approaches in terms of the personality characteristics of buyers. Similarly, attempts have been made in marketing research to develop market segmentation criteria based upon what buyers *are* in terms of psychological characteristics, on the assumption, presumably, that such characteristics determine what buyers will do.[16]

Undoubtedly, some correlation can be found between the

behavior of some buyers and the personality characteristics imputed to them by researchers; indeed, the premise here is that the psychological makeup of any given individual will have some influence upon his behavior.

Level 3: Instrumental Performance

The third level of competence refers to the individual's ability to develop a functionally related repertoire of behaviors which together constitute a performance. The individual operating at this level is capable not only of reacting to cues in terms of his personality characteristics, but is also able to substitute and connect creatively a variety of behaviors into a coherent performance. His behavior acquires purpose or function and is not purely responsive. Performances are not necessarily deliberate or conscious forms of behavior decided upon or planned in advance by individuals, yet they may attain the quality of highly regular and systematic sequences of behavior. While the previous two levels of competence are relatively easily induced or attained by means of rules or instruction, the level of performance cannot be induced and attained in this manner. The use of participative training techniques to supplement the natural process of learning by imitation will be taken up in Chapter XIII.

At the level of performance the buyer is relating buying behavior to other behaviors significant for his goal attainment. The objects purchased take on meaning as *possessions* and are functionally related to other possessions of the buyer. It is thus postulated that the buyer operating at this level takes into account a wider scope of influences than buyers operating on the previous two levels. On the other hand, the requirement of a functional relationship among the elements of the buyer's assortment of goods and services imposes certain limitations upon what is acceptable. Since the choice process is more elaborate than at the first two levels, there is reason to believe that brand loyalty is of some importance to the buyer operating at this and higher levels of competence.

Several writers impute a higher degree of "rationality" to the industrial purchasing process than to that of the final buyer. Despite this apparent difference in the "rationality" underlying industrial and consumer purchasing, however, little or no research has been conducted to establish the specific nature of the final buyer's purchasing system and the criteria which he applies to the development and maintenance of a suitable assortment of possessions. Clearly, economic limitations establish the effective constraints on the purchasing activities of final buyers; but within these constraints, it may be hypothesized that the household purchasing agent's competence becomes an important and deciding factor:

The consumer purchasing agent is highly rational within the limits of her information. Rationality is reflected in her ability to learn and to avoid repeating the same mistakes. Studies reflecting consumer learning can apply to learning about a class of products, learning to use products, learning to evaluate the competitive appeals of retailers.[17]

Level 4: System Integration

The system level of competence refers to an individual's repertoire of performances. The meanings attached to objects in the environment at this level are generally intuitive and indicate sensitivity to or empathy with the environment. One of the important signs of a fully integrated personality system is a quality which has been called social effectiveness:

Social effectiveness can be developed. For some people, dealing with feelings is as easy as recognizing and manipulating facts. For others, the world of emotions is mysterious indeed. The improvement of social skills is a many-sided challenge. Neither intellectual learning nor emotional experience alone suffice. Nor is the heightening of social sensitivity the sole sacrosanct cure-all. Experiences are needed that reach the full personality. Increased social effectiveness depends on a "toolkit" of appropriate behaviors, in addition to enhanced understanding of social situations.[18]

It should be noted here that social effectiveness is not necessarily the same as "popularity." Social awareness and effectiveness are the ability of any given actor to determine and influence (establish, maintain, or modify) those conditions of the environment vis-à-vis another individual or group (or those conditions of the individual or group vis-à-vis the environment) *conceived* to be relevant to the accomplishment of the acting individual's objectives.

The system level of competence encompasses the so-called "sociological buyer."[19] The buyer operating on this level takes into account the implications of his purchasing behavior upon the social system of which he is a part. The industrial purchasing agent is a clear case in point; but even the final buyer is presumed to take into account the perceived opinions of reference groups, that is, other individuals significant to his social position, and professional groups, that is, individuals in similar occupations. The important point here is that *the buyer makes his decisions on the basis of his own socialized point of view,* and not that these reference groups, as such, *determine* his behavior. The buyer's problem is one of developing what is to him a socially meaningful system of possessions. In other words, he wants to "communicate" something about himself through his behavior and possessions; and therefore he must take into account the various social meanings of economic products.

The industrial purchasing agent's problems at this level are only superficially different from those of the final buyer. Empirical evidence derived from the study of industrial purchasing behavior indicated the importance of the information-seeking aspects of the buyer's job. The buyer may be thought of as the focal point of an information network receiving information from a variety of internal and external sources, interpreting and perhaps modifying that information, and transmitting it to key people both inside and outside the company.[20]

Level 5: Value Integration

The fifth and last level of competence refers to the value commitments of an individual. The relevant ability is one of relating behavior to some set of moral values. Values in this sense are different from behavioral and cultural standards applicable to all levels of behavior since *standards constitute the internalized behavior rules of individuals governing efficiency of interactive behavior, while moral values pertain to notions of right or wrong regardless of efficiency.* Moral values may nevertheless be considered within the same framework as other behavior standards, since, functionally speaking, they have similar effects of acting as limitations upon the number and variety of actions an individual will perform. Allport discusses the process of development of moral values or conscience in the personality as follows:

> The theory I am here suggesting holds that the must-consciousness precedes the ought-consciousness, but that in the course of transformation three important changes occur. (1) External sanctions give way to, internal — a change adequately accounted for by the processes of identification and introjection familiar in Freudian and behavioral theory. (2) Experiences of prohibition, fear, and "must" give way to experiences of preference, self-respect, and "ought." This shift becomes possible in proportion as the self-image and value systems of the individual develop. (3) Specific habits of obedience give way to generic self-guidance, that is to say, to broad schemata of values that confer direction upon conduct. [21]

It should be noted that moral values are not necessarily religious. The moral personality possesses an ability to behave with reference to, and an ability to resolve behavior conflicts in terms of, a set of values relevant to the individual's concept of an "ideal self-image."

Each of the preceding levels of competence contains its own peculiar standards on the basis of which the buyer attributes utility to a given product or service. A topic which has received only scant attention in the marketing literature is the influence of the buyer's moral values upon purchasing behavior. The increasing legislative attention to the marketing process clearly indicates some public concern with this area. Most marketers know that an "anything goes" attitude may be dangerous even within legal limits, but very little is known about the influence of dubious claims and sharp practices on either the deliquent's image or the image of the marketing process as a whole. The large mail-order houses have apparently decided that "overselling" can be dangerous for sales in the long run, but what about personal selling? Is the salesman who introduces himself as a market researcher engaging in personal *selling* or personal *intimidation*? Perhaps this question can be settled legislatively only, but for the purposes here the assumption will be made that the role of personal selling is to establish communicative relationships with potential and actual customers within the general confines of accepted moral values.

SOME IMPLICATION OF THE BUYING SYSTEM ANALYSIS

The basic complexity of the individual personality should be apparent from the above outline. Moreover, individuals vary on a multitude of points; and an individual may be primarily socially conscious, primarily morally conscious, or primarily conscious of the self. Obviously, the model, at least in its present state, is capable of providing only a crude basis for differentiation of individual behavior. Even so, it represents progress since in much marketing literature, and particularly that of personal selling, there is a tendency to gloss over the basic complexity of the human personality with reference to both buyers and sellers. The fact of the matter is that an individual's buying or selling behaviors are elements of a much more complex whole; and while individuals apparently adhere to certain rules common to most, they are not definable as "bundles of needs"[22] bent on immediate satisfaction. The human being is a highly complex and dynamic system, engaging in various types of activities for the purpose of achieving a goal or a set of goals.

The COMPACT matrix (shown in Figure 19) represents a "mapping" of a generalized buying situation from an observer's point of view. In other words, the matrix constitutes an attempt to operationalize the notion of "discovering and satisfying customers' needs" which is so commonly used in market literature. In and of itself, the matrix does not provide a full-fledged guideline for product development and promotion. It does provide, however, a basis for further research into the relationship between product concepts and utility, and buyer values. Each level of competence implies a differentiated set of variables, influences, and standards entering into a buyer's decision making. Consequently, the matrix may be used either as a means of differentiating among buyers with reference to the level of competence most prevalent in their behavior, or it may be used as a means of separating, for analytical purposes, the various influences and standards underlying the behavior of any given buyer. Each of the smaller squares of the matrix (Figure 19) constitutes a specific motivational orientation at a roughly defined level of complexity and competence of a given buyer or group of buyers. The promotional task from a marketing point of view is that of relating a given product to one or more such motivational orientations at one or more levels of buyer competence.

The purpose of a structural analysis of the buying system is thus to provide a classification of the significant motivational orientations of individual buyers. The COMPACT matrix offers, on the one hand, a classification of the major aspects of the buying act; and on the other, it provides a rough classification of the significant categories of meanings an individual attaches to his situation.[23]

The matrix taken as a whole represents a black box: "buyer." A message beamed at this box will clearly be understood by only that part of the audience which is oriented toward that message. More research is required to develop the full and specific implications of the COMPACT model; but the major communicative implications are established and discussed in the following chapter, while some of the implications for marketing and personal selling are discussed in Part Four.

SUMMARY

The purpose of the present chapter has been to develop the COMPACT model further to include the dimension of individual buyer behavior. The individual considered as an information and decision system exists within a complex environment composed partly of his own physiological environment and partly of physical, social, and cultural objects around him. It is postulated that a significant property of the individual personality system is its competence, conceptual and interpersonal, in dealing with these various environmental elements.

The COMPACT model was applied to the individual buying system, partly to outline the significant relationships among the various environmental influences, and partly to develop some structural reference points for the following discussion of communicative relationships.

One of the conclusions which can be drawn from the generalized framework of buyer behavior presented in the preceding chapter is that buyers are continually engaged in problem solving or "disambiguation" of their situation; in other words, buyers tend to sell themselves upon a given course of action. In doing so, the individual relies on a number of motivational standards and behavior rules which have been internalized as a result of past experience in dealing with the environment. The general nature of these standards was stated in terms of the following five categories:

Level 1: Activity standards related to the level of "doing," or concern with extensions of the organism.

Level 2: Adaptive behavior standards related to the level of behavioral interaction, or concern with extensions of the mind.

Level 3: Performance standards related to the level of functional requirements or concern with functional integration of self and situation.

Level 4. Social standards related to the level of social function and status, or concern with integration of the self in a social system.

Level 5: Moral standards related to the level of values, or concern with right and wrong.

The concept of individual competence is a significant third dimension to the generally accepted hierarchical model of organizational structural relationships. Since the essential tie between an organization and any one individual member is communicative, there is no doubt that conceptual and interpersonal competence is at least partly determinative of organizational effectiveness. Moreover, unlike personality characteristics, an individual's competence can be altered by means of certain training methods, thus enabling the individual to increase his performance effectiveness:

Training influences decisions "from the inside out." That is, training prepares the organization member to reach satisfactory decisions himself, without the need for the constant exercise of authority or advice. In this sense, training procedures are alternatives to the exercise of authority or advice as means of control over the subordinate's decisions.[24]

X

Communication
in a Marketing Context

THE SEVERAL LEVELS of individual competence discussed in the previous chapter imply a set of *models* in terms of which an individual *receives, processes. and transmits* information.[1] It was proposed that an individual, considered as an information and decision system will "organize" the communication events occurring around him on the basis of one or more of the following categories of models:

1. The physiological capacities and incapacities of his biological system.
2. The psychological abilities and inabilities of his personality system.
3. The perceived functional relationship between himself and his environment.
4. The social or interpersonal relationships and affiliations (the "significant others") perceived as reference groups in terms of which an individual decides to behave or not behave in a certain fashion.
5. The perceived cultural definition of the environment.

It is postulated that an individual perceives, interprets (takes account of), and accumulates information and knowledge in terms of the above categories of models; and consequently, communication is not limited as to time and space. Therefore, that which gets communicated in any given situation is not solely a result of the events occuring in that situation; nor are the cues perceived in a specific situation by any given individual necessarily causally related to his subsequent behavior. The necessary condition for the occurrence of communication is the individual's possession of one or more of the above categories of "models" or orientations while his competence represents his ability to organize and relate to his environment.

Communication, in this connection, can be defined as *an operation involving the organization of raw sensory data into information for eventual use in behavior or for psychological consumption.*[2] It should be stressed that communication as defined here is not a "sharing of ideas" and that it may occur entirely independent of the sender's or communicator's "will" and "intention."

THE TOOLS OF COMMUNICATION

The notions of cause-effect and stimulus-response which are popularly used to explain interpersonal influence seemingly derive from the physical and observable manifestations of communication. It appears that there are three principal ways in which human beings communicate with each other:[3]

1. By actual physical touch—individuals attempt to make themselves understood with, for example, a tap on the shoulder, a pat on the back, and the ritualistic extension of the handshake.
2. By visible movements—a great deal of communication occurs by means of a finger pointing, a wink of the eye, a nod of the head, a shrug of the shoulders, a smile, a grimace, or a scowl.
3. By symbols—audible and visible symbols constitute important tools of communication. Individuals attempt to transfer information by means of, for example, spoken symbols (noisemaking), written symbols (marks on a page), and pictures (color patterns).

Clearly the transmission of some sort of signal or sign, audible, visual, or tactile, is a necessary condition for interpersonal communication, but it is by no means a sufficient condition.

The suggestion that words are symbols for things, actions, qualities, re-lationships, et cetera, is naive, a gross simplification. Words are slippery customers. The full meaning of a word does not appear until it is placed in its context, and the context may serve an extremely subtle function — as with puns, or *double entendre.* And even then the meaning will depend upon the listener, upon the speaker, upon their entire experience of the language, upon their knowledge of one another, and upon the whole situation. Words do not "mean things" in a one-to-one relation like a code. Words, too, are empirical signs, not copies or models of anything.[4]

To be sure, communication does depend on the existence of commonly recognized sound patterns (language) and light patterns (movement and pictures). But, as Oscar Wilde once observed, people can easily be separated by their common language, merely because they do not attribute similar meanings to words and signs.

Sounds, movement, touch, and marks on a page are the basic tools of communication, at least for the purposes here. Linking together sounds in a certain way produces a set of sounds which is labeled "word." It is useful here to differentiate between spoken words (phonetics) and written words, primarily because the former is normally accompanied by visual and occasionally tactile cues while the written word generally stands alone. Words linked together in a certain fashion make up a pattern usually labeled a sentence.

Each of these basic tools or combinations of them will be referred to in the following as *events* which an individual must create or interpret in the course of interacting with other individuals.

A *communication* event, then, is the attachment of meaning to sounds or sequences of sounds and acts or sequences of acts. The originator of a message must choose from his store of sounds and then act to elicit his *intended* meaning in a given receiver. The translation of meaning into transmittable signals is nearly always subject to a certain degree of uncertainty and so is the reverse process of influence or interpretation with respect to a receiver. The reason that this extremely complex process works at all is that each individual possesses a store of habits and past experiences which enable him to draw inferences from the cues in his environments.

THE NATURE OF DATA

Data essentially comprise the physical or observable evidence gathered from events and behavior. For example, a buyer selecting a jar of coffee in a supermarket engages in a sequence of acts. While the buyer, by behaving in a certain fashion, makes available a set of data to an observer, the observer's report will not contain data emanating from the buyer, *but rather it will contain data emanating from the observer.* [5] Data in this sense are *perfect* indicators of the nature and content of the events of the behavior occurring, but the imperfections in the observer's ability to detect and attribute meaning to all the data limit his understanding of that behavior. And though only the buyer possesses the full set of data regarding his purchasing behavior, even he is incapable of explaining it fully. As stated earlier, purchasing behavior is not solely a function of the data transfer occurring at the point of purchase. It is impossible, both physically and conceptually, for the individual to plan consciously (or "mentalize" about) all his activities, and as a consequence he acts upon internalized or nonconscious guidelines which are an integral part of his systems.

Observation of behavior is a communicative operation centering on the observer whose level of competence, while enabling him to draw certain conclusions, also *limits* his ability to discriminate among data. The psychological and conceptual limitations upon man's communicative abilities are quite severe. A human being can process data conceptually at a rate somewhere between 1/10,000th and 1/100,000th the rate at which he can handle it as sensory data.[6]

THE NATURE OF INFORMATION

Information is data which are "consumable" or to which an individual can ascribe meaning and significance. It is evident that a one-to-one relationship seldom if ever exists between the *data* in the "real world" and *information* in the individual or organizational systems. Data consumption is heavily influenced by the individual's predilections to act in a certain manner. Such predilections arise partly from what the individual "knows" to be the case from generally accumulated past experiences and partly from the manner in which the given situation has been defined by the participants or some common organizational framework. The manager or supervisor who is subjected to a course in "Human Relations" and has acquired some rules about "how to communicate" is likely to run into severe difficulties when he attempts to implement his new framework because of his peers' and subordinates' past experiences and present predilections to act toward him in a certain manner. Even though the manager or supervisor is emitting a different set of data as a result of his new "knowledge" (on the assumption that the course was successful in changing his behavior), these data do not necessarily become information to the individuals around him.[7] In other words, "better communication" is some function of all the individual participants and the nature of their relationship in any given situation, and cannot be defined apart from these factors.

It should not be inferred that people's expectations and predilections never change, since they evidently do; but the physiological and psychological thresholds or barriers against data in combination with the difficulty of behaving in a new situation or in a differently defined situation make such changes both slow and often imperceptible to an observer.

THE NATURE OF DECISION MAKING

The process of decision making has been subjected to increasingly rigorous examination in recent years, the main impetus being the growing interest in the application of mathematical tools to problem solving. The following points approximate a typical description of the decision making process:

1. There are two or more alternative courses of action possible (which may be symbolized by A_1, A_2, . . . etc.). Only one of these lines of action can be taken . . . .
2. The process of decision will select, from these alternative actions, a single course of action which will actually be carried out . . . .
3. The selection of a course of action is to be made so as to accomplish some designated purpose. [8]

In many respects, decision making is not as straightforward and conscious as the above description might indicate. Not only does action presuppose a sequence of many decisions, but the actual outcome of any given decision making process is co-determined by the purposes or objectives of the individual or the organization *and* the situation in which the choice occurs. Even without directly attacking the philosophical issue of rationality versus irrationality, it is thus evident that the physiological and psychological constraints upon the individual information and decision system effectively limit, for example, a manager's or a buyer's ability to take into account those aspects of any given situation which he does not have as information.

The fact that an individual's or an organization's behavior is a continuous "things-always-lead-to-other-things" process should thus not be taken to imply that the intervening decision sequences are necessarily fully volitional and conscious. This latter point does not detract from the "rationality" of an individual's decision in a philosophical sense insofar as that is, at least partly, dependent upon an *observer's* ability to infer or discover the reasons behind the individual's decisions. [9]

COMMUNICATION SYSTEMS

Two basic communication systems are of interest in the context of this study: the individual and the organization. In general, the term communication system describes a functional system of action. The COMPACT model may thus be construed as a conceptual "map" of the communication system which serves any living system (individual or organization) and which constitutes the system's means for establishing and maintaining communicative metabolism with its environment. Similar to the physiological energy-processing system, the basic functions of an individual's or an organization's communication system are:

1. To establish, confirm, exploit or change the *internal structure* of the living system with reference to some aspect of its interdependent or symbiotic relationship with its environment (learning and market research).
2. To establish, confirm, exploit or change some aspect of the living system's interdependent or symbiotic *relationship*

with its environment by affecting some aspect of the environment (teaching and selling).[10]

From the point of view of any one individual or organization, only the second of the above functions is generally thought of as communication. The communicative implications of marketing research, for example, are often not fully realized. The "objectivity" methodology of researchers are related to their ability to verbalize their models and assumptions and are not always an indication of the "truth" of their statements with regard to the "real" world. This is not to say that researchers are necessarily deceiving themselves; on the contrary many of them are only too well aware of the limitations of their models. It is rather to say that the *basic* nature of research, whatever its aims, is that of a communication system subserving a given individual or organization.

The communication system is an integral part of the living system which it subserves and it encompasses the individuals or the organization's activities devoted to the dissemination and acquisition of information. It is important to keep in mind that these activities are not necessarily conscious, controlled, planned, or intended, nor do the dissemination activities of one system necessarily match the acquisition activities of any other system. In the case of both individuals and organizations, however, the principal criterion of effectiveness of their respective communication systems is the flexibility and viability of the relationship each of the communication systems maintains with its data environment.

COMMUNICATIVE ENCOUNTERS

The interaction of two or more communication systems may give rise to a number of different patterns of behavior two of which are outlined in Figure 20. The diagram labeled (a) represents essentially one-way communication, while the diagram labeled (b) represents the case of two-way communication. In the latter pattern individual systems alternately occupy the roles of sender and receiver, thus creating a form of feedback loop. This loop does not, however, constitute a closed loop in the sense that the communication occurring is solely a function of the events occurring at the time and place of the encounter.

The underlying basis for communicative interaction between two or more living systems (individual or organization) is the process of socialization discussed in the previous chapter. This process gives rise to a mutuality or complementarity (and thus facilitates the synchronization) of both conceptual competence and communicative subfunctions (dissemination and acquisition

FIGURE 20

Diagrams of Two Communication Patterns

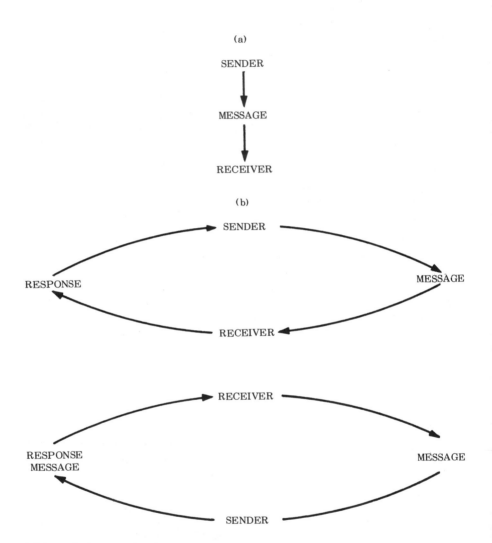

*Adapted from: The Kaiser Aluminum and Chemical Corporation. "Communications," *Kaiser Aluminum News*, Vol. 23. (1965), p. 25

of information). That is, the socialized point of view of an individual implies *a set of predilections or inclinations to agree with, to understand, to accept or to believe the information disseminated.* Such mutual or complementary inclinations constitute *metacommunicative facilitation.* The impetus or motivation to engage in the encounter, on the other hand, is *some function of the possible gains to be achieved from the encounter as perceived by each individual participant.* That is, to the extent that the informational or behavioral consequences of a message or encounter are mutual or complementary (e.g., when the implied consequences do not favor one participant at the expense of the other, or when the "costs" anticipated by each do not exceed the anticipated "pay-off"), or to the extent that there is a matching of output and input activities (e.g., the dissemination subfunction of one participant matches the acquisition subfunction of the other participant), there is *communicative facilitation.*

The metacommunicative and the communicative abilities of individuals constitute the bases for what might be termed *intercommunication* as well as for *mass communication. Intercommunication* refers to the evolutionary encounter of two living systems (superior-subordinate, salesman-buyer, or husband-wife) oriented toward one or more of the following goals: (1) the development of mutual and self serving control (authority, sanctions), (2) the development of a dynamic and viable *relationship,* (3) the achievement of the anticipated *consequences* of the relationship. *Mass communication* is aggregated communication and intercommunication modified by the characteristics of the medium involved. In other words, *inter*communication roughly pertains to personal relationships while mass communication pertains to a relationship between living systems via the social, physical and technological environment. If the socialization process were perfect, idiosyncratic concerns and abilities would presumably be limited to relatively peripheral and inconsequential matters. As it is, all living systems are characterized by idiosyncratic concerns and abilities which vary outside generally predictable limits. These indirectly serve to preclude both complete redundancy in any communicative encounter *and* prediction of the total range of consequences or outcomes beyond some vague generalities which may hold *en masse* in some particular culture.

THE DATA DISSEMINATION-ACQUISITION INTERFACE

It was indicated earlier that awareness in the communication sense goes deeper than the concept of selective perception and its corollary, selective communication. It is evident that people do not take into account all available data, but that does not explain why people *do* take into account *some* of the available data. The answer to this problem must be found in the conceptual models in terms of which individuals perceive the world. Given that an individual has a basic inclination to engage in certain activities (in his capacity as a living system), and given that he is limited by his physiological and psychological capacities (competence) to take account of internal and external cues, he must necessarily "choose" from among a vast number of cues and courses of action. Moreover, in making such choices the individual is barred, again by limitations on his capacities, from taking into account more than the most "obvious" alternatives. The process of selection involved is based not only on the past experiences of the individual (i.e., the things he knows), but is also frequently based on such secondary criteria or rules as time (visit customer X once a month), place (it is always done that way here), and object (never flirt with the customer's secretary). Some rules have developed to the point where they have become institutionalized and thus represent a broad basis for predicting certain ranges of behavior. For example, certain things are done at Christmas which are not done at any other time of the year, the behavior expected in a church is different from that expected in a tavern, and the behavior expected of a teacher is different from that expected of a student. The rules may, of course, "interact" to modify each other and certain behaviors may be expected of the student in relation to the teacher at a given time and in specific places.

The rules pertaining to time, place, and object constitute metacommunicative facilitators or barriers depending upon the specific rules involved. *Communicative* facilitators and barriers on the other hand are essentially transactional.[11] In other words, even though metacommunicative facilitation may exist between a sales manager and his salesmen in that a set of mutual role expectations exists, the institution, for example, of a new bonus scheme providing salesmen with an incentive for "trying harder" may have little or no effect as a result of a lack of communicative facilitation. If the salesman "knows" that trying harder is likely to result in his becoming a decided nuisance for his customers, his expected cost of the bonus scheme may well exceed his expected pay-off.

Ability to perceive the existence of metcommunicative and communicative facilitators and barriers is an important element of a communicative awareness. The occurrence of overselling, for example, provides an interesting instance of inability on the part of a salesman to take into account a buyer's *positive* attitude toward the product or service in question. Since the salesman expects the buyer to resist (metacommunicative barrier) he may perceive a difference between actual and expected behavior (since the buyer exhibits a positive attitude). Consequently, if the salesman proceeds to elaborate on the utilities of his product (attempts to create communicative facilitation), the buyer may perceive the salesman's apparent disagreement with his (the buyer's) point of view (metacommunicative barrier) as a sufficient reason for reconsidering his original (positive) attitude.

From the communicator's point of view, then, awareness must pertain to both metacommunicative facilitation (is the buyer inclined to agree and believe or disagree and disbelieve?) and communicative facilitation (what is the buyer's utility for the given product or any specific message?). These two elements of intentional communication will be further discussed in Chapter XII with reference to the salesman's competence as a communicator.

It is clearly the responsibility of the initiator of a communicative relationship to establish not only the state of the intended receiver's prior predilections, but also the degree to which the receiving system is committed to its present store of knowledge. It will be recalled from previous chapters that the competence dimension as applied to the buyer referred to his ability to conceptualize and deal with his environment. The individual's "profile" in terms of the COMPACT matrix roughly indicates the extent and classification of his prior experiences as well as the extent of his commitments to these experiences. Thus, the more extensive a buying system's commitments, the more difficulty one would expect in trying to influence it. For example, if the president of an industrial concern has given instructions to use a certain supplier, a few small mistakes on the part of that supplier are not likely to bring about a change. Also, considerable effort will be required on the part of competitive suppliers to effect such a change.

There are other, more general metacommunicative facilitators available to the marketer which can serve as enablers in creating, modifying, exploiting, or maintaining the relationship between buyers and sellers. The functional, social, and cultural implications of certain media, for example, are well-known to some marketers.

The medium is often said to be instrumental in "delivering" or "selecting" the audience. But it is more likely, I think, that "audience selection" is the result of the interaction between media characteristics and audience predispositions and that in the final analysis the audience selects the media rather than vice versa. Available research evidence would seem to support two closely related generalizations about media:

1. The process of audience selection of media is not random. Any particular medium will have more appeal for some groups than for others.
2. Within the larger group which is attracted to a particular medium some subgroups will be more attracted than others. [12]

Ultimately, the effectiveness and efficiency of marketing communication is some function of the inherent commonalities or complementarities in any communication encounter and not of the "will," "intention," and "expertise" of the sender. Even a bad advertisement may communicate to readers who are inclined to agree with the advertiser and who are looking for data of the type included in the ad. Similarly, a good advertisement may fail to communicate in the face of either metacommunicative or communicative barriers or both. Yet the criteria for the "perfect" or the "effective" sales presentation or the "eloquent" speech remain as vestiges of the myth that the *how* of communication is more or even as important as the *what.* Consequently, there is an unmistakable tendency for ads to look like ads and for sales presentations to sound like sales presentations regardless of the receivers' requirements. It is seldom the prepared speech which enables the suitor to win the coveted lady, and often it is the spontaneous and perhaps incoherent declaration which carries the day, not as a result of what it *is,* but as a result of what it *does.*

COMMUNICATIVE INTENSITY

In the previous sections of this chapter an attempt has been made to outline some concepts of the facilitators and barriers to communication inherent in communication systems and communicative relationships. It has been postulated that communication systems (individual and organizational) possess certain "natural" inclinations or predilections to exchange information, and that these inclinations broadly determine the consequences of communicative interaction ranging from the more or less inevitable (positive metacommunicative and communicative facilitation) to the impossible (negative facilitation). Within this range of consequences, however, it is apparent that the quality and dynamics of the communicative relationship, in terms of intensity of participation, at least partly determines the outcome of any specific interaction. Thus, a typology of communicative relationships involves at least the following three categories:

1. Persuasive or influence relationships.
2. Educational or training relationships.
3. Change agent—client system relationships.

These categories of communicative relationships are hierarchically related in terms of the degree of participation required by the communication systems involved.

The necessary conditions for influence, learning, and change are the processes of *data* dissemination and acquisition. The process of converting data into information (communication), however, can frequently not be accomplished merely by making data available to an individual. If the sender is interested in retaining at least some control as to the information which gets communicated in an interaction, a more intensive process of relating the intended meaning to the receiver's communication system is often required.

In recent years, the term information has gained unprecedented popularity. Organizations are subjected to minute scrutiny to discover the existing information flows and to devise information systems which purportedly will provide members of the organization with the optimum amount of information. It is never quite clear what is intended by the expression "optimum amount of information;" and, as Patrick J. Robinson has repeatedly pointed out:

The answer is often found, not in more information but in a different approach. Perspective and problem-solving go hand in hand; and the person *with* the problem is in this sense a part of the problem.[13]

The point is that the implementation of a "better" information system does not in and of itself improve the performance of individual members of the organization. Information systems are usually understood to constitute data distribution networks; as such they provide information only insofar as the individual user is capable of taking into account and acting upon the data. Similarly, the communicative impact of much advertising and personal selling is entirely dependent upon the degree to which it matches the data acquisition and consumption abilities and procedures of the buying public. In such situations, the marketer has little influence over the actual interpretation which the buying public attributes to the data although sensitivity to cultural and social commonalities enables him to predict broadly the utility of a given message. This means that the effectiveness of much advertising is almost entirely a function of the existing meta-communicative and communicative complementarities between marketing and buying systems. As already indicated, the idiosyncratic differences among individual buyers preclude complete ineffectiveness *as well as* perfect effectiveness of any specific advertisement or campaign.

Persuasive or Influence Relationships

Persuasion differs from simple data dissemination in the sense that it involves a conscious or nonconscious effort on the part of the persuader to *influence* the behavior of the receiver in a given direction. The process is often thought of as one of "making people do what they do not really want to do." That is, however, an oversimplification of the notion of persuasion. *Unless the communicator employs coercive force, he has no way of "making" an individual act contrary to the proclivities of that individual.*

The requirement for persuasion arises when a communicator perceives an incentive for changing an individual's behavior in a specific direction. While it is undoubtedly fair to assume that people are favorably disposed toward buying[14] and can be expected to engage in a certain amount of self-persuasion, more complex or subtle product or service differences may not present themselves as *clear-cut* reasons for the purchase of one product or one brand over another. It is thus possible to speak of persuasive advertising insofar as it helps the buyer in the process of self-persuasion.[15] In general, however, it is primarily the more specific aid offered by personal relationships (salesmen, neighbors, and friends) which falls into the category of persuasive relationships.

The strategy of the persuader must be to increase the importance of his intentions *in terms of the receiver's present concepts.* Consequently, persuasive communication requires a greater degree of competence on the part of the communicator than mere data dissemination since he must be capable of gauging the receiver's concept structure, or, in other words, what is and what is not important to the receiver. Persuasion thus involves a more receiver-oriented process of information giving than that pertaining to data dissemination.

Educational or Training Relationships

Training has variously been referred to as the process of acquiring a set of skills, a process of accumulating knowledge, and as a process of acquiring certain conceptual abilities. Yet, apparently little is known about the nature of the process involved. A number of participative training methods have been developed including case analysis, role playing, sensitivity training or so-called T-group interaction, and operational gaming. It is important to note that while the method used may vary, *participation* is an important feature of education or training. While persuasion implies only a minimal level of participation on the part of the receiver, educational or training relationships presuppose a trainee-helper relationship in which the receiver meets the communicator at least halfway.

The requirement for participative training or learning arises from the nature of the human communication system. It was suggested in an earlier chapter that the competence, interpersonal and conceptual competence, of an individual is to a large extent nonconscious. Therefore, modification or alteration of individual concepts and abilities cannot easily, if at all, be achieved by means of a little "talk" or even by means of "reasoning" or persuasion. Training is thus not a matter of *telling* trainees how they *should* behave:

We have to stop telling supervisors how they should behave and what their attitudes should be . . . . Let us remember that our new objective is to assist people in learning from their own experience. We are no longer trying to change them; we are giving them the opportunity to change themselves, if they wish, by reflecting upon and re-evaluating their own experience . . . . We are not interpreting their own experience *for them;* we are not telling them *our* personal experience. Instead, *we are allowing them to examine and re-evaluate their own experience.*[16]

The case discussion, role playing, sensitivity training, and gaming methods are all potentially capable of achieving a high degree of trainee participation, or empathy, and all rely to a greater or lesser extent upon interaction of individuals in groups. [17] With reference to the personal selling function, participative training finds its most obvious application in the development of salesmanship, but systems selling and management consulting are also areas where such techniques may be utilized in the salesman-buyer relationship. In any case, a successful training process involves a process of conceptual change (development of superior orientations) as well as integration for the individual, a process which is often both psychologically painful and exhilarating. Most important of all, both the process and its content must be related to the problems and goals perceived by the trainees.

The Change Agent-Client System Relationship

Communication in the context of a dynamic relationship between buyer and seller involves the communicator's taking into account the total buying system. The concept of a change agent-client relationship is derived from the behavioral sciences where it is defined as follows:

[A change relationship is] a conscious, deliberate, and collaborative effort to improve the operations of a system, whether it be a self-system, social system, or cultural system, through the utilization of scientific knowledge. [18]

In a continually changing world, an individual or an organization occasionally becomes involved in a situation where it is difficult to understand the conflicting cues arising from the internal state of the system being at odds with its environment. In one case, the organization or the individual may become aware of a difficulty itself; and so a change agent, be it a management consultant in the case of the organization or a psychiatrist in the case of an individual, is invited into the system for the purpose of resolving the apparent problem.

In other cases, the client system itself may not be aware of change requirements whereas an outsider may be able to detect symptoms of difficulties. Finally, the change agent may be faced with an unusually tough selling problem, as in the case of a capital equipment salesman or possibly a salesman facing a buying committee. The change agent-client system concept as used here is akin to management consulting in its nature and process. The change process is aimed at changing the formal or informal aspects of the individual's or a group of individuals' beliefs and attitudes. That is, the aim is an accelerated process of change in the behavior rules which the individual has acquired through trial and error or through imitation over long periods of time. Normally, an individual or an organization has a vested interest in an existing set of behavior rules, and any serious attempt to change these from the outside often will be viewed as a threat to the system. Resistance to change may, of course, be interpreted in several ways, depending upon the context in which it occurs, but for present purposes, the following description will suffice:

Perhaps the most familiar notion of resistance is that of clinging to existing satisfactions. This includes the situations in which subparts with vested interests know they benefit from the status quo and want to keep it that way, as well as the situation in which the client system as a whole is reluctant to give up familiar types of satisfaction. The familiar satisfactions may be ways of getting reward, ways of avoiding pain or anxiety, *ways of thinking about itself, or even ways of thinking about the external world.* Any one of these may be threatened by the proposed change. We might also include among familiar satisfactions *the modeling of present behavior on past traditions,* for the conviction that things are being done now as they have always been done can be a source of great pleasure and security.[19]

In bringing about substantial change in an individual or an organization, it is utmost importance that a change agent take into account all the related aspects of an individual or an organization when attempting to bring about change of a given set of behavior rules or a given part of an organization.

The theory and research available on change agent–client system relationships or the process of planned change[20] provide a useful background for considering both the organizational relationships within the personal selling organization and the organizational relationships and problems confronting the industrial and trade salesmen. The important point is that the institutional variables of an organization cannot be influenced substantially without involving a major part of the organization. A well-planned and well-executed training program, for example, may be effectively counteracted by an unchanged and unchanging organizational structure. Similarly, the salesman who fails to take account of both the hierarchical and the individual competence dimensions of any specific organizational buying system is likely to achieve only random matching of information with buying decision makers.

The role or function of the change agent or salesman vis-à-vis the buying system is here conceived as one of a helper contributing to the buying system's own efforts in the direction of some goal or set of goals. From this point of view, the elements of the salesman–buying system relationship may be outlined as follows:

Phase 1: Discovery or development of complementary goals, or metacommunicative facilitation between the selling and the buying system.

Phase 2: Establishment of a dynamic and viable helping relationship between the salesman and the buying system.

Phase 3: Attempts at establishing, exploiting, modifying, or maintaining those environmental and organizational conditions conceived to be mutually advantageous to both selling and buying systems.

Phase 4: Harmonization, generalization, and stabilization of the relationship.

Phase 5: Maintenance of a continuing relationship between the selling organization and its salesmen and buying system.

This brief outline of the selling system-buying system relationship is designed to indicate the potential scope of the personal selling function. Whether or not this function is assigned to a single salesman, a sales team, or distributed in a hierarchical organization consisting of sales managers, supervisors and salesmen, the central objective must be to establish cooperative and helping relationships between selling and buying systems.

In the old days selling was a matter of pushing or even of bludgeoning the prospect into buying by the use of fast words and pretentious claims — though even then the best salesmen instinctively mixed in a strong dose of solicitude for the customer. But, as time went on, buyers became more sophisticated, if only because they had to be to survive the increasing barrage that came at them from press and radio. Also, business itself was slowly becoming more professional. Whether in dismay at the lessening effectiveness of high-pressure selling or because of a serious desire to find a more constructive approach, the discovery was made that there was hidden resource in the prospect himself. He *liked* to buy from you provided you gave him a chance to trust and respect you, which could only happen if he didn't feel he was being kept from considering your proposition fairly and rationally.[21]

SUMMARY

The dynamic factor in all human behavior is the phenomenon of communication. The purpose of the present chapter has been to outline the elements of communication that apply at the interface of buying and selling systems. It was postulated that communication essentially constitutes that process or operation which is inferred when a living system (organization or individual) takes something into account. That which the system takes into account is ultimately a product of its own communication system. That is, an external event may be a necessary condition for communication, but the sufficient conditions are ultimately conditions of the receiving system.

The fact that selling and buying systems are parts of, and have developed in, a substantially similar culture and social environment gives rise to certain complementarities in the form of metacommunicative and communicative facilitation of interaction. Beyond these general enablers and barriers, more participative intercommunicative relationships must be developed to accommodate the transfer of information from one system to another.

The general purpose of Chapters V through X has been to formulate a model or conceptual framework representing the elements of the marketing function as defined in Chapter II. The COMPACT model draws attention to the functional elements of buying and selling systems and at the same time constitutes an attempt to integrate relevant concepts from the several behavioral disciplines. A critical element of the COMPACT model is the concept of levels of competence and motivational orientation. The five analytical levels reflect different orientations (cultural, social, and psychological), yet each maintains the behavior of individuals as the focal point of analysis.

In Part Four, attempts will be made at developing some implications of the preceding material. Chapter XI contains a discussion of the marketing mix and the roles of its various elements. In Chapter XII the salesman's role as a communicator will be explored. Chapters XIII and XIV are devoted to a discussion of the roles of selection, training, and compensation in the relationship between the selling organization and the salesman. Chapter XV examines some problems of organizational control and effectiveness. Part Five contains some concluding remarks as well as a prospectus for future research.

PART FOUR

Implications
of the COMPACT Model

XI

The Marketing Mix
and Some Conceptual Issues

THE FUNCTION of marketing was defined in Chapter II as one of "creating, modifying, exploiting, or maintaining a communicative relationship between a utility producing and one or more utility consuming systems." On the basis of the concepts presented in Part Three, it is now possible to be more specific about the relationship between these two systems. It may be postulated that, ideally, the functions of marketing and promotion are to establish, maintain, exploit, or modify (*conceptually* or *communicatively*) a *functional* relationship between the utility consumer and the product or service involved, consistent with the utility producing functions of the producer.

The concept of the marketing mix, in this context, encompasses the *data transmission* activities at the interfaces of utility producing and utility consuming systems. The purpose of this chapter is to explore some implications for the planning and implementation of the marketing mix based upon an application of the COMPACT model to the buyer–seller interface.

Descriptive analysis of the marketing mix is generally approached from the point of view of the activities or media involved. That is, the marketing mix is taken to consist of such efforts as advertising, merchandising, sales promotion and market research. This descriptive approach to a definition of the marketing mix, however, has neither led to an operational differentiation between, advertising and personal selling, for example, nor has it produced any operational guidelines for planning and allocation. Personal selling clearly differs in several respects from mass communication, but these differences cannot be operationally defined without some concept of the relationship between marketers and buyers. In other words, *personal and mass communication must be differentiated in terms of the requirements and conditions imposed by the marketing environment rather than in terms of each other.*
The immediate and short run cost of a message distributed by means of personal selling may be considerably higher than the

cost of the same message delivered by mass media. Yet, as indicated earlier, the efficiency of a given promotional element, is dependent upon effectiveness as well as cost, and effectiveness in turn *is some function of the degree to which the data distributed match the data required by the buying public.* Moreover, the various media available to the marketer do not "interact" with each other, such as is often assumed in the case of the cybernetic "black box" model. Instead, they disseminate data of differing levels of conceptual complexity, at differing times or points in the purchasing cycle, and at differing locations. To the extent that the economic laws of supply and demand apply to the media market one would expect at least a partial relationship between the cost of a unit of promotion in a given medium and the perceived effectiveness of that medium. Actually very little is known about the influence of economic cost models upon either the number of alternatives taken into account or the perceived effectiveness of a promotional medium. It is apparent, however, that the cost of promotion is not *necessarily* related to its effectiveness:

An individual does not remain unaffected by a rumor that is spontaneously circulated in his milieu by a growing number of persons. Obviously, he pays no attention to it unless he is already personally interested. In fact, no rumor can circulate if the individual is not concerned. He may be concerned, or feel he is, simply on the basis of the judgment—or what he thinks is the judgment—of his milieu. This is where we find fashion. But it may be objected that the decisive element is a commercial mechanism: a fashion is launched by the producers, and advertising plays the biggest role (in the form of an organized rumor launched by propagandists). This is true in the majority of cases, even in the case of such absurd fashions as the Yo-Yo, the Hula Hoop, or Davy Crockett. But it is not always that way: sometimes an absurd fashion spreads without advertising, from only one point of departure, such as in the astonishing case of the Scoubidou [a toy made from molding plastic]. Beginning with an article in a children's magazine, and without any commercial interest being involved, France was submerged within a month by Scoubidous made by children and adults. Evidently, we are face to face with the phenomenon of imitation, pure and simple, but to the extent that this imitation is caused by an article that reaches only a limited number of children, it is an example of the individual's extreme susceptibility, his capacity to be influenced and propagandized. Even if he defies it, even if he stiffens in the presence of true propaganda, he still is extremely vulnerable.[1]

It is this susceptibility, or capacity to be influenced, which constitutes the basis for the effectiveness of all promotion. The susceptibilities and inclinations of an individual to be influenced are neither exclusively a property of his communication system, nor exclusively a property of his data environment; rather, they are properties of the specific transaction involved. Thus the individual is susceptible to influence by certain advertisements and not by others, or he may be inclined to believe the words of certain salesmen and not those of others. Furthermore, an analysis of media effectiveness solely in terms of the media or solely in terms of buying behavior is likely to miss some essential transactional aspects of the influence process.

The descriptive approach to the definition of the marketing mix is proven further inadequate as evidenced by the type of research it has inspired. Research has been directed toward establishing correlational measures between promotional expenditures and such alleged indicators of effectiveness as sales, attitude change and recall of a given message. Such correlational measures may not only obscure any neutral or negative effects of promotion, but by isolating one single factor the influence of all other factors is automatically discounted. Consequently, future research must adopt a broader framework of influential relationships to establish *what the role of promotion is in terms of the totality of a marketing environment,* rather than be satisfied with measuring arbitrarily selected cause and effect relationships across a cybernetic "black box."

THE MARKETING MIX
IN THE LIGHT OF THE COMPACT MODEL

It is possible to stipulate a number of *requirements* which must be met at the interface of the marketing and buying systems if viable relationships are to develop and be maintained between the systems. The point is that a given minimum of information, however transmitted, is necessary for all action. Classification systems have been developed which seek to define information requirements by product class (characteristics of goods theory)[2] or by the nature of the buying situation (the Marketing Science Institute's study of industrial purchasing behavior)[3] Although both of these classification systems are valid in certain specified instances, in a more general sense *the information requirements of both buying and marketing systems will be some function of the past experiences of the systems and their resultant conceptual competence.*

The *bases* or *requirements* for communication and exchange between marketing and buying systems across the physical and conceptual space separating them may be outlined as follows:

1. A certain minimum level of mutual or complementary awareness.
2. A certain degree of complementarity of dissemination and acquisition patterns.
3. A minimum degree of complementarity of goals.
4. A certain level of complementarity of product concepts across a population of buying systems.
5. A minimum level of mutual or complementary value commitments.

The extent to which individualized (that is noncomplementary) motivational orientations govern the purchase and utilization of any given product or service establishes the broad criteria for determining the use and effectiveness of nonpersonal and personal media. Each of the above conditions will be briefly discussed in the following sections; and in later sections the differences between personal and nonpersonal media will be explored in terms of the nature of the marketer-buyer relationship.

Mutual or Complementary Awareness

The concept of awareness as used here refers to the mutual awareness of marketers and buyers of the same or similar problem situations for which a given product concept may be a solution.

It may be helpful here to iterate some earlier remarks. It has been stated that individual members of a society learn to behave in a certain fashion with respect to environmental events, both physical and social. The individual's accumulated experiences, many of which are held in common by the other members of a society, constitute the basis for his ability to communicate with others. The existence of such commonalities of concepts and values between groups of individuals should not be construed as meaning that the individual is an inherently passive entity engaging only in reactions. On the contrary, *the adoption or learning of a set of institutionalized behavior rules by all individuals (including marketers) constitutes both a necessary and an efficient means for an autonomous decision system to simplify the apparent complexity of the environment.* In any case, the accumulated past experiences of an individual buying system substantially influence its inclinations to engage in certain behaviors and not in others.

The individual's internalized experiences and behavior rules represent a distinct type of competence; namely, the ability to deal with certain events without deliberate attempts at problem solving (automatistic or habitual behavior). A capable machine operator is not continually making conscious decisions to move his arms in a certain pattern. He has accumulated a capacity to perform a certain task and is highly competent in the sense that he has internalized the meaning of the cues his machine emits as well as the appropriate responses to these cues.

A great deal of individual behavior is of this internalized type. The purchasing agent who is in charge of reordering has established certain cues which for him are indicative of the soundness of his activity. The very essence of such modern concepts as management by exception and electronic information systems is the development of a selective perception and decision making process based on someone's conclusions about the importance of various data or indicators.

The apparent irrationality of certain individual behaviors

arises partly from the fact that these behaviors acquire a functional autonomy of their own. An individual buys brand X "because" he buys brand X. Similarly, of course, marketers advertise "because" they advertise. The fact that an individual is unable to verbalize the basic reasons for all his actions does not necessarily mean that he did not have a perfectly good reason for the action in the first place. It may mean merely that the original motive has been forgotten and that the action itself has become the subject of commitment.

The presence of this internalized competence does not necessarily imply that the individual buying system is oblivious to new information. It does imply, however, that *certain sales are going to get made regardless of what the marketer does, just as certain marketing activities will be carried on regardless of what the buyer does.* In this sense, buyers and sellers will be acting out their mutual expectations across the interface of the two sets of systems.

From one point of view, the internalized awareness of an individual is represented by the concept of selective perception. On the other hand, however, internalized awareness also signifies a certain degree of conceptual "input-ability." That is, an individual will pay attention to and be able to understand and relate certain cues to the neglect of others. The important problem from the marketer's viewpoint is the determination of the boundaries of the commonalities of awareness (input-ability) between groups or populations of individuals. The competence dimension of buying systems is specifically relevant to this problem.

Apart from internalized awareness, individual buyers possess a certain competence to engage in overt problem solving. It is this competence which has brought so much frustration to market researchers. The individual faced with a direct question pertaining to his preference for a given product is faced with a problem situation which not only is new to him, but which also differs in some essential aspects from any given buying situation. In the familiar surroundings of, a supermarket, for example, the product selection problem perhaps would barely enter the interviewee's consciousness, while in the interviewing situation the question of preference is not only hypothetical — and thus of little or no consequence to the interviewee — but it is also subject to the personal influences of the interviewer.

This combination of automatistic and problem solving in the individual buying system is of crucial importance in the planning and execution of a marketing mix. Product concepts which are well within the internalized capacities of the individual will require a different approach from those which represent a totally new problem situation to the individual. A simple example will indicate the parameters of the problem facing the marketer.

Consider for a moment a selling situation involving a computer. The diagram in Figure 21 represents a hypothetical individual

FIGURE 21

Simplified Conceptual Network of an Individual

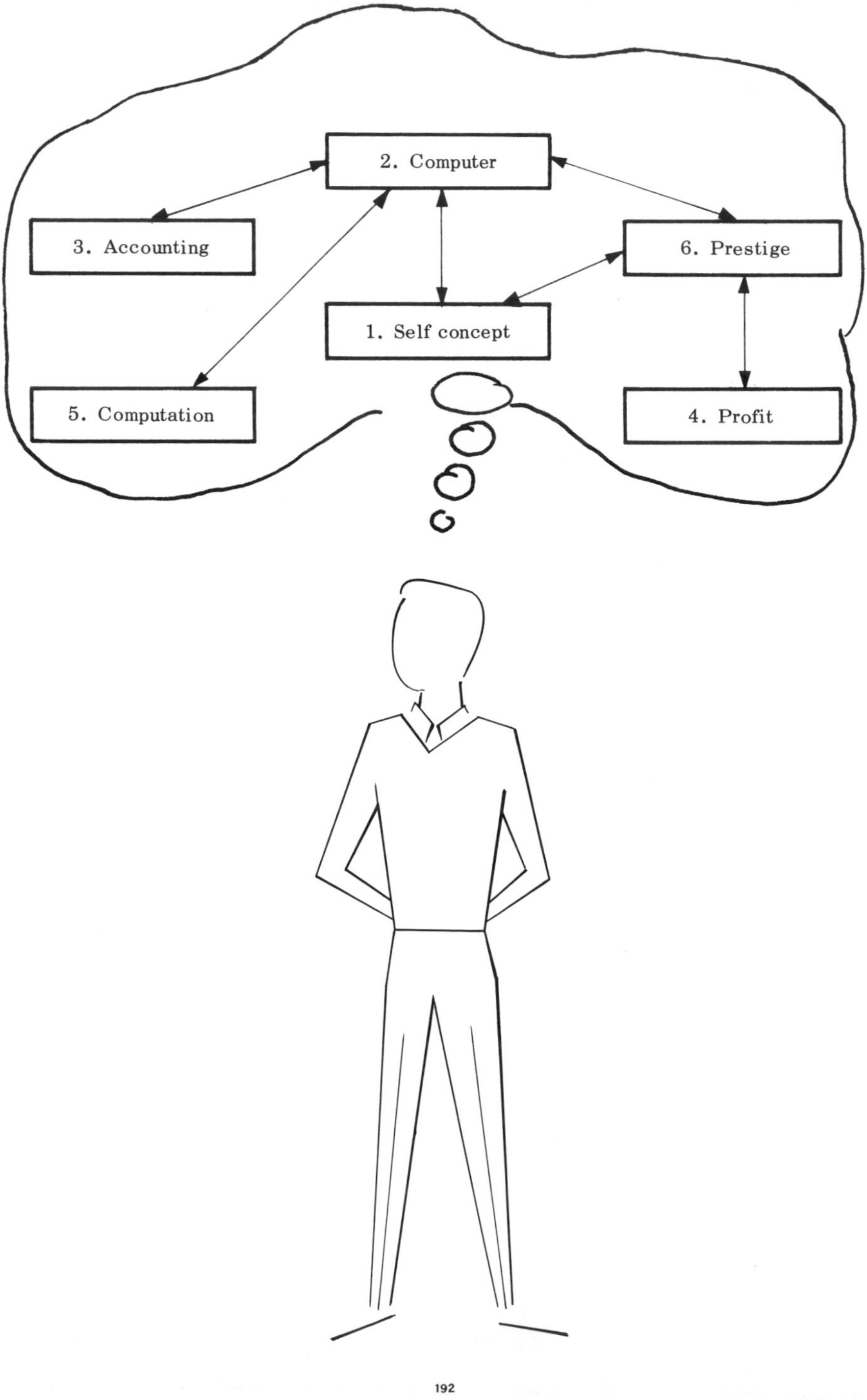

who possesses six concepts. A small number of concepts has been selected for the purpose of simplicity and it bears no relationship to the number of levels in the COMPACT model. Similarly, the content of the concepts has been arbitrarily selected as follows:

1. The individual's self-concept which is central to his network of concepts.
2. A concept of the computer as a machine.
3. A concept of accounting and control requirements.
4. A concept of profit as a requirement for survival and prestige.
5. A concept of computation as a clerical activity.
6. A concept of prestige as a function of the perceived respect of the individual's peers.

An individual may for example connect these concepts as shown in Figure 22. The concept of a computer is connected with his concept of prestige but it is not entirely clear to him what the connection is between a computer and profit.

The problem for the marketer, who of course does not have this kind of information, is to predict what strategy to utilize in attempting to sell this individual on acquiring a computer. In fact, the situation gives rise to the following questions:

1. What is the level of awareness of this prospective buyer? (What does he "know?")
2. What means are required to reach him?
3. What are his relevant goals?
4. How will he evaluate the product?
5. On what basis should he be encouraged to commit himself?

The strategic choice here is essentially between two alterna tives:

1. Utilize the buyer's present conceptual framework and hope his problem solving capacity is sufficient to carry the sale through.
2. Establish an interpersonal relationship with the prospective buyer for the purpose of helping him with the purchase and integration of the product.

The buyer in the above example is, for the sake of simplicity, depicted as a single individual. *In the case of industrial and retail buying systems several individuals may, of course, be involved in the decision making process, each with his own specific level of competence and each with a specific scope and direction of decision making authority as defined by the perceived organizational framework.* Indeed the inherent complexity of the organizationally circumscribed buying process has led to a concentration of personal selling efforts in these types of markets, while nonpersonal selling efforts have been concentrated in the organizationally less complex consumer market.

The degree of mutual awareness between marketers and buyers determines the ability of each to predict the behavior of the other. The higher the degree of mutuality (and therefore predictability), the greater the potential effectiveness and efficiency of nonpersonal media. On the other hand, the lower the degree of mutuality (and therefore predictability), the greater the requirement for some personal relationship whether in the form of market research or personal selling.

Complementarity of Data Dissemination and Acquisition Patterns

When buying systems are considered as information and decision systems in their own right, it becomes clear that what the marketer transmits to the buyer's environment is not information as such; it is data which the marketer hopes and expects will be of use to the buying system. The buyer, on the other hand, engages in a search for meaningful data to help him develop solutions to problems. The actual search pattern will be some function of the past experiences of the buying system as well as of the complexity and importance of the purchase.

The COMPACT model presented earlier provides a structural framework on the basis of which inferences may be made about the "why" of buying patterns—inferences which must necessarily be based on the observable aspects of that behavior. *Just as it is evident from studies of industrial purchasing behavior that purchasing agents maintain systems to guide them in the search for information so, it may be concluded, do final buyers.* In many cases, of course, the industrial purchasing agent is not responsible for all the rules and constraints of his purchasing system in that his decision making is limited by the organizational framework. The organizational aspect of industrial purchasing perhaps exhibits a greater degree of influence in the case of repeat purchases where previous experiences establish a set of relatively explicit standards for decision making. The fact that no such explicit standards are apparent in the cases of infrequent or new purchases should not be taken to imply however, that no standards exist or that the buying system does not behave according to a pattern of acquisition behavior. [4] One of the most important elements of industrial selling competence is the strategic ability to discern the relevant "nodes," or decision makers, and the nature of the "links," or communication lines among them.

The organizational aspects of industrial purchasing behavior are usually obvious to a discerning observer. In the case of consumer buying behavior, however, little attention has been paid to the existence of systemic or interrelated patterns of behavior. The concern here has been primarily with the discovery of single "causes" underlying certain behavior, that is, latitudinal studies of behavior, rather than with the understanding of influential relationships, or longitudinal studies of behavior processes. The Marketing Science Institute is presently planning a series of research projects designed to explore the systemic aspects of buying behavior with specific reference, at least initially, to final buyers. In the present context however, it is sufficient, to suggest *that buying behavior, whatever the context,* represents a pattern, the complexity of which is some function of the conceptual competence of the buyer.

The COMPACT model suggests five categories of influences, some or all of which may be applicable in any given buying situa tion. In other words, it is possible that some buyers take into account the full spectrum of perceived influences ranging from physiological to cultural or moral values (consciously or unconsciously) whenever a purchase is made. The possibility also exists that the purchases of certain products (e.g., certain durables) are subject to a greater array of influences than purchases of other products (e.g., certain nondurable household goods). Further research remains to be done before specific referents can be named, but in any case, the "why" of buying behavior is not solely a function of such vague causes as "needs" and "desires" but represents a combination of past experiences and communicative relationships, which make up a certain systemic pattern or order. Research in this direction promises an opportunity to push back the borders of the "rational" rather than satisfy itself with a process of dichotomizing behavior into the two classifications of "rational" and "irrational."

Further development of the systemic aspects of buyer behavior should also lead to a better understanding of the relationship between buyer behavior and the evolution of distribution channels as well as enable marketers to improve the effectiveness and efficiency of both product and data dissemination.

Complementarity of Goals

The essence of the marketing concept is *the creation and maintenance of a relationship between buyers and sellers which takes into account the goals of both systems.* The concept does not necessarily advocate that producers must produce only what buyers "need." On the contrary, it recommends a greater degree of involvement between buyers and sellers for the purpose of exploiting technological innovation. As a matter of fact, it has occurred to industrial buyers just recently that the marketing concept has a corollary: the procurement concept. [5]

The utility of a given product or service depends on the degree
to which the individual buying system can attribute meaning to
it. In the absence of better measures, price often becomes the
decision factor for the buyer primarily on the basis of his past
experiences and not necessarily, if ever, on the basis of the producer's expectations with respect to utility.

The market cannot be cleared unless the price is right, but neither can it
be cleared unless other essential items of information are right. Is the dress
an acceptable shade of red? Does the machine part have the right dimensions? Will the synthetic detergent actually get clothes clean under the given
laundry conditions? Price is not the only essential item of non-product information. For example: Will the store deliver if I buy a refrigerator? This
store is scarcely a practical source of supply for me if it will not deliver
and if I have no means of picking up the refrigerator. Will the store finance
the purchase of the refrigerator with monthly payments? If not, this store
may not be a practical source of supply in the present state of my pocket-
book.[6]

The point is that no product, however simple, has the same
utility to two different buyers. Even a highly complex camera can
be used as if it were a simple box camera (low utility attribution)
or it can be used to the full extent of its potential capacity (high
utility attribution). The price of such a camera would be "high"
in the former case and perhaps "right" or even "low" in the
latter case. At least two alternatives present themselves to the
camera manufacturer faced with the above situation: namely; (1)
attempt to educate buyers to appreciate the intended qualities of an
intricate and complex camera, or (2) develop a product which combines the low price of the box camera with the important features
of the complex camera in such a manner that little or no education
is required to utilize the full potential of the camera. Innovations in
the camera industry indicate that the latter alternative has been
chosen and implemented with substantial success (e.g., Eastman
Kodak's Instamatic).

In general the marketing concept—building as it does on the
complementarity of goals of buyers and sellers,—essentially
requires that marketers sell *functions,* utilities, and relationships
(ownership), and not physical objects. To be able to do this, the
marketer requires more than socioeconomic data describing the
observable behavior of individuals: he requires data pertaining to
the present and potential competence of buyers and users. Many
products never clear the hurdle of market acceptance primarily
because they are considered a source of profit by the marketer and
producer but are of little or no use to buyers and users.

Unfortunately, the solution does not often lie in more interviews
and market tests. Well planned interviews can certainly provide
useful data about the utility of various products to the user, *but the
buyer can predict the future no better than the marketer.* With
present techniques, market research can at best supply answers to
tactical questions. The significance of a marketer's competence

is his ability to anticipate the strategic complementarities, present and future, between marketing and buying systems.

Complementarity of Product Concepts

The communicative and distributive means or channels which the marketer utilizes must be related to a set of relevant properties of the potential buying systems in terms of some communicable set of product concepts. That is, the same product concepts can be related to different buying systems in terms of similarities between these systems. Examples of such groups of buying systems might be industries, occupations or the range of products carried by an intermediary.

The determination of the nature of product concepts held by an individual or group of buying systems has proven to be a particularly difficult task. The difficulty arises not so much from the complexity of the concepts held by buyers but from the difference in their viewpoints or knowledge about a product. In many cases marketers are taken in by their own propaganda, thereby losing the ability to see the product as would a potential buyer. This partiality on the part of marketers also contributes to a tendency to interpret all sales as a direct result of existing marketing efforts. The apparent inability of market research, as presently conceived, to cross this communication "barrier" inherent in the differing viewpoints of marketers and buyers is evident in the importance marketers attribute to competitive products and promotion. Consequently, *one company's marketing mix is as likely to be related and perhaps even modeled upon those of competing companies as it is likely to be related to the data and information requirements of its potential buyers.*

There is no easy solution to the problem of determining the necessary conceptual standards for creating a marketing mix which relates to the communicative requirements of buying systems. The COMPACT model, as it stands, provides no more than a way of thinking about and organizing the data which buyers make available about themselves. However, with the aid of the model, the problem facing the marketer can be defined as one of creating, modifying, changing or exploiting the relationship between the various aspects of a buying system or set of buying systems and product and service concepts and utilities. The point is that the efficiency of a given marketing mix will depend upon the marketer's ability to define the product concept of a group of buying systems and select that medium which will most efficiently and effectively cover this group.

Mutuality of Values

Marketing literature is notoriously short on discussions of the moral and ethical values which ultimately govern human behavior. Such

questions are usually left to philosophers and social critics such
as William H. Whyte Jr.[7] and Vance Packard.[8] Some communication
researchers have concerned themselves with the problem of credibility of data originating in various marketing media. Certainly
bias does exist in many of these data, but if communication bias
must be taken into account, so must its corollary—bias correction
by the receiver. The credibility of an advertisement is not some
hidden quality of the ad itself; but is related to of the individual
reader's expectations with reference to the intentions of the
advertiser's statements. In the final analysis *the buyer believes
what he wants to believe and is capable of believing, and attributes
meaning to the available data accordingly.*

The question of moral values goes beyond the mere violation
of a few behavior rules, primarily because such violations cannot
really be committed without the participation of both buyers and
sellers.[9] The important questions of values are related to the
future role of marketing and its various elements. If the role of
marketing is to inform a society and to expedite the diffusion of
technological and social innovations in a primarily free enterprise
economy, then more effort must be expended to develop an understanding of the interplay between moral values and economic
activity. This quest for guiding values in a world where the technological communication enablers are rapidly surpassing man's
capacities to acquire and consume information should be less
directed toward legislation of morality and the institutionalization
of behavior rules and more directed toward the development of a
philosophy of organization and communication.

THE MARKETING MIX—SUMMARY

The preceding outline of the elements of the relationship between
marketers and buyers deliberately points up conceptual issues
rather than enumerates the possible elements of any given mix.
A substantial volume of literature already exists on the allocation
of the various elements of the marketing mix from the point of
view of "things to do." It is evident from the preceding that the
activities performed and the efforts expended by marketers to
reach buyers must, in view of the state of the art, follow from a
largely qualitative assessment of the pertinent variables. The
essence of the COMPACT model in this connection is a conceptual
integration, albeit tentative, of all the influence underlying the
behavior of an individual. The primary limitation of quantitatively
oriented experiments (such as those described in Chapters III and
IV) is that to treat a problem using this technique it must be removed
from its psychological, functional, social, and cultural connections
and reduced to its simplest state:

This would be barely acceptable if it were admitted that the results are rather thin and relatively insignificant. But because they are expressed in figures, and because we have a maniacal faith in the exactness of mathematics, it is claimed that such methods produce the truth itself, and that the rest is literature. But it is precisely the rest that is most important, so long as we do not have a total "robot" image of man. It is the rest that is important, so long as we do not discount man altogether, as do the Kinsey report and others. What is particularly serious in this connection is that the socio-psychologists, who use mathematical methods, are quick to claim that what cannot be reached by their methods does not exist . . . . I must add that the results, attained and the figures arrived at never go beyond what is already obvious and merely common sense. To prove with figures, after long statistical inquiries, that women are more receptive to emotional propaganda than men is hardly an astounding revelation. Common sense also tells us that man has a certain psychic stability that cannot be altered radically by propaganda; figures, charts, and ratios add little to that.[10]

It is clearly not the exactness of mathematical methods which is being disputed here; what is of concern is the lack of integration between conceptual and methodological disciplines. Much remains to be done in this connection, and until a more substantial body of marketing science has been developed out of available and future conceptual and methodological contributions, the essence of a marketing manager's competence will be his ability to intuit the relevant complementarities and differences between marketing and buying systems. The COMPACT model is offered as a means of taking into account a wide range of buying influences while still enabling the marketer or researcher to differentiate such influences, thus avoiding the circularity of analysis involved in explaining one level of behavior in terms of another.

THE NATURE OF NONPERSONAL MEDIA

In transmitting messages, the marketer has essentially two alternatives. He can attempt to exploit the commonalities among a specified group of buyers by transmitting messages in anticipation of sufficient mutuality of information requirements among these buyers. This process of supplying answers in anticipation of questions was outlined by Wroe Alderson:

While [advertising] is an aid to search it is not search. The questions which [advertising] anticipates may not be the questions for which consumers want answers. They may be questions which the supplier hopes the consumer will ask or which he believes are uppermost in the consumer's mind.[11]

One alternative available to the marketer then, is to utilize what is generally called nonpersonal or mass media as a means of distributing messages which satisfy buyer information requirements.

The second alternative available to the marketer is the use of personal media in the form of salesmen, service agents, or perhaps top management contacts. Without implying either that nonpersonal or mass media should be used to the exclusion of personal media or vice versa, or that these two types of media are interchangeable, it is possible to outline the characteristics of each class of media and to identify some qualitative differences which may be crucial for their effective use.

The process of mass communication derives its effectiveness from the existence of similarities or commonalities among individual members of the population. Advertising *taps the inclinations or potential responses of individuals but does not create these potential responses in other than possibly the very long run.* Thus, an advertiser attempting to inform buyers can only tell them what *he* knows, and these data become information only when related to the buyer's own system of standards and values, whether negatively or positively. In other words, the advertiser who presents arguments for the purchase of a product is not making up the buyer's mind. He is providing data which the buyer can use, in conjunction with his existing knowledge, to reach a decision. [12]

The effectiveness of an advertising campaign is thus some function of the degree to which it relates product concepts to the values and motivational standards of the population of buyers at which it is directed. When it is claimed, however, that attitudes of potential buyers have changed as a result of an advertising campaign, one must logically question (1) the definition of attitude; (2) the technique of questioning, and (3) the criterion by which change is detected. An example of the inability of mass communication to create or even change attitudes, where no prior inclination to learn from the campaign exists is provided by an experiment concerning public knowledge of the nature and operation of the United Nations. [13] This experiment, undertaken in an eastern metropolitan area, included the following steps.

1. Interviews of a randomly selected sample of 745 people were conducted. These revealed a very low level of knowledge about the United Nations.
2. An intensive educational campaign on the United Nations was subsequently conducted in television and radio.
3. Interviews of a randomly selected sample of 758 people after the campaign was carried out. (This second sample did not include any of the individuals interviewed in step 1.) These interviews also revealed a low level of knowledge about the United Nations.
4. Reinterviews of 592 of the original 745 individuals interviewed in step 1 revealed a substantial increase in knowledge about the United Nations subsequent to the educational campaign.

To conclude from the above that the educational campaign "resulted" in a substantial change in the attitudes or the knowledge of the sample of individuals misses an essential element of the experimental design. The very fact that the initial interviews called attention to the interviewees' lack of knowledge about the United Nations clearly constitutes an important influence toward the result obtained in step 4. The campaign may have been of some aid in providing the data, but any inclinations to consume these data were undoubtedly awakened by the initial personal interview. Since information about the United Nations is obtainable from a number of readily available sources, it is perhaps reasonable to assume that the increase in knowledge might have occurred even without the campaign.

Mass media essentially constitute static links between senders and receivers, and whatever communication occurs and mass media do communicate, related to the receiver's ability and willingness to interpret the messages. The efficiency of mass communication will depend, at least in part, upon the efficiency of any specific medium vis-à-vis a specified group of buyers, and can be appraised from two points of view: (1) from the point of view of the originator or (2) from the point of view of the receiver. The data can be originated and transmitted efficiently, and they can be received and understood efficiently. In this sense, then, the total efficiency of intentional communication should be measured *by considering the expenditure (money and effort) of both the originator and the receiver as well as the effectiveness of the communication process itself.* [14]

The results of the extensive efforts which have been expended on the measurement of the advertising effectiveness have been far from conclusive. Research findings, notably Katz and Lazarsfeld, [15] suggest a number of intervening variables between the actual message and its effect such as exposure, nature of media, content, and predispositions of the audience. In any case, the number of potential buyers which will react to a given campaign will depend upon (1) *the generalizability of the message,* that is, the number of individuals to whom the message will mean something as a result of their metacommunicative inclinations and past experiences, (2) *the efficiency of the medium,* that is, the correspondence between potential buyers and readers or viewers of the medium, (3) the competence of buyers to derive the potential utility from the product, that is, the *generalizability of the product concept,* (4) *the motivational orientation of the buying system,* that is, the relevance of the product to the buyer's existing assortments, and (5) *the strength of existing commitments of the buying system.*

Future research into advertising or mass communication effectiveness must be based on a consideration of the whole spectrum of influences or effects and not just on those considered meaningful to the communicator. Arbitrarily selected criteria of effectiveness are as likely as not to miss the "real" effect or influence of mass communication upon buying behavior.

THE NATURE OF PERSONAL MEDIA

Personal or direct selling differs from mass media in that the former is dynamic rather than static in character. The competent salesman basically represents a marketing mix by himself in the sense that he can relate to the buying system and determine both the appropriate strategic (metacommunicative) and tactical (communicative) approach to the solution or the buyer's conflict or problems. The competent salesman can thus detect and appeal to the *differences* among buying systems, where as mass communication must rely on their *similarities* among buying systems.

The reason that some "matches" between buyers and products cannot be made without the presence of a change agent is that the buying system tends to meet new situations on the basis of its internalized past competence. While the buyer may be attempting to sell himself, his past experiences act as a block for change. Hence, the potential utility of the personal selling function is greatest where the buyer is experiencing the greatest difficulty in selling himself.

As will be shown in later chapters, the effectiveness of the personal selling function is not measurable directly in terms of sales. The relevant competence of the salesman is *his ability to do that which no other communication medium can do;* consequently, some measure relevant to that task must be developed. In terms of the variables of the relationship between marketing and buying systems, the personal selling function is potentially most effective and efficient when:

1. Potential buyers are unaware of a given product and no other means can achieve awareness.
2. The search patterns of potential buyers are such that no other channel will bring the given product into the purview of the buyer.
3. Potential buyers' goals are so specific and different that no general function can be established.
4. The number of potential buyers is relatively restricted and individual buying systems can be defined.
5. Potential buyers are so strongly committed, legally, economically, or psychologically to competitive suppliers or existing and traditional practices (in the case of a new product or service) that any other medium is rendered ineffective.

In other words, the effectiveness of the personal selling function increases rapidly with the effort required to bridge the interface between marketing and buying systems within the constraints imposed by functional (product) and economic (resource) limitations.

The role of personal selling in the marketing mix, then, *is that of establishing or providing a dynamic and flexible communicative relationship with individual buying systems.* The function is potentially more effective and economical when strategically relevant messages (metacommunicative facilitation) cannot be predicted or when no other medium is capable of providing the information or the catalysis required for the buying system to resolve the ambiguity of a problem situation. In many respects, the roles of personal and nonpersonal media are not and should not be divided as sharply as the above description indicates. The point is *that the effectiveness and, therefore, the efficiency of personal selling depend on the extent to which the potential competence of the salesman is utilized,* a problem which will be further explored in the following chapter.

SUMMARY

This chapter has dealt with some conceptual issues related to the planning and implementation of the marketing mix. From the content of Part III it was concluded that the relationship between marketing and buying systems is multidimensional and subject to both limiting and facilitating conditions which are neither exclusively properties of either of the systems, nor exclusively environmental, but are properties of the interactions or transactions between the systems. It was also concluded in this that a definition of any one element of the marketing mix in terms of some other element is insufficient for the purposes of understanding the relevant properties of any given element.

The metacommunicatively facilitating conditions for interaction between marketing and buying systems were classified and discussed under the following headings:

1. Mutual or complementary awareness,
2. Complementary data dissemination and acquisition patterns,
3. Complementarity of goals,
4. Complementarity of product concepts across a population of buying systems,
5. Mutual or complementary value systems

Mass communication, or what is popularly known as one-way communication, depends for its effectiveness and efficiency on a relatively high level of complementarity of the five types mentioned above. The lower the degree of complementarity at the interface of marketing and buying systems — and consequently the more difficult the predictive process — the more effective and efficient is personal selling or two-way communication, within the limitations imposed by functional (product) and economic (resource) constraints. While it has not been the purpose here to discuss in detail all the possible elements of a marketing mix, the analytical framework is applicable to a wide variety of data dissemination techniques. In the following chapter the role of the salesman as a communicator will be outlined and discussed from the point of view of the COMPACT model and the concepts of communication presented earlier.

XII

The Salesman and His Competence as a Communicator

IT FOLLOWS from Part Three that communication is not something an individual *does* to another. It is a relationship, or a system state between an individual and certain aspects of his environment. As an autonomous information and decision system the individual combines his accumulated experiences with environmental cues according to some goal structure which to him is unique and is generalizable across individuals only by virtue of similarities in the process of socialization.

The purpose of the present chapter is to outline a particular approach to the analysis of the role of the salesman as a communicator. The implications of this approach for the management of the personal selling function will be further explored in subsequent chapters. The remaining chapters of Part Four have been arranged deliberately to proceed from the specific to the general, mainly because it is useful to develop a concept of the salesman-buyer relationship on which to base an analysis of the processes of selection, training, compensation, and measurement of effectiveness.

THE SALESMAN AND THE SYSTEM OF ACTION CONCEPT

The bulk of the existing literature on personal selling considers the salesman from the point of view of *what he does* or should be doing. Several attempts have thus been made to provide detailed descriptive and prescriptive handbooks of selling performance on the basis of the author's personal experiences or observations. Yet, the exact qualities which differentiate the successful from the unsuccessful salesman have still escaped full description or verbalization. Moreover, it is highly unlikely that empirical observation alone can provide the key to this problem since the conclusions derived from such observation can never be any better than the observer's ability to draw relevant inferences.

The primary advantage of personal selling as an element of the marketing mix is that *the salesman is an autonomous entity capable of interacting with and adapting to other autonomous entities (buyers).* Consequently, the key to the effective utilization and management of the personal selling function is an understanding of what influences a salesman to behave and perform in a given manner. Just as there is no single indicator of selling or communication competence, there is no single motive which governs selling behavior. It has occasionally been maintained that the "typical" salesman is primarily motivated by money, a statement which, if true, may also be taken to mean that selling organizations provide no other incentive, and therefore attract individuals who *do* tend to see money as an important incentive. The fact that some or even many salesmen consider money an important incentive can thus not be taken to mean that the *best* salesmen necessarily are money oriented. The amount or quantity of effort which a given salesman exerts (that is, number of calls made and time spent with each buyer) may correlate with the intentions of some given incentive scheme, but, as was apparent in the experimental situations described in Part Two, the quantity of effort expended is not directly related to either the quantity or the quality of results achieved.

There is no reason whatever to expect that a salesman possesses a less complex personality system than, say, a buyer, a manager, or a researcher. One of the upshots of the increasingly popular role concept has apparently been a tendency to confuse the relationship of job requirements and personality characteristics. For example, the fact that a salesman's role differs from that of a sales manager or a buyer does not imply that his personality system must also be different. As explained earlier, the role is a facilitator and not a determinant of behavior. Few people would maintain that the best manager is the individual who can play the role of manager to perfection. On the contrary, a good manager must be characterized on the basis of his ability to achieve the objectives he sets for himself or his organization. In other words, the managerial task involves the total range of competencies and standards of the individual. Similarly, the selling task, even though it may be organizationally more circumscribed for the sake of coordination, also involves the total range of competencies and standards of the individual salesman whether or not this is organizationally facilitated. Clearly, the salesman as an individual has capacities and commitments which are neither directly related to his tasks nor defined organizationally, and he does not necessarily leave these behind when he puts on his salesman's hat. Willy Loman's problem, in Arthur Miller's *The Death of a Salesman* is not his failure as a salesman but his failure as an individual and as a man; in other words, the point of the play is the *personality,* not the *occupation.* Whatever objectives the individual salesman pursues on the job, they are only a part of and are subordinate to his objectives as an individual.

THE SELLING SYSTEM OF ACTION

It will be helpful here to define the word "selling" as it is used in this volume. Too often this word has been associated with a military analogy in such expressions as "being on the firing line" and other similarly aggressive terms. The advent of the term "soft sell" as opposed to "hard sell"[1] has perhaps also added to the confusion in the meaning and uses of the word selling.

While "selling" is frequently used to describe that which the salesman does to the buyer, the fact that in many cases mass communication and mass distribution have taken the place of the personal selling function is ample indication that selling cannot be limited to the salesman's activities. Even apart from this and other substantial changes in the personal selling environment, the nature of the *communicative process* is such that selling cannot be solely a function of the salesman. As used in this volume, *selling is an operation performed by the buying system.* The salesman emits noises and gestures (data) the informational content and relevance of which is some function of the salesman's competence in relating to and understanding the motivations of the buying system. Ultimately *the buying system provides the sufficient condition for a sale with, without or despite the assistance of the salesman's efforts.*

The increasing complexity and sophistication of many buying systems clearly tends to emphasize the advisory or consultative capacity of the salesman. In the broader context, then, selling is communication oriented toward the development of dynamic, mutually beneficial relationship, or toward the achievement of some mutually compatible goals between producers and users. It is important to note that *selling (or communication) may occur without any intentional data dissemination or data acquisition on the part of either producers or users.* Conversely, intentional data dissemination and data acquisition do not necessarily imply that the intended selling (or communication) is occurring.

Within the context of the total organizational framework, the objective of any one individual salesman need not be limited to the achievement of sales as such. The development of a viable and dynamic relationship between a producer and a user, for example, may itself be an acceptable objective for the personal selling function. This is not to say that the guiding principle for the selection of potential buyers should not be anticipated sales, it means that sales constitute a poor measure of the effectiveness of salesmen as salesmen, unless the *total* process of potential buyer selection and selling is controlled and influenced by the salesman.

These problems of integrating the measurement of individual effectiveness and managerial or organizational control will be further discussed in Chapters XIV and XV. For the present purposes, it is sufficient to keep in mind that effectiveness of performance cannot be evaluated apart from the existing organizational structure *and* objectives.

The functional phases of a selling system of action with reference to the *individual* salesman can be outlined as follows (Figure 22):

FIGURE 22

The Selling System of Action with
Reference to the Individual Salesman

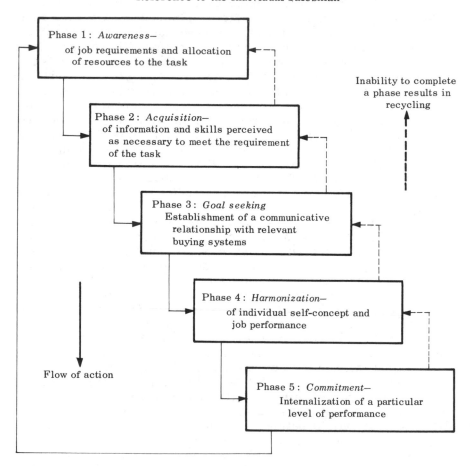

Phase 1: Awareness of job requirements and allocation of resources to the perceived task.

Phase 2: Acquisition of required skills and information to meet the perceived requirements of the task.

Phase 3: Establishment of a communicative relationship with a specified set of buying systems.

Phase 4: Harmonization of the individual's self-concept and job performance.

Phase 5: Internalization of and commitment to a specific level of performance.

These functional phases constitute categories of action components each of which can be analyzed in terms of the five categories of models, or levels of competence, described in Part Three. Figure 23 outlines the variables involved in each of these levels of analysis. In the following sections, both the categories of action components and the levels of competence will be discussed with reference to the functions of a salesman at the interface of marketing and buying systems.

Phase 1: Awareness of Job Requirements

Clearly, selling behavior requirements differ from buyer to buyer, from industry to industry and from industry to final buyer. A very basic requirement for the performance of a *successful* selling job, whatever the buying system, *is awareness of the function to be fulfilled by the salesman.* This requirement is not as simple as it may sound, primarily because of the peculiarly dual role of the salesman at the interface of the two systems.

The salesman enters his job with a certain awareness of a discrepancy between an apparent and a desired state of himself as a personality system. That is, the individual entering a job or occupation brings with him a certain predilection to perform that job. This predilection or motivation may, of course, vary widely among individuals and range from a requirement for money, to a need for personal achievement and self-fulfillment. The individual's motivation to work may also attain a certain functional autonomy in itself: that is, people work because they work, in the sense that motives have been internalized so that individuals are no longer fully aware of them. The point is *that the complexity of motivation an individual brings to a task is related to his concepts of the world.* In general, the more conceptually competent the individual, the more complex his motivational framework.

Awareness of job requirements as defined by the selling organization is only one part of the problem facing the salesman. It is with reference to the buying system that he must perform his task whether with the support of, or in spite of, the selling organization behind him. Since the motivation of an individual (as shown in Chapter V) reflects the degree to which he perceives his values satisfied by his efforts, *his level of awareness has a direct*

FIGURE 23

Outline of the Concept of Selling Competence

Direction of Competence ⟶   Direction of Control ⟶

Flow of action	Level 1 Activity	Level 2 Behavior	Level 3 Performance	Level 4 System	Level 5 Values
Awareness	"Things to do" with regard to buyers	Types of buyers and buyer expectations	Differences between own and buyer's goals	Indicators of strategically relevant buying systems	Differences among own, buying systems', and selling system's goals
Acquisition	Memorization of presentation and rules for place and object of presentation	Development of ability to adapt to buyer's viewpoint	Acquisition of information and skills relevant to perceived goals	Acquisition of information and ability to creatively analyze buying situations	Development of information and skills relevant to achievement of buyer's, seller's, and own goals
Goal seeking	Flawless delivery of presentation, in a *prescribed* number of situations	Achievement of *prescribed* goals	Achievement of *self-approved* goals	Establishment of communicative relationships with relevant set of buying systems	Selection of strategically relevant buyer relationships
Harmonization	Quality of delivery of sales presentation	Quality of performance measured against prescribed standards	Evaluation of performance in relation to self-concept	Evaluation of communicative effectiveness in relation to own and organizational goals	Strategic effectiveness of relationships
Commitment	Rhetorical competence	Adaptive competence	Performance competence and achievement of buyer satisfaction	Buying systems and communicative relationships involved	Integrated value structure with reference to all relevant systems

bearing upon his motivation to perform. Motivating salesmen, therefore, is essentially an act of communication which may or may not be achieved by means of a single class of *messages* such as money. In any case, the messages or incentives provided by an organization must clearly be related to the effort required of the salesman, rather than to the results of that effort, if the selling organization is to have any influence upon the quality of performance of the salesman.

A description of the job does not necessarily foster awareness of the salesman's function since the conceptual framework underlying a sales manager's verbal expressions of the job concept is likely to be quite different from that of the salesman. The communicative implications of both job descriptions and generalized "pep-talks" are entirely dependent upon what the salesman "knows" about the following elements of his environment:

1. The job of a salesman.
2. The requirements of buyers.
3. The requirements and objectives of the selling organization.
4. His own potential resources relevant to the several elements of the selling task.

The salesman's awareness of these elements and their relationships serves as both an enabling and a limiting factor in his communicative interactions with buyers and sales managers. *A technically good job description, from the point of view of completeness and well-chosen language may thus be communicatively irrelevant or even have negative import to the salesman, depending upon the things he "knows."*

In summary, the salesman's awareness proceeds not necessarily from a detailed, formal description of the possible situations he might encounter, but from a conceptual framework establishing the relevance or irrelevance of environmental cues. This conceptual competence will be treated in somewhat more detail in a later section of this chapter.

Phase 2: Acquisition of Perceived
Required Skills

The old controversy centering on the question of whether salesmen are born or made has proven itself largely inapplicable to the problem of establishing why some salesmen are better than others. Building as it did on a one-dimensional concept of competence, this controversy could never be resolved in terms of the premises underlying the two sides of the argument. The answer to the riddle is: *Salesmen are made and they make themselves.* This does not mean that training programs are useless. On the contrary, many salesmen probably require the presence of a change agent or trainer to perceive the requirement for additional skills and to internalize those skills as part of their behavior repertoire.

Those individuals who appear to be born salesmen have learned from their previous experiences various advantageous ways of relating to and communicating with other people, and this competence has become internalized to the extent that these individuals are unable to verbalize it. By the same token other individuals may be unable to describe or imitate the performances of these highly competent salesmen, primarily because the communication resulting from observation is highly dependent upon the observer's conceptual abilities.

The process of acquiring the necessary communication skills has been considered at several levels both in theory and practice as ranging from rote memory of a canned sales talk to experimentation with the so-called T-group (training group) approach. If the potential effectiveness of the salesman is to have any meaning, however, the individual must be taken into account in the design of training methods. *That is, the central purpose of the training process must be to enable the salesman to determine the relevant approach to different buying systems and not to "program" him with a preplanned message.*

The basic advantage of the salesman as a promotional medium is his potential or actual ability on the spot to determine and implement a strategically relevant approach to any given buying system. The salesman whose efforts consist of delivering a preplanned and prerehearsed sales pitch is achieving sales, if any, on the basis of a more or less random or fortuitous match of data dissemination and data acquisition processes.

The individual salesman's willingness and ability to seek and acquire new and improved skills or competence is closely related to the challenges and opportunities he perceives in his environment. Similarly, *the salesman's achieved level of competence is closely related to the amount and type of organizational control.* Clearly, the sales manager who prefers to write his salesmen's presentations is exercising a greater degree of control over them than the manager who restricts his activities to the assignment of territories, relying on the salesmen's competence for the selection and development of individual accounts. The superior approach depends partly upon the objectives of the specific personal selling function and partly upon the quality of available resources with reference to both salesmen and training facilities.

Phase 3: Establishment of
Communicative Relationships

*The purpose of the personal selling function is communication,*as defined in this volume. An exchange or sale *is one possible* *outcome* of the salesman's *and* the buyer's efforts, aided by a host of other variables including the suitability of the product. A necessary condition for the establishment of a communicative relationship is an understanding of or "feel" for the processes of problem definition and decision making of any specific buying system. Acquisition of the necessary information and establishment of viable contacts have often been overlooked as key factors in the development of a relationship between a salesman and a buying system. In large and complicated organizations, it is frequently a laborious undertaking to find and establish contact with the relevant decision makers with reference to the purchase of a given product. Yet, this is an absolute necessity if the salesman's efforts are going to make any difference whatever.

The exchange of data at the interface between buying and selling systems is clearly a two-way street, or, in other words, a cooperative activity. Just as the buying system requires information about suppliers and products, so the selling system requires information about buyers and their requirements. Unless suppliers and salesmen can show that the buyer stands to gain from providing data about himself and his system, however, this two-way street is liable to remain a one-way thoroughfare for salesmen.

The relevance of the salesman's communicative competence is established at one extreme by the functional and economic limitations on the buying system which preclude some communicative consequences, and at the other extreme by the transactional facilitators which render some communicative consequences inevitable. *At either extreme, the communicative competence of the salesman, however well developed, is largely irrelevant to the outcome of the interaction.* Examples of one extreme include situations where a particular product is unsuitable for the buyer's purposes, or the buying system's resources are insufficient to allow an exchange, or where the buying system is so strongly committed to competitive suppliers legally, economically, or psychologically, that no reasonable amount of effort on the part of the salesman will bring about the desired results. Examples of the other extreme include situations where the buying system already has decided to buy, or the buying system has no feasible alternative supplier, or where legal, economic or psychological commitment already exists.

Between these two extremes are situations in which the outcome, depends largely upon the quality of the salesman's efforts. Consequently, *the relevance of a salesman's competence, and therefore his effectiveness and efficiency,* is heavily dependent upon the strategic selection of buying systems. This selection may or may not be performed by the salesman, depending upon the organizational division of responsibility.

Phase 4: Harmonization of
Self and Job Concepts

At the center of the individual salesman's behavior is a self-concept in terms of which he acts upon (or does not act upon) the messages which he receives from his environment. This integrative element of selling behavior implies *that the messages a salesman receives from his superiors (e.g., job descriptions, pep talks, and compensation plans) are interpreted by the salesman in terms of his self-concept as well as the task he is to perform. The* salesman consciously or unconsciously assesses his own performance and attaches values to it based on his perception of the job as it relates to his self-concept. He utilizes the messages received from sales managers and supervisors to confirm or disconfirm his own assessment and not to replace it.

In sum, the primary influence exerted by the so-called motivational efforts undertaken by sales management is to confirm or disconfirm the salesman's expectations and evaluations of his own efforts. To the degree that organizational rewards tend to confirm the individual salesman's expectations and evaluations, commitment to the given and existing level of performance and competence is likely to follow. On the other hand, disconfirmation of the salesman's expectations, whether in a positive or in a negative direction *will not necessarily bring about a change in performance.* The human ability to rationalize away negative feedback provides a degree of "slack" in terms of responses to the environment, but outright "disunderstanding" may occur. "Disunderstanding" is essentially "willful misunderstanding" and occurs primarily in the face of messages which appear threatening to the systemic integration of the personality system. In effect, *the possible influences of compensation and reward systems external to the individual, in general are limited to a confirmation of existing levels of performance.* Improvement of competence and performance is a *training* problem; and, as shown in Chapter X, training is a participative process involving the total personality system of the salesman.

Phase 5: Internalization and
Commitment

One of the real difficulties in evaluating a salesman's competence arises from the fact that this competence is almost totally internalized. Very successful salesmen have attempted to verbalize or even write down the "secrets" of their success and the result has invariably been less than spectacular. One of the reasons for this is that the ability to communicate or sell is primarily achieved by imitation, that is by observation and adaptation.

In any case, the *quality* of performance is not necessarily *positively* related to the process of internalization and commitment. *Ineffective performances get internalized as often as effective ones.* Indeed, at lower levels of competence the performance which has been internalized is the one which the salesman perceives to be confirmed by the system of rewards and punishments existing in his environment. The sales manager who puts great emphasis on paper work may well be awarded with a high output of paper work possibly at the expense of other aspects of the performance.

Again, it is important to recognize that a *good performance cannot be legislated* by managerial decree. On the contrary, a salesman will internalize and commit himself to the level of performance which satisfies *his* standards. Different or higher standards can be achieved through an effective learning process but, in general, cannot be achieved by merely imposing rules and regulations. Commitment may occur at varying levels of competence and it is consequently these levels of competence which provide the proper concept of effectiveness. To evaluate salesmen according to the number and amount of sales occurring in their relevant territories is equivalent to treating the personal selling function as if it were essentially an advertising function. The potentially attainable function of the salesman is not limited to data dissemination, but represents a capacity to serve as a change agent for selected buying systems. *Encouraging salesmen to commit themselves to a performance based on sales output as the sole measure of competence may produce sales which could have been achieved more efficiently by some other means.*

To reiterate, the potential competence of a salesman as an element of the marketing mix, is to do that which no other promotional tool can do. Hence, the effectiveness, and the efficiency of the personal selling function increase as the difficulty of the communication task increases, and personal selling attains its full potential effectiveness at the point where all other media become ineffective.

THE COMPETENCE DIMENSION OF PERSONAL SELLING

Figure 23 (page 210) outlines the relationships among the categories of action components and the levels of competence. The sequence and labeling of the columns from left to right indicates the direction of increasing competence and, thus, the direction of increasing control exerted upon behavior resulting from the influence of successive levels of standards. For example, a highly competent salesman requires less organizational control than a salesman operating at a lower level of competence. An individual may combine all levels of competence in a single action or he may utilize only part of his potential competence. Each of these levels will be explained briefly in the following section with reference to the salesman. In the following chapters, their implications will be discussed with reference to the management of the personal selling function.

Level 1: Physical Activity

This competence level represents the lowest degree of ability to communicate. An example may be the salesman who memorizes a pitch and merely delivers it whenever a suitable occasion arises. In some cases, this is all that is required of the salesman, and all that the organizational training program prepares him for. From the point of view of the concepts outlined in Chapter VI the salesman operating at this level of competence is utilized primarily on the basis of his physiological capacities. That is, the competence required is limited to the salesman's ability to memorize, his ability to convey himself from one point to another, and his ability to speak and gesticulate.

Quite apart from the fact that the selling organization which utilizes its salesmen primarily as "wandering loudspeakers" is liable, from the human relations point of view, to experience personnel problems and high turnover, there are certain obvious inefficiencies inherent in such an approach. Notwithstanding the sales manager's ability to create an excellent presentation for his salesmen to memorize and enunciate, *there is a crucial difference between a "good" sales presentation—in the sense that the salesmen do and say the things they "should" do and say—and an effective selling performance in the sense that the salesman attempts to establish a strategically advantageous relationship.* Most readers have undoubtedly been subjected to a flawlessly delivered speech without recalling a word afterwards, and have probably also been subjected to a badly delivered speech which nevertheless left a lasting imprint.

The point is that a flawlessly delivered sales talk, evaluated from the point of view of things to say and do, is not much better than a well-presented advertisement. It communicates if the buyer wants it to communicate and for no other reason. Moreover, the salesman's objective tends to become the delivery of the talk itself, with little or no consideration for the buyer's information requirements.

Level 2: Adaptive Behavior

While perhaps few sales managers would go as far as to assume that there is a one best sales pitch, some seem to believe that salesmen must at least be provided with a range of presentations which can be adapted to any buying situation. The following quotation illustrates this point:

The truth is that the salesman needs a well-defined structure, a prepared "pitch" to follow in making his presentations. In spite of years of practice, even the best specialty salesmen experience great difficulty in originating a presentation or coping unaided with a new or unusual objection or resistance. They often have very retentive memories and have acquired a substantial storehouse of answers and ploys which they can use as the occasion may demand, but practically none of this material is ever original. [2]

The view expressed in the above quotation appears to be based on the following assumptions:

1. Salesmen have relatively narrowly defined and recognizable personalities.
2. Years of experience can be equated with training as a factor in increasing competence.
3. The key factor in the achievement of sales is the form of the sales presentation.

In view of the conceptual framework presented in Part Three, a framework which is primarily derived from modern developments in the behavioral sciences, the above assumptions are entirely unwarranted. The personality characteristics of a salesman may well influence his effectiveness but they are not the sole determinant of selling performance. It was also shown earlier that while repetition of a given activity or system of action is likely to result in internalization of, and commitment to, the performance of that action *at any given level of competence,* the attainment of a higher level of competence involves a learning experience which is essentially different in nature and method from habit formation. With reference to the third assumption underlying the quoted statement, it has been shown repeatedly that it is the *what* as much as it is the *how* of data dissemination which helps establish a dynamic communicative relationship between a buyer and a salesman. Moreover, the relevance of the data disseminated by the salesman is some function of the *buyer's* conceptual framework and only indirectly of the frameworks of either the salesman or the sales manager.

In any case, this level of competence does not exhaust the salesman's *potential* competence. In some respects, the use of completely packaged sales presentations relegates the salesman to a level only slightly above a wandering advertisement, and while the method may "work" in certain cases, the salesman and his sales presentation are hardly the most important ingredients.

Level 3: Instrumental Performance

This level of competence involves a coherent communicative

performance on the part of the salesman. The primary difference between the adaptive and the performance levels of competence lies in *the inclusion of individual goals as standards for performance implementation and assessment.* In many respects, the performance level of competence signifies managerial ability on the part of the salesman. As a communicator he chooses his own approaches and is capable of varying these substantially, depending on the specific buying system. Yet, the fact that his own goals are involved ensures not merely adaptive behavior but also purposive behavior.

From an organizational point of view, the performance level involves less directive control and a greater degree of reliance upon the salesman's ability to develop and maintain a set of accounts. It was shown in Chapter X that with reference to any given buying system, two categories of communication enablers and barriers can be identified. The first of these is termed metacommunicative facilitators or barriers and encompasses the overriding cultural, social, and functional or economic opportunities and constraints which exist in any intercommunicative relationship. The second category of communication enablers and barriers is termed communicative facilitators and constraints and encompasses the perceived utility for either participant of any intercommunicative encounter.

With reference to a salesman's competence, each of these two categories of enablers and constraints implies a criterion (or a set of criteria) for selecting buying systems as potential accounts. The performance level of competence involves the salesman's selection of selling approaches on the basis of his judgment concerning available communicative facilitators, or utilities and disutilities in any given relationship. The salesman is thus capable, of not only delivering a set of messages, but also of selecting a communicative approach which will "optimize" the possible outcomes of any given relationship. The competence involved here pertains to an ability to operationalize the objectives of the selling function with respect to the buying system by developing, changing or maintaining a relationship between the qualities of the buying system and the utilities of the products involved.

Level 4: System Integration

While Level 3 competence involves ability to optimize the outcome of any given interaction, Level 4 competence involves ability to select an optimal set of buying systems: that is, to develop a system of contacts or relationships with buying systems on the basis of organizational objectives and with reference to metacommunicative (i.e., higher order) criteria. The salesman who seeks to become a member of the community in which he operates, to develop personal contacts, and otherwise to take into account the importance of social relationships is essentially operating on the system level of competence. So is the member of top management who puts on his salesman's hat and plays a round of golf with a prospective buyer.

The problem involved in matching salesmen and buying systems is generally "solved" in literature and practice by developing and implementing a set of rules for assignments (market segmentation). Some of the criteria frequently used are:

1. *Geographical.* Salesmen are assigned to geographical areas and are required to cover all relevant buying systems within that area.
2. *Type of Product.* Salesmen are assigned a given product or product class, and consequently several salesmen may visit a given buying system.
3. *Type of Situation.* Salesmen are specialized with reference to new accounts (development sales) and existing accounts (maintenance sales).[3]
4. *Type of Account.* Salesmen are specialized on the basis of a functional differentiation of buying systems.

Each of these rules for assigning and specializing salesmen is based on a specific set of assumptions about the role of salesmen. The geographical or territorial assignment of salesmen is perhaps the most popular, and several techniques have been developed around the problem of measuring selling effectiveness across inherently dissimilar territories.[4] The territorial assignment enables the salesman, if given sufficient time, to develop a network of contacts and relationships with existing and prospective customers. Assignment on the basis of product or product class is primarily justified on the basis of very complex products or product concepts, while specialization on the basis of type of situation has been justified with reference to differences in required communicative skills. Specialization on the basis of functional differentiation of buying systems is justified on the basis of differences in the buyer's requirements attributable to the organizational or environmental peculiarities of the buying system. Each of the above specialization criteria may, of course, be supplemented by one or more of the others. Thus, for example, salesmen may be specialized with reference to type of account and type of product or product class.

Any criterion of specialization will undoubtedly have certain advantages, *but the very existence of an essentially arbitrary rule is also bound to have serious disadvantages.* The fact that it has been found in many cases that a large part of the sales force produced only a small percentage of the sales of a given company[5] is evidence of a certain inflexibility in the selection and maintenance of relationships between sellers and buyers. A salesman who specializes with reference to a given product is less likely to take into account the peculiar organizational aspects of a buying system than one who specializes on the basis of class of trade or type of account.

As pointed out consistently in this study, the primary function of personal selling is to establish a viable communicative relationship between the selling organization and a relevant set of buyers. Within the broad economic and functional parameters imposed by the size and product strategies of selling and buying systems, the consequences of any given relationship are partly dependent upon the strategic and tactical capacities of the personal selling function. The competence required here is not exclusively one of product or technical orientation, nor is it, of course, determined by the geographical location of the buying system. The required competence is primarily communicative and comprises the salesman's ability to take into account and influence significant elements of the buying system's environment, or significant elements of the internal structure of the buying system. These elements may be psychological, functional, economic, social, or cultural (i.e., they are ultimately conceptual) depending upon the state of the buying system.

Ideally, then, the salesman is not a specialist in the usual technical sense of that word; *he is a generalist capable of playing many roles while relying on organizational backing for more specialized competencies.* Performance on this level is not only a question of training, but also a question of organizational status and function, a concept which will be further explored in Chapter XV.

Level 5: Value Integration

Ultimately, the effectiveness of a salesman is dependent upon the degree to which his personal values and purposes can be integrated with those of the organization. The growing tendency to refer to a "professional" salesman is perhaps evidence that the importance of this value integration is being recognized. Yet, the serious deprivation of self-determination accorded many salesmen, beyond the most elementary activities, has contributed greatly to the decrease in prestige which the personal selling function has experienced in recent decades. One of the factors influencing the high turnover of salesmen, the aversion of college students to selling careers, and the clamor among salesmen for advancement into managerial position is a basic desire for a responsible function. As Peter Drucker has said:

In a time of change and challenge, new vision and new danger, new frontiers and permanent crisis, suffering and achievement, in a time of overlap such as ours, the individual is both all-powerless and all-powerful. He is powerless, however exalted his station, if he believes he can impose his will, that he can command the tides of history. He is all-powerful, no matter how lowly, if he knows himself to be responsible. [6]

If the future of personal selling is to make any difference, the trend must be toward greater competence and higher involvement than has been evidenced in the past. While the simple data dissemination can be accomplished both efficiently and effectively by mass communicative means or intercompany electronic links, the change-agent function must still be accomplished by people. These people must be capable of communicating with other people, not as duplicators of electronic equipment and advertising, but as consultants and change agents providing viable, dynamic links between buyers and sellers. Moreover, the solution to the problem of the prestige of personal selling as an occupation cannot be solved by means of semantics. That is, it is not a matter of revising titles from salesmen to territory or resident managers. *Responsibility without authority is as ineffective and frustrating as competence without responsibility.* An individual's full involvement in and contribution to the performance of any occupation is contingent upon the degree to which he perceives that occupation as conferring function and status upon him as an individual.

SUMMARY

The purpose of the present chapter has been to outline an application of the COMPACT model to the role of the salesman as a communicator at the interface of buying and selling systems. The primary distinguishing characteristic of personal as compared with nonpersonal data dissemination is the dynamic two-way interaction of the participants. Consequently, the salesman is first and foremost a communicator subject to the metacommunicative and communicative facilitators and constraints inherent in human relationships.

The general functional elements of the salesman's performance were outlined as follows:

Phase 1: Awareness of job requirements and allocation of of resources to the perceived task.

Phase 2: Acquisition of required skills and information to meet the perceived requirements of the task.

Phase 3: Establishment of a communicative relationship with a specified set of buying systems.

Phase 4: Harmonization of the individual's self-concept and job performance.

Phase 5: Internalization of and commitment to a specific level of performance.

These action components may be acted out at different levels of competence. The actual level of competence at which a salesman operates partly depends on the effectiveness of available

training procedures, and partly upon the responsibility and authority accorded him by the organizational framework. Five distinct
levels of competence were outlined and discussed. In the following
two chapters, the implications of the COMPACT framework will
be examined with reference to selection, training, and compensation. In Chapter XV a discussion of the enabling and limiting factors of the organizational framework will be presented.

XIII

Selection and Training
of the Salesman

THE PECULIAR NATURE of the personal selling function as an intermediary between utility-producing and utility-consuming entities gives rise to a set of problems which perhaps is unique in the business world. There appears to be general agreement that the personal selling function is an important one, but there is controversy about the nature of this importance. On one side are those who justify the personal selling function in terms of its economic implications for the welfare of society, while others seek to justify it on the basis of its superiority over other elements of the marketing mix, with primary reference to the competitive strengths it affords one company over other companies in the same or similar industries.

The primary emphasis in this volume is on the *cooperative* rather than the *competitive* view of the strengths and weaknesses of the personal selling function. Clearly, personal selling is a factor in the competition between individual firms in the same industries, but defeat of competitors' purposes is not necessarily a useful objective nor criterion of effective performance of the personal selling function.

From a strategic point of view, *the function of personal selling is to promote the potential commonalities between sellers and buyers, whatever their position in the distribution channel.* This objective may, of course, have as its by-product the defeat of competitors' purposes, but it is reached by means of a cooperative relationship with buyers rather than by means designed solely for the purpose of one-upmanship over competition. In any case, since competitive claims are seldom interpreted similarly by buyers and sellers, their effect depends on the degree to which they influence the buyer's knowledge about available alternatives. It is on the basis of this knowledge that a salesman must relate to buyers for the purpose of advancing his conceived objectives.

The outline in the previous chapter of the potential competencies of the salesman provides a perspective in which to view the various aspects of sales management: selection, training, and compensation of individual salesman as well as the strategic development of the selling function. The purpose of the present chapter is to explore the nature of selection and training problems in light of the COMPACT model; in the following chapter the problems of compensation and measurement of effectiveness will be discussed.

SELECTION, TRAINING, AND COMPENSATION
AS ELEMENTS OF A SYSTEM OF ACTION

As an autonomous information and decision system, the salesman provides a *potentially* flexible and dynamic communicative link between the selling and buying systems. Thus, he ideally should be able to link conceptually the buying and selling systems as well as retain a balance of commitments with which he, as an individual, can operate effectively.

Selection, training, and compensation are two-way processes, the effectiveness of which depends upon their relevance to the objectives of the task and to the competencies and standards of the salesman. If the relationship between a selling organization and a salesman is considered as a system of action, the following functional phases (or categories of action components) obtain:

Phase 1: Awareness on the part of salesmen and sales management of job requirements in terms of communicative ability and organizational objectives. What function is the salesman to perform and at what level of competence?

Phase 2: Acquisition or recruitment and selection of the desired number and quality of salesmen.

Phase 3: Training of new and existing salesmen with reference to the requirements of both buying and selling systems.

Phase 4: Evaluation and measurement of effectiveness of relevant performances.

Phase 5: Development and maintenance of a system of compensation and other rewards as they relate to both organizational and individual interests.

The criteria utilized in the selection process must be dependent upon the level of competence required as well as upon the outcome of the choice between selecting already trained versus potentially trainable salesmen. The cost involved in training salesmen may be a sufficient reason for an organization with a relatively small sales force to attempt to find fully trained salesmen. On the other hand, the possibility of recruiting salesmen with training relevant for the specific sales situation of a given organization is often difficult and expensive, quite apart from the problems involved in having little or no control over and knowledge about the competence of salesmen trained by another organization.

The diagram shown in Figure 24 represents a generalized application of the COMPACT model to the selection, training, and compensation system of action. The remainder of this and the following chapter are devoted to a discussion of various elements outlined in this diagram.

PHASE 1: AWARENESS OF JOB REQUIREMENTS

A prerequisite for any selection, training and compensation program is an awareness of the role or task the salesman is to perform. This basic awareness and the resultant job descriptions are all too easily confused, however, by a failure to discriminate among the several levels of concepts involved. In general, job requirements, with reference to the personal selling function, may be considered on the basis of one or more of the following viewpoints or levels of concepts:

Level 1. The physical requirements of a given task. This is the "things to do" approach from which derives the notions of required appearance, mechanical dexterity, and verbal acumen of the salesman.

Level 2: The adaptive requirements of a given task. At this level the concern is with the range and typology of situations which the salesman is likely to encounter. Attempts have thus been made to match job requirements and individual psychological traits.

Level 3: The performance requirements of a given task. At this level job requirements are defined in terms of the function or role the salesman is required to fill. The concern here is primarily with the purposes of the salesman's activities rather than with a specification of these activities as such.

Level 4: The integrative or systemic requirements of a given task. At this level job requirements are expressed in terms of the relationship between the selling organization and some specified category of buyers.

Level 5: The strategic requirements or the value dimensions of a given task. That is, the extent to which the salesman must be potentially or actually capable of determining the strategically most effective use of his time and competence.

Clearly, the more detailed the job description, the more circumscribed the salesman's activity; the more specific the

FIGURE 24

A Compact Outline of Selection, Training, and Compensation

——— Direction of Competence ———→

Flow of action	Level 1 Activity	Level 2 Behavior	Level 3 Performance	Level 4 System	Level 5 Values
Awareness of job requirements	Awareness and definition of "things to do"	Awareness and description of range of situations	Awareness and definition of salesman's function	Awareness and definition of salesman's role within marketing mix	Awareness and definition of strategic implications of marketing mix
Acquisition or selection criteria	Physical appearance	Psychological traits or typology	Relationship of individual's goals to goals of selling function and	Diagnostic and communicative abilities of salesman	Individual's capacity for responsible behavior
			ability and willingness to learn		
Goal seeking or training	Memorization and rehearsal of a "canned" sales presentation	Specification and teaching of behavior rules	Various participative training methods (case discussion, role playing, and T-group) directed toward developing both strategic and tactical communicative competence		
Harmonization or evaluation of performance	Effectiveness of the sales presentation and efficiency of the individual	Effectiveness of behavior and efficiency of individual	Effectiveness of performance	Effectiveness of integrated system of approach	Effectiveness of strategic direction of system of approach
Commitment or compensation criteria	Efficiency in performing prescribed activities	Efficiency in and ability to perform prescribed roles or behaviors	Relationship between individual and organizational goals	Relationship between individual managerial ability and organizational goals	Ability of individual to relate organizational goals to cultural and social environment

job description, the less reliance on the salesman's competence. In this sense it appears that job descriptions and selection techniques are often combined as an alternative to training. While such an approach may "work" in certain cases, it hardly does justice to the full competence, actual or potential, of individual salesmen.

PHASE 2: ACQUISITION OR SELECTION PROCEDURES

The problems involved in recruiting potential salesmen are undoubtedly greatly influenced by the nature of generally held expectations and stereotypes. Perhaps no other occupation has been subjected to quite so much amateur analysis and pseudo-psychology as personal selling, without moving one step closer to an understanding of the problems and influences involved. The function or purpose of personal selling is only vaguely defined, if known at all, as compared with, for example, the accounting function. The basic assumption held by many writers and practitioners that the salesman is essentially an intruder, a nuisance, and a fast talker, has perhaps contributed more to the unfavorable stereotype of personal selling than any other single factor.

In any case, it is highly likely that companies obtain the recruits they bargain for. A company which becomes known for its high paid messenger boys, or order takers, rather than its competent and responsible salesmen will, in all likelihood, obtain recruits who are prepared and willing to become order takers. In many respects a certain circularity of behavior appears to have developed. Insecurity on the part of sales managers about their own ability to communicate leads to increasing emphasis on management and control which in turn leads to a decrease in the salesmen's competence requirements. As salesmen perceive the apparent unimportance of their jobs, performance falls off, leading to more management and control. This circular trend cannot be broken without substantial changes in the concept of the role of personal selling. Moreover, if this image of the salesman is not revised through some real changes in the concept and responsibilities of the job, companies will find themselves selecting progressively weaker salesmen from a decreasing number of applicants.

The Nature of the Problem
of Selection

Selection of personnel is perhaps the most controversial problem within the field of personal selling. Countless techniques ranging from rules of thumb to intricate psychological tests have been advocated as solutions to a problem which is only vaguely understood, even, one suspects, by the authors of the screening tests. This does not mean that psychological testing is necessarily useless as a technique of differentiating among individual applicants for a given job; on the contrary, many of these tests are constructed by serious scholars who meticulously test their instruments against a number of standards. On the other hand, no competent psychologist will maintain that any one or even a battery of tests will do more than differentiate among individuals with reference to certain characteristics.

The area of controversy however, is not centered differentiation among characteristics of individuals, but rather on the problem of establishing the relevance of these characteristics to the requirements of a given task. Numerous lists of "required" or "preferable" characteristics of the successful salesman have been tendered by writers on personal selling. Yet all such lists specify characteristics of *a primarily static* nature with little or no reference to the dynamic nature of the *relationship* between buyers and sellers. The search for a unique "sales type" appears to be based on the assumption that both the *buyer* and the *relationship* between the buyer and the salesman are definable in a never changing typological checklist. Attempts have, for example, been made to define tactical approaches to "types" of buyers or prospects (the "silent," the "procrastinator," the "overcautious," the "grouch").[1] It would appear, however, that such classifications have been made on the basis of observable behavior in specific situations, but the buyer who is silent in one situation may be talkative in another. In any case, personality characteristics of the above type constitute only one variable among many influencing the outcome of any interpersonal interaction.

Since the basic advantage of the personal selling function, as compared with other promotional tools, is the ability of salesmen to establish a dynamic and flexible relationship between selling and buying systems without the necessity of an analysis of mass markets or more specific forecasts of probable buyer behavior, the relevance of selection criteria must be established on the basis of a dynamic concept of that relationship. It was concluded in earlier chapters that the creation, modification, or maintenance of a relationship between sellers and buyers is essentially a communication process. Consequently, it is *the potential or actual competence of an individual to communicate which the various selection techniques must aid in establishing.*

It is important to keep in mind here the nature of the individual as an information and decision system. Psychological tests, for example, are one-way communication devices, apart, of course, from the impressions or stereotypes a candidate derives from a selection procedure based on tests. Since the applicant does not have comparable aids at his disposal, he thus must make *his* selection on the basis of advertisements, general stereotypes, and whatever information the personnel department may offer. The various selection techniques are in general designed to screen out those who do not conform to some predetermined "norm" or "role" based on the test designer's perception of the world. Whether or not personality traits bear any relationship to ability to achieve goals is still a highly controversial question. *The popularity of psychological tests is perhaps more a result of a feeling of uncertainty on the part of recruiters than of the relevancy of the data provided by these tests.*[2] In any case the validity of interpretations of test results are entirely a dependent on the interpreter's ability to assess the relationship between the job requirements and the competence of the applicant.

Several volumes have been produced on the topic of interviewing and application forms[3] and the purpose here is not to provide another set of forms. Whatever means are utilized in the process of selection the following constitute the minimum requirements of the process as a system of action:

Phase 2.1: Determination of the level of awareness of the candidate with reference to both general and specific job requirements. Past experience may or may not be indicative of awareness, nor does age bear any necessary relationship to awareness. The problem is primarily one of determining the kinds of data and messages which the individual considers important as opposed to those which he ignores. The individual who expects to be told what to do may show a tendency to ignore messages not originating with a superior, whereas the individual who expects to be able to act on his own may have a predilection against messages originating with a superior; *which individual is* actually chosen depends clearly upon the ability of the existing organization to compensate for the weaknesses while utilizing the strengths of the individual.

Phase 2.2: Determination of the willingness and ability of the individual to acquire new capacities. The majority of individuals are able to learn and acquire new behavior repertoires, but if the individual does not perceive the requirement for learning in terms of his perception of the job, the change influence required may well be beyond the capacities of a company training program. The existing capacity of the individual beyond a certain level becomes an important element of the selection process only if the company does not intend to provide training. Some executives report that they have had good results with high school graduates while others prefer to hire only university graduates. However, few high schools or universities provide specific or even general training in interpersonal communication and consequently ability and willingness to learn may be a more significant selection criterion than past achievements.

Phase 2.3: Determination of the goal structure of the individ-

ual. Much ink has been spilled in advocacy of money goals versus so-called subjective goals. It is highly unlikely that an individual will have only one specific goal which he pursues relentlessly. If an organization provides its rewards primarily through money it is clearly of some importance that its salesmen be interested in money as a goal. The organization which is prepared to be flexible in its reward structure, however, must make an attempt to determine the relevant goal structure of both its new and existing employees. There is no doubt that for many individuals money loses its primary goal position beyond a given standard of living, or, to put it another way, money as a communication medium carries only a limited amount of "meaning" for many individuals.

Phase 2.4: Determination of the individual's ability to harmonize the job requirements with his existing framework of standards and affiliations. This, as well as the previous requirements, can be considered on several levels. The obvious consideration is the individual's willingness and ability to live a salesman's life. Beyond the obvious, however, the job may have adaptive, performance and value requirements with which the individual is unwilling and unable to come to terms. On the other hand the specific job may not provide a sufficient outlet for the total spectrum of his competence and motivation. The organization which insists on hiring university graduates to perform sales jobs which do not require a sufficient outlet for the individual's perceived competence may, among other things, run into the problem of having to reward individuals for what they believe they can do, rather than for what they actually do.

Phase 2.5: Determination of the individual's ability and willingness to commit himself to the performance of a given task. The majority of people will develop a commitment to that concept or organization which they perceive as giving them status and function. The power and authority necessary for the management and coordination of organizational activities are entirely dependent upon the degree to which individual members commit themselves to the purpose and activities of the organization. The development of commitment is a two-way communicative process in the sense that the organization gives meaning to the individual efforts and the individual gives substance to the organizational framework.

The above five requirements of the selection process are outlined in general only, primarily because the specific situation must determine the level and content of these requirements (Figure 24). Similarly, the extent to which psychological testing

aids in establishing an applicant's profile within the competence-
activity matrix is primarily a function of the meaning the recruiter attaches to test results. If, for example, the recruiter
feels an "aggressive" and "dominant" salesman has a tendency
to: (1) be more aware, (2) be more willing to learn, (3) have a
simpler goal structure, (4) be better prepared to harmonize job
requirements, and (5) be more willing to commit himself, than a
salesman with some other personality configuration, then is
clearly justified in using his battery of tests. The quality of a
salesman is in any case a relative measure; consequently no test,
however elaborate, is any better than the sample upon which it is
constructed, combined with the constructor's ability to observe.

Selection and Training as
Alternative Strategies for the
Development of a Sales Force

The selection procedure utilized may be designed to achieve one
of two alternative results. It may be designed to select individuals
who are potentially capable of being trained as salesmen or it may
be designed to select individuals who are already trained. On the
basis of a general cost comparison it is not possible to prove con-
clusively that one approach is cheaper than the other.[4] In any
case, the failure of the general educational system to provide
training in communication skills dictates that some organizations
must train salesmen even though a few companies may depend
upon other companies' training programs as a source of trained
personnel.

In a rapidly changing environment, however, the use of selection techniques as an alternative stragegy to the institution of
training programs has several disadvantages which should not be
overlooked despite apparent savings. *Training, or learning, is an
ongoing process which the salesman may or may not be able to
negotiate on his own.* Even though the individual may be aware
of the requirement for continuous learning, the process is not a
simple one where each new piece of information is simply added
to the existing store of knowledge. Learning is an evolutionary and
integrative process involving both unlearning of some existing
knowledge and integration of some new knowledge before the individual can act upon the acquired behavior repertoire.

In this sense then, the existing competence of a given individual
salesman will act as both a bridge and a barrier to the acquisition
of new skills. The process of training or learning is essentially
one of communication designed to help the individual attain a
higher order of competence. The individual who operates on one
level of competence (e.g., the adaptive level) must go through
some learning process to attain the next higher level of competence (the performance level). To the extent that an organization

intends to utilize salesmen as order takers, relying on sales managers for higher level planning and decision making, the cost and effort of a full fledged training program may well be too high compared to the results actually derived from it.

If, however, an organization is dependent upon its salesmen for both the planning and the execution of an integrated personal selling function, or if an organization considers its salesmen as potentially promotable to managerial positions, an effective training program is not only preferable but a requirement. *Cases abound of salesmen who have been rewarded by being promoted to supervisors or sales managers and then failed miserably in the new assignment.* In terms of the COMPACT model, a good salesman may have attained a high degree of internalized competence with regard to a specific performance level. This internalized competence may be of little use and perhaps even a barrier against effective operation on a higher level of responsibility. The process of changing from one level of competence to another is thus a learning process involving unlearning of some previous, and integrating and internalizing new behavior repertoires.

PHASE 3: THE TRAINING PROCESS

The word training is often used in connection with two dissimilar kinds of processes. The first of these is based on the assumption that learning is a passive process. The bulk of "how to sell" literature as well as some company training programs are built on this assumption which relegates people to the role of sponges and places the means to the end in the forefront. It was shown however, in Chapter X that training is an intensified form of communication, consequently whatever learning experience occurs in the course of the training process is some function of the learner and not solely are of the teacher or the books with which the learner is confronted. This does not mean that one can do away with the trainer; on the contrary, he occupies an important helping role in the learning process. It does mean *that learning is ideally a participative process with both the salesman and the trainer learning from and influencing each other.* The learning process itself is influenced by the following elements: [5]

1. What the trainee brings to the situation;
2. What the trainer brings to the situation;
3. The objective or goal of the learning process;
4. The method used to bring about the learning process;
5. The method of evaluation of the training process.

Insufficient attention to the above requirements may easily preclude a learning experience. Clearly, each individual learner brings to the situation a background of past experiences and behavior repertoires which must be taken into account in determining both the content and method of learning. On the other hand, learning is not separate from the content of a training program. The problem is thus one of striking a balance among content, method, and past experiences rather than engaging in a dogmatic advocacy of one method or one set of materials versus another.

Phase 3.1: The Trainee's
Awareness

In a general sense the trainee brings to the training situation his accumulated past experiences, the elements of which are:

1. A certain level of awareness and perception of the training process and his own place in it, as well as a set of expectations concerning the benefits he is likely to receive from the process. *The resources which an individual is willing to allocate to the learning process will in large measure determine the outcome of the process.* In the case of nonvolunteers one of the first tasks of the training process may well be the development of such awareness.
2. An attitude toward the specific trainer or trainers in general and an internalized concept of learning in relation to himself. *The individual's attitudes toward the learning process and teachers may have either a positive or a negative influence on the learning process itself.* In general, learning is a disturbing experience to the individual primarily because it involves him in a change of his existing modes of thought and behavior. In the case of a negative attitude to trainer and learning, the trainer may have to "sell" both himself and the process to the individual learner.
3. A concept of a desired outcome of the learning experience and a set of expectations about the value of the exercise for the trainee.

    In general, it may be postulated *that individuals will accept a higher degree of responsibility for their own learning if the experience is related to their goal structure.* In a limited number of cases learning may take on a functional autonomy in itself and the individual will be learning for the sake of learning. In most cases, however, the learning experience is probably perceived as a means to an end. In such cases it is important that the individual's perceived purpose is recognized. Training for the sake of improving company profits may, after all, not ring a bell with the trainee unless he perceives a direct and purposive relationship between company profits and his behavior.

4. A certain ability and willingness to internalize the results of the training process. The process of learning involves the whole personality and is in no sense limited to the individual in the role of a salesman. Indeed, *the essence of a learning process is the transfer of new knowledge and behavior repertoires from an overt to an internalized state.* The achievement of this transfer may be a difficult and painful process which in any case involves the participation of the trainee. The process of internalization may break down for several reasons, such as the individual's attitude toward the usefulness of the content of the learning experience, his unwillingness and perhaps inability to change his existing framework, or lack of sufficient problem-solving competence with which to approach and understand the content of the training material.

5. A certain predisposition for or against committing himself to the outcome of the process. One of the real and yet largely unsolved problems in training and education is that of developing a reliable measure of the value of the learning experience. Theoretically, *learning has not occurred until the trainee has identified with or committed himself to the results of the experience.* The process of commitment is not a mere exercise in memorization but an identification and internalization of the acquired knowledge as a "useful" and "reliable" guide for future behavior. The test of commitment is the individual's ability to generalize the experience to new situations, a process which most existing testing methods are unable to measure.

The above brief outline is intended to draw attention to some of the more important aspects of the individual learner's problems in a training situation. There is no one way to overcome the barriers to a learning experience, but attention to possible problem areas may go a long way in avoiding an impasse and a consequent waste of both time and resources.

Phase 3.2: The Trainer's
Awareness

The second element of the training process is the trainer, and as in the case of the trainee, the relevant factors of the trainer's abilities and background may be considered within the context of the COMPACT model. Among the abilities and predispositions he brings to the situation are:

1. A certain level of awareness of himself, the training process, and the requirements of the trainees. *The trainer who is not consciously aware of the requirements of the*

trainees may easily fall back on a process of maintaining a "system or method of training" or perhaps even concentrate on making the trainees like him in some way.

A teacher who is always ingratiating, for example, may develop his students' dependence and admiration at the cost of their skill to learn. Or the teacher who equates agreement with esteem may indicate such anxiety in the face of *dis*agreement and work so hard to achieve agreement with his students that they soon learn it is more comfortable for everyone if they appear always in accord.[6]

2. A certain level of understanding of means and methods of training and their employment as well as a certain level of understanding of the subject matter. Quite frequently, the one-way message stream of the lecture fails more or less completely to communicate. Role playing may similarly fail to bring about a useful learning experience particularly if trainees end up acting out the trainer's expectations. In any case, *the primary purpose of any training process is change in the learner and not the acting out of any given teaching method.*

3. A certain perception of the goal of the learning process. Quite apart from the organizational goal relevant to the training process the trainer as an individual has goals which may be more or less influenced by professional considerations. The trainer may have a requirement for overt satisfaction of his goals by trainees or he may teach for the sake of teaching, that is, perceive his goal as achieved when a certain sequence of events has occurred. The learning process is often quite imperceptible in its slowness, despite the occasional occurrence of so-called "eureka" learning, and it may often be difficult for the trainer to get proof of his goal attainment. Consequently, *training process may easily degenerate into an exercise in satisfying the trainer's goal in some overt fashion unrelated to a genuine learning experience.*

4. A certain level of ability to bring about personal involvement of the trainees. In the words of James Clark:

It involves . . . the skill to respond to the student on the level at which he is talking. If he believes he is discussing a printed case and you believe he is simply projecting his own assumptions, perceptions, and feelings onto it, you had best engage him first at the level of the case, and only later introduce some further complexity, and then only tentatively. Else he will tend not to feel confirmed, will feel misunderstood, alone, anxious, and defensive.[7]

Just as the training process involves the total personality of the trainee, so does it involve the totality of the trainer's personality, and the participative nature of the process, if at all successfully achieved, should, in general bring about a learning experience for both trainer and trainee.

5. A certain level of commitment to the purpose and process of training. In this, as in the previous four elements, there are several possible levels at which the trainer can operate, *ranging from a commitment to a set of activities, to a commitment to a set of values.*

The preceding outlines of trainee and trainer participation process show the interactive nature of the training process. There is no "how to" description of training which can possibly cover all the contingencies, nor is there an absolute measure of success. Yet the effectiveness of the salesman as a communicator depends upon a training process which is capable of providing him with the necessary factual or technical knowledge as well as the communicative skills, verbal and nonverbal, on which his success is predicated.

Phase 3.3: The Objective of
the Training Process

Problems easily arise in the goal phase of the training process as a result of conflict between the several goals of trainers, trainees, and the organization. A training process which does not take into consideration these different goal orientations while attempting to coordinate them is likely to bog down in a situation consisting of alternate monologues between the participants. It is important, of course, to recognize that significant learning experiences cannot be legislated by managerial decree.

The nature of the organizational goals or metagoals of the training process will clearly depend upon the basic conception of the role of training. That is, if the role of training is conceived by trainers and management as primarily one of imparting information to trainees, then the goals of the process will differ from those governing a training process that is conceived as a means of influencing the trainees' conceptual frameworks. It is undoubtedly possible to train or condition individuals to do or say certain things in specified situations, but this places the trainer in the position of having to specify all or most of the situations which the salesman is likely to encounter.

A much more effective set of goals, which also is much more difficult to achieve relates to individual self-determination or ability to cope with a wide variety of communicative interactions without a detailed exposition of "how to behave." Warren G. Bennis suggests four central metagoals or values related to T-group or sensitivity training methods:

1. Expanded consciousness and recognition of choice: that is, the development of an ability to question generally accepted assumptions.

2. A "spirit of inquiry." That is, the development of a predilection to examine observable behavior; to ask "why."
3. Authenticity in interpersonal relations: that is, the development of an ability to relate to other individuals in
   terms of the several dimensions of interaction.
4. A collaborative conception of authority relationships: that
   is, the development of a predilection for self-control with
   reference to organizationally circumscribed relationships. [8]

While the values of metagoals suggested above are possible
overall outcomes of a participative training process, a more explicit set of training objectives might be outlined as follows:

1. Development of self-insight or increase of self-knowledge;
2. Development of an understanding of the conditions which
   inhibit interpersonal interaction (e.g., metacommunicative
   facilitators and barriers);
3. Development of an understanding of the process of interpersonal interaction (e.g., communicative facilitators and
   barriers)
4. Development of competence in diagnosing individual and
   organizational behavior. [9]

In any case, it is important that the goals of the training process be related to the organizational structure and objectives and
the resulting job requirements.

Thus the above should be taken as suggested goals only and not
as a set of normative or absolute objectives. Clearly, the individual
who has been subjected to training in diagnosing individual and
organizational behavior and subsequently finds himself restocking
supermarket shelves is liable to experience more than a minimal
amount of frustration as a result either of overtraining or under-
utilization.

Phase 3.4: Selection of
Training Methods

Training methods range from a provision of written materials for
study at the trainee's discretion to the use of the highly participative sensitivity training methods in the form of T-groups or other
open-end methods. Clearly, the choice of a specific training
method must be dependent upon the availability of resources and
the time limitations. On-the-job training, for example, has long
been considered an acceptable alternative in cases where cost
or time requirements of off-the-job training are considered too
high. The main limitation of on-the-job training, which essentially
involves a process of imitation, is the relatively narrow sample of
experience to which the trainee is normally exposed.

The choice of off-the-job training methods must be partly dependent upon the specific objective, and partly dependent upon the intended content of the training process. Certain factual knowledge, technical and procedural data, may be transferred by means of written materials or lectures. Salesmanship or ability to communicate, however, is not so easily imparted. Some of the available methods are briefly described below. The procedure involved, as well as the relative advantages and disadvantages of these methods have been treated at length in the literature, references to which will be found in the Bibliography.

1. The case method. The case discussion method offers a means of bringing trainees face to face with a complex problem situation without involving the expense associated with trial and error learning on the job:

Case methods involve the confrontation of people in training with concrete human situations, situations with some temporal and developmental span, in which a whole complex of determinants of behavior are at work. Trainees are asked to diagnose these situations, to analyze them in terms of why events happen as they do, why the people involved act as they do. If the trainees are asked to prescribe and test verbally alternative behaviors for managing the situation confronted, they are asked to do so in terms of the diagnosis made of the evidence available as to the dynamics of the situation, including the dynamics of the "manager" in it. Diagnosis and prescription are thus tied together in any adequate case analysis.[10]

No training method, however "realistic," will in and of itself bring about a learning experience, and the case method is no exception. *The most important element of learning is trainee participation* and the case method offers a means of fostering such participation and involvement. Learning is, however, ultimately dependent upon the trainee and not the method.

2. Role playing. Role playing as a training method lacks the direction and order which is inherent in case discussion by virtue of the case:

A major advantage of role playing as an educational method is that it can bring out data about human behavior and human relations which are not made available by more traditional methods. Written records or lectures may give a group useful data and may stretch the boundaries of the group's previous experience, but the data they bring is limited by the fact that it must always be presented to the group through the medium of words. They cannot provide the group with direct common experience of what is being talked about. Role playing, so to speak, caters to the whole person of the learner. He not only hears about a problem or tells about it; he *lives through it* by acting it out—he experiences it emotionally and then uses this experience to produce and test insights into the problem and generalizations about ways of dealing with it. [11]

Role playing as an educational technique easily loses its value if it is used primarily as a basis for judging "right" and "wrong" behaviors, *particularly if the evaluating criterion is the trainee's ability to satisfy a set of predetermined "answers."* The basic advantage of role playing is the opportunity it affords the trainee of improving his performance with reference to objectives that he himself has conceived, and in terms of the strengths and weaknesses apparent to him as an individual.

3. The T-group method. Perhaps one of the most open-ended training methods available is the so-called T-group or training group. Essentially, the training group method is designed to further the individual member's understanding of interpersonal interaction—not only by discussion of the topic as such, but by actual *interaction*. Normally, the T-group has no objective imposed upon it and consequently cannot be evaluated apart from the possible increases in mutual understanding and performance of the individuals involved.

Training goes well in a group setting because different individuals can provide widely varied resources for intelligent behavior change by any particular learner. Many different ideas about job innovations can emerge. Ingenious procedures for learning can be devised more quickly. There is greater possibility of penetrating, mistake-correcting analysis. In addition, because of group support, each person can hear and respond to group suggestions about his behavior which he might ignore if they were the suggestions of an outside expert or status figure.[12]

The primary value of the T-group, as well as of the previously outlined training methods, is the opportunity afforded the trainee to develop his interpersonal or communicative competencies. The choice of method must be made with reference to the existing capacities and preferences of trainer and trainees as well as the specific purpose of the training process.

4. Operational gaming. The concept and method of operational gaming or management games as applied to the development of strategic and tactical marketing and selling competence are still in the experimental stage. Operational gaming, which employs a computerized or manually operated model of a given organization or environment, affords trainees an opportunity to exercise and improve their analytical and decision making competence with the benefit of rapid feedback on the results of their decisions. Gaming can thus be described roughly *as combining the "reality" of the case method with the flexibility and change characteristics of role playing.*

In management games, the concentration on decision making produces many of the same advantages as do case studies. In both, there is great emphasis on the effective selection of information from a large mass of data, and its subsequent organization and analysis which result in the framing of alternate problem solutions. Both can be used to illustrate decision making under uncertainty or conditions of inadequate information. Both can be employed to give the trainee practice in the use of certain accounting or analytical tools such as budgeting and statistical analysis. Both require consideration of the possible responses which might be made by competitors to certain decisions, and expose the student to the different viewpoints of his classmates. *However, management games add two extremely important elements to the case study and approach—the objectivity of the feedback and the new use of the time dimension—*and these two factors are the key to the great potential effectiveness of this technique.[13]

Management games have been primarily applied to problems involving strategic decision making in a competitive environment. In view of efforts directed toward developing more and better models, however, there is no doubt that operational gaming eventually will be of significant utility in the improvement of salesmen's ability to recognize and deal with the various communicative facilitators and barriers which were discussed in Chapter X. Until such models have been developed, however, operational gaming must be seen as complementary to the case method, role playing, and T-group training methods.

Phase 3.5: Evaluation of the
Training Process

A training process can be evaluated at various levels, and it is important to keep in mind, and carefully distinguish among these levels. If the objective of the process is the trainee's memorization of certain technical information, various written tests may be sufficient to establish the effectiveness of the process. If, however, the objective is to impart various levels of communication skills, evaluation of the process is somewhat more difficult. *Basically, the evaluative criterion of any training process is subsequent performance.* Clearly, only the most elementary training processes can be evaluated on the basis of off-the-job performance on tests and examinations. The real and crucial measure of competence, existing and acquired, is the individual's *ability to interact and communicate in basically different situations.* This problem of measuring communicative or selling effectiveness will be discussed at some length in the following chapter.

SUMMARY

The purpose of the present chapter has been to structure the basic relationship between the salesman and the sales organization of which he is a part. The various aspects of this relationship were outlined as follows:

Phase 1: Awareness, on the part of salesmen and sales management, of job requirements in terms of communicative ability and organizational objectives. What function is the salesman to perform and at what level of competency?

Phase 2: Acquisition or recruitment and selection of the desired number and quality of salesmen.

Phase 3: Training of new and existing salesmen with reference to the requirements of both buying and selling systems.

Phase 4: Evaluation and measurement of effectiveness of relevant performances.

Phase 5: Development and maintenance of a system of compensation and other rewards with regard to both organizational and individual interests.

Each of these aspects of the individual salesman–organization relationship (of which only Phases 1 through 3 were discussed in this chapter) may be analyzed and influenced on several conceptual levels as outlined in Figure 24. The specific level applicable to any given organization will depend upon the existing organizational structure and the available resources available for the personal selling function.

The problems involved in the development of job requirements as well as selection and training objectives and methodology were discussed in the present chapter. In the following chapter the remaining two elements, measurement of effectiveness and development of a compensatory scheme, will be discussed.

Each of the above-mentioned elements: job description, selection, training, measurement of effectiveness, and compensation serves a specific purpose in the relationship between organization and individuals—and these purposes overlap only to a limited extent. Job description provides the setting or awareness of the general relationship, selection provides a given actual or potential ability to perform the specified task, and training provides a means to actualize potential or to maintain actual competence. *The measurement of effectiveness aspect comprises the means for relating individual efforts to organizational objectives, while compensation and reward structures comprise the means for relating organizational objectives to individual value structures.*

XIV

Measuring Sales Effectiveness
and Planning Compensation

IT WAS CONCLUDED in the preceding chapter that each of the elements — job description, selection, training, measurement of effectiveness, and compensation — represents a structural component of the relationship between a selling organization and its salesmen. A successful relationship over time is dependent upon the relevancy and consistency of the messages conveyed by each of these elements. The COMPACT model provides a framework for establishing the relative levels of these structural elements. As examples of extreme cases, the salesman who is required to deliver a preplanned message does not present the same problems in selection, training, and compensation as the salesman who is required to operate primarily on his own, tactically and even strategically.

It remains in the present chapter to examine Phases 4 and 5 of the individual-organization interface; namely, the problems of evaluating salesmen's performance and of developing an appropriate compensation scheme. The approach in this chapter as in preceding ones is to explore the *conceptual* implications of effectiveness and compensation, and to construct a general framework which a sales manager may use to develop the specific tools and methods which best serve his particular situation. Thus, the point here is not to prescribe a set of "things to do" with reference to the measurement of effectiveness and the development of compensation plans. While one sales manager may feel that gross profit derived from personal selling activity is a meaningful measure of effectiveness, the meaning he attributes to this measure is necessarily tempered by his experience with and knowledge about his product and industry. *What therefore is a meaningful measure to one man may be a mere column or row of figures to another.* Of course, concepts are not in themselves "right" or "wrong" but merely "useful" or "not useful;" and even a useful concept may lead the manager to doing the right things for the wrong reasons. Thus, the sales manager who plans and acts as if his salesmen were passive robots which must be screened, motivated and evaluated may be quite successful as a manager, not because of his concept or reasons, but because of the things he does. Similarly, of course, the "right" reasons may lead to the "wrong" activities.

In any case, the fact that a salesman achieves a predicted quota or sales goal is not necessarily an indication of his competence. There is no doubt, for example, that many salesmen obtain sales in spite of what they do rather than as a result of their activities. Similarly, sales managers may obtain results in spite of their activities rather than because of them.

It may be argued that if results are obtained it makes little difference what the underlying concepts are. Yet, since results depend on the collective competencies of the selling organization, the salesman, and the buying system, failure to take into account incapacities or incompetencies in one or more of these systems is likely to influence the conclusions derived from any measure of effectiveness. In other words, since results, or sales, depend upon the total performance of the selling organization-salesman-buying system chain, measurement of a salesman's performance must be based upon variables that are controllable by the salesman. The development of appropriate criteria and measuring scales is no easy task, but must nevertheless be attempted. Mere availability of certain quantitative data such as number of visits, sales, and profit are not in themselves adequate measures of effectiveness. Though number of calls made, time spent, and total expenses may be countable (and consequently compared and assessed) they are not necessarily operationally relevant. With reference to the measurement of effectiveness, it is useful to keep in mind that all that is countable does not necessarily count, and all that counts is not necessarily countable.

PHASE 4: MEASUREMENT OF EFFECTIVENESS AND EFFICIENCY

Within the context of the various organizational limitations over which the salesman has no control, his effectiveness is a direct function of his competence. *Efficiency* of the individual salesman is defined here as *that measure which relates his actual competence to the required competence as established by the general and specific requirements of buying systems and by the organizational structure within which the salesman operates.* This definition of efficiency differs from the normally accepted economic definition, stated in terms of sales-cost relationships, insofar as it explicitly takes into account the dimension of individual competence. Since the economic measure of efficiency combines sales obtained with, without, or in spite of the salesman's efforts it takes into account only implicitly the competence of the individual salesman.

A salesman's competence is not measurable in terms of a single variable, however much one may desire to simplify the measurement process. The number of variables to be taken into account is at least partly dependent upon the degree of control maintained by a sales organization. The more limitations an organization imposes upon a salesman's performance, the more irrelevant becomes his competence. This is so because a sales organization which determines the salesman's movements down to his detailed itinerary is in a sense replacing a significant part of the salesman's potential competence. The personal selling function, as will be shown in the following chapter, can be structurally organized so as to operate either by means of control or by means of training. The more effective and efficient method must be found by analyzing the strengths and weaknesses of the organization and the significant elements of the task to be performed.

In any case, the communicative competence of the salesman and, therefore, the problem of measuring his effectiveness does not become relevant until it can be clearly established that his competence makes any difference. If the salesman is merely handing out messages with little or no freedom to operate on his own, the relevant competencies must be found in the sales manager or the buying system.

The Problem of Measuring Individual Competence

The primary concern here is with the process of evaluating individual competence, the elements of which were outlined in Chapter XII. Although competence and action can be differentiated conceptually, it is through the quality of the latter that competence must be defined and measured. As indicated in the previous chapter, there are still some real doubts about the ability of psychological tests, whether personality, aptitude, or intelligence tests, to predict reliably the dynamics of an individual's performance from an essentially static assessment of individual characteristics. The primary reason for this must be found in the nature of communicative interactions. The outcomes of communicative *interaction are neither exclusively a function of the communicator or sender nor are they exclusively a function of the receiver, but they are codetermined by the qualities of both sender and receiver and the specific properties or circumstances of the communicative transaction.*

The state of the art with reference to the measures of effectiveness thus dictates that individual competence be inferred from observable performance. Basically, this observational procedure can be divided into the following structural elements:

Phase 1: Awareness of a set of relevant criteria for the assessment of competence on the basis of an observation of performance.

Phase 2: Acquisition of relevant information in terms of the specified criteria and feasible action for improvement.

Phase 3: Development of a competence pattern for each salesman with reference to the significant aspects of his task.

Phase 4: Organization of communication channels and lines of authority to compensate for existing strengths and weaknesses of both the salesman and the aggregate sales force with regard to the task to be performed.

Phase 5: Commitment to a given evaluation procedure for the purpose of maintaining consistency of feedback and measurement.

Figure 25 outlines the criteria for assessment of an individual salesman's competence. The following discussion is centered on the COMPACT model and its possible application to the development and implementation of evaluative procedures.

Phase 4.1: Awareness of a set of relevant criteria. The competence of a salesman relfects his conceptual and physical abilities to perform a given task. Competence and success, however, are related only insofar as success constitutes a measurement of the salesman's ability to *achieve the goals and objectives he sets for himself.* In other words, the *measure* of communicative competence is the degree to which an information and decision system can achieve a self-approved goal vis-à-vis other information and decision systems. Sales results, however, measured, basically represent the combined competencies of the selling organization and its salesmen to help buying organizations or buyers sell themselves. That is, sales are a result of both the *existing* or inherent as well as the *created* mutuality among the participating systems.

The criteria for evaluating a task can be classified in terms of the COMPACT model. The five resulting levels of criteria are (Figure 25):

Level 1: Physical activity or efficiency criteria. That is, the appearance of the salesman, number of calls made, number of presentations made, amount of time spent with buyers and amount of expenses over a given time period. Essentially, these criteria are related to the "busyness" of the salesman, but not necessarily to the quality, effectiveness and efficiency of his efforts.

Level 2: Adaptive behavior criteria. That is, the salesman's ability to adapt to different buying situations. Given certain products or services, can the salesman be expected to understand differences in a given range of buying situations clearly enough to provide a message sufficiently relevant to a given buying system to be persuasive? Persuasive ability is not a mere function of verbal acumen,

FIGURE 25

Summary of the Proposed Set of Criteria for Performance Evaluation

Direction of Individual Competence ⟶

Direction of Organizational Control ⟶

Action components	Objects of orientation	Level 1 Activity	Level 2 Behavior	Level 3 Performance	Level 4 System	Level 5 Values
Level of awareness of:	Buying system Selling system Selling task Product or service	Awareness of objects and their physical extensions. High degree of control provided or required	Awareness of psychological typologies. Organization determines behavior rules	Awareness of functional or utility concepts of the various interacting systems	Awareness of social and affiliative influences upon relevant systems	Awareness of moral or strategic value implications of the selling function
Ability to acquire information and analyze	Buying system Selling system Selling task Product or service	Information acquisition with reference to immediately observable data	Information acquisition with reference to observation of psychological typologies	Ability to analyze systems with reference to functional or utility concepts and implications	Ability to analyze systems with reference to implications of social relationships	Ability to analyze and predict strategically relevant implications of the selling function
Ability to attain goal with reference to:	Buying system Selling system Selling task Product or service	Goal seeking with reference to the performance of certain activities	Goal seeking with reference to the performance of certain behaviors	Goal seeking with reference to the optimization of product and service utilities	Goal seeking with reference to the establishment of a communicative relationship	Goal seeking with reference to the strategic relevance of participating systems
Ability to harmonize requirements with reference to:	Buying system Selling system Selling task Product or service	Harmonization on the basis of physical requirements and standards	Harmonization on the basis of psychological requirements and standards	Harmonization on the basis of functional requirements and standards	Harmonization on the basis of affiliative requirements and standards	Harmonization on the basis of value of strategic requirements and standards
Level of commitment to:	Buying system Selling system Selling task Product or service	Commitment to a set of physical activities	Commitment to a set of behavior rules	Commitment to a set of functional or utility standards	Commitment to a set of affiliative or social interaction standards	Commitment to a set of moral or strategic values

but first and foremost a function of ability to size up and
adapt to a given set of buying systems.

Level 3: Instrumental performance criteria. That is, a set of
criteria based on a concept of ability to pursue a given
goal without the requirement for intermittent control and
direction. Has the salesman developed a system of selling
or communicating which enables him to influence significantly buying systems or certain elements of buying systems? This level of competence involves an ability to size
up systems creatively and constructively for the purpose
of offering guidance in problem solution. Since the buying
system may want to consider alternative solutions, the
salesman, at this level of competence, should be aware of,
and willing to discuss, the merits of competitive products.

Level 4: System integration criteria. That is, a set of criteria
pertaining to the salesman's competence to integrate a
variety of performances and behaviors and bring them to
bear on a given problem situation. Is the salesman capable
of operating as a change agent? That is, can he analyze a
buying system, point out potential and actual problems,
develop feasible alternative solutions, create awareness,
and help the buying system sell itself on the requirement
for a solution to such problems?

Level 5: Value integration criteria. That is, criteria based on
a concept of competence to perform the total selling job
from selecting potential buying systems to relating a given
product or service to a specific problem within that buying
system. Performance at this level involves the salesman's
commitment to the strategic or metagoals of the organization and his ability to relate his own value structure to
these goals.

The purpose of competence or performance evalution, with
reference to the individual salesman, must be to establish some
concept of his ability to achieve certain objectives with respect to
specified buying systems *in terms of criteria which can be translated into specified training and control requirements.* The dynamic and multidimensional nature of this salesman–buyer
interaction precludes the use of sales as a measure of competence
and effectiveness with reference to the performance of an *individual salesman.* A low sales attainment by a salesman may be indicative of a serious problem, but neither the nature of the problem
nor its solution can be established without an understanding of the
structure and function of the communicative interactions comprising the personal selling task. Also, as will be shown in the
following chapter, the information and control network of a personal selling organization will be dependent upon the relative
competence of salesmen and sales managers. The sets of criteria
used in the assessment of performance thus *should be related*

*partly to the job requirements and partly to the degree to which
the organizational structure has been designed to compensate for
planning and decision making by salesmen.*

*Phase 4.2: Acquisition of relevant information for evaluative
purposes.* The process of assessing a salesman's competence
to perform a given task is a subjective one involving observation
and inference. The observer, whether a sales supervisor or an
outsider, has several options when observing an interaction among
two or more individuals:

1. He can attempt to record everything he sees and hears, and
   attempt to describe performance on the basis of the activity
   he observes.
2. He can attempt to distill his impressions about the kinds
   and qualities of behavior exhibited. Since a process of influence is involved the question is one of establishing the
   relevance of the salesman's behavior in view of the buyer's
   actions as perceived by the observer.
3. He can conjecture as to what he thinks was achieved in the
   interaction and which of the participants were instrumental
   in achieving it.
4. He can attempt to judge the interaction with reference to
   the degree to which the outcome is satisfactory in view of
   the apparent objectives of the participants.
5. He can attempt to evaluate his impressions about the strategic effectiveness of the interaction and the degree to
   which the interaction was relevant to the apparent outcome.

If the above outline is considered as points on a scale, the
points essentially constitute successively higher levels of inference with reference to a set of observable data. As an integral part
of the evaluation process, the observer himself possesses a competence level which will influence the outcome of the evaluation,
and different observers will tend to come to different conclusions
about an individual's competence on the basis of their respective
interests and orientations. A salesman considered competent by
his sales supervisor may appear a complete novice to the engineer or the production technician who are concerned primarily
with product knowledge. Similarly, the sales manager's image of
a good salesman may differ in some essential aspects from the
buyer's image of the same individual.

Although the majority of sales managers are aware of this
"subjectivity" of observation a great many evaluation programs
fail to specify the level and content of the salesman's relevant
competence. Salesmen who are never called upon to do any more
than make predigested presentations are evaluated on characteristics and competencies ranging from personal appearance to
"marketing planning," although perhaps only a few of these

salesmen are ever called upon to exhibit any more than the most elementary competence.

It is important to keep in mind the multidimensionality of competence. As an example, "listening ability" is occasionally listed as a characteristic which a competent salesman must possess. Some of the dimensions involved in the ability to listen have been investigated with reference to the psychotherapeutic profession which in certain respects resembles the selling "profession":

If it is true that the therapist has to avoid reacting to the patient's data in terms of his own life, this means that he must have enough sources of satisfaction and security in his nonprofessional life to forego the temptation of using his patient for the pursuit of his personal satisfaction or security. If he has not succeeded in getting the personal fulfillments in life which he wanted and needed, he should realize this. His attitude toward the sources of dissatisfaction and unhappiness in his life must then be clarified and integrated to the extent that they do not interfere with his emotional stability and *with his ability to concentrate upon listening to the patient.*[1]

Ability to listen is thus not a characteristic that is measurable apart from such dimensions as the satisfaction which the salesman, as an individual, derives from his function, the social and organizational pressures upon the salesman, and his conceptual and interpersonal competence. From an observer's point of view, a salesman may be listening whenever he does not speak, but his listening may have results ranging from merely hearing what is said to the achievement of understanding on the basis of which action may proceed. There is reason to believe, for example, that a salesman who does not perceive his goals and aspirations satisfied with respect to the selling organization, may seek to achieve what might be termed "communicative satisfaction" with respect to the buying systems. Such a situation may involve the salesman's efforts to "make people like him," or it may involve the salesman's exercise of unwarranted authority in the face of perceived excessive organizational control. Thus the selling organization, its salesmen, and its prospective buyers may become involved in a self-defeating round of misdirected efforts, frustrations, and transferred aggressions.

Individual competence and communicative effectiveness are thus not isolated phenomena and, consequently evaluation of a salesman's performance will remain a subjective undertaking for a long time to come. On the other hand, most normal individuals are capable of evaluating both their own and others' performances in general terms. That is, the majority of, if not all, sales managers *intuitively* "know" a good salesman when they see one. Unfortunately, since it is not yet possible to define explicitly a good performance, within the context of a structural framework such as the COMPACT model, intuition still remains an important ingredient in the process of evaluating performance.

Countless attempts have been made to verbalize the intuitive aspects of performance appraisal, presumably on the basis of the assumption that if something can be named, it can be understood. A list of fifteen words taken from a number of existing evaluation "inventories" is shown below. While the lists differ from company to company, variations are generally slight:

Appearance	Patience	Empathy
Verbal Ability	Dependability	Ego Drive
Initiative	Stability	Enthusiasm
Imagination	Resistance	Aggressiveness
Ambition	Flexibility	Judgment

Apart from the fact that many of the above terms are difficult to define operationally, such characteristics are not likely to be exhibited by the competent salesman in all situations and certainly do not exist apart from the psychological, functional, social, and cultural aspects of a dynamic communicative interaction. A salesman may fail to exhibit aggressiveness or initiative either because he does not possess such characteristics, or because he perceives them as being detrimental to the achievement of his objectives in some specific situation.

The important point here is *that the competent salesman does not necessarily exhibit a specifiable set of characteristics in some regular fashion.* As stated repeatedly, competence is not a measure of a salesman's ability to reproduce faithfully a specific set of behaviors. On the contrary, it is a measure of the salesman's ability to relate communicatively to a set of more or less diverse buying systems.

Phase 4.3: Development of a pattern of individual competence. Given the subjective nature of performance evaluation, how is it possible, then to achieve relevancy and consistency in evaluation? Since it is never possible, of course, to achieve complete agreement on a given individual's performance quality, it is necessary for the sales manager to decide which and how many viewpoints he wants to take into account for the purpose of rating selling performance. Repeated rating of salesmen by only one person, the supervisor for example, may well produce consistency of appraisal, but it will not necessarily ensure the accuracy of the evaluation. Consequently, the process of acquiring both relevant and consistent information about performance quality begins with a choice of appropriate information souces.

The basic determinants of the outcome of any personal selling interaction are:

1. The structure and competencies of the specific buying system involved.
2. The structure and competencies of the selling organization.

3. The competencies of the individual salesman.
4. The nature of the potential transaction as established by the product or service concepts and utilities involved with regard to the above systems.

There are thus, at least four basic orientations or objects in terms of which any specific salesman's performance competence may be considered. The diagram shown in Figure 25 (page 246) outlines a set of evaluation criteria with reference to the four objects listed above and the five categories-of-action components at each of the proposed five levels of competence. It should be noted that Figure 25 combines and abridges much of the discussion in Part Three of this volume. It is also important to keep in mind that the level of competence *actually* exhibited by a salesman is partly dependent upon the extent of organizational enablers and constraints. Some of the problems inherent in the interaction between organizational control and individual competence will be discussed further in Chapter XV.

Each of the four objects included in Figure 25 represents a specific viewpoint or orientation on the basis of which competence may be determined. Ideally, each rating, whether with respect to an object or a category of action components, should be made by the individual or individuals most competent to evaluate the salesman's knowledge of a given subject. Thus, the production engineer might rate the salesman's product knowledge, buyers could rate the salesman's knowledge of buying systems, and the sales manager or supervisor or trainer should rate the salesman's competence within terms of the selling organization and its requirements. Similarly, the salesman should be given an opportunity to rate, not necessarily his own performance as has occasionally been suggested, but the various elements of his task with respect to himself as an individual.

In many cases such a broad approach to the evaluation process is not used. The salesman's performance is rated by one individual, usually the supervisor, across all of these qualities and the result is fed back to the sales manager. The latter must then attempt to judge the salesman on a combination of data which partly pertains to the salesman's competence as a salesman and partly to the supervisor's competence as an evaluator.

An increase in the number of evaluators does not, of course, eliminate the bias introduced by any one observer's capacity or incapacity to evaluate. Nevertheless, more points of view can provide the sales manager with a pattern or profile of the salesman's competence which is at least related to the individuals and products with which the salesman must deal. In addition, such broader evaluation should reveal the salesman's possible strengths and weaknesses in terms which are operational in the sense that something can be done about them. While the salesman who is weak on product knowledge can be more readily educated, the

salesman who is weak on aggressiveness or stability is not as
amenable to this alternative and may eventually end up being re-
leased or transferred.

The purpose of evaluation is, after all, not just to pass judgment on individuals or to classify them in all possible ways. The
central purpose must be to relate competence to some meaningful
and operational standards which can indicate corrective measures
to be taken in cases where existing competence falls short of the
required competence.

Phase 4.4: Organization of lines of authority and communication.
The role of management and organization in personal selling is not
a simple and clear-cut one. In an article entitled "Sales Managers
Must Manage," Raymond Loen makes the following statement:

> It is easy to confuse selling with managing because one who sells is expected
> to get sales results through customers and prospects. Selling is not man-
> aging, however. The essential difference is that a person in a managerial
> position has authority and responsibility to get a job done through others
> in the same organization—and these others are expected to recognize his
> authority and responsibility to help accomplish the over-all objectives of
> the enterprise.[16]

The writer's main point in the article from which the above
quote is taken, is that sales managers have a tendency to do the
salesman's job for him rather than act in a capacity of director
and coordinator of the salesman's activities. Authority and responsibility, however, are not inherent qualities of some specific
individual but are essentially functions of both the organizational
definition of interpersonal relationships and the relative competence of the individuals involved. Herbert Simon put it this way:

> An analysis of organized behavior of all sorts will demonstrate that such
> behavior results when each of the coordinated individuals sets for himself
> a criterion of choice that makes his own behavior dependent upon the be-
> havior of others. In the simplest cases he makes his own decision at each
> point as to what those adjustments should be. In slightly more complex
> forms of organization, *he sets himself a general rule which permits the
> communicated decision of another to guide his own choices* (i.e., to serve
> as a premise of those choices) *without deliberation on his own part on the
> expediency of those premises.*[3]

The frequently encountered "definition" of management as
"planning, directing, and coordinating" basically represents a
substitution of one set of words for another. There is no inherent
reason whatever why a salesman cannot plan, direct, and coordinate nor is there any reason why a manager cannot sell. The
purpose of an organization is not to exercise authority as such,
but rather to facilitate cooperation and organized behavior. To
achieve effectiveness and efficiency in an organization some attention must be paid to the coordination of the activities of *all* of

its members. In other words, the basic advantage of an organization with sales managers, supervisors, and salesmen occupying
different hierarchical positions lies in the degree to which these
complement each other and not in the degree to which they overlap.

In this connection, the purpose of evaluation procedures must
be to develop an awareness of the strengths and weaknesses of a
given sales organization so that compensatory measures can be
taken. The sales manager with a sales force which is strong on
planning but weak on customer contracts, may indeed find himself
making more contacts than the manager whose sales force is
strong on contact but weak on planning. This is not to say that the
former should or should not be selling. The creation and maintenance of an effective training program may prove, however,
both a more effective and a more efficient means of compensating
for weaknesses than the sales manager's or supervisor's direct
participation in the selling task.

The standards and values underlying organizational relationships are thus relative and no one specific system of information
or communication channels and lines of authority is applicable to
all organizations. Whether a given report from salesman to manager or a given instruction or list of procedures from the manager
to the salesman are necessary or unnecessary, is not solely a
question of operational relevance. In terms of the organization,
a given report may well appear operationally irrelevant, and yet
the specific individual receiving it may consider it quite useful.
The most effective organization, therefore, may not be the one
with the least "noise" in its communication channels, an assumption occasionally made by systems engineers. Indeed the multidimensional nature of interpersonal interaction makes it difficult,
and perhaps undesirable, depending on the competence of the
members, to develop more than a minimum of organizational
rules and standards with reference to communication and authority.

Phase 4.5: Commitment to a set of evaluative criteria. Individual
behavior constitutes a continually changing process which cannot
be evaluated once and for all. Periodic evaluation on the basis of
a framework such as the COMPACT model should indicate the
direction of change and so provide a basis for adaptation of organizational structure and administrative procedures. Evaluation of
a salesman's competence, as described in the previous section,
should lead to the emergence of a pattern of competence relating
the salesman's capacities and incapacities to the relevant aspects
of his position as a communicator between selling and buying systems. On the basis of such patterns, it should be possible to plan
and implement relatively specific improvement programs and
avoid subjecting the whole sales force indiscriminately to a
blanket training program. That is selective training and instruction becomes a possibility. Quite apart from the possible savings

involved in a selective training program, the indiscriminate sub-
jection of all salesmen to a training session "because it is there"
may create insurmountable communicative barriers to the occurrence of a learning experience.

If company support of salesmen's efforts is to have any practical significance, *training and control should be based on an evaluation procedure which is sufficiently general to be meaningful,
sufficiently relevant to make any difference, and sufficiently consistent to ensure detection of improvement.* It should be noted here
that detail in evaluation inventories is not necessarily a virtue.
Even though it is possible to classify individuals according to
dozens of personality traits, such detailed classifications are not
necessarily more meaningful and exact than evaluations based on
broader and less explicitly defined, but intuitively well understood classifications which represent total behavior processes.

PHASE 5: DEVELOPMENT OF COMPENSATION PLANS

Performance evaluation and compensation plans together make up
a two-way communicative relationship between an organization and
its individual members. Performance thus represents the individual's contribution to the organization and its purposes, while
compensation, as defined here, comprises the organization's
contribution to the individual's objectives. The results of a given
performance evaluation are not, of course, directly related to the
effectiveness of the existing compensation plan. Such results are
related to the level of individual competence to perform in the
specified environment, including the individual's willingness and
ability to take into account the communicative implications of a
compensation or reward structure.

Economic requirements constitute one basis for a relationship
between an individual and business organization. An individual
entering into an organizational relationship certainly does so with
a purpose in mind, even if it is nothing other than to make a living.
The more competent the individual, however, the more varied one
would expect his motivational framework to be and the more complex the individual's perception of the organizational reward and
penalty structure. The basic nature of a compensation or incentive
plan is, therefore, that of a communication medium which accommodates a certain set of messages, the meaning or communicative implications of which is some function of individual receivers—in this case, salesmen. In this connection, at least, the
following criteria are important in the development of a compensation plan:

*Level 1: The basic or minimum economic or resource re-
quirements of the individual.* This criterion may at first

glance appear to be obvious, but cases have been noted where salesmen were "promoted" to territorial or resident managers without receiving the necessary remuneration to meet the raised expectations of buyers and contacts.

Level 2: The psychological requirements of the individual. Incentives, or more generally, rewards and penalties, are partly dependent for their effect upon the psychological aspects of the individual personality system.

It is important to distinguish between rewards administered in relation to individual effort and performance and the system rewards which accrue to people by virtue of their membership in the system. In the former category are piece-rate incentives, promotion for outstanding performance, or any special recognition bestowed in acknowledgement of differential contributions to organizational functioning. The category of system rewards includes fringe benefits, recreational facilities, cost-of-living raises, across-the-board upgrading, job security, and pleasant working conditions.[4]

The point here is that there are certain idiosyncratic aspects of individual motivation and commitment which may render a general compensation plan ineffective. Moreover, the compensation or reward structure involved here is not limited to monetary payments, but may involve such individual requirements as security, approval, and confirmation of self-esteem.

Level 3: The functional relevance of reward structures. The utility of any given compensation structure is partly dependent upon the degree to which it rewards behavior relevant to the achievement of organizational goals.

Obviously, the value of a specific element or combination of elements [of a compensation plan] depends on the objectives sought: First the executive needs to have a clear idea of the tasks for which he wishes to compensate salesmen; otherwise he may share the experience of many other executives who have found the salesman resisting or failing to perform satisfactorily certain types of work for which the rewards provided by the plan are not sufficiently interesting to him. Next the problem is to determine what particular features will prove to be useful in attaining the particular objectives. [5]

The primary difficulty here is that the effects of any given reward structure can never be completely predetermined; nor are such effects necessarily obvious, even after the fact. The supervisor who keeps a sharp eye on expense accounts may, wittingly or unwittingly, reward the salesmen who manage to spend the least regardless of their effectiveness. Similarly, the retail store supervisor who prefers that sales personnel constantly "look busy" may get his preferences satisfied at the expense of effective and efficient customer service.

Level 4: The social or interpersonal implications of a reward structure. The extent to which an individual will accept and develop commitment to organizational objectives is partly dependent upon the degree to which he perceives his personal goals, with reference to social function and status or prestige, as being satisfied by the organization. A conflict easily arises here if both the limiting and enabling factors of social relationships are not carefully considered. The existence of certain social standards with reference to status and prestige enables the organization to attract and hold individual members by providing a reward structure which generally satisfies these standards. On the other hand, the influence of social standards serve as a limiting factor upon the possible individual rewards that the organization can provide.

Since there is such a high degree of collective interdependence among rank-and-file workers the attempts to use individual rewards are often perceived as inequitable. Informal norms develop to protect the group against efforts which are seen as derisive or exploitive. Differential rates for subsystems within the organization will be accepted much more than invidious distinctions within the same subgrouping. Hence promotion or upgrading may be the most potent type of individual reward. The employee is rewarded by being moved to a different category of workers on a better pay schedule. Some of the same problems apply, of course, to this type of reward.[6]

Even though both individual and, to an extent, group or system rewards are based on the conscious or nonconscious performance evaluation of superiors, it is nevertheless important that deliberate attempts be made to base such evaluation on a set of operationally relevant and differentiating criteria with respect to the quality of individual performance. In the absence of such criteria, a tendency easily develops to reward conformity to organizational rules such as delivering reports on time, beginning and ending a day's work at certain times, and keeping expense accounts to a specified minimum.

Level 5: The implications of individual values structures. Ultimately, an organizational reward structure constitutes a means of relating organizational objectives and structural requirements to the goals and behavior modes of individual members.

It might be helpful . . . to distinguish between *intrinsic* and *extrinsic* motivational sequences. Most activities are self-motivating—that is, they provide their own intrinsic rewards. People *like* to create, eat, play, work, use their muscles, solve problems, do crossword puzzles, help others and do almost anything that is not inherently abhorrent or that they have not learned to dislike. Unfortunately, in our ignorance of the principles of learning, and in our defensive distrust, we often do things as parents, teachers and "managers" that deliberately "train in" avoidance reactions. Activities that are intrinsically rewarding, that allow us to feel we've accomplished something (running a lathe, writing a poem, reading a book) become "work" when we are paid money for doing them. School activities that are basically challenging and fun in and of themselves become "school work" when they are "rewarded" by grades, and hence become something to dislike and avoid. Parents, teachers, and other managers are then caught in the problem of having to continue manipulating the grades or wages or praise in order to bolster the motivations artificially. In fact, the manager actually defeats his own intentions. The recipient . . . becomes dependent upon the anticipated external reward—and upon the rewarder. He looks upon activities as something to barter rather than as intrinsically exciting, developmental, rewarding and fulfilling.[7]

A question may thus be raised with reference to the usefulness of the occasionally frantic search for new innovations in "motivational techniques." As a set of purely extrinsic rewards, compensation plans and reward structures can lead only to a greater *amount* of activity at any given level of competence, and even that is dependent upon the individual's understanding of the plan or structure. Quality of performance, on the other hand, is entirely dependent upon the individual's value structure, his feeling of participation and interdependence, and the relationship between individual and organizational goals. The problem involved here is not so much that of rewarding "right" and "wrong" behavior as it is that of facilitating the development of individual competence and participation.

On the basis of the criteria outlined above the following general guidelines with reference to the development of organizational compensation plans or reward structures can be stated:

1. The effectiveness of any general compensation plan *cannot be predicted* insofar as that effect depends primarily upon the individual.
2. The primary requirement of any reward structure is that it be *flexible and designed to meet individual requirements* rather than be allowed to grow into an inflexible structure with a functional autonomy of its own.
3. The primary purpose of a reward structure should be *to facilitate individual participation* rather than to determine or even influence the direction of individual behavior.
4. The basic nature of compensation and rewards *is that of communicative facilitators,* subject to the enablers and constraints inherent in all communicative interaction.
5. Compensation and rewards are not limited to financial and other concrete material payments but *encompass the entire organizational structure* and the interpersonal relationships facilitated by that structure.

In a number of interviews made in connection with earlier work of the Marketing Science Institute involving organizational structures in marketing, two points were frequently made by the executives interviewed. First, executives stressed that they were actively searching for employees to strengthen their organizations and were having to accept people less qualified than formerly. More good people were leaving than they were able to recruit. Salary, fringe benefits, and other compensation factors were not reported to be factors in this problem. Instead genuine interest was reported as lacking in most instances. Second, the executives often stressed the opportunities for growth that they considered their firms to have and would emphasize that company expansion plans were not being realized for lack of managerial talent. The general feeling appeared to be that there was not sufficient time to train new employees who did not have the background and experience necessary to carry out assignments without much explanation or guidance.

The specific reasons behind the problem situation described above have yet to be established, but on the basis of the concepts developed earlier, it would seem that organizational inflexibility and a consequent lack of of opportunity for individual self-determination are major factors. That is, *an individual's perception and feeling of function and status, and, therefore, individual interest and desire for self-improvement, is closely related to the perceived rewards and constraints imposed by any given organizational framework.* Whether or not this perception is "correct" is not the central point. The point is that the nature of individual perception and its influence upon individual motivation must be taken into account. Failure to do this may well result in a decreasing availability of potentially and actually competent individuals, or alternatively there will be an increase in requirements for direction and control, the implementation of which will tend to further aggravate the situation.

Ideally, the function of the organizational framework should be to coordinate and differentiate individual performance with reference to individual abilities or competencies while *compensating* for individual inabilities or incompetencies. Or, to put it differently, the organizational control and reward structure should be designed to facilitate individual goal attainment and not to determine it. Some of the implications of this compensatory approach to organizational control and reward structures will be discussed in the following chapter.

SUMMARY

The purpose of this chapter has been to discuss the implications of the COMPACT model and communication theory with reference to evaluation of performance and the development of compensatory or reward structures. The basic operational elements of performance evaluation were outlined as follows:

Phase 4.1: Awareness of a set of relevant criteria for the assessment of competence on the basis of observation of performance.

Phase 4.2: Acquisition of relevant information in terms of the specified criteria and feasible action for improvement.

Phase 4.3: Development of a competence pattern for each salesman with reference to the significant aspects of his task.

Phase 4.4: Organization of communication channels and lines of authority to compensate for existing strengths and weaknesses of both the individual salesman and the aggregate sales force with respect to the task to be performed.

Phase 4.5: Commitment to a given set of evaluative criteria for the purpose of maintaining consistency of feedback and evaluation.

The implications of each of these phases were outlined and it was concluded that the following categories of criteria were relevant to the evaluation of a salesman's performance:

1. The structure and competencies of the specific buying systems involved.
2. The structure and competencies of the selling organization.
3. The competencies of the individual salesman.
4. The nature of the potential transaction as established by the product or service concepts and utilities involved with regard to the above systems.

The diagram in Figure 25 outlines the basic criteria used in the performance evaluation scheme proposed here.

The basic function of compensatory or reward structures is that of relating organizational objectives to individual behavior standards and value structures. The following criteria for the development of such structures were outlined as follows:

1. The minimum instrumental or resource requirements of the individual.
2. The psychological requirements of the individual.
3. The functional relevance of reward structures.
4. The social or interpersonal implications of a reward structure.
5. The implications of individual value structures.

Compensation is thus not limited to monetary rewards but pertains to all elements of the relationship between an individual and an organization. This same relationship or interface will be examined further in the following chapter with reference to organizational control requirements.

XV

The Concept
of Compensatory Control

ON THE BASIS of the concepts outlined previously, the role of personal selling in the marketing mix can be defined as *that of establishing a set of relevant intercommunicative relationships between sellers and buyers of economic goods and services or utilities.* The unique advantage or strength of personal selling, as contrasted with other promotional media, *is the potential or actual capacity of the salesman to provide a dynamically evolving two-way communicative link between selling and buying systems.* The attainment of an "optimum" effectiveness and efficiency of this dynamic two-way link depends upon the competence of individual members of the selling organization, aided by an effective organizational information and control system, to establish the following:

> Level 1: The "best feasible" approach to any given buying system with reference to the nature of the potential transaction and the structural and functional nature of the buying system.
> Level 2: The "optimum" specialization of tasks and responsibilities with regard to the nature of product or service concepts and buying systems, as well as with regard to the individual salesman's or sales manager's requirement for organizational function and status.
> Level 3: The operational relevance and economic efficiency of the personal selling function as established by the information requirements of both selling and buying systems.
> Level 4: The "optimum" integration of available marketing resources with reference to the strengths and weaknesses of the various systems or entities involved.
> Level 5: The strategically relevant buying systems with reference to the economic niche within which the selling organization operates and the strategic strengths and weaknesses of the selling organization.

The interrelationships among the above outlined levels of planning, problem solving, decision making, and action give rise to certain organizational information and control requirements, and it is the purpose of the present chapter to explore the nature and implications of these requirements. Information requirements will be considered from the point of view of a data *acquisition* and *consumption* process underlying planning and decision making, while control will be considered from the point of view of a process of integrating individual efforts within an organizational framework—that is, a data *generation* and *dissemination* process. The diagram in Figure 26 outlines briefly the conceptual relationships among the three dimensions: organizational framework or hierarchy, individual competence, and information requirements.

THE INDIVIDUAL-ORGANIZATION INTERFACE

The essential functions of a social organization, such as a business firm, are its communication networks (information and control systems) *and its decision centers* (information conversion nodes). The existence of an interpersonal organization is dependent upon a sufficient commonality among individuals' definitions of goals and relationships to permit intercommunication. The commonalities or agreements involved here are essentially transactional (from the point of view of the individual) in the sense that the acceptance of certain organizational rules of behavior enables the individual to achieve certain instrumental *goals* with reference to his self concept. The individual accepts certain constraints (costs) to achieve certain benefits (pay-offs).

The effectiveness of the relationship between an individual and an organizational system is partly dependent on the individual's competence to perform his organizationally defined function, and partly dependent on the organizational constraints imposed. The managerial task in this connection is that of optimizing the trade-off between individual competence and organizational control with reference to some organizationally defined and predetermined goal or subgoal. The best approach to the performance of this managerial function has by no means been definitely established, but several schools of thought have developed around the problem of determining the "optimum" relationship between the individual and the collective. These range from the so-called Classical School, building mainly on a mechanistic model of organization, to the so-called Human Relations School, building mainly on a "people-oriented" approach:

The search for greater effectiveness and efficiency in organizations gave rise to the *Classical Theory* of Administration, perhaps more appropriately

FIGURE 26

The Basic Requirements of an Information and Control
System with Reference to a Personal Selling
Organization

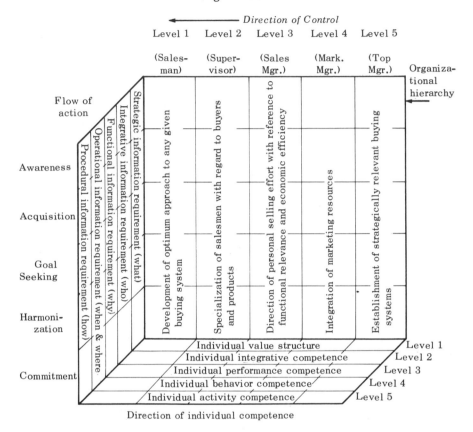

Direction of individual competence

called *Scientific Management,* since this latter title expresses the emphasis of this organizational approach: Workers were seen as motivated by economic rewards, and the organization was characterized by a clearly defined division of labor with a highly specialized personnel and by a distinct hierarchy of authority. Out of this tradition comes the characterization of the *formal organization* as a blueprint according to which they ought to adhere.

Arising in part as a reaction to Scientific Management, another school of thinking gained prominence in the United States—*Human Relations.* In contrast to *Classical Theory,* Human Relations emphasized the emotional, unplanned, non-rational elements in organizational behavior. It discovered the significance of friendship and social groupings of workers for the organization. It also pointed out the importance of leadership in the organization and of emotional communication and participation. From these observations the concept of *informal organization* was developed. This is sometimes viewed as what there is to organization beyond the formal structure; sometimes, as what the organizational life is really like, as distinct from blueprints and charts.[1]

The Classical School or Scientific Management,[2] thus is based on an assumption of complete economic rationality on the part of individual members of an organization, while the Human Relations approach to organizational control is based on an assumption of an almost complete lack of economic rationality on the part of individual organizational members. In other words, one approach assumes away the existence of potential or actual conflict between individual and organizational goals, while the other not only recognizes the existence of such conflict, but develops its theory on the premise that all such conflict is bad and should therefore be avoided at all costs. More recently, it has become evident that organizations are neither completely formal and separate from individuals, nor are they a completely informal "sharing" of goals:

The two views were only different in substance of the balance they depicted: whereas Scientific Management saw the balance as natural if restraints were removed, Human Relations believed the ideal state had to be deliberately constructed . . . . It remained, therefore, for the *Structuralists to point out that alienation and conflict are both inevitable and occasionally desirable,* and to emphasize that social science is not a vehicle to serve the needs of either worker or organization. It is no more concerned to improve the organization of management than it is to improve organization of the employees.[3]

The general objective of an economic organization thus is neither exclusively that of furthering individual goals as such, nor exclusively that of furthering organizational goals at the expense of individual goals: it is rather to coordinate both sets of goals in the pursuit or what Peter Drucker terms "economic performance."[4] Consequently an organizational information and control system should be designed so as to be flexible enough to accommodate individual differences while providing a sufficient structural definition of the organizational relationships to ensure the necessary coordination of productive efforts.

The problem involved here is primarily conceptual or, in other words, it is a communication problem. One basic assumption underlying the framework presented in Part III is that *all* behavior is *organized behavior* and that a necessary condition for the occurrence of communicative interaction is the individual's possession of some conceptual framework in terms of which he ascribes, or does not ascribe, meaning and significance to any given message. The conceptual frameworks of two different individuals overlap to the extent that agreement has been reached, consciously or nonconsciously, about certain rules of behavior. It is this requirement for interpersonal agreement about significant behavior rules which is at the root of organizational control systems. The objective function of a control system is neither to "make" all individual members of an organization follow some prescribed behavior manual, an approach which is liable to give rise to all sorts of communication "problems," nor is it to attempt to accommodate *all* individual viewpoints, thereby providing few or no structural guidelines. Its function is *to provide a system of behavior rules which primarily complements rather than overlaps existing individually internalized behavior rules.* For the highly competent individual, the compensatory control requirement may be filled by providing him with a statement of organizational objectives, whereas the conceptually less competent individual may require a more specific control structure. In any case, an individual's contribution to, and the rewards gained from the pursuit of, any given organizational objective are dependent upon the existence of some mutually acceptable structure in terms of which he can determine the direction, extent, and consequent value of his efforts.

THE NATURE OF AN INFORMATION AND CONTROL SYSTEM

The term control has several connotations ranging from a purely manipulative and authoritarian concept to a more global concept of activities devoted to the coordination of individual efforts to achieve certain common objectives in light of the various environmental opportunities and constraints. In the present context, information systems and control systems are considered as two elements of a single process: namely, that of acquiring, consuming, and disseminating information with respect to the past, present, and future operations of an economic organization. In this sense, control is an *attribute* of the organization, and as such is dependent upon the degree to which the organizational information and control system *enables* each individual member to utilize his competence rather than the degree to which the organizational information and control system develops and maintains hierarchical dominance. In terms of the COMPACT model, a generalized information and control system thus must satisfy the following requirements:

Phase 1: Awareness. The effectiveness of an information and control system is highly dependent upon the degree to which the system can take into account and compensate for individual capacities and incapacities with reference to the function and objectives of their performance.

Phase 2: Acquisition. The instrumental function of an information and control system is to provide external and internal data relevant to the achievement of organizational objectives and the communicative competence of individual members.

Phase 3: Goal Seeking. The ultimate objective of an information and control system is to facilitate the allocation of
individual effort to the most productive activities with a
minimum expenditure of energy.

Phase 4: Harmonization. Organizational effectiveness is directly dependent upon the degree to which the process of
matching available and required information is integrated.

Phase 5: Commitment. A meaningful integration of the information acquisition and dissemination processes is based
upon a commitment to the purposes of the information
and control system rather than a commitment to the *means*
or techniques of the system.

Essentially, an organizational information and control system
is embodied in the data flows among individual members of the
organization. In this connection there is a frequently encountered
tendency to ascribe importance to only the operationally relevant,
or formal data flows. That is, data considered directly pertinent
to the development and implementation of organizational objectives.
Indeed, informal or unofficial data flows have frequently been
designated as mere "noise" in the organizational communication
channels and its elimination has been thought to bring about an
automatic improvement in organizational effectiveness.

Application of the COMPACT model to the analysis of intraorganizational information and control systems, however, would
indicate that informal, unofficial data flows represent not only
a more complex network than the formal and official flows, but
also a significant influence on organizational effectiveness and
viability.

Phase 1: The Compensatory Information and Control System.

The prevailing information and control system in an organization
strongly influences, if not indirectly determines, the task-related
things which will be taken into account by individual employees.
The concepts or models underlying an information and control
system are thus closely related to, and some would suggest,
even determinative of organizational effectiveness and efficiency.
The now well-known dichotomy of assumption structure with reference to managerial control of human behavior provided by Douglas
McGregor is relevant here:

The conventional conception of management's task in harnessing human
energy to organizational requirements can be stated broadly in terms of
three propositions. In order to avoid the complications introduced by a
label, I shall call this set of propositions "Theory X:"

1. Management is responsible for organizing the elements of productive enterprise—money, materials, equipment, people—in the interest of economic ends.

2. With respect to people, this is a process of directing their efforts, motivating them, controlling their actions, modifying their behavior to fit the needs of the organization.

3. Without this active intervention by management, people would be passive—even resistant—to organizational needs. They must, therefore, be persuaded, rewarded, punished, controlled—their activities must be directed. This is management's task in managing subordinate managers or workers. We often sum it up by saying that management consists of getting things done through other people. [5]

In contrast to his above quoted ''Theory X,'' McGregor outlines a concept of human motivation which he terms ''Theory Y.''

1. Management is responsible for organizing the elements of productive enterprise-money, materials, equipment, people—in the interest of economic ends.

2. People are *not* by nature passive or resistant to organizational needs. They have become so as a result of experience in organizations.

3. The motivation, the potential for development, the capacity for assuming responsibility, the readiness to direct behavior toward organizational goals are all present in people. Management does not put them there. It is responsibility of management to make it possible for people to recognize and develop these human characteristics for themselves.

4. The essential task of management is to arrange organizational conditions and methods of operation so that people can achieve their own goal *best* by directing *their own* efforts toward organizational objectives.[6]

The theory or assumption structure pertaining to human motivation and behavior underlying this volume was treated at length in Part Three, but it might be helpful to summarize it briefly here. The central concept in this theory is that of the individual as an information and decision system possessing a certain intuitively determinable level of conceptual competence which enables him to engage in certain activities and constrains him from engaging in others.

The predilection or motivation to act is inherent in the individual as a living system, while the direction of this action is dependent upon his ''definition'' of the environment in relation to his self-concept and value structure. In other words, it is postulated that an individual's ability and willingness to act in a certain manner in a specific situation is determined by the conceptual meaning he attributes to the situation. *Control in this sense is always a function of both the individual and of the system.* This does not, of course, prevent individuals from doing or not doing certain things and making or not making certain decisions *because* the system is perceived to dictate it. On the contrary, it appears that the more entrenched a given information and control system becomes the more things tend to be done "because" of the system.

In any case, the point to be made here is not that control is unnecessary and "bad"; rather the point is that a control system is only a means to an end. The activity devoted to the maintenance or observance of the system as a system is as likely to contribute to organizational ineffectiveness as to organizational effectiveness, since it is as likely to *limit* as it is to *enable* the individual in exercising his competence. As a means to an end, however, an information and control system, and therefore an organizational structure, can serve a real and important purpose as a communication enabler in organizational relationships:

It is clear in any discussion of organizations that controls are necessary to keep an organization viable and efficient in performing the purposes for which it was designed. To understand controls, the existence of uncertainty is one of the key factors—perhaps the key factor. Uncertainty arises for two reasons. One, the more essential in the sense that it must inevitably occur in any sizeable organization, is that the different parts cannot be perfectly acquainted with each other. All the discussion about centralization and decentralization has to do with precisely that fact. A given part in an organization may know what it is doing, and it may know a certain set of facts which come up in a natural way as a result of engaging in its activities. The transmission of this information is always costly, in greater or lesser degree. The result is that it does not by any standards pay other parts of the organization and particularly top management to know everything . . .

A second uncertainty, which is not basic from a definitional point of view but which is important from a practical point of view, is the uncertainty about the external environment. [7]

The potentially best information and control system *is one which enables each member to utilize his actual competence while compensating for his inabilities whether physical or conceptual.* The problem inherent in the development of an information and control system is thus not one of creating a system which will provide a guideline for every possible contingency. The important problem is one of creating and maintaining a system which supplements the individual's competence and function.

This concept of a *compensatory control system* is an attempt to take into account the values and competencies of individuals in the interest of organizational effectiveness and efficiency and is thus *both task* and *people* oriented. Since individual competence is subject to continual change, partly as a result of outside influences, compensatory control calls for a system which is both dynamic and flexible enough to accomodate individual differences and structurally consistent enough to maintain direction of effort.

Phase 2: The Role of an Information
Acquisition System

The problems involved in the development of an organizational
information or data acquisition system have received extensive
descriptive and prescriptive or normative treatment in the literature.[8] The following discussion will therefore be centered primarily on the issues peculiar to the personal selling function.
Organizational control, with reference to personal selling, is
dependent upon each individual member of the selling organization possessing one or more of the following categories of information:

> *Level 1: Procedural information* that pertains to the tactical
> or "how to sell" activities of the salesman.
> *Level 2: Operational information* that pertains to the types
> of buying systems to which personal selling is relevant
> as well as the optimum call frequency and the location
> of the relevant decision maker(s) in the buying system.
> *Level 3: Functional information* that pertains to the function
> or purpose of the personal selling activities vis-à-vis
> both the selling organization and the relevant buying
> systems.
> *Level 4: Integrative information* that pertains to the inte-
> gration of the personal selling function with the various
> elements of the marketing mix.
> *Level 5: Strategic information* that pertains to the develop-
> ment and implementation of marketing strategies.

The conceptual relationship among these five categories of
information, the various levels of the organizational hierarchy,
and the several levels of individual competence is briefly outlined
in Figure 26. While there is no reason why a single individual
cannot possess all of this information, the size and geographical
dispersion of the buying systems relevant to any given organization generally makes a division of responsibility and a specialization of tasks more effective than a one-man effort.

The existence of a system of responsibility division and task
specialization has given rise to several complex issues, the
nature of which is outlined below with reference to the several
phases of the information control system:

> *Phase 2.1* Individual awareness or "knowledge" and motiva-
> tion, tend to be equated with organizationally hierarchical
> divisions on the basis of some intuitive concept of "quantity."
> In other words, responsibilities and information require-
> ments tend to be *ranked* rather than *divided.* It is essentially
> this tendency on which the "participative management"
> school is focusing its attention partly basing its conceptions

on the observed relationships among the parts of the biological system.

The kind of organization we find [in man's internal environment] is a patterned activity in which all the specialized organ systems and functional processes constitute the organization and maintain the organized whole by the way each articulates, synchronizes, compensates and otherwise operates in relation to all others.[9]

Phase 2.2 Information acquisition systems tend to become technique and methodology oriented as a result of a lack of involvement in, and understanding of organizational objectives. Moreover, the quite substantial data available to the salesman by virtue of his close relationship with buying systems are quite often not taken into account in the course of decision making at higher levels. Apparently, the salesmen's observational bias for some curious reason is thought to be less related to organizational objectives than that of the market researcher.

Phase 2.3 Externally generated data tend to become replaced by internally generated data, particularly in the planning and decision making of lower echelon individuals. Salesmen perform in a certain manner and according to a certain schedule, not because they perceive this performance to be an optimum vis-à-vis the environment, but because they perceive it to be an optimum vis-à-vis their superiors, who in turn do not normally have access to the same data environment as the salesman.

Phase 2.4 Information and control systems tend to be highly fragmented and overlapping. The responsibility for information acquisition relevant to marketing is partly assigned to market research (surveys), accounting (sales and cost data), advertising agencies (advertising effectiveness), and sales supervisors (effectiveness of salesmen). A lack of integration was evident in the majority of companies interviewed in connection with the present study since no data were available for making even the simplest comparisons between the effectiveness of personal selling and the effectiveness of advertising.

Phase 2.5 An information acquisition system tends to become an object of commitment. Data acquisition not only tends to be concentrated on data of which the *acquirer,* who is not necessarily the *user,* is aware; it also tends to be concentrated on the perpetuation of a given form and content of the process itself.

The problems involved in developing an information acquisition system, which is flexible enough to provide decision makers with relevant information, are not necessarily solved by either complete centralization or decentralization of the acquisition function. Indeed, the objective of an information system is not only to achieve efficiency of the system itself. It is also to facilitate the development and achievement of organizational and individual goals.

Much research has yet to be done before definitive statements can be made about the "best" information acquisition system for any given organization. Consequently, the management of information, or to put it differently, the facilitation of individual performance with a minimum of constraint upon individual competence, is, despite the revolutionary implications of technological innovations in information acquisition and processing, one of the most important areas of concern for the modern manager. Moreover, it is an area where conceptual and interpersonal competence has more relevance and promises greater potential effectiveness than the institution of general rules and guidelines for behavior.

Phase 3: The Purposes of an Information and Control System

The ultimate goal of an information and control system (and therefore of the organizational structure itself), is to facilitate integration of individual performances. Insofar as the organizational structure defines the individual's environment it enables him to communicate with that environment. On the other hand, the greater the area of overlap of the organization's and the individual's definitions of the environment, the greater the possibility of conflict. Since such conflict is likely to be resolved in favor of the organization it may result in restriction or frustration of the individual's motivation and competence. In this context *the individual member of the organization must be considered as an integral part of the organizational information and control system. He is the information consumption and decision system or node in the organizational framework of communication channels.*

The concept of organizational synergy may be helpful here as a means of expressing the potential outcomes of the interaction among several organizational elements. The concept of synergy involves a matching of the strengths and weaknesses of organizational elements in such a manner that the combined performance of these elements in a given environment is greater than the sum of its parts. This synergistic effect has also been described as the "2+2=5" effect.[10] In actuality, of course, the effect of a matching of resources may be positive, neutral, or negative depending upon the mutual fit of the resources. For example, the sales manager whose main strength is his ability to deal directly with customers may produce an organizationally negative effect when matched with a salesman with a similar strength. That is, the sales manager does not add sufficient strength to the combination to produce an effect equal to that which would have resulted had the sales manager and the salesman operated independently of each other. Similarly, the effect of checking upon, "second-guessing" and controlling, salesmen's utilization of time may be neutral or even negative in the case of an otherwise fully competent salesman.

Perhaps the most important implications of the concept of synergy lie in the area of integrating salesmen's efforts into the organizational information acquisition and dissemination system. For example, a relationship of *direct* interaction between salesman and market researchers may prove far more fruitful than one in which hierarchically dominant individuals act as sole coordinators and interpreters of data. Similarly, a hierarchical division of responsibility among individual members of the selling organization may well be less effective than a horizontal division on the basis of action orientation.

In any case, the emphasis of the concept of synergy is upon attempts *to optimize the consequences of various organizational combinations of available resources with reference to environmental opportunities and constraints.* From the point of view of the organizational information and control system the emphasis is upon an *experimental* approach to information acquisition and control rather than upon the establishment of routine data flows and controls.

The experimental studies reported in Part Two are examples of a type of nonroutine control studies which are capable of revealing significant inefficiencies precisely because they are nonroutine. Moreover, such experimental studies can be designed to investigate combinations of performance which may appear too unorthodox or promise too small a return to warrant the institution of routine controls. Indeed, *the tendency for routine controls to create their own organizational structure may be an argument in favor of more emphasis upon nonroutine experimental data acquisition with reference to intraorganizational performance evaluation.*

Routine data collection concerning external influences upon and results from organizational performance exhibits weaknesses similar to those of intraorganizational control. Not only does external data acquisition tend to be limited to relatively superficial surveys, but few attempts have been made, for example, to relate studies of promotional effects over time to capture any evolutionary trends and patterns of change in buyer behavior. Those few attempts that have been made include an approach termed "adaptive control" which may be defined as follows:

When faced with uncertainties . . . the common sense approach is to learn from experience. As the process unfolds, we should be able to learn more and more about the unknown structures and unknown parameters . . . . Processes of this type . . . will be called *adaptive control processes.*[11]

Adaptive control models are still in the developmental stage [12]

and further work is required to verify empirically their predictive capacities. Suffice it here to say that adaptive control
models essentially constitute attempts to optimize the synergistic effect of combinations of promotional decisions over time.
Developments in this area combined with the increasing sophistication of operations research techniques and experimental design
should provide a useful addition or alternative to existing routine
information acquisition and control techniques.

Phase 4: Integrating Information and Control Systems

*The effectiveness of the personal selling organization is
directly dependent upon the degree to which externally and internally
generated data can be integrated so as to fit the individual member's
ability to convert the resulting messages into meaningful and
effective action.* The elements of this integrative phase may
be summarized from the previous discussion as follows:

Phase 4.1: Awareness of the interaction among internal and
external variables and the means and methods of influencing this interaction in the direction of organizational
objectives.

Phase 4.2: Adaptive acquisition and consumption of internal and
external data, or ability to take account of and learn from
a changing internal and external environment.

Phase 4.3: Orientation toward goal seeking activities designed
to improve organizational performance in economic terms
while maintaining the ability of the organization to continue
to do so in the long run.

Phase 4.4: Integration of organizational goal seeking activities
with individual goal seeking activities so as to minimize
the degree of distrust and necessary control measures
while improving organizational input–output relationships
with reference to both human and nonhuman resources.

Phase 4.5: Individual commitment to organizational purposes
rather than to existing rules and control measures.

The organizational analysis and the measures of organizational
effectiveness underlying an operational application of the above
criteria of effectiveness must necessarily be both broader and
more flexible than many of those presently in use. It has been
repeatedly maintained in this volume that accounting measures
such as sales, cost of traveling, cost of training, and cost of
incentive schemes are insufficient for the purpose of measuring
effectiveness since they are primarily based on a mechanistic
model of individual performance, and at the very best provide
feedback of only short term usefulness.

The solution to the problems of measuring and improving organizational effectiveness does not nessarily, if at all, lie in more control—that is, internally generated messages to salesmen; it may well lie in *less control* coupled with *more participative training* to enable salesmen to perform more effectively in the face of a changing environment. The more a sales manager can rely on the judgment of his salesmen in the field, the more he can concentrate on integrating the salesman's activities with other organizational performances and goals, such as market research and new product research.

The concept of responsibility division and specialization involved here is less hierarchical in the sense of dominance, and more horizontal in the sense of cooperation, than that generally encountered. A competent salesman constitutes a resource and a spokesman as well as the eyes and ears of an organization. The problem involved in linking the salesman with the organization is neither one of "telling the salesman what to do," however subtly or enthusiastically, nor is it one of developing reward schemes which foster conformity to an organizationally established norm. It is one of *establishing a two-way link between organization and salesmen facilitating the attainment of the synergistic effect deriving from the positive interaction of individual and organizational goals.*

The effectiveness of the selling organization is thus neither exclusively a function of the salesman, nor is it exclusively a function of the selling organization; *it is a measure of the strategic integration of buying systems, salesmen, and selling organization as well as of the type of interaction involved with reference to the product or product class.* Each of these elements influence the overall effectiveness of the personal selling function, but the measure of this influence is neither fixed nor absolute.

For purposes of distributing organizational funds it has often been found useful to forecast or budget sales expenses against expected sales. Insofar as attempts to predict cash flows are necessary, forecasting and budgeting may be here to stay. However, forecasts used as organizational measuring sticks against which to gauge the effectiveness of selling activities leave a great deal to be desired. Not only are forecasts limited by the forecaster's ability to anticipate future events, but they tend to become substantive goals in themselves. The achievement of a forecast, regardless of the means or the reasons for the success, becomes something to be rewarded.

In a perceptual situation of complexity, that is in any social situation of the kind we deal with in business enterprise, the act of measurement is, however, neither objective nor neutral. It is subjective and of necessity biased. It changes both the event and the observer. For it changes the perception of the observer—if it does not altogether create his perception. Events in the social situation acquire value by the fact that they are being singled out for the attention of being measured. No matter how "scientific" we are, the fact that this or that set of phenomena is singled out for being "controlled," signals that it is being considered to be important. Everybody who ever watched the introduction of a budget system has seen this happen. For a long time—in many companies forever—realizing the budget figures becomes more important than what the budget is supposed to measure, namely economic performance. This goes often so far that managers, upon their first exposure to a budget system, deliberately hold back sales and cut back profits rather than be guilty of "not making the budget." It takes years of experience and a very intelligent budget director to restore the balance.[13]

The measure of a salesman's effectiveness is *not the number of sales he makes or the amount of expenses he reports anymore than the measure of an accountant's effectiveness is the number of entries he makes in a given time period.* Similarly, the effectiveness of an aggregate sales force as compared with some other promotional medium cannot be measured in terms of a simple revenue-cost comparison, and particularly not over short-term periods such as a year or less.

Basically *the measure of an individual salesman's effectuveness is his ability to communicate or interact with relevant buying systems.* The effectiveness of the aggregate sales force must be the return it provides on the organization's investment as compared with the possible return on investment which may be derived from the use of alternative media in the same or similar markets. Such comparisons of investment returns require a significant degree of integration and improvement with respect to available accounting techniques, a problem which is briefly highlighted in the last section of this chapter.

Phase 5: The Problem of Individual Commitment and Loyalty

In a recent article, David Mayer and Herbert M. Greenberg[14] arrive at the conclusion "that a good salesman must have at least two basic qualities: empathy and ego drive:"

Industry must improve its ability to select top salesmen. Failure to date has stemmed from such errors as: the belief that interest equals aptitude; the fakability of aptitude tests; the crippling emphasis on conformity rather than creativity; and the subdivision of a man into piecemeal traits, rather than understanding him as a whole person. Experience appears to be less important than a man's possession of the two central characteristics of empathy and ego drive, which he must have to permit him to sell successfully. Training can only succeed when the raw material is present.[15]

Empathy, or ability to relate to another individual, is essentially the communicative competence with which much of this volume has been concerned. Ego drive, on the other hand, is defined essentially as task orientation:

The second of the basic qualities absolutely needed by a good salesman is a particular kind of *ego drive* which makes him want and need to make the sale in a personal or ego way, not merely for the money gained.[16]

Ego drive would thus appear to be a type of commitment which is essentially composed of two parts, namely (1) the basic motivation or physical energy of the individual and (2) the psychological understanding which provides direction for the action.

This second part of the so-called ego drive appears largely similar to the concept of loyalty which has gained a great deal of popularity in personal selling literature. Loyalty, however (and presumably ego drive), is not a quality exclusively dependent upon the individual. It is essentially based upon a feeling of participation, function, and importance or status which is not normally fostered by the development of simple goals and elementary guidelines but is partly a function of the degree of self-determination and interpersonal trust fostered by the salesman's organizational environment:

People naturally tend to share their feelings and concerns with those whom they trust, and this is true at the simplest and most direct level of interpersonal relationships as well as at more complex levels of organizational communication. Thus a high-trust managing system may institute open planning meetings and evaluation meetings; public criteria for promotion; easily available information on salaries, cost figures and budgets; open stock rooms, and easy access to material in the files. There is comparatively little concern with public relations, with the corporate or family "image," or with "communications" programs. Communication in such a system is a *process* rather than a program.[17]

The best salesman, on this basis, is the one who has been able to attain a large measure of his potential competence and who knows that his competence makes a difference with reference to both buying and selling systems. He has perceived that the organizational structure behind him is designed to support and further the consequences of his efforts as opposed to the frequently encountered perception that organizational controls are designed to limit and frustrate the salesman's competence through what, to the uninformed, may easily appear to be arbitrary rules and control measures.

An organizational climate of the latter type is not easily changed. It requires more than a human relations course for sales managers and supervisors to foster the type of organizational support and interpersonal trust which leads to effective individual commitment and loyalty to organizational goals and purposes. It requires an organizational framework designed to facilitate rather than dominate individual performance.

SOME NOTES ON COST ANALYSIS
OF THE PERSONAL SELLING EFFORT

The preceding discussion has examined some of the conceptual and interpersonal issues involved in the development and maintenance of individual and organizational effectiveness. It is evident at this point that the usual accounting models are entirely inadequate as means of collecting and processing data relevant to the assessment of organizational and individual effectiveness. It is not only highly unlikely that the cost of keeping a salesman in the field bears any meaningful relationship to the consequences of his efforts, the conclusions delivered by an accounting report are also ambiguous and do not in and of themselves indicate the direction for improvement. As Peter Drucker expresses it:

> . . . a control reading "profits are falling" does not indicate, with any degree of probability, the response "raise prices" let alone by how much; the control-reading "sales are falling" does not indicate the response "cut prices," and so on. There is not only a large—a very large—number of other equally probable responses—so large that it is usually not even possible to identify them in advance. There is no indication in the event itself which of these responses is even possible, let alone appropriate, not to mention its being right. The event itself may not even be meaningful. [18]

The mere provision of cost and sales data then, without an attempt to integrate these data with other significant decision variables, may be a hindrance rather than a help to the receiver. Moreover, the value of a sales force depends partly on the strategic decisions made by the marketing manager, partly on the integrative decision making by the sales manager, and partly on the communicative effectiveness of the salesmen. *If the control data provided by the accounting function are to be of any use at any of these levels of decision making, they must necessarily be collected and reported on the basis of a concept relevant to the marketing and selling functions rather than on the basis of inflexible accounting principles and methods.*

A recent study by Michael Schiff and Martin Mellman[19] sponsored by the Financial Executives Research Foundation assesses the state of the art with reference to the provision of useful cost data for decisions affecting the personal selling function. The study, which included 28 major U.S. companies (22 of which are among *Fortune's* listing of the 500 largest corporations in the United States) focuses upon the controllership function, which the authors view as planning and control, specifically including:

1. To establish, coordinate and administer, as an integral part of management, an adequate plan for the control of

operations. Such a plan would provide, to the extent required by the business, profit-planning programs for capital investing and for financing sales forecasts, expense budgets and cost standards.

2. To compare performance with operating plans and standards, and to report and interpret the results of operations to all levels of management.

3. To consult with all segments of management responsible for policy or action concerning any phase of the operation of the business as it relates to attainment of objectives and the effectiveness of policies, organization structure and procedures. [20]

The study specifically does *not* address itself to sales analyses related to the establishment of marketing strategy and planning and controlling of marketing effort *that are not directly related to cost analysis.* Thus, marketing research, operations research, and sales forecasting are not included. Rather, the basic objective is to evaluate the appropriateness to marketing and selling decisions of regularly conducted budgeting procedures and cost analysis within the firm. Among the conclusions and observations relevant to personal selling activities are:

The tools of capital budgetary control can and should be extended to expenditures for securing markets if the controller would forget generally accepted financial accounting principles, for this management purpose. The planned expenditures of developing markets are known and, if treated as an investment, can be related to profitability in the same way that the plant turns out the goods sold in the market.[31]

Among the companies visited, very few had comprehensive planning; a few had partial planning (long range) of varying scope, but the majority confined their planning or forecasting to the year ahead.[22]

Many of Schiff and Mellman's findings and conclusions point to areas where the comptroller function could perform useful services in connection with marketing decisions. Among those relating to the personal selling function are:

1. Analyses of customers, channels, salesmen, and order sizes are not usually prepared.

2. Distinctions between fixed and variable costs resulting in marginal earnings are rarely used.

3. Distinctions between controllable and non-controllable costs, with but few exceptions, are not carefully developed. [23]

4. Where the field organization is responsible for developing estimates of future sales . . . the importance of product mix and profitability needs to be stressed. [24]

5. Very few instances [were found] where the controller had combined

the variable costs of both production and marketing at various volume levels for the use of the marketing man.[25]

6. The field study indicates that, of all marketing personnel served by the controller, the needs of special managers [i.e., sales managers with responsibility for sales of an entire line to a given distribution channel or industry class,] are most frequently overlooked. [26]

7. A noteworthy fact is the lack of integration between the measures used by the field organization and the controllers' reports relative to salesmen's activity. [27]

Organizational control is first and foremost an attribute or a process of organization. Secondly, it involves the question of *what* to measure to enable decision makers at the various levels to assess the effectiveness of their activities. This latter question cannot be answered generally since the answer depends not only upon the function involved but also upon the decision maker's ability to take account of the data supplied him, that is, it involves communication:

The problem of communication between marketing and the control function is fundamental. While the view is still held in many places that marketing executives, being primarily sales and promotion minded, are not inclined to the use of quantitative information, our study reveals the contrary to be the case. As members of the management team, they well comprehend the need for quantitative financial reports and analyses and they use them. One might say that the problem of communication stems from the failure of the controller to recognize fully the marketing problem of the corporation, the nature of the marketing organization, and the specific channels and geographic operations. The field study shows that reporting is of a most advanced nature and liaison is excellent where a member or members of the controller's staff is in the marketing department with line responsibility to marketing management but with a close working relationship with the controller.[28]

SUMMARY

The purpose of the present chapter has been to examine some of the conceptual problems involved in developing and maintaining an information and control system which serves the selling organization rather than dominates it. The key issue in this connection is that of achieving flexibility of data acquisition consumption and dissemination within the organization, while maintaining sufficient structure to provide a basis for communication where individual competencies fall short.

The elements of an information and control system were outlined and described as follows:

Phase 1: Awareness. The efficiency and effectiveness of an information and control system is highly dependent upon

the degree to which the system can take into account and
compensate for individual capacities and incapacities with
reference to the function and objectives of their performance.

Phase 2: Acquisition. The instrumental function of an information
and control system is to provide external and internal
data relevant to the achievement of organizational objectives
and the communicative competence of individual members.

Phase 3: Goal Seeking. The ultimate objective of an information
and control system is that of facilitating the allocation of
individual effort to the most productive activities with
a minimum expenditure of energy.

Phase 4: Harmonization. Organizational effectiveness is directly
dependent upon the degree to which the process of matching
available and required information is integrated.

Phase 5: Commitment. A meaningful integration of the information acquisition and dissemination process is based upon
a commitment to the purposes of the information and control
system rather than a commitment to the means or techniques of the system.

A brief examination of the state of the art in the development
and use of accounting data, based upon a study conducted by Schiff
and Mellman, revealed that a great deal of research and experimentation has yet to be done before definitive statements can be
made about the "best" accounting model. *It is evident from the
earlier discussion in this volume, however, that control is essentially an attribute of an organizational system and that the key
questions are what to measure and control as well as how to
measure and control.*

PART FIVE

In Summary

XVI

A Review

THE PRIMARY PURPOSE of this volume is to outline a theory, or a set of concepts, and to discuss some of the implications of these concepts for the role and performance of personal selling as an element of the marketing mix. In so doing it has become evident that a number of areas are in need of continued research and development. It is the purpose of the present chapter to outline a prospectus for further exploration. First, however, it will be helpful to summarize briefly the content of the preceding chapters for the purpose of focusing on the concepts presented.

The following four orientations have formed the basic structure of the volume:

1. The content and trends apparent in the existing literature on personal selling.
2. The state of the art in experimental methodology relevant to measuring and controlling personal selling effectiveness and efficiency.
3. Development of a structural-functional classification of behavior systems and definition of a communication theory of the relationships between these systems on the basis of available behavioral science concepts.
4. Establishment of some of the practical implications of a functional classification and a communication theory of human behavior in the context of marketing and personal selling.

THE PERSONAL SELLING LITERATURE

Despite the considerable volume of literature on personal selling only implicit, and apparently highly mechanistic, viewpoints of human behavior and interpersonal influence are available. The bulk of the literature is oriented toward the establishment of generalized "right" behaviors on the part of the salesmen or alternatively the manager and it tends to ignore the idiosyncratic nature of individual motivation. There are several reasons for questioning the simplistic and essentially nonintegrated approach to the problems of the personal function encountered in the existing literature:

1. The concern with the development and institution or memorization of specific rules regarding behavior in sales situations negates the basic advantage of the salesman as a promotional medium. Such rules tend to hamper him as a flexible and dynamic communicative link between selling and buying systems.

2. The emphasis upon psychological characteristics almost to the complete exclusion of other elements of interpersonal competence is evidence of a failure to take into account and turn to full advantage the basic nature of human learning and concept formation.

3. The emphasis upon control in personal selling tends to minimize the basic complexity and motivational significance of individual goals and standards. This failure results in both misleading and inadequate guidelines for the management and performance of the personal selling function.

4. The frequent failure of selling organizations and much selling literature to take into account and encourage full individual participation in the selling process is evidence of a relatively shallow understanding of the roles of selling and salesmen. This, in turn, has hampered the efforts of many companies in recruiting competent and potentially competent sales people.

5. The existing literature generally exhibits a lack of understanding of the interdependence of individual performance and organizational structures. Even though much remains to be learned on this point, there is evidence, deriving from work in organizational theory and behavior, that the quality of individual motivation and performance is at least partly dependent upon the nature of the organizational framework within which the individual performs.

EXPERIMENTAL ANALYSIS OF SELLING OPERATIONS

The experimental cases summarized in Part Two, in addition to providing examples of an operations research approach to the analysis of the personal selling function, resulted in a number of tentative conclusions. These conclusions, while specific in origin, illustrate the possible gains to be realized from supplementing, and perhaps even substituting studies of a nonroutine nature for, regular and routine controls.

The experimental approach, if utilized with reasonable care, can uncover ineffectiveness and inefficiency in the operation of the personal selling function. However, variations in quantitative input-output relationships depend ultimately for their meaning and implication upon the researcher's theory of the behavior of the variables used in experimentation. Introducing variations into the input mix and observing changes in outputs (that is, treating and selling relationship as a mysterious black box) may enable the researcher to establish some range of "best" input-output relationship at any given point in time and with reference to any given situation. Nevertheless, both the experimental design (that is, the quality and quantity of variations introduced) and the interpretation of the outcomes are entirely dependent upon the realism of researcher's assumptions about the system.

Experimentation, then, constitutes a means of testing and quantifying "known" and suspected relationships. The usefulness of experimentation is dependent upon the degree to which it facilitates the attainment of relevant goals and not upon the techniques involved, as such. Any given set of objectives and concepts is not "right" or "wrong," but merely useful or not useful. *There are thus no absolute concepts of human behavior,* nor are there, at least within the current state of the art, any generalizable operational statements or guidelines which hold across all selling situations. Developments in systems engineering have shown that it may be feasible to design a mechanically and technologically efficient organizational information and control system. When introduced into actual situations, however, such theoretically elegant systems almost invariably run into difficulties because of the failure or inability of the systems designer to take into account human factors. Moreover, control requirements, such as the specification of certain routine reports to be completed by salesmen, have a tendency to become the center of a functionally autonomous reward structure and, as such, are in danger of becoming a structural necessities whether or not they contribute to the attainment of organizational goals. The experimental approach to the analysis of organizational effectiveness and efficiency avoids such problems but brings up a number of other issues which will be discussed later in this chapter.

THE COMPACT MODEL

The experiments recounted in Part Two basically rely on a black box model of the selling relationship. Part Three constitutes an attempt to map or outline the content of this black box in the form of a set of structural and functional concepts which describe the

qualitative influences governing the economic input–output relationships with reference to both marketing and personal selling.
The COMPACT model, while representative of an exceedingly
complex system of essentially communicative interactions has
been designed to take into account only the more significant of
these behavioral influences. In any case, the purpose of Part
Three is not to legislate concepts but rather to propose elements
of a possible theory of marketing and personal selling. These
basic theoretical elements can be summarized as follows:

1. There are essentially two sources of energy related to
   individual motivation and behavior. First, the *physiological*
   process of metabolism, and, second, the *psychological* process of metabolism inherent in the acquisition and consumption of information. The physiological process of
   energization accounts for the fact that individuals act as
   living systems, while the psychological process of information aquisition and consumption accounts for the direction
   of an individual's action.
2. The process of psychological metabolism, or communication, is not limited as to any specific time and place insofar
   as it is influenced by the individual's past experiences which
   in turn make up the models and concepts that enable him to
   communicate or prevent him from communicating with the
   world around him. Thus, the ability of an individual to take
   into account any specific set of cues is neither exclusively
   dependent upon his environment, nor is this ability exclusively dependent upon him as an individual, but is codetermined by him and his environment according to the nature
   of the transaction or communicative situation in which he
   is engaged.
3. Human behavior is basically purposive or goal–oriented
   behavior. That is not to say that all human behavior is
   consciously planned and determined, on the contrary, the
   greater part of an individual's behavior is automatistic in
   the sense that it is based primarily on unconscious or
   internalized goals and value structures.
4. A process of socialization accounts for the integration of an
   individual into a group, an organization, or a society. This
   process of socialization essentially constitutes a learning
   or "in-forming" of "appropriate" rules for behavior and
   response to behavior. The resulting "knowledge" accounts
   for the individual's ability or inability to act in various
   situations.
5. An individual attains stability with respect to his environment by forming commitments to certain values and standards of behavior. That is, through the process of socialization the individual acquires a value structure which in turn,
   through a process of internalization, becomes a possession
   and an integral part of his personality system.

For purposes of operationalizing these theoretical elements, a three-dimensional COMPACT model was developed to account for the structural and functional interrelationships among the following three constructs:

1. *A structural differentiation of continuous individual and organizational behavior processes.* This differentiation is achieved by means of a system of action analysis which, while accommodating analysis of isolated behavior segments, provides a means of mapping the essential interrelationships among individual behavior sequences and environmental influences.

2. *A conceptual differentiation of the scope and orientation of individual communicative competence.* This differentiation calls attention to five basic levels of models and standards which, it is postulated, together account for the form and direction actually taken by individual behavior. Each of the competence levels accounts for certain behavior influences inherent either in the individual as a physiological and a psychological system or in the external social and physical environment. It is highly doubtful that a given individual behavior sequence can be explained in terms of any one of these levels of competence, and a substantial amount of research is required before the interrelationships among the levels can be examined analytically.

3. *A conceptual differentiation of the interrelationships between individual competence and organizational structures.* It is postulated here that the efficiency and the effectiveness of an organizational structure is highly dependent upon the conceptual or communicative competence of the individuals comprising that organization. This postulate gives rise to a number of researchable questions which will be briefly outlined in a later section of this chapter.

The merging of the first two theoretical constructs produces a matrix matching the structurally differentiated *behavior sequences* (the system of action) with a conceptually differentiated scale of *communicative competence.* This matrix, or COMPACT model, subsequently serves as a basis for both descriptive and normative analysis of individual behavior in the context of an *organizational framework.* In a broad conceptual sense an organizational framework serves as both an enabler of, and a constraint upon, individual behavior. It serves as an enabler insofar as it *complements* individual competence, and as a constraint insofar as it *directs* individual behavior toward any goal that is in conflict with other goals.

XVII

The Implications

THE IMPLICATIONS OF THE concepts previously summarized can now be categorized as follows:

1. The strategic significance of the personal selling function derives from its potential role in the development and maintenance of intercommunicative relationships between selling and buying systems. Consequently, insofar as the personal selling function provides a set of dynamic and flexible channels of communication between the selling system and one or more buying systems it constitutes a distinct capital investment, the return on which is at least partly dependent upon the organizational product policies.

2. In the context of the marketing mix, the unique characteristic of the personal selling function is that it is a two-way communicative medium. Consequently, if properly integrated into the marketing function the salesman can serve as both an information disseminator and an information acquirer. The effectiveness and efficiency of the personal selling function in the context of the marketing mix are partly dependent upon the degree to which its unique characteristics or potential capacities are utilized. The cost per message of advertising is generally sufficiently lower than the cost per message of personal selling to render the latter comparatively inefficient in situations where advertising can serve the information dissemination requirements of the selling organization.

3. The relationship between the individual salesman and the selling organization is manifested in the task definition, selection, training, measurement of effectiveness and compensation systems of the organization. The essentially communicative nature of these systems implies a necessity of taking into account the competence of the individual salesman when attempting to establish the effectiveness of the individual-organization relationship.

4. An individual salesman's effectiveness is a function of his conceptual and communicative competence. Selling, in this sense, constitutes an establishment of an intercommunicative relationship for the purpose of exploiting, establishing, changing, or maintaining the actual or potential commonalities between selling and buying systems.

5. Motivation and competence are closely related and are integral elements of the individual personality system. It seems evident, therefore, that the salesman who is permitted to participate in decision making concerning the orientation and coordination of his task will also experience the motivation necessary to do so. Furthermore, the motivation usually bought through various compensation plans may be more easily achieved by enabling the salesman to exercise self-determination within the limits of his competence.

One of the fundamental lessons to be learned from a behavioral framework, such as that presented here, is that all systems of behavior are integrally related at one or more conceptual levels. For example, a salesman's loyalty is partly dependent upon the value he perceives a given organizational or interpersonal relationship to hold for him. Yet, merely manipulating the organizational framework is not likely to produce loyalty; it is the individual's *perception* of that framework which is the crucial element. Similarly, the institution of a training program designed to influence and change individual behavior is not likely to be successful if the salesman's values remain at odds with the organizational framework.

This interdependence of organizational structure and individual competence suggests a requirement for structural flexibility in organizational relationships. The purpose of an organizational framework is neither to establish rules and regulations circumscribing all individual behavior nor to avoid the specification of rules and regulations altogether. An *organizational framework is a means to an end.* and as such it should be sufficiently stable to permit the definition of individual relationships, and thereby facilitate communication. It should also be sufficiently flexible to enable individual members to contribute their competence to organizational pursuits as fully as possible. A structure of this type can not be established once and for all, but must be based on managerial willingness and facility for experimentation.

SOME NOTES ON EXPERIMENTATION

The dynamic nature of the personal selling function makes it peculiarly well-suited to an experimental approach to planning and decision making concerning the organization and performance of the function. Moreover, a direct requirement for an experimental approach both to the exploitation of opportunities and the solution of problems in marketing and personal selling arises from the need for organizational flexibility, mentioned above, and from a number of factors inherent in any planning and decision making process including:

1. The exceedingly large number of possible strategies in any given situation.
2. The impossibility of establishing unique estimates of the effectiveness of any given strategic course of action.
3. The constantly changing environment which makes any given strategic plan obsolete before it can be implemented.
4. The difficulty inherent in measuring even the relative effectiveness of any given performance.

These and other similar factors combine to make model building and planning in marketing and personal selling impossible to reduce to a few hard and fast rules. Yet the most imposing problem facing the modern marketing manager is not the technical one inherent in the development of planning models and control techniques, however difficult these tasks may appear. It is that of developing a concept or a theory of marketing which will enable him to interpret and evaluate performances and activities vis-à-vis a long-range conceptions of the marketing function. The key facilitating condition underlying an experimental approach to the performance and evaluation of marketing activities is the marketing manager's ability to conceptualize or organize the world of marketing as it pertains to his operations. It is in terms of such a conceptual organization that the manager must decide where he is, where he wants to be, how to get there, and how to measure whether or not he reached his goal.

With reference to the marketing function considered as a communication system subserving both producing and buying systems, several structural categories of the marketing manager's conceptual system can be identified. Each of these structural elements, which are outlined below, may be interpreted at several levels, and the complexity of the interpretation is directly related to the marketing manager's conceptual competence.

1. Awareness of a concept of marketing and personal selling as the communicative link between the process of technological innovation and the process of social innovation. The marketing manager's value structure cannot and should not be limited to economic values but must take into account the total range of standards and values governing human behavior. The measure of the effectiveness of any given marketing function is the degree to which it facilitates communication between producers and users of economic goods

and services as measured from the point of view of *both* producers and users.

2. An experimental approach to the acquisition of data relevant to and facilitating the allocation of available resources on the basis of the unique strengths and weaknesses of these resources. The key concept here is that of experimentation since routine collections of data have a tendency to create their own environment and structure, and consequently seldom prompt reallocation of resources but merely lead to an increase in the amount expended on any given approach.

3. Perhaps one of the most difficult problems facing the marketer is that of implementing his plans and strategies. In view of the tremendous expansion in efforts and techniques devoted to problem solving, comparatively little attention has been paid to the problem of translating plans into action. Yet, even the best plan is useless unless someone understands it and acts upon it. Some of the communication problems involved here are discussed in Chapter XIV.

4. A necessary requirement of any effective planning function is the feedback of relevant information. Relevance is determined by the theory underlying the plan as well as the operational implications of the feedback information. The increasing availability of data processing equipment has fostered such concepts as "real time" feedback based on an analogy to mechanical systems such as servomechanisms. Here, as elsewhere, the concern has been primarily with the techniques involved in developing feedback information rather than with the more crucial issues of meaning and operational implication.

5. The marketer's object of commitment is an important issue which has received little attention in the literature. Most writers and theorists avoid this issue by considering marketing as an end in itself. The practicing marketing manager, however, is ultimately faced with the issues of purpose and commitment with reference to marketing as a communication system. The economist attempts to solve the issue by means of a technique designed to measure marketing's contribution to the profit of the economic enterprise, a solution which appears conceptually unsatisfactory since marketing generates influences far beyond those accounted for in any given profit and loss statement. Even apart from the economic issue, however, a question still remains with reference to the professional marketer's loyalties, a question which is becoming more and more pressing of consideration in view of the lengthening shadow of government intervention and regulation.

The conceptual content of these structural categories essentially amounts to a strategic planning function. It is in this context

that the marketing manager must coordinate and direct the efforts
of the various information acquisition and dissemination functions
of the marketing system. It is often reported in the literature that
market researchers and controllers have a tendency to pursue
their data acquisition activities on the basis of standards and concepts which are technically correct but which have little or nothing
to do with the objectives of the marketing function. This situation
is not exclusively a function of the theoretical orientation of these
individuals, but is partly due to the absence of a viable theory of
marketing.

Perhaps it is useful here to step back and consider the basic
function of research and experimentation in the context of the
marketing system. The function of research and experimentation
is that of a communication system subserving the strategic and
tactical decision-making function of the marketing system. Clearly,
the researcher's or the controller's tasks are not those of generating an increasing *amount* of data with ever-decreasing time
intervals, but to improve upon the information content of the data
made available to the decision maker.

Improvement of the information content of data derived from
market research and experimentation is not, of course, exclusively a function of the techniques and methods utilized in the process
of collecting the data. The well-known communication barrier separating managers and researchers primarily results from the
limited degree of commonality in their respective goals and purposes. In this connection, the staff-line division of personnel and
of functional responsibility is carried to such lengths in many organizations that communication often is inhibited rather than
facilitated by the organizational framework.

The maximum benefit of research and experimentation cannot
be obtained unless intercommunicative relationships between managers and researchers are permitted and encouraged to develop.
It matters little that managers are pragmatically oriented and
researchers theoretically oriented if their respective competencies can be coordinated to produce a synergistically positive effect
in the direction of the achievement of strategically sound planning
and organizational activity.

The potential problems involved in experimentation with the
personal selling function are clearly more complex than in many
other experimental situations since not only the environmental
variables are continually changing, but also the object of experimentation, namely the salesman, continually modifies his behavior.
Moreover, any given sales force constitutes a much less flexible
quantity than say an advertising budget. Consequently, research
and experimentation in personal selling is dependent for its use-
fullness upon the communicative involvement of researchers and
sales personnel, not only for the purpose of avoiding conscious
or nonconscious resistance to experimental objectives by salesmen and sales managers, but also to enable researchers to go
beyond mere counting such as that evidenced in the time and duty

study recounted in Chapter IV. Moreover, the experimental objectives should not be limited to the development of ways and
means of manipulating the efficiency of the salesman's efforts
with reference to any given buying system, or set of buying
systems, but should also include investigations of the influence
exerted by the selling organization upon the salesman.

As emphasized throughout the study, the essential aspects of
research and experimentation, with reference to both marketing
and personal selling, are communicative. Consequently they are
subject to the theoretical considerations presented in Chapter X
and preceding chapters. Sound research and experimentation in
marketing must be relevant to and oriented toward the establishment, modification, or maintenance of those organizational and environmental conditions relevant to the accomplishment of the
conceived objectives of the organization or the subsystem within
the organization under consideration. Since the key factor here is
"conceived to be relevant," no marketing or sales effort can be
evaluated apart from conceived objectives, except in the abstract.
Thus, any real contribution of research and experimentation to the
operational effectiveness of marketing or personal selling must be
relevant to the models or assumptions upon which the existing
allocation and deployment of resources is based. Failure by the
researcher to take into account these underlying models and assumptions, or failure of the organizational framework to facilitate
the development of intercommunicative relationships between
managers and researchers to that end, is likely to be evident in
the form of communication "problems" regardless of the intrinsic quality of the research effort.

A PROSPECTUS FOR FUTURE RESEARCH

The concepts presented in the previous chapters, and primarily
those developed in Part Three, comprise a framework for viewing
the opportunities and problems of marketing and personal selling
in the context of behavioral theory, especially the theory and research developing in the fields of interpersonal and mass communication. Some of the broad implications of this approach to the
analysis of personal selling are discussed in Part Four.

In the present section, some of the future research opportunities relevant to both the generic concept of information acquisition
and consumption and the more specific research possibilities
relevant to marketing and personal selling will be discussed. The
general areas which appear to offer both interesting and valuable
research and development opportunities may be classified as
follows:

1. Exploration of and experimentation with the concept of mutuality or complementarity for the purpose of establishing

the empirical parameters of the concept and its implications for selling competence and training.

2. *The process of communicative interaction.* That is, the generation, dissemination, acquisition and consumption of information . . . seller-buyer relationship.

3. The empirical parameters establishing the *strengths and weaknesses of personal selling* (intercommunicative processes) and *advertising* (mass communicative processes) and their interaction effects.

The general purposes behind each of these possible research opportunities are to establish the operational usefulness of the concepts involved and to develop a basis for further conceptual advancement of the marketing and personal selling functons.

The Concept of Mutuality

The concept of mutuality was shown in Chapter X to be of central importance to a communication concept of marketing relationships. Any given economic enterprise, by virtue of its explicit or implicit strategic decisions is faced with essentially four general classes of communicative outcomes:

1. Those that are given or *inevitable* by virtue of the latent mutuality among the systems involved;

2. Those that are *possible* given a certain amount of promotional effort on the part of the marketer, or given a certain amount of search effort on the part of buyers, or given a combination of both;

3. Those that are *impossible* by virtue of a direct conflict between the objectives of selling and buying systems;

4. Those that occur *serendipitously* without intentional effort on the part of either seller or buyer.

The primary problem to be faced in future research is that of empirical verification of each of these conditions. Such empirical study should help establish guidelines for the allocation of intercommunicative and mass communicative efforts, and also contribute to a process of developing some measures of the nature and requirements of strategic selling competence. These measures may in turn help to establish an individual's ability to recognize and differentiate among the inevitable, the possible, and the impossible; and consequently to apply his tactical competencies where these will be most effectively and efficiently utilized.

A successful research program of this type should also be directly relevant to the problem of the skewed distribution of outcomes, given any set of inputs, as defined by Peter Drucker:

Any sales organization I have ever seen has the bulk of its salesmen—and especially the good men—working on the 90 per cent of the customers who, together, buy 10 per cent of the output, or on the 90 percent of products by number which together produce 10 per cent of the company's revenue and markets, and so on. Any technical service force—one of the most expensive and most valuable resources of a company—in the absence of the right information regarding market structure and customers, will put its men on the smallest and least valuable accounts, if only because these are the people who have the least technical competence themselves and therefore seem to need technical help the most. In fact this constant drift towards the irrelevant and unproductive is so great, and the weight behind it so heavy, that a "controls" system which did nothing but focus attention on the central events—the events which under normal probability statistics are not seen at all—would give any manager a great deal more control and very much better performance and results than the most elaborate simulation and quantification can possibly produce.[1]

Further clarification of the empirical elements of interpersonal and interorganizational mutuality of purpose and behavior should provide not only a partial solution to the problem outlined above, but also some guidelines with reference to the required content of training programs. This can enable salesmen to achieve more effective and efficient performance with a minimum of organizational direction and control. Recently developed techniques and methods of computer simulation, for example, appear to offer a useful stepping stone in the process of establishing and testing the nature and influence of mutuality as an intercommunicative enabler and constraint.[2]

The Communication Process

The personal selling function is composed of a number of subsystems (individuals and departments), each engaged in a basic communication process involving the generation, dissemination, acquisition, and consumption of information. In this connection, the basic elements of the personal selling function can be outlined as follows:

1. The organizational communication system manifest in the organizational information and control system;
2. The individual salesman considered as an information and decision system processing a given conceptual and communicative competence;
3. The buying system, organizational or individual, the communication system of which is manifest in the organizational information and control system and/or the conceptual competence of individuals influencing the buying process.

The generic communication process involved at the interfaces of these three system categories subsumes a number of research and theory areas such as decision making, problem solving, concept formation search strategies, conceptual structuring and the various interrelationships among these areas.

While some thought and research have been devoted to the generation and dissemination of data aspects, of the communication process, as well as the problems involved in storage and retrieval, much remains to be done in studying the acquisition and consumption aspects of the communication process. These are particularly important *since it is the acquisition and consumption subphrases which determine the relevance and value of the generation and dissemination subphrases.*

The basic purpose of a research program in the area of communication processes is that of developing generalizable answers to questions such as the following:

1. In what way does the manner, content, form, or extent to which the selling organization maintain contant with and control of the salesman influence the outcome of any given interaction between salesmen and buyer?
2. What is the effect, vis-à-vis the selling organization and any given buying system of a change in the salesman's competence, and how may this change be brought about most effectively and efficiently? The problem involved here is partly one of establishing the empirical usefulness of the competence dimension by determining the degree to which it can be measured and manipulated by means of various communicative techniques.
3. What empirical implications do the COMPACT model and the concomitant communication theory have for the analysis and prediction of the behavior of buying systems, as well as for the possibilities of influencing that behavior?

The COMPACT model should facilitate the development and structuring of a research program designed to establish and evaluate the flow of influences among these various systems and in addition it should provide a standard on the basis of which to detect improvement in performance. The aims of this research extend beyond the means and methods of such mathematical information theory concepts as channel capacity and signal-to-noise ratio, and will include contributions from fields as widely different in approach as those of physiological psychology (the study of intrapersonal communication processes) and sociology and cultural anthropology (the study of inter- and intra-organization and society communication). It is evident from the conceptual content of the COMPACT model that contributions from several disciplines will be required to further the understanding of the processes of intercommunication and mass communication.

The Interaction Between Personal and Nonpersonal Communication

The third experimental case recounted in Chapter IV constitutes an attempt to separate the effects of personal selling and advertising. It will be recalled that the researchers attributed the difference in effect to the relevant buyers rather than to the media as such. Undoubtedly, research into the communication process, as outlined above, will serve to further clarify the empirical boundaries of differential effects of promotional media. At the present time, viewpoints range from Marshall McLuhan's,"the medium is the message"[3] to a complete dismissal of any intrinsic media qualities. Whether or not any given medium modifies a specific message, however, must ultimately be determined by analyzing the receiver's ordering of the world and not by analyzing the medium as such.

Some of the questions which should be addressed by research in this area can be outlined as follows:

1. What unique consequences can be directly attributed to intercommunicative influences in any given interaction?
2. What unique consequences can be directly attributed to mass communicative influences in any given interaction?

It is quite possible, of course, that most consequences of any given set of interactions must be attributed to the fact that *both* personal and nonpersonal communicative media are used. In any case, the problem remains of developing empirical guidelines for the achievement of a synergistic effect of the allocation of resources to various media. The COMPACT model may serve as a useful structural device to supplement or even replace the black box model usually employed in such experiments. The aim of the research should be to establish the communicative boundaries of the interaction between the two types of media, that is, to develop some empirically useful concept of the unique characteristics of personal and mass communicative media, or a combination of both, as means of exploiting the interface between selling and buying systems.

The research areas outlined above are closely interrelated via the theory of communication and interaction developed in earlier chapters. Moreover, they are formulated so as to enable the researcher to draw upon several disciplines (i.e., economical behavioral sciences) to answer questions specifically relevant to marketing and personal selling. This is in keeping with the role of marketing science and the Marketing Science Institute, namely that of a communication system supporting the marketing community by acquiring and consuming widely dispersed concepts and research findings, and then generating and disseminating con-

ceptual and operational guidelines relevant to marketing as a
professional discipline.

SUMMARY

The purpose of the present chapter has been to summarize briefly
the concepts developed earlier and to outline a set of promising
research areas. The purpose of this book, as stated in the introduction is to contribute to the development of a theory of marketing
and more specifically personal selling. Basically the following
theoretical constructs have been advanced and described:

1. A structural-functional model designed to classify individual
   and organizational selling and buying behavior.
2. A communication theory designed to account for, and to
   serve as a basis for, explaining interpersonal and interorganizational influence.

While some of the implications of these two theoretical constructs are presented in Part Four, further research and development is clearly required to establish their empirical usefulness.
The potential research areas were broadly outlined as follows:

1. Investigation of, and experimentation with, the concept of
   mutuality of individual purposes and standards as a facilitator, of, and a barrier to, communication.
2. Development of the empirical parameters of the communication process itself as manifest in the selling organization—
   salesmen—buying system chain of influence.
3. Investigation of, and experimentation with, the unique and
   combined effects of personal and non-personal communication media at the interface of seller and buyer.

The ultimate aim of this report and the purposed research is
to develop a dynamic and viable theory of marketing as the
mediator or communication system between the realm of technological innovation and the realm of social innovation. That is the
meaning of the marketing concept, and the present volume is
offered as a contribution to the development and understanding of
the opportunities and limitations of this vital concept in its capacity as a philosophy of management.

Glossary

ACQUISITION denotes activities, behaviors, or performances directed at the mobilization of resources which can be used to facilitate the system's goal attainment.

ACTIVITY LEVEL is a concept encompassing competencies or abilities based primarily upon the physiological capacities of the individual (e.g., memory, manual dexterity, and appearance).

ACTOR is a term denoting an individual or an organization in their capacities as elements of systems of action.

APACS is the acronym for Adaptive Planning and Control Sequence described in Patrick J. Robinson and David J. Luck, *Promotional Decision Making: Practice and Theory.* (New York: McGraw-Hill Book Co., Inc., 1964, Chapter III).

AWARENESS denotes a condition or latent ability of a given system (individual or organization) to perceive and take account of its environment.

BEHAVIOR LEVEL is a concept comprising the adaptive competencies or abilities of an individual as manifested in the psychological characteristics of his personality system.

BUYING SYSTEM is a system of action oriented toward the acquisition and use of economic products or services.

CAUSE-EFFECT refers to a relation assumed between two events in order to explain one in terms of the other.

CHANGE AGENT is a catalytic agent, such as a management consultant, a trainer or a salesman, who has been trained to, and is oriented toward, the achievement of deliberate change in some other system.

CLOSED SYSTEM refers to a system which is self-sustaining and which does not normally engage in transactions across system boundaries (e.g., servo-mechanisms).

COGNITIVE DISSONANCE is a concept used to account for the conflict an individual experiences in the face of two equally acceptable alternatives, or in the case of an action which is perceived as incompatible with the individual's self-concept.

COMMITMENT denotes a gradually evolving process of internalization, or taking possession of certain concepts or behavior rules which in turn become conditions for the future activities of a given system.

COMMONALITIES refer to the motivational orientations and standards held in common by the majority of members of a given group.

COMMUNICATION is a term referring to an operation involving the organization of raw sensory data into information for eventual use in covert and overt behavior.

COMMUNICATION SYSTEM encompasses the value and concept structure which enables an individual or an organizational system to establish and maintain communicative metabolism with its environment.

COMMUNICATIVE FACILITATORS denote the transactional "costs" or "pay-offs" inherent in any communicative encounter.

COMPACT MODEL an acronym for the Competence-Activity matrix described in Chapter VI.

COMPENSATORY CONTROL SYSTEM denotes a system of authority and control which is designed to complement (or compensate for) the strengths and weaknesses of each member of the system being controlled.

COMPETENCE is a term describing the conceptual capacities of an individual to achieve his own purposes vis-à-vis his environment.

COMPLEMENTARITY is a concept referring to the mutual or overlapping aspects of the goals and standards of two or more individuals.

CONCEPTUAL FRAMEWORK See MODEL.

CONSTRAINT is a term used in allocation problems to refer to stated limitations on the range and alternative combinations of various resources.

CONTROL denotes a state of affairs as well as a future expectation. (Something is in or out of control.)

CONTROLS denotes the activities of measuring, analyzing and directing the operations of a social system.

CUES refer to data which are automatically recognized by the individual with reference to meaning and action requirements.

CULTURAL OBJECT denotes an institution, behavior rule, or tradition which must be taken into account by an individual in dealing with his environment.

CYBERNETICS is a Greek word meaning "steermanship" and pertains to the study of control in man and machine. The word was introduced by the mathematician Norbert Wiener.

DATA are manifestations of events or behavior occurring in the physical or social environments of a system.

DATA ACQUISITION refers to the information search or retreival activities and efforts of an information and decision system.

DATA CONSUMPTION See COMMUNICATION.

DATA DISSEMINATION refers to the transmission and distribution of data through channels of communication.

DATA GENERATION refers to a translation of concepts and ideas into transmittable data. (See also COMMUNICATION)

DIS-UNDERSTANDING refers to a receiver's deliberate or selective understanding of certain messages in the face of a perceived requirement for behavior change.

ENTROPY is a term deriving from the Second Law of thermo-dynamics, which states that "systems can only proceed to a state of increased disorder;" as time passes, "entropy can never decrease."

EPIPHENOMENON is a phenomenon which is secondary to, or a by-product of, one or more other phenomena.

FEEDBACK is a term used to relate the response of a system to the system's inputs and goals for the purpose of controlling the process according to desired standards.

FUNCTIONALISM is a method of explaining or classifying activities and social events by specifying the function or system oriented effect they serve.

FUNCTIONAL ANALYSIS comprises a description, normative or observational, of the system relevant effects of given activities or variables.

FUNCTIONAL REQUISITE denotes a set of operational conditions, or components of action, which must be satisfied if a given social system is to continue to exist.

GAMING See OPERATIONAL GAMING.

GOAL ATTAINMENT denotes activities, behaviors or performances directed at the achievement of certain possible and desired relationships between a system and its environment.

HARMONIZATION refers to the requirement for external and internal coordination of the various elements constituting the system with reference to a central concept or purpose.

HOLISM refers to the view that cause and effect analysis is inadequate as a method of cognition, because certain phenomena can be understood only if viewed in their entirety.

INFORMATION is data which have been "consumed" or to which an information and decision system has attributed meaning.

INTEGRATION denotes a systematic order or organization of related parts into a whole with reference to some overriding purpose.

INTERCOMMUNICATIVE RELATIONSHIP refers to the evolutionary (diachronic) encounter of two living systems (superior-subordinate, salesman-buyer, or husband-wife).

INTERFACE denotes a common boundary, for example, the boundary between two systems or, in computer terminology, two devices.

INTERNALIZATION refers to the process by which the individual acquires and integrates information as knowledge into his personality system.

INTUITIVE KNOWLEDGE refers to knowledge which cannot easily be verbalized. This inability to verbalize is not inherent in the situations involved and it is one objective of science to categorize or verbalize otherwise intuitive knowledge.

KNOWLEDGE is internalized and conceptually organized information which constitutes an integral part of the system structure (individual or organization).

LATITUDINAL ANALYSIS refers to the analysis of the behavior of two or more individuals at a given point in time for the purpose of discovering similarities and dissimilarities among these individuals.

LEARNING is a process of acquiring and integrating concepts and values additional to, or different from, the individual's existing concept and value structures.

LONGITUDINAL ANALYSIS refers to analysis of an individual's behavior over time for the purpose of gaining some understanding of the evolutionary characteristics of competence and behavior.

MACRO-ECONOMICS deals with the study of phenomena — consumption, investment — at the level of the total economy.

MARKETING is a process designed to create, modify exploit, or maintain a communicative relationship between utility producing and utility consuming entities of a social system.

MARKETING CONCEPT denotes the concept underlying customer oriented marketing efforts.

MARKETING MIX denotes a set of activities designed to provide a link between a producing entity and one or more consuming entities or systems with reference to a given product or product class.

MASS COMMUNICATION is a combination of communication and intercommunication modified by the characteristics of the medium involved.

MEANING refers to the conceptual and evaluative implications which an individual attributes to symbols and data.

MESSAGE denotes a transmitted series of words or cues *intended* to convey information.

METACOMMUNICATIVE FACILITATORS denotes the predilections of any given individual to agree, understand, accept or believe the statements of some other individual quite apart from the content of such statements.

MICROECONOMICS is the study of phenomena—price, output, income—at the individual, firm, and industry level.

MODEL refers to an abstract representation of the state of affairs under consideration to allow the application of deductive reasoning.

MOTIVATION denotes an individual's inherent drive or desire to engage in activities of various types as well as the direction such activities take.

MUTUALITY See COMPLEMENTARITY.

NORMATIVE or prescriptive theories differ from descriptive theories in that they tend to include norms or standards for the "best" behavior or course of action to follow under the given conditions.

OPEN SYSTEM refers to a system which engages in transactions with its environment across system boundaries.

OPERATIONAL GAMING is a type of simulation in which a human operator plays an active part in determining the output of the simulated situation or interaction.

OPERATIONAL RELEVANCE refers to a conceptualization or categorization of elements of a system in such a manner that remedial action is facilitated by the analysis.

PARAMETER is a factor in a mathematical or statistical equation which remains constant for one or more computations but is subject to alteration on the basis of a change in assumptions, or to reflect new reference conditions.

PERFORMANCE LEVEL is a concept encompassing a set of behaviors, or adaptively oriented activities, coordinated with reference to some overriding or future purpose.

PERSONAL SELLING is interpersonal, face-to-face interaction for the purpose of creating, modifying or maintaining a communicative relationship between utility producing and utility consuming entities or systems.

PERSUASION refers to a conscious or unconscious effort on the part of a communicator to influence the behavior of one or more individuals.

PHYSIOLOGICAL SYSTEM denotes the structure and function of the neurological communication system of living organisms.

PROCESS denotes a continuous forward or progressive movement or course of action.

PROMOTIONAL MIX denotes a set of promotional activities designed to disseminate data to buyers with reference to economic goods and services.

PROPERTIES are essentially the observable aspects or characteristics of the empirical world.

PSYCHOLOGICAL SYSTEM is a concept denoting an orderly arrangement (hierarchical levels) of the concepts and value structures which provide the orientation or direction of individual motivation.

QUALITATIVE refers to system properties which have not been quantified.

ROLE CONCEPT is an abstraction from the concrete behavior of people at given points in a social system and refers to commonalities of behavior and expectations among such similarly situated individuals.

SELECTIVE PERCEPTION is a concept used to account for the abilities and inabilities of individuals to take account of their environments.

SELF-CONCEPT is a term denoting the family of concepts an individual holds of himself vis-à-vis his environment.

SELLING SYSTEM is a system of action oriented toward the production and distribution of economic products or services.

SOCIALIZATION is a process of learning or informing by means of which an individual acquires a capacity to perceive and act "appropriately" in social interactions.

SOCIAL OBJECT denotes an individual, group, or organization which is capable of engaging in interaction with any other individual, group, or organization.

STIMULUS-RESPONSE denotes a theory of communication which basically assumes individual behavior to occur in response to stimuli originating in the individual's environment.

STRATEGIC DECISION MAKING denotes the determination of the basic long-term goals and objectives of a system, and the allocation of resources necessary for carrying out these goals.

STRUCTURAL MODEL is a description or classification of a pattern of interrelated activities, behaviors or performances.

STRUCTURAL-FUNCTIONAL MODEL of a system is a description of a certain order of determinate relationships, with reference to the systemic functions or effects of these relationships.

SYNERGISM refers to the interaction of factors in any activity so as to yield aggregate effects that are beyond the effects attainable by a simple addition of individual factors.

SYSTEM is a concept denoting an orderly arrangement of interdependent activities on the basis of some specified criterion, such as the function served by these activities.

SYSTEM LEVEL is a concept encompassing the integrative capacities of a given system with reference to both internal and external variables and vis-à-vis some specified objective.

SYSTEM OF ACTION denotes the configuration of activities and effects generated by any process of interaction between two or more individuals.

TACTICAL DECISION MAKING encompass short-term planning and decision making necessary for efficient and smooth operation of a system of action (organization).

THRESHOLD pertains to a sensation (physiological) or perception (psychological) barriers to an individual's data acquisition.

TRADE OFF is a term used in value theory to denote the amount of some resource or objective which a decision maker is willing to give up to acquire some other resource or achieve some other objective when both cannot be simultaneously obtained.

TRANSVECTION is the unit of action by which a single end product moved through all the intermediate sorts and transformations from raw material to consumption.

VALUE LEVEL is a concept encompassing the capacities or competencies of a given system to relate itself and its activities to a coherent set of moral or ethical values.

VERBAL ACUMEN denotes ability to speak or write fluently and lucidly.

Footnotes

CHAPTER I. THE OBJECTIVES

1. Patrick J. Robinson and David J. Luck, *Promotional Decision Making: Practice and Theory* (New York: McGraw-Hill Book Co., Inc., 1964).
2. *Ibid.,* p. 96.
3. Edward B. Weiss, *The Vanishing Salesman* (New York: McGraw-Hill Book Co., Inc., 1962).

CHAPTER II. AN UP-TO-DATE VIEW OF PERSONAL SELLING

1. This definition is closely related to that offered by William C. McInnes in "A Conceptual Approach to Marketing," *Theory in Marketing,* ed. Reavis Cox, Wroe Alderson, and Stanley J. Shapiro (Homewood, Illinois: Richard D. Irwin, Inc., 1964), p. 57.
2. The assumption of a homogeneous market is familiar in economic theory. However, the late Professor Wroe Alderson in his book *Dynamic Marketing Behavior* (Homewood, Illinois: Richard D. Irwin, Inc., 1965), pp. 23-51, adopts the opposite assumption: that of a heterogeneous market. (The heterogeneous market is assumed to be cleared by information rather than price.)
3. Harry R. Tosdal, *Principles of Personal Selling* (New York: McGraw-Hill Book Co., Inc., 1925), p. 4.
4. Paul W. Ivey, *Salesmanship Applied* (New York: McGraw-Hill Book Co., Inc., 1937), p. 9.
5. Albert Wesley Frey (ed.), *Marketing Handbook* (2d ed; New York: Ronald Press Co., 1965), p. 9.1.
6. Franklin B. Evans, "Selling as a Dyadic Relationship—A New Approach," *American Behavioral Scientist,* Vol. 6 (May, 1963), pp. 76-79.
7. Carl I. Hovland, Irving L. Janis, and Harold H. Kelley, *Communication and Persuasion* (New Haven: Yale University Press, 1953).
   Carl I. Hovland *et al., The Order of Presentation in Persuasion* (New Haven: Yale University Press, 1957).
   Irving L. Janis and Carl I. Hovland, *Personality and Persuasibility* (New Haven: Yale University Press, 1959).
8. Raymond A. Bauer, "The Communicator and the Audience," *Journal of Conflict Resolution,* Vol. 2 (March, 1958), pp. 67-77.

9. Theodore Levitt, *Industrial Purchasing Behavior* (Boston, Mass.: Harvard Business School, 1965).

10. Edward C. Bursk, "Low-Pressure Selling," *Harvard Business Review*, Vol. 25 (Winter, 1947), pp. 227–42.

    _____. "Opportunities for Persuasion," *Harvard Business Review*, Vol. 36 (September–October, 1958), p.p. 111–19.

11. Howard G. Sawyer, "Can Ads Sell as Well as Salesmen?" *Printer's Ink*, Vol. 248 (July 16, 1954), pp. 28–29.

12. "Cost of an Industrial Salesman's Call," McGraw-Hill Research Laboratory of Advertising Performance (New York: July 7, 1966).

13. H. Deane Wolfe and Gerald Albaum, "Inequality in Products, Orders, Customers, Salesmen, and Sales Territories," *Journal of Business*. (July, 1962), pp. 298–301.

14. Several authors have contributed to the development of this theory. In 1923, H.T. Copeland ("Relation of Consumer Buying Habits to Marketing Methods," *Harvard Business Review*, Vol. 1 [April, 1923], pp. 282–89) became curious about the disparity of buying motives as related to classes of goods, that is, convenience, shopping, and specialty goods. More recently, Richard H. Holton ("The Distinction between Convenience Goods, Shopping Goods, and Specialty Goods," *Journal of Marketing*. Vol. 23 [July, 1958], pp. 53–56) has written on the same subject. Both articles suggest, but do not explore thoroughly, the relationship between buying motives and a firm's marketing mix. Some attempts have also been made to explain interproduct differences in promotional mix, pricing, and channel policy as related to product and marketing characteristics.
    Leo V. Aspinwall ("The Characteristics of Goods Theory," *Managerial Marketing: Perspectives and Viewpoints*, ed. William Lazer and Eugene J. Kelley, [Homewood, Illinois: Richard D. Irwin, Inc., 1962], pp. 633–43) and more recently Gordon E. Miracle ("Product Characteristics and Marketing Strategy," *Journal of Marketing*, Vol. 29 [January, 1965], pp. 18–24) have written on this subject.

15. E.H. Lewis, "Sales Promotion Decisions," *Business News Notes* (Minneapolis: University of Minnesota) (Nov., 1954), p. 2.

16. Peter F. Drucker, *Managing for Results* (New York: Harper & Row Publishers, 1964), p. 10.

17. "Salesman's Nemesis: The Computer," *Sales Management*, Vol. 90 (April 5, 1963), p. 46.

18. Michiel R. Leenders, *Improving Purchasing Effectiveness Through Supplier Development* (Boston, Mass.: Harvard Business School, 1965), p. 7.

19. J. Porter Henry, Jr., "The Ten Biggest Mistakes Field Sales Managers Make," *Sales Management*, Vol. 90 (Titles of a series of ten articles published from July 5, 1963 through Nov. 15, 1963.)

20. Raymond O. Loen, "Sales Managers Must Manage," *Harvard Business Review*, Vol. 42 (May–June, 1964), p. 107.

21. "Attitudes Toward Selling; A Survey Among a Thousand College Men," *Sales Management*, Vol. 89 (Oct. 5, Oct. 19, and Nov. 2, 1962).
    See also: John L. Nelson, "The Low Prestige of Personal Selling," *Journal of Marketing*, Vol. 29 (October, 1965), pp. 7–10.

22. Whitney King, Jr., "Exploding Seven Myths About Salesmen," The *American Salesman* (November, 1962), pp. 26–30.

23. "Are There Enough Good Salesmen?" *Sales Management*, Vol. 87, No. 4 (August 18, 1961), p. 42.

24. "The Salesman's Role at P&G," *Sales Management*, Vol. 89, No. 9 (October 19, 1962), p. 71.

25. Roger H. Zion, *Keys to Human Relations in Selling* (Englewood Cliffs, N.J.: Prentice-Hall, Inc., 1963), p. 15.

26. Walter Horvath, *How to Overcome Objections in Selling* (Englewood Cliffs, N.J.: Prentice-Hall, Inc., 1954).
    Abbott P. Smith, *How to Sell Intangibles* (Englewood Cliffs, N.J.: Prentice-Hall, Inc., 1958).
    Elmer Wheeler, *Tested Ways to Close the Sale* (New York: Harper & Row Publishers, 1957).

27. Ray C. Brewster, "More Psychology in Selling," *Harvard Business Review*. Vol. 31 (July-August, 1953), p. 96.

28. David Mayer and Herbert M. Greenberg, "What Makes a Good Salesman," *Harvard Business Review*, Vol. 42 (July-August, 1964), p. 121. (Italics removed).

29. J. Russell Doubman, *Salesmanship and Types of Selling* (New York: Appleton-Century-Crofts, 1939), p. 117.

30. "Attitudes Toward Selling; A Survey Among a Thousand College Men," *op. cit.*

31. Samuel N. Stevens, "The Application of Social Science Findings to Selling and the Salesman," *Marketing Management and Administrative Action*, ed. Steuart Henderson Britt and Harper W. Boyd, Jr. (New York: McGraw-Hill Book Co., Inc., 1963), pp. 603-04. (Italics removed).

32. See for example: Elihu Katz and Paul Lazarsfeld, *Personal Influence* (New York: The Free Press, 1955).

33. Two recent contributions toward the alleviation of that problem are: Edgar Crane, *Marketing Communications: A Behavioral Approach to Men, Messages, and Media* (New York: John Wiley & Sons, Inc., 1965), and Joseph W. Thompson, *Selling: A Behavioral Science Approach* (New York: McGraw-Hill Book Co., Inc., 1966).

34. Merle Thorpe, *The Greatest Opportunity in the World: Selling* (New York: Hawthorn Books, Inc., 1957), pp. 26–27.

35. John Maynard Keynes, *The General Theory of Employment, Interest and Money* (London: Macmillan Co., 1961), pp. 96–97.

36. Sidney Weintraub, *Intermediate Price Theory* (Philadelphia: Chilton Books, 1964), pp. 232–33.

37. Talcott Parsons and Neil J. Smelser, *Economy and Society: A Study in the Integration of Economic and Social Theory* (New York: The Free Press, 1956).

38. Andreas G. Papandreou, "Some Basic Problems in the Theory of the Firm," *A Survey of Contemporary Economics*, ed. Bernard F. Haley (Homewood, Illinois: Richard D. Irwin, Inc., 1952) Vol. II, p. 184.

39. One of these exceptions is:
    D. Maynard Phelps and J. Howard Westing, *Marketing Management*, (Rev. ed.; Homewood, Illinois: Richard D. Irwin, Inc., 1960) which for several years has offered the only general approach to the problems of personal selling as an element of marketing.

40. Michael H. Halbert, *The Meaning and Sources of Marketing Theory* (New York: McGraw-Hill Book CO., Inc., 1965).

CHAPTER III. ANALYSIS OF SELLING COSTS AND RETURNS

1. George A. Miller, *Mathematics and Psychology* (New York: John Wiley & Sons, Inc., 1964).

2. It may, for example, be postulated that sales revenue (R), is some function of territory characteristics (T), characteristics of salesmen

(S), and various other elements of a company's marketing activities (C). A wholly explanatory "quantitative" representation of the above statement might be: $R = f(T + S + C)$.

3. It may thus be possible to organize the relevant sales revenue data, establish company inputs of dollars, measure the territorial characteristics by some reliable indexes, and use psychological test measurements and production records to define the salesman's characteristics. In this manner, the above discursive statement may be altered to $X_1 = a + b_2 X_2 + b_3 X_3 + b_4 X_4 + e$, where X_1 is dollars of sales revenue, X_2 is territorial characteristics, X_3 is salesman's characteristics, X_4 is a term combining the elements of company supportive activities, a is a constant (intercept term), and b_2, b_3, and b_4 are parameters or weights (net regression coefficients) associated with each of the independent variables of the equation. This so-called multiple regression equation constitutes a statistical model which purports to explain or predict the values of the dependent variables (sales revenue) when the values of the independent variables are known or estimated and "plugged into" the equation along with the regression coefficients.

4. See for example, Mordecai Ezekiel and Karl A. Fox, *Methods of Correlation and Regression Analysis* (New York: John Wiley & Sons, Inc., 1959).

5. A.M. Weitzenhoffer, "Mathematical Structures and Psychological Measurements," *Psychometrika*, XVI (December, 1951); p. 401.

6. John A. Howard, *Marketing Management: Analysis and Decision* (Homewood, Illinois: Richard D. Irwin, Inc., 1957); p. 368.

7. Paul E. Green and Donald S. Tull, *Research for Marketing Decisions* (Englewood Cliffs, N.J.: Prentice-Hall, Inc., 1966), p. 370.

8. *Ibid.*

9. The work of the Task Force is described in "Five-year Planning for an Integrated Operation," by Walter S. Glover and Russell L. Ackoff, *Proceedings of the Conference on Case Studies in Operations Research*, Case Institute of Technology, (1956) pp. 38-47.

CHAPTER IV. MEASURING EFFECTIVENESS AND DEVELOPING INCENTIVE PLANS

1. The input-output concept of promotional allocation is amenable to mathematical analysis by means of the so-called linear programming technique. This formulation of the promotional allocation problem is briefly outlined below:

Promotional Mix Equations	Inputs (Economic)	Outputs (Psychological)
I	$d_{11} y_1 + d_{12} y_2 \cdots + d_{1n} y_n$	$\geq B_1$
II	$d_{21} y_1 + d_{22} y_2 \cdots + d_{2n} y_n$	$\geq B_2$
Objective Function	$e_1 y_1 + e_2 y_2 \cdots + e_n y_n$	= a minimum

The d's are coefficients translating the input units into units of output. The first, d_{11}, stands for the units of psychological output, B_1, produced by one input unit of promotion type y_1. Equation I, then, describes a relationship between the output of B_1 derived from employing any given input mix y_1 and y_2. The least cost input mix is stated in the objective function equation, where the e's are the monetary cost per unit of each input. The d's termed technological coefficients, here represent the *effectiveness* of promotional inputs in terms of psychological outputs which are "translated" into economic outputs as follows:

Markets	Inputs (Psychological)	Outputs (Economic)
I	$a_{11}B_1 + a_{12}B_2 \cdots + a_{1n}B_n$	$\geq S_1$
II	$a_{21}B_1 + a_{22}B_2 \cdots + a_{2n}B_n$	$\geq S_2$

Objective Function	$c_1 B_1 + c_2 B_2 \cdots + c_n B_n$	= a minimum

For example, a minimum sales goal in market I of S_1 and in market II of S_2 might be specified. The a coefficients represent sales return per unit of psychological input of the specified kind in the specified market, and equations I and II are consequently economic output equations. The objective function specifies the "values" of the psychological inputs that will minimize an economic cost function within the constraints of the specified sales objective.

2. Patrick J. Robinson and David J. Luck, *Promotional Decision Making: Practice and Theory* (New York: McGraw-Hill Book Co., Inc.,1964).

3. Patrick J. Robinson, "R&D in Marketing Management," *Proceedings from the Membership Conference of the Marketing Science Institute* (Philadelphia, Pa.: May 25, 1965), p. 16.

4. Among the territorial variables which appeared to be significantly related to sales were the following:

x_1 = total population

x_2 = population of age 21 or over

x_3 = population living in cities

x_4 = average per capita income

The forecast took the form of an equation in which territorial sales in a period is equal to:

$$a_0 + b_1 x_1 + b_2 x_2 + b_3 x_3 + \cdots + b_n x_n$$

where the x's represent the values of the relevant territorial characteristics and the b's are regression coefficients obtained from the statistical analysis.

5. Joseph W. Thompson, *Selling: A Behavioral Science Approach* (New York: McGraw-Hill Book Co., Inc., 1966).

6. *Ibid.*, pp. 28-29.

7. Noble Hall, "Productivity Standards–Sales," Speech delivered before the Association of Sales and Marketing Executives, New York, November, 1950. The Atlantic Refining Co. Study is the most comprehensive under review and is based on studies of over one hundred salesmen in considerable detail.

8. James H. Davis, *Increasing Wholesale Drug Salesmen's Effectiveness* (Columbus, Ohio: Bureau of Business Research, College of Commerce and Administration, The Ohio State University, 1948).

CHAPTER V. SYSTEMS, COMMUNICATION, AND MOTIVATION

1. Lawrence C. Lockley, "An Approach to Marketing Theory," *Theory in Marketing,* ed. Reavis Cox, Wroe Alderson, Stanley J. Shapiro (Homewood, Ill.: Richard D. Irwin, Inc., 1964), p. 38.

2. For an excellent account of the role of functionalism in the social

sciences the reader is referred to: *Functionalism in the Social Sciences,* ed. Don Martindale, Monograph 5 in a series sponsored by the American Academy of Political and Social Science (Philadelphia, February, 1965).

3. A.R. Radcliffe Brown, *Structure and Function in Primitive Society* (New York: The Free Press, 1952).

4. Talcott Parsons, *The Structure of Social Action* (New York: McGraw-Hill Book Co., Inc., 1937).

5. Warren S. Torgerson, *Theory and Methods of Scaling* (New York: John Wiley & Sons, Inc., 1958), p. 9.

6. Wroe Alderson, *Dynamic Marketing Behavior* (Homewood, Illinois: Richard D. Irwin, Inc., 1965).

7. *Ibid.,* p. 24

8. Robert F. Spencer, "The Nature and Value of Functionalism in Anthropology," *Functionalism in the Social Sciences, op. cit.,* p. 13.

9. A system of action is any individual or social system considered from the point of view of the property: action.

10. Donald E. Payne (ed.), *The Obstinate Audience* (Ann Arbor, Mich.: Foundation for Research on Human Behavior, June, 1965), p. 1.

11. Lee Thayer, "On Theory-Building in Communication: Some Conceptual Problems," *Journal of Communication,* Vol. XIII, (December, 1963), p 219.

12. Nathan Maccoby, "Arguments, Counter-Arguments and Distractions," *The Obstinate Audience, op. cit.,* p. 37.

13. In connection with this definition, the authors gratefully acknowledge the insights of Lee Thayer, Director of the Center for the Advanced Study of Communication, University of Missouri at Kansas City.

14. D.O. Hebb, *The Organization of Behavior: A Neuropsychological Theory* (New York: John Wiley & Sons, Inc., 1949), p. 171.

15. Abraham H. Maslow, "Deficiency Motivation and Growth Motivation," *Nebraska Symposium on Motivation,* ed. Marshall R. Jones (Lincoln, Neb.: University of Nebraska Press, 1955), pp. 1-30.

16. David C. McClelland, "Notes for a Revised Theory of Motivation," *Studies in Motivation,* ed. David C. McClelland (New York: Appleton-Century-Crofts, 1955), pp. 231 & 233.

17. Lee Thayer, "Communication and Organization," *Human Communication Theory,* ed. Frank E.X. Dance (New York: Holt, Rinehart & Winston, Inc., 1967).

18. Donald W. Taylor, "Toward an Information Processing Theory of Motivation," *Nebraska Symposium on Motivation,* ed. Marshall R. Jones (Lincoln, Neb.: University of Nebraska Press, 1960), p. 67.

19. *Ibid.,* p. 68.

20. Bernard Berelson and Gary A. Steiner, *Human Behavior: An Inventory of Scientific Findings* (New York: Harcourt, Brace & World, Inc., 1964), p. 100.

CHAPTER VI. THE SYSTEM OF ACTION

1. John A. Howard, *Marketing: Executive and Buyer Behavior* (New York: Columbia University Press, 1963).

2. The following discussion is based in part on the structural model developed in *Toward a General Theory of Action,* ed. Talcott Parsons and Edward A. Shils (Cambridge, Mass.: Harvard University Press, 1952), although significant modifications have been made in the framework as presented here.

3. Reprinted with permission of The Macmillan Company from *Administrative Behavior* by Herbert A. Simon. Copyright The Macmillan Company, 1957.

4. Amitai Etzioni, *Modern Organizations,* © 1964. Reprinted by permission of Prentice-Hall, Inc., Englewood Cliffs, New Jersey.

5. Patrick J. Robinson and David J. Luck, *Promotional Decision Making: Practice and Theory* (New York: McGraw-Hill Book Co., Inc., 1964).

6. Patrick J. Robinson and Charles W. Faris, "Industrial Buying and Creative Marketing," (unpublished manuscript, Marketing Science Institute, Philadelphia, Pa., October, 1966).

7. Simon, *op. cit.,* p. 154.

8. Chester I. Barnard, *The Functions of the Executive* (Cambridge, Mass.: Harvard University Press, 1938), p. 187.

9. Based on a combination of the initial letters of the words *com*petence and *act*ivity.

10. Marshall McLuhan, *Understanding Media: The Extensions of Man* (New York: McGraw-Hill Book Co., Inc., 1965), p. 350.

11. *Ibid.,* p. 354.

CHAPTER VII. MARKETING AND COMMUNICATION

1. Daniel Katz and Robert L. Kahn, *The Social Psychology of Organizations* (New York: John Wiley & Sons, Inc., 1966), p. 262.

2. Alfred D. Chandler, Jr., *Strategy and Structure: Chapters in the History of the Industrial Enterprise* (Garden City, N.Y.: Doubleday & Co., Inc., 1966), p. 16.

3. Peter F. Drucker "The Executive's Job in Its Three Dimensions," and "Entrepreneurship in Business Enterprise," of the *Commercial Letter,* Canadian Imperial Bank of Commerce, Toronto: March, 1965.

4. William C. McInnes, "A Conceptual Approach to Marketing," *Theory in Marketing,* ed. Reavis Cox, Wroe Alderson, and Stanley J. Shapiro (Homewood, Ill.: Richard D. Irwin, Inc., 1964), p. 56.

5. Patrick J. Robinson and David J. Luck, *Promotional Decision Making: Practice and Theory* (New York: McGraw-Hill Book Co., Inc., 1964), p. 11.

6. The concept of a buying system will be discussed further in the following chapter.

7. Ernest Dichter, *Handbook of Consumer Motivations: The Psychology of the World of Objects* (New York: McGraw-Hill Book Co., Inc., 1964).

8. Wroe Alderson, *Dynamic Marketing Behavior* (Homewood, Ill.: Richard D. Irwin, Inc., 1965), p. 78.

9. Patrick J. Robinson and Charles W. Faris, "Industrial Buying and Creative Marketing" (unpublished manuscript, Marketing Science Institute, Philadelphia, Pa., October, 1966).

10. Alderson, *op. cit.,* p. 86.

11. *Ibid.,* p. 90

12. McInnes, *op. cit.,* p. 59.

13. Robinson and Faris, *op. cit.*

14. Herbert A. Simon, *Administrative Behavior* (2d ed.: New York: Macmillan Co., 1957), pp. 225–26.

15. Peter F. Drucker, "Controls, Control and Management," *Management Controls: New Directions in Basic Research,* ed. Charles P. Bonini, Robert K. Jaedicke and Harvey M. Wagner (New York: McGraw-Hill Book Co., Inc., 1964), p. 287.

16. Alexander H. Leighton, "The Functional Point of View," *Organizational*

Behavior and Administration: Cases, Concepts and Research Findings, ed. Paul Lawrence et al., The Irwin-Dorsey Series in Behavioral Sciences in Business. (Homewood, Ill.: Dorsey Press, Inc. and Richard D. Irwin, Inc., 1961), pp. 28-29.

CHAPTER VIII. A CONCEPT OF BUYING SYSTEMS

1. Clyde K. Kluckhohn, *Mirror for Man* (New York: Fawcett World Library, 1960), p. 57.
2. Edward T. Hall, *The Silent Language* (Garden City, N.Y.: Doubleday & Co., Inc., 1959).
3. *Ibid.,* p. 66.
4. *Ibid.,* p. 73.
5. Howard Baumgartel, "The Concept of Role," *The Planning of Change: Readings in the Applied Behavioral Sciences,* ed. Warren G. Bennis, Kenneth D. Benne, and Robert Chin (New York: Holt, Rinehart and Winston, Inc., 1962), p. 374.
6. Reprinted with permission of The Macmillan Company from *Administrative Behavior* by Herbert A. Simon. Copyright The Macmillan Company, 1957.
7. Patrick J. Robinson and Charles W. Faris, "Industrial Buying and Creative Marketing" (unpublished manuscript, Marketing Science Institute, Philadelphia, Pa., October, 1966).
8. W.T. Tucker and John J. Painter, "Personality and Product Use," *Dimensions of Consumer Behavior,* ed. James U. McNeal (New York: Appleton-Century-Crofts, 1965), pp. 75-76.
9. Kenneth E. Boulding, *The Image: Knowledge in Life and Society* (Ann Arbor, Mich.: Ann Arbor Paperbacks, University of Michigan Press, 1961), p. 84.
10. Adapted from: Wroe Alderson, *Dynamic Marketing Behavior* (Homewood, Ill.: Richard D. Irwin, Inc., 1965), p. 60.
11. *Ibid.,* pp. 60-61.
12. Robinson and Faris, *op. cit.,* p. 159.
13. *Ibid.,* p. 157-58.
14. *Ibid.,* p. 160.
15. *Ibid.*
16. Edward B. Weiss, *The Vanishing Salesman* (New York: McGraw-Hill Book Co., Inc., 1962), p. 104.
17. Marshall McLuhan, *Understanding Media: The Extensions of Man* (New York: McGraw-Hill Book Co., Inc., 1965), p. 354.
18. *Ibid.,* p. 219.
19. Weiss, *op. cit.*
20. See for example:
    Chris Argyris, *Integrating the Individual and the Organization* (New York: John Wiley & Sons, Inc., 1964).

CHAPTER IX. A CLASSIFICATION OF INDIVIDUAL BUYING BEHAVIOR

1. Reprinted with permission of The Macmillan Company from *Administrative Behavior* by Herbert A. Simon. Copyright The Macmillan Company, 1957.
2. Lee Thayer, *Administrative Communication* (Homewood, Ill.: Richard D. Irwin, Inc., 1961), p. 19.

3. Intentional communication means the intended meanings of the sender. As will be seen later, however, unintentional communication, or noise, may not be entirely dysfunctional.

4. Talcott Parsons, "Present Position and Prospects of Systematic Theory in Sociology," *Essays in Sociological Theory,* (Rev. ed.; New York: The Free Press, 1954), p. 234.

5. Patrick J. Robinson and Charles W. Faris. "Industrial Buying and Creative Marketing" (unpublished manuscript, Marketing Science Institute, Philadelphia, Pa., October, 1966).

6. Talcott Parsons, "Pattern Variables Revisited: A Response to Robert Dubin," *American Sociological Review,* Vol. 25 (August, 1960), pp. 467–83.

7. Robinson and Faris, *op. cit.*

8. Simon, *op. cit.,* p. 3.

9. Colin Cherry, *On Human Communication: A Review, Survey, and a Criticism.* (New York: John Wiley & Sons, Inc., 1957), p. 214.

10. Paul J. Brouwer, "The Power To See Ourselves", *How Successful Executives Handle People* (Boston, Mass.: Harvard Business School, 1965), p. 58.

11. Talcott Parsons and Edward A. Shils (eds.), *Toward A General Theory of Action* (Cambridge, Mass.: Harvard University Press, 1952), p. 133.

12. A discussion of the nature and effects of organizational "slack" can be found in: Richard M. Cyert and James G. March, *A Behavioral Theory of the Firm* (Englewood Cliffs, N.J.: Prentice-Hall, Inc., 1963), pp. 36-38.

13. Leon Festinger, "The Theory of Cognitive Dissonance," *The Science of Human Communication,* ed. Wilbur Schramm (New York: Basic Books, Inc., 1963)., pp. 19-20.

14. Gordon W. Allport, *Becoming: Basic Considerations for a Psychology of Personality* (New Haven: Yale University Press, 1955), p. 48.

15. Chris Argyris, "Interpersonal Competence and Organizational Effectiveness," *Interpersonal Dynamics: Essays and Readings on Human Interaction,* ed. Warren G. Bennis *et al.* (Homewood, Ill.: Dorsey Press, Inc., 1964), p. 631.

16. Morris J. Gottlieb, "Segmentation by Personality Types," *Marketing Management and Administrative Action,* ed. Steuart Henderson Britt and Harper W. Boyd, Jr. (New York: McGraw-Hill Book Co., Inc., 1963), pp. 134-42.

17. Wroe Alderson, *Dynamic Marketing Behavior* (Homewood, Ill.: Richard D. Irwin, Inc., 1965), p. 356.

18. Robert Tannebaum, Irving R. Weschler, and Fred Massarik, "The Process of Understanding People," *Interpersonal Dynamics: Essays and Readings on Human Interaction,* ed. Warren G. Bennis et al. (Homewood, Ill.: Dorsey Press, Inc., 1964), p. 940.

19. John A. Howard, *Marketing: Executive and Buyer Behavior* (New York: Columbia University Press, 1963), Chapter V.

20. Robinson and Faris, *op. cit.,*

21. Allport, *op. cit.,* p. 73.

22. James U. McNeal (ed.), *Dimensions of Consumer Behavior* (New York: Appleton-Century-Crofts, 1965), p. 1.

23. In a recent article, Professor Philip Kotler discusses five different models of the buyer's "black box" which may have some interesting connections with the system presented here. Professor Kotler discusses the following models:

Economic Model (economic motivations)
Pavlovian Model (learning or conditioning)
Freudian Model (psychoanalytic motivation)
Veblenian Model (social-psychological factors)
Hobbesian Model (organizational factors)
Philip Kotler, "Behavioral Models for Analyzing Buyers," *Journal of Marketing*, Vol. 29 (October, 1965), pp. 37-45.
24. Simon, *op. cit.*, p. 15.

CHAPTER X. COMMUNICATION IN A MARKETING CONTEXT

1. The authors gratefully acknowledge the substantial contribution to the development of the concepts in this chapter by Lee Thayer, Professor and Director of the Center for the Advanced Study of Communication, University of Missouri at Kansas City, Missouri.
2. Lee Thayer, "Communication and Organization," *Human Communication Theory*, ed. Frank E.X. Dance (New York: Holt, Rinehart and Winston, Inc., 1967).
3. The following paragraphs are adapted from: Kaiser Aluminum and Chemical Corporation, "Communications," *Kaiser Aluminum News*, Vol. 23 (1965), p. 15.
4. Colin Cherry, *On Human Communication: A Review, a Summary and a Criticism* (New York: John Wiley & Sons, Inc., 1957), p. 10.
5. Lee Thayer, "Data, Information, Decision: Some Perspectives on Marketing as a Communication System," *Concepts for Advertising*. Proceedings from the 8th Annual Meeting of the American Academy of Advertising, at Miami Beach, June, 1966.
6. *Ibid.*
7. Ronald Lippitt, Jeanne Watson, and Bruce Westley,*The Dynamics of Planned Change: A Comparative Study of Principles and Techniques* (N.Y.: Harcourt, Brace & World, Inc., 1958), p. 78.
8. Irwin D.J. Bross, *Design for Decision* (New York: Macmillan Co., 1953), pp. 19-20.
9. Michael H. Halbert, *The Meaning and Sources of Marketing Theory* (New York: McGraw-Hill Book Co., Inc., 1965), p. 23.
10. Acknowledgement is due Lee Thayer for both the content and the formulation of this definition.
11. Raymond A. Bauer, "Communication as Transaction," *The Obstinate Audience*. ed. Donald E. Payne (Ann Arbor, Mich.: Foundation for Research on Human Behavior, June 1965), pp. 3-12.
12. Donald F. Cox, "Clues for Advertising Strategists,"*Harvard Business Review*. Vol. 39 (September-October, 1961), p. 172.
13. Patrick J. Robinson, "R & D in Marketing Management," *Proceedings of the Membership Conference of the Marketing Science Institute*(Philadelphia, Pa., May 25, 1965), p. 4.
14. Edward C. Bursk, "Opportunities for Persuasion," *Harvard Business Review*. Vol. 36 (September-October, 1958), p. 112.
15. See for example:
John C. Maloney, "Is Advertising Believability Really Important?" *Journal of Marketing*. Vol. 27 (October, 1963).
16. F.J. Roethlisberger, "Training Supervisors in Human Relations," *Harvard Business Review*, Vol. 29 (September-October, 1951), p. 51.

17. See for example:
Leland P. Bradford, Jack R. Gibb, and Kenneth D. Benne (eds.), *T–Group Theory and Laboratory Method* (New York: John Wiley & Sons, Inc., 1964).
Herbert A. Shepard, "The T-Group as Training in Observant Participation," *The Planning of Change: Readings in the Applied Behavioral Sciences,* ed. Warren G. Bennis, Kenneth D. Benne, and Robert Chin (New York: Holt, Rinehart and Winston, Inc., 1962), pp. 637-43.
Grace Levit and Helen H. Jennings, "Learning Through Role Playing," *ibid.*, pp. 706-10.
Kenneth D. Benne, "Case Methods in the Training of Administrators," *ibid.*, pp. 631-36.
18. Bennis, Benne, and Chin (eds.), *op. cit.* p. 3.
19. Ronald Lippitt, Jeanne Watson, and Bruce Westley, *The Dynamics of Planned Change: A Comparative Study of Principles and Techniques* (N.Y.: Harcourt, Brace and World, Inc., 1958), pp. 84-85. (Italics added).
20. See for example:
Ibid.
Bennis, Benne, and Chin, *op. cit.*
21. Edward C. Bursk, "Thinking Ahead: Drift to No-Pressure Selling," *Harvard Business Review,* Vol. 34 (september-October, 1956), p. 26.

CHAPTER XI. THE MARKETING MIX
AND SOME CONCEPTUAL ISSUES

1. Jacques Ellul, *Propaganda: The Formation of Men's Attitudes,* translated by Konrad Kellen and Jean Lerner (New York: Alfred A. Knopf, Inc., 1965) p. 294.
2. See Chapter 1.
3. Patrick J. Robinson and Charles W. Faris, "Industrial Buying and Creative Marketing" (unpublished manuscript, Marketing Science Institute, Philadelphia, Pa., October, 1966).
4. *Ibid.*
5. Bruce D. Henderson, "Purchasing's Part in Corporate Strategy," *Purchasing,* Vol. 60 (January 13, 1966), pp. 76-78.
6. Wroe Alderson, *Dynamic Marketing Behavior* (Homewood, Ill.: Richard D. Irwin, Inc., 1964), p. 98.
7. William H. Whyte, Jr., *The Organization Man* (Garden City, N.Y.: Doubleday Anchor Books, Doubleday & Co., Inc.), 1957.
8. Vance Packard, *The Hidden Persuaders* (New York: Pocket Books, Inc.), 1958.
Vance Packard, *The Waste Makers* (New York: Pocket Books, Inc.), 1963.
9. See for example: Pierre Berton, *The Big Sell* (New York: Alfred A. Knopf, Inc., 1963), for a discerning analysis of "sharp" practices in Canada.
10. Ellul, *op. cit.,* pp. 275-76.
11. Alderson, *op. cit.,* p. 73.
12. *Ibid.,* p. 128.
13. Shirley A. Star and Helen M. Hughes, "Report on an Educational Campaign: The Cincinnati Plans for the United Nations," *American Journal of Sociology,* Vol. 55 (January, 1950), pp. 389-400. On the basis of the survey completed in connection with the campaign, it was concluded that individual interest is a necessary requirement for the success of

informational campaigns (propaganda), and that the information disseminated must be functional (perceived as being of use) to be heeded and retained.

14. Lee Thayer, *Administrative Communication* (Homewood, Ill.: Richard D. Irwin, Inc., 1961), pp. 93–94.

15. Elihu Katz and Paul Lazarsfeld, *Personal Influence* (New York: The Free Press, 1955).

CHAPTER XII. THE SALESMAN
AND HIS COMPETENCE AS A COMMUNICATOR

1. Edward C. Bursk, "Low Pressure Selling," *Harvard Business Review*, Vol. 25 (Winter, 1947), p. 227–42.
   _____. "Thinking Ahead: Drift to No-Pressure Selling," *Harvard Business Review*, Vol. 34 (September-October 1956), pp. 25–30.
   _____. "Opportunities for Persuasion," *Harvard Business Review*, Vol. 36 (September-October 1958), pp. 111–19.

2. Robert N. McMurry, "The Mystique of Super Salesmanship," *Harvard Business Review*, Vol. 39 (March-April, 1961), p. 119.

3. George N. Kahn and Abraham Shuchman, "Specialize Your Salesmen!" *Harvard Business Review*, Vol. 39 (January-February, 1961), pp. 90–98.

4. *Sales Management* Magazine's Survey of Buying Power Index is perhaps the best known example.

5. Peter F. Drucker, *Managing for Results* (New York: Harper and Row Publishers, 1964), p. 9.

6. Peter F. Drucker, *Landmarks of Tomorrow* (New York: Harper and Row Publishers, 1959), p. 270.

CHAPTER XIII. SELECTION AND TRAINING
OF THE SALESMAN

1. See for example: Charles L. Lapp, *Successful Selling Strategies* (New York: McGraw-Hill Book Co., Inc., 1957) and Steven J. Shaw and Joseph W. Thompson, *Salesmanship: Modern Viewpoints on Personal Communication* (New York: Holt, Rinehart and Winston, Inc., 1960).

2. See for example:
   Martin L. Gross, *The Brain Watchers* (New York: The New American Library, Inc., 1962).

3. See example: Benjamin Balinsky and Ruth Burger, *The Executive Interview: A Bridge to People* (New York: Harper & Row Publishers, 1959); R.L. Kahn and C.F. Cannell, *The Dynamics of Interviewing: Theory, Techniques and Cases* (New York: John Wiley & Sons, Inc., 1957); and D. Maynard Phelps and J. Howard Westing, *Marketing Management* (Rev. ed.; Homewood, Ill.: Richard D. Irwin, Inc., 1960), Chapter XXI.

4. *Ibid.*

5. Adapted from: Leland P. Bradford, "The Teaching-Learning Transaction," *The Planning of Change: Readings in the Applied Behavioral Sciences*, ed. Warren G. Bennis, Kenneth D. Benne, and Robert Chin (New York: Holt, Rinehart and Winston, Inc., 1962), p. 494.

6. James V. Clark, *Education for the Use of Behavioral Science* (Los Angeles, California: Institute of Industrial Relations, University of California, 1962), pp. 39–40.

7. *Ibid.* p. 45.
8. Paraphrased from: Warren G. Bennis, "Goals and Meta-Goals of Laboratory Training," *Interpersonal Dynamics: Essays and Readings on Human Interaction,* Warren G. Bennis *et al,* (Homewood, Ill.: Dorsey Press, Inc., 1964), pp. 692-98.
9. *Ibid.* p. 693.
10. Kenneth D. Benne, "Case Methods in the Training of Administrators," *The Planning of Change: Readings in the Applied Behavioral Sciences, op. cit.,* p. 634.
11. Grace Levit and Helen H. Jennings, "Learning Through Role Playing," *ibid.,* p. 707.
12. Matthew B. Miles, "The Training Group," *ibid.,* pp. 724-25.
13. Joel M. Kibbee, Clifford J. Craft, and Burt Nanus, *Management Games: A New Technique for Executive Development* (New York: Reinhold Publishing Corporation, 1961), p. 41.

CHAPTER XIV. MEASURING SALES EFFECTIVENESS AND PLANNING COMPENSATION

1. Frieda Fromm-Reichmann, "On Listening," *Interpersonal Dynamics: Essays and Readings on Human Interaction,* ed. Warren G. Bennis *et al.* (Homewood, Ill.: Dorsey Press Inc., 1964), p. 718. (Italics added)
2. Raymond O. Loen, "Sales Managers Must Manage," *Harvard Business Review,* Vol. 42 (May-June, 1964), p. 109.
3. Reprinted with permission of The Macmillan Company from *Administrative Behavior* by Herbert A. Simon. Copyright The Macmillan Company, 1957.
4. Daniel Katz and Robert L. Kahn, *The Social Psychology of Organizations* (New York: John Wiley & Sons, Inc., 1966), p. 352.
5. Harry R. Tosdal, "How to Design the Salesman's Compensation Plan," *Harvard Business Review,* Vol. 31 (September-October, 1953), p. 64.
6. Katz and Kahn, *op. cit.,* p. 354.
7. Jack R. Gibb, "Fear and Facade: Defensive Management," *Science and Human Affairs.* ed. Richard E. Farson (Palo Alto, California: Science and Behavior Books, Inc., 1965), p. 201.

CHAPTER XV. THE CONCEPT OF COMPENSATORY CONTROL

1. Amitai Etzioni, *Modern Organizations,* © 1964. Reprinted by permission of Prentice-Hall, Inc., Englewood Cliffs, New Jersey.
2. Normally associated with Frederick W. Taylor and his work: *The Principles of Scientific Management* (New York: Harper & Row Publishers, 1911).
3. Etzioni, *op. cit.,* p. 40. (Italics added)
4. Peter F. Drucker, *Managing for Results* (New York: Harper & Row Publishers, 1964).
5. Douglas M. McGregor, "The Human Side of Enterprise," *The Planning of Change: Readings in the Applied Behavioral Sciences,* ed. Warren G. Bennis, Kenneth D. Benne, and Robert Chin (New York: Holt, Rinehart and Winston, Inc., 1962), p. 423.
6. *Ibid,* p. 428.
7. Kenneth J. Arrow, "Research in Management Controls: A Critical Synthesis," *Management Controls: New Directions in Basic Research,* ed.

Charles P. Bonini, Robert K. Jaedicke, and Harvey M. Wagner (New York: McGraw-Hill Book Co., Inc., 1964), pp. 317-18.

8. The Marketing Science Institute is presently engaged in an extensive study of and experimentation with, the role of information and control systems in management. This study is tentatively entitled: "Management Information and Control Requirements."

9. Lawrence K. Frank, *Nature and Human Nature: Man's New Image of Himself* (New Brunswick, N.J.: Rutgers University Press, 1951), p. 53.

10. See for example: H. Igor Ansoff, *Corporate Strategy: An Analytic Approach to Business Policy for Growth and Expansion* (New York: McGraw-Hill Book Company, Inc. 1965), Chapter 5.

11. Richard Bellman, *Adaptive Control Processes* (Princeton, N.J.: Princeton University Press, 1961), p. 201.

12. See for example:
John D.C. Little, *A Model of Adaptive Control of Promotional Spending*. Working Paper (Cambridge, Mass.: Alfred P. Sloan School of Management, Massachusetts Institute of Technology, July 1, 1965) and
Peter T. FitzRoy, "An Adaptive Model of Promotional Expenditure Determination," *Proceedings of the Fall Conference* (Washington, D.C.: American Marketing Association, 1965), pp. 370-76.

13. Peter F. Drucker, "Controls, Control and Management" *Management Controls: New Directions in Basic Research, op. cit.,* pp. 288-89.

14. David Mayer and Herbert M. Greenberg, "What Makes a Good Salesman," *Harvard Business Review,* Vol. 42 (July-August, 1964), pp. 119-25.

15. *Ibid.*, p. 125.

16. *Ibid.*, p. 120.

17. Jack R. Gibb, "Fear and Facade: Defensive Management," in *Science and Human Affairs,* ed. Richard E. Farson (Palo Alto, California: Science and Behavior Books, Inc., 1965), p. 207.

18. Drucker, "Controls, Control and Management," *op. cit.,* p. 287.

19. Michael Schiff and Martin Mellman, *Financial Management of the Marketing Function,* (New York: Financial Executives Research Foundation, 1962).

20. *Ibid.*, p. 34.

21. *Ibid.*, p. 49.

22. *Ibid.*, p. 58.

23. *Ibid.*, p. 134.

24. *Ibid.*, p. 142.

25. *Ibid.*, p. 144.

26. *Ibid.*, p. 141.

27. *Ibid.*, p. 134.

28. *Ibid.*, p. 146.

CHAPTER XVI. A REVIEW

No footnotes.

CHAPTER XVII. THE IMPLICATIONS

1. Peter F. Drucker, "Controls, Control and Management," *Management Controls:* New Directions in Basic Research, ed. Charles P. Bonini, Robert K. Jaedicke, and Harvey M. Wagner (New York: McGraw-Hill

Book Co., 1964), p. 291.

2. See for example: Russell L. Ackoff (ed.), *Progress in Operations Research*. Vol. I. (New York: John Wiley & Sons, Inc. 1961), particularly Chapter IX.

3. Marshall McLuhan, *Understanding Media: The Extensions of Man* (New York: McGraw-Hill Book Co., Inc. 1965).

Bibliography

Abelson, Herbert I. *Persuasion; How Opinions and Attitudes Are Changed.* New York: Springer Publishing Co., Inc., 1959.

Ackoff, Russell L. "Allocation of Sales Effort," *Proceedings of the Conference on "What is Operations Research Accomplishing for Industry?"* Cleveland: Case Institute of Technology, April 1955, pp. 23-30.

____(ed.). *Progress in Operations Research,* Vol. I, New York: John Wiley & Sons, Inc., 1961.

Alderson, Wroe. *Marketing Behavior and Executive Action.* Homewood, Ill.: Richard D. Irwin, Inc., 1957.

____. *Dynamic Marketing Behavior.* Homewood, Ill.: Richard D. Irwin, Inc., 1965.

____. and Green, Paul E. *Planning and Problem Solving in Marketing.* Homewood, Ill.: Richard D. Irwin, Inc., 1964.

____. and Shapiro, Stanley J. (eds.). *Marketing and the Computer.* Englewood Cliffs, N.J.: Prentice-Hall, Inc., 1963.

Allport, Gordon W. *Becoming: Basic Considerations for a Psychology of Personality.* New Haven: Yale University Press, 1955.

Anderson, Harold H. (ed.). *Creativity and Its Cultivation.* New York: Harper and Row Publishers, 1959.

Ansoff, H. Igor. *Corporate Strategy: An Analytic Approach to Business Policy for Growth and Expansion.* New York: McGraw-Hill Book Co., Inc. 1965.

"Are There Enough Good Salesmen?" *Sales Management,* Vol. 87 (August 18, 1961), pp. 42-43.

Argyris, Chris. *Personality and Organization.* New York: Harper & Row Publishers, 1957.

____. *Integrating the Individual and the Organization.* New York: John Wiley & Sons, Inc., 1964.

____. "Interpersonal Competence and Organizational Effectiveness," *Interpersonal Dynamics: Essays and Readings on Human Interaction.* Edited by Warren G. Bennis, *et al.* Homewood, Ill.: Dorsey Press, Inc., 1964, pp. 624-38.

Arrow, Kenneth J. "Research in Management Controls: A Critical Synthesis," *Management Controls: New Directions in Basic Research.* Edited by Charles P. Bonini, Robert K. Jaedicke, and Harvey M. Wagner. New York: McGraw-Hill Book Co., Inc., 1964, pp. 317-27.

Aspinwall, Leo V. "The Characteristics of Goods Theory," *Managerial Marketing: Perspectives and Viewpoints.* Edited by William Lazer, and Eugene J. Kelley. Homewood, Ill.: Richard D. Irwin, Inc., 1962, pp. 633-43.

"Attitudes Toward Selling: A Survey Among a Thousand College Men." *Sales Management,* Vol. 89 (October 5, October 19, and November 2, 1962).

Balinsky, Benjamin, and Burger, Ruth. *The Executive Interview: A Bridge to People.* New York: Harper & Row Publishers, 1959.

Barnard, Chester I. *The Functions of the Executive.* Cambridge, Mass.: Harvard University Press, 1938.

Bass, Frank M., *et al.* (eds.). *Mathematical Models and Methods in Marketing.* Homewood, Ill.: Richard D. Irwin, Inc., 1961.

Bauer, Raymond A. "The Communicator and the Audience," *Journal of Conflict Resolution,* Vol. 2 (March, 1958), pp. 67-77.

——. "Communication as Transaction." *The Obstinate Audience.* Edited by Donald E. Payne. Ann Arbor, Mich.: Foundation for Research on Human Behavior, June, 1965, pp. 3-12.

Baumgartel, Howard. "The Concept of Role," in *The Planning of Change: Readings in the Applied Behavioral Sciences.* Edited by Warren G. Bennis, Kenneth D. Benne, and Robert Chin. New York: Holt, Rinehart and Winston, Inc., 1962, pp. 373-76.

Baumol, William J. *Economic Theory and Operations Analysis.* 2d ed. Englewood Cliffs, N.J.: Prentice-Hall, Inc., 1965.

Beer, Stafford. *Cybernetics and Management.* New York: John Wiley & Sons, Inc., 1959.

Bellman, Richard. *Adaptive Control Processes.* Princeton, N.J.: Princeton University Press, 1961.

Benne, Kenneth D. "Case Methods in the Training of Administrators," *The Planning of Change: Readings in the Applied Behavioral Sciences.* Edited by Warren G. Bennis, Kenneth D. Benne, and Robert Chin. New York: Holt, Rinehart, and Winston, Inc., 1962, pp. 631-36.

Bennis, Warren G. "Goals and Meta-Goals of Laboratory Training," *Interpersonal Dynamics: Essays and Readings on Human Interaction.* Edited by Warren G. Bennis, *et al.* Homewood, Ill.: Dorsey Press, Inc., 1964, pp. 692-98.

——. *Changing Organizations.* New York: McGraw-Hill Book Co., Inc., 1966.

——. Benne, Kenneth D., and Chin, Robert (eds.). *The Planning of Change: Readings in the Applied Behavioral Sciences.* New York: Holt, Rinehart, and Winston, Inc., 1962.

——. *et al.* (eds.). *Interpersonal Dynamics: Essays and Readings on Human Interaction.* Homewood, Ill.: Dorsey Press, Inc., 1964.

Berelson, Bernard, and Steiner, Gary A. *Human Behavior: An Inventory of Scientific Findings.* New York: Harcourt, Brace & World, Inc., 1964.

Berlo, David K. *The Process of Communication.* New York: Holt, Rinehart and Winston, Inc., 1960.

Berton, Pierre. *The Big Sell.* New York: Alfred A. Knopf, Inc., 1963.

Blake, Robert R., and Mouton, Jane S. *The Managerial Grid: Key Orientations for Achieving Production Through People.* Houston, Texas: Gulf Publishing Company, 1964.

Bliss, Perry (ed.). *Marketing and Behavioral Sciences.* Boston: Allyn and Bacon, Inc., 1963.

Bonini, Charles P., Jaedicke, Robert K., Wagner, Harvey M. (eds.). *Management Controls: New Directions in Basic Research.* New York: McGraw-Hill Book Co., Inc., 1964.

Boulding, Kenneth E. *The Image: Knowledge in Life and Society.* Ann Arbor, Mich.: Ann Arbor Paperbacks, The University of Michigan Press, 1961.

Box, George E.P. "Evolutionary Operation: A Method for Increasing Industrial Productivity," *Applied Statistics,* Vol. 6 (June, 1957), pp. 81-101.

Bradford, Leland P. "The Teaching-Learning Transaction," in *The Planning of Change: Readings in the Applied Behavioral Sciences.* Edited by Warren G. Bennis, Kenneth D. Benne, and Robert Chin. New York: Holt, Rinehart and Winston, Inc., 1962, pp. 493-502.

——, Gibb, Jack R., and Benne, Kenneth D. (eds.). *T-Group Theory and Laboratory Method.* New York: John Wiley & Sons, Inc., 1964.

Brewster, Ray C. "More Psychology in Selling," *Harvard Business Review*, Vol. 31 (July-August, 1953), pp. 91-99.

Britt, Steuart Henderson, and Boyd, Harper W., Jr. *Marketing Management and Administrative Action.* New York: McGraw-Hill Book Co., Inc., 1963.

Brooks, Robert C., Jr. "Relating the Selling Effort to Patterns of Purchase Behavior," *Business Topics*, Vol. 11 (Winter, 1963), pp. 77-79.

Bross, Irwin D.J. *Design for Decision.* New York: Macmillan Co., 1953.

Brouwer, Paul J. "The Power to See Ourselves," *How Successful Executives Handle People.* Boston, Mass.: Harvard Business School, 1965, pp. 58-65.

Brown, Arthur A., Hulsmit, Frank T., and Kettelle, John D. "A Study of Sales Operations," *Operations Research*, Vol. 4 (June, 1956), pp. 296-308.

Brown, A.R. Radcliffe. *Structure and Function in Primitive Society.* New York: The Free Press, 1952.

Bruner, J.S., Goodnow, J.J., and Austin, G.A. *A Study of Thinking.* New York: John Wiley & Sons, Inc., 1956.

Burns, T., and Stalker, G.M. *The Management of Innovation.* London: Tavistock Publishers, Ltd., 1961.

Bursk, Edward C. "Low-Pressure Selling," *Harvard Business Review*, Vol. 25 (Winter, 1947), pp. 227-42.

——. "Thinking Ahead: Drift to No-Pressure Selling," *Harvard Business Review*, Vol. 34 (September-October, 1956), pp. 25-30.

——. "Opportunities for Persuasion," *Harvard Business Review*, Vol. 36 (September-October, 1958), pp. 111-19.

Buzzell, Robert D. *Mathematical Models and Marketing Management.* Boston, Mass.: Harvard Business School, 1964.

Canfield, Bertrand R. *Sales Administration: Principles and Problems.* 4th ed. Englewood Cliffs, N.J.: Prentice-Hall, Inc., 1961.

Caswell, W. Cameron. "Marketing Effectiveness and Sales Supervision." *California Management Review* (Fall, 1964), pp. 39-44.

Chandler, Alfred D., Jr. *Strategy and Structure: Chapters in the History of the Industrial Enterprise.* Garden City, N.Y.: Doubleday & Co., 1966.

Cherry, Colin. *On Human Communication: A Review, Survey and a Criticism.* New York: John Wiley & Sons, Inc., 1957.

Clark, Donald F., and Ackoff, R.L. "Allocation of Sales Effort in the Lamp Division of the General Electric Company." *Operations Research*, Vol. 4 (December, 1956), pp. 629-47.

Clark, James V. *Education for the Use of Behavioral Science.* Los Angeles, Calif.: Institute of Industrial Relations, University of California, 1962.

Cleveland, E.A. "Sales Personnel Research, 1935-1945: A Review," *Personnel Psychology*, Vol. 1 (1948), pp. 211-55.

Collins, Barry E., and Guetzkow, Harold. *Social Psychology of Group Processes for Decision Making.* New York: John Wiley & Sons, Inc., 1964.

Cooper, W.W., Leavitt, H.J., and Shelley, W.W. II (eds.). *New Perspectives in Organization Research.* New York: John Wiley & Sons, Inc., 1964.

Copeland, H.T. "Relation of Consumer Buying Habits to Marketing Methods," *Harvard Business Review*, Vol. 1 (April, 1923), pp. 282-89.

"Cost of an Industrial Salesman's Call." McGraw-Hill Research Laboratory of Advertising Performance, New York, July 7, 1966.

Couch, D.D. "Measuring, the Effectiveness of Your Salesman," (Marketing Series, No. 93), New York: American Management Association, 1954.

Cox, Donald F. "Clues for Advertising Strategists," *Harvard Business Review* Vol. 39 (September-October, 1961), p. 172.

Cox, David R. *Planning of Experiments.* New York: John Wiley & Sons, Inc., 1958.

Cox, Reavis, Alderson, Wroe, and Shapiro, Stanley J. (eds.). *Theory in Marketing.* Homewood, Ill.: Richard D. Irwin, Inc., 1964.

Crane, Edgar. *Marketing Communications: A Behavioral Approach to Men, Messages, and Media.* New York: John Wiley & Sons, Inc., 1965.

Crisp, Richard D. *Sales Planning and Control.* New York: McGraw-Hill Book, Co., Inc., 1961.

Crissy, W.J.E., and Cash, H.C. *Psychology of Selling.* 12 Vols. Flushing, N.Y.: Personnel Development Associates, 1957-1965.

Cyert, Richard M., and March, James G. *A Behavioral Theory of the Firm.* Englewood Cliffs, N.J.: Prentice-Hall, Inc., 1963.

Davis, James H. *Increasing Wholesale Drug Salesmen's Effectiveness.* Columbus, Ohio: Bureau of Business Research, College of Commerce and Administration, The Ohio State University, 1948.

Dichter, Ernest. *Handbook of Consumer Motivations: The Psychology of the World of Objects.* New York: McGraw-Hill Book Co., Inc., 1964.

Dirksen, Charles J., Kroeger, Arthur, and Lockley, Lawrence C. *Readings in Marketing.* Homewood, Ill.: Richard D. Irwin, Inc., 1963.

"Do Salesmen Like Their Jobs," *Sales Management,* Vol. 89 (December 21, 1962), pp. 34-35.

Dorsey, John T. "A Communication Model for Administration," *Administrative Science Quarterly,* Vol. 2 (December, 1957), pp. 307-24.

Doubman, J. Russell. *Salesmanship and Types of Selling.* New York: Appleton-Century-Crofts, 1939.

Drucker, Peter F. *Landmarks of Tomorrow.* New York: Harper & Row Publishers, 1959.

——. "Controls, Control and Management," in *Management Controls: New Directions in Basic Research.* Edited by Charles P. Bonini, Robert K. Jaedicke, and Harvey M. Wagner. New York: McGraw-Hill Book Co., Inc., 1964, pp. 286-96.

——. *Managing for Results.* New York: Harper & Row Publishers, 1964.

——. "The Executive's Job in Its Three Dimensions" and "Entrepreneurship in Business Enterprise" in Canadian Imperial Bank of Commerce, *Commercial Letter,* Toronto (March, 1965).

——. *The Future of Industrial Man: A Conservative Approach.* New York: The New American Library, Inc., 1965.

Duncan, Delbert J. "Top Management Attitudes Toward Salesmanship in Our Economy." A Survey conducted for the Klein Institute for Aptitude Testing, New York, 1966.

Ellul, Jacques. *Propaganda: The Formation of Men's Attitudes.* Translated by Konrad Kellen and Jean Lerner. New York: Alfred A. Knopf, Inc., 1965.

Etzioni, Amitai. "Authority Structure and Organizational Effectiveness," *Administrative Science Quarterly* (June, 1959), pp. 43-67.

——. *Modern Organizations.* Englewood Cliffs, N.J.: Prentice-Hall, Inc., 1964.

Evans, Franklin B. "Selling as a Dyadic Relationship—A New Approach," *American Behavioral Scientist,* Vol. 6 (May, 1963), pp. 76-79.

Ezekiel, Mordecai, and Fox, Karl A. *Methods of Correlation and Regression Analysis.* New York: John Wiley & Sons, Inc., 1959.

Farley, J.U. "An Optimal Plan for Salesmen's Compensation," *Journal of Marketing Research.* Vol. 1 (May, 1964), pp. 39-43.

Festinger, Leon. *The Theory of Cognitive Dissonance.* New York: Harper & Row Publishers, 1957.

——. "The Theory of Cognitive Dissonance," in *The Science of Human Communication.* Edited by Wilbur Schramm. New York: Basic Books, Inc., 1963, pp. 17-27.

FitzRoy, Peter T. "An Adaptive Model of Promotional Expenditure Determination" Proceedings of the Fall Conference (Washington, D.C.: American Marketing Association, 1965) pp. 370-76.

——. "A Quadratic Adaptive Control Model for Purposive Processes." Unpublished Ph.D. thesis, Purdue University, 1966.

Frank, Lawrence K. *Nature and Human Nature: Man's New Image of Himself.* New Brunswick, N.J.: Rutgers University Press, 1951.

Frey, Albert Wesley (ed.). *Marketing Handbook.* 2d ed. New York: Ronald Press Co., 1965.

Fromm-Reichmann, Frieda. "On Listening," *Interpersonal Dynamics: Essays and Readings on Human Interaction.* Edited by Warren G. Bennis, et al. Homewood, Ill.: Dorsey Press, Inc., 1964, pp. 715-24.

Gadel, M.S. "Concentration by Salesmen on Congenial Prospects," *Journal of Marketing,* Vol. 28 (April, 1964) pp. 64-66.

Gibb, Jack R. "Fear and Facade: Defensive Management," *Science and Human Affairs.* Edited by Richard E. Farson. Palo Alto, Calif.: Science and Behavior Books, Inc., 1965, pp. 197-214.

Goffman, Erving. *The Presentation of Self in Everyday Life.* Garden City, N.Y.: Doubleday Anchor Books, Doubleday & Co., Inc., 1959.

Gottlieb, Morris J. "Segmentation by Personality Types," *Marketing Management and Administrative Action.* Edited by Steuart Henderson Britt and Harper W. Boyd, Jr. New York: McGraw-Hill Book Co., Inc., 1963, pp. 134-42.

Glover, Walter S., and Ackoff, Russell L. "Five Year Planning for an Integrated Operation," *Proceedings of the Conference on Case Studies in Operations Research.* Cleveland: Case Institute of Technology (1956), pp. 38-47.

Green, Paul E., Robinson, Patrick J., and FitzRoy, Peter T. "Advertising Expenditure Models: State of the Art and Prospects." *Business Horizons* (Summer, 1966), pp. 72-80.

——, and Tull, Donald S. *Research for Marketing Decisions.* Englewood Cliffs, N.J.: Prentice-Hall, Inc., 1966.

Gross, Martin L. *The Brain Watchers.* New York: The New American Library Inc., 1962.

Halbert, Michael H. "A Practical and Proven Measure of Advertising Effectiveness," *Proceedings: 6th Annual Conference,* Advertising Research Foundation (N.Y.) (October, 1960), pp. 77-82.

——. *The Meaning and Sources of Marketing Theory.* New York: McGraw-Hill Book Co., Inc., 1965.

Haley, Bernard F. (ed.). *A Survey of Contemporary Economics,* Vol. II, Homewood, Ill.: Richard D. Irwin, Inc., 1952.

Hall, Edward T. *The Silent Language.* Garden City, N.Y.: Doubleday & Co., Inc., 1959.

Hall, Noble. "Productivity Standards—Sales." Speech delivered before the Association of Sales and Marketing Executives, New York, November, 1950.

Harding, Murray. "Who Really Makes the Purchasing Decision?" *Industrial Marketing,* Vol. 51 (September, 1966), pp. 76-81.

Hayakawa, S.I. *Our Language and Our World.* New York: Harper and Row Publishers, 1954.

Hebb, D.O. *The Organization of Behavior: A Neuropsychological Theory.* New York: John Wiley & Sons, Inc., 1949.

Heider, Fritz. *The Psychology of Interpersonal Relations.* New York: John Wiley & Sons, Inc., 1958.

Henderson, Bruce D. "Purchasing's Part in Corporate Strategy," *Purchasing,* Vol. 60 (January 13, 1966), pp. 76-78.

Henry, J. Porter Jr. "The Ten Biggest Mistakes Field Sales Managers Make," *Sales Management,* Vol. 90 (Series of tentatives published from July 5, 1963 through November 15, 1963.)

Herzog, Donald R. "Setting Sales Quotas," *California Management Review,* Vol. III, No. 2 (Winter, 1961) pp. 47-52.

Hileman, Donald G., and Rosenstein, Leonard A. "Deliberations of a Chain Grocery Buying Committee," *Journal of Marketing,* Vol. 25 (January, 1961), pp. 52-55.

Hirsch, Werner F. "Decision Making in Industrial Marketing," *Journal of Marketing,* Vol. 24 (January, 1960), pp. 21-27.

Holton, Richard H. "The Distinction Between Convenience Goods, Shopping Goods, and Specialty Goods," *Journal of Marketing,* Vol. 23 (July, 1958), pp. 53-56.

Homans, George C. *The Human Group.* New York: Harcourt, Brace & World, Inc., 1950.

———. *Social Behavior: Its Elementary Forms.* New York: Harcourt, Brace & World, Inc., 1961.

Horvath, Walter. *How to Overcome Objections in Selling.* Englewood Cliffs, N.J.: Prentice-Hall, Inc., 1954.

Hovland, Carl I., Janis, Irving L., and Kelley, Harold H. *Communication and Persuasion.* New Haven: Yale University Press, 1953.

———, et al. *The Order of Presentation in Persuasion.* New Haven: Yale University Press, 1957.

Howard, John A. *Marketing Management: Analysis and Decision.* Homewood, Ill.: Richard D. Irwin, Inc., 1957.

———. *Marketing: Executive and Buyer Behavior.* New York: Columbia University Press, 1963.

Howton, F. William, and Rosenberg, Bernard. "The Salesman: Ideology and Self-Imagery in a Prototypic Occupation. *Social Research* (Autumn, 1965), pp. 277-98.

Hughes, Lawrence M. "When Salesmen Sound Off," *Sales Management,* Vol. 93 (February 15, 1963), p. 42.

Hummel, Francis E. *Market and Sales Potentials.* New York: Ronald Press Co., 1961.

Huntington, Virginia R. "Some Applications of Statistical Analysis in the Development of Accounting Information for Control." Unpublished Ph.D. dissertation, University of Texas, Austin, Texas, 1962.

Ivey, Paul W. *Salesmanship Applied.* New York: McGraw-Hill Book Co., Inc., 1937.

Janis, Irving L. and Hovland, Carl I. *Personality and Persuasibility.* New Haven: Yale University Press, 1959.

Johnson, Richard A., Kast, Fremont E., and Rosenzweig, James E. *The Theory and Management of Systems.* New York: McGraw-Hill Book Co., Inc., 1963.

Kahn, George N., and Shuchman, Abraham. "Specialize Your Salesmen," *Harvard Business Review,* Vol. 39 (January-February, 1961), pp. 90-98.

Kahn, R.L., and Cannell, C.F. *The Dynamics of Interviewing: Theory, Techniques and Cases.* New York: John Wiley & Sons, Inc., 1957.

Kaiser Aluminum & Chemical Corporation, The. "Communications." *Kaiser Aluminum News,* Vol. 23, No. 3 (1965).

Katz, Daniel, and Kahn, Robert L. *The Social Psychology of Organizations.* New York: John Wiley & Sons, Inc., 1966.

Katz, Elihu, and Lazarsfeld, Paul. *Personal Influence.* New York: The Free Press, 1955.

Kelley, Eugene J., and Lazer, William (eds.). *Managerial Marketing: Perspectives and Viewpoints.* Homewood, Ill.: Richard D. Irwin, Inc., 1958.

Keynes, John Maynard. *The General Theory of Employment, Interest and Money.* London: Macmillan Co., 1961.

Kibbee, Joel M., Craft, Clifford J., and Nanus, Burt. *Management Games: A New Technique for Executive Development.* New York: Reinhold Publishing Corporation, 1961.

King, Whitney Jr. "Exploding Seven Myths about Salesmen," *The American Salesman* (November, 1962), pp. 26–30.

Klapper, Joseph T. *The Effects of Mass Communication.* New York: The Free Press, 1960.

Kluckhohn, Clyde K. *Mirror for Man.* New York: Fawcett World Library, Inc., 1960.

Koontz, Harold. *Toward a Unified Theory of Management.* New York: McGraw-Hill Book Co., Inc., 1964.

Koopman, Bernard O. "The Optimum Distribution of Effort," *Operations Research,* Vol. 1 (February, 1963), pp. 52–63.

Kotler, Philip. "Behavioral Models for Analyzing Buyers," *Journal of Marketing,* Vol. 29 (October, 1965), pp. 37–45.

Langhoff, Peter (ed.). *Models, Measurement and Marketing.* Englewood Cliffs, N.J.: Prentice-Hall, Inc., 1965.

Lapp, Charles L. *Successful Selling Strategies.* New York: McGraw-Hill Book Co., Inc., 1957.

Lawrence, Paul R., *et al. Organizational Behavior and Administration: Cases, Concepts, and Research Findings.* Homewood, Ill.: Dorsey Press, Inc. and Richard D. Irwin, Inc., 1961.

Lawson, Chester A. *Language, Thought and the Human Mind.* East Lansing, Mich.: Michigan State University Press, 1958.

Lazer, William. "The Role of Models in Marketing," *Journal of Marketing,* Vol. 26 (October, 1961), pp. 59–62.

——, and Kelley, Eugene J. "Interdisciplinary Horizons in Marketing," *Journal of Marketing,* Vol. 25 (October, 1960), pp. 24–30.

Leavitt, Harold J. *Managerial Psychology: An Introduction to Individuals, Pairs, and Groups in Organizations.* Chicago: Phoenix Books, University of Chicago Press, 1962.

Lee, Irving J., and Lee, Laura L. *Handling Barriers in Communication.* New York: Harper & Row Publishers, 1956.

Lee, Lauren E. "Guiding and Controlling a Small Scattered Sales Force," *Industrial Marketing,* Vol. 50 (October, 1965), pp. 78–82.

Leenders, Michiel R. *Improving Purchasing Effectiveness Through Supplier Development.* Boston, Mass.: Harvard Business School, 1965.

Leighton, Alexander H. "The Functional Point of View," *Organizational Behavior and Administration: Cases, Concepts and Research Findings.* Edited by Paul Lawrence, *et al.* The Irwin-Dorsey Series in Behavioral Science in Business. Homewood, Ill.: Dorsey Press, Inc. and Richard D. Irwin, Inc., 1961, pp. 26–29.

Levit, Grace, and Jennings, Helen H. "Learning Through Role Playing," *The Planning of Change: Readings in the Applied Behavioral Sciences.* Edited by Warren G. Bennis, Kenneth D. Benne, and Robert Chin. New York: Holt, Rinehart and Winston, Inc., 1962, pp. 706–710.

Levitt, Theodore. *Industrial Purchasing Behavior.* Boston, Mass.: Harvard Business School, 1965.

Lewis, E.H. "Sales Promotion Decisions," *Business News Notes.* Minneapolis: University of Minnesota (November, 1954), pp. 1–5.

Likert, Rensis. *New Patterns of Management.* New York: McGraw-Hill Book Co., Inc., 1961.

Lionberger, Herbert F. *Adoption of New Ideas and Practices.* Ames, Iowa: Iowa State University Press, 1960.

Lippitt, Ronald, Watson, Jeanne, and Westley, Bruce. *The Dynamics of Planned Change: A Comparative Study of Principles and Techniques.* New York: Harcourt, Brace & World, Inc., 1958.

Little, John D.C. "A Model of Adaptive Control of Promotional Spending." Working Paper. Cambridge, Mass.: Alfred P. Sloan School of Management, Massachusetts Institute of Technology, July 1, 1965.

Livingston, J. Sterling, and Davis, Robert T. *Cases in Sales Management*. Homewood, Ill.: Richard D. Irwin, Inc., 1962.

Lockley, Lawrence C. "An Approach to Marketing Theory," *Theory in Marketing*. Edited by Reavis Cox, Wroe Alderson, and Stanley J. Shapiro. Homewood, Ill.: Richard D. Irwin, Inc., 1964, pp. 37-50.

Loen, Raymond O. "Sales Managers Must Manage," *Harvard Business Review*, Vol. 42 (May-June, 1964), pp. 107-14.

Luck, David J. *Marketing Education in the United States*. Philadelphia, Pa.: Marketing Science Institute, 1964.

Maccoby, Nathan "Arguments, Counter-Arguments and Distractions," *The Obstinate Audience*. Edited by Donald E. Payne. Ann Arbor, Mich.: Foundation for Research on Human Behavior, June, 1965, pp. 33-41.

Magee, John F. "The Effect of Promotional Effort on Sales," *Journal of the Operations Research Society of America*, Vol. 1 (1952-53), pp. 64-74.

Maloney, John C. "Is Advertising Believability Really Important?" *Journal of Marketing*, Vol. 27 (October, 1963), pp. 1-8.

March, James G., and Simon, Herbert A. *Organizations*. New York: John Wiley & Sons, Inc., 1958.

Martindale, Don (ed.). *Functionalism in the Social Sciences*. Monograph 5 in a series sponsored by The American Academy of Political and Social Science, Philadelphia, February, 1965.

Maslow, Abraham H. *Motivation and Personality*. New York: February, Harper & Row Publishers, 1954.

——. "Deficiency Motivation and Growth Motivation," *Nebraska Symposium on Motivation*. Edited by Marshall R. Jones. Lincoln, Neb.: University of Nebraska Press, 1955, pp. 1-30.

Mason, John L. "The Low Prestige of Personal Selling," *Journal of Marketing*, Vol. 29 (October, 1965), pp. 7-10.

Masters, Dexter. *The Intelligent Buyer's Guide to Sellers: A Moral Reader in Three Parts*. Mt. Vernon, N.Y.: Consumers Union, 1965.

Mayer, David, and Greenberg, Herbert M. "What Makes a Good Salesman," *Harvard Business Review*, Vol. 42 (July-August, 1964), pp. 119-25.

Maynard, Harold H., and Davis, James H. *Sales Management*. 3d ed. New York: Ronald Press Co., 1957.

McClelland, David C. "Notes for a Revised Theory of Motivation," *Studies in Motivation*. Edited by David C. McClelland. New York: Appleton-Century-Crofts, 1955, pp. 226-34.

McDonough, Adrian M. *Information Economics and Management Systems*. New York: McGraw-Hill Book Co., Inc., 1963.

McGregor, Douglas M. "The Human Side of Enterprise," *The Planning of Change: Readings in the Applied Behavioral Sciences*. Edited by Warren G. Bennis, Kenneth D. Benne, and Robert Chin. New York: Holt, Rinehart and Winston, Inc., 1962, pp. 422-31.

McInnes, William C. "A Conceptual Approach to Marketing," *Theory in Marketing*. Edited by Reavis Cox, Wroe Alderson, and Stanley J. Shapiro. Homewood, Ill.: Richard D. Irwin, Inc., 1964, pp. 51-67.

McLuhan, Marshall. *Understanding Media: The Extensions of Man*. New York: McGraw-Hill Book Co., Inc., 1965.

McMurry, Robert N. "The Mystique of Super Salesmanship," *Harvard Business Review*, Vol. 39 (March-April, 1961), pp. 113-22.

McNeal, James U. (ed.). *Dimensions of Consumer Behavior*. New York: Appleton-Century-Crofts, 1965.

Miles, Lawrence D. *Techniques of Value Analysis and Engineering*. New York: McGraw-Hill Book Co., Inc., 1961.

Miles, Matthew B. "The Training Group," *The Planning of Change: Readings in the Applied Behavioral Sciences*. Edited by Warren G. Bennis, Kenneth D. Benne, and Robert Chin. New York: Holt, Rinehart and Winston, Inc., 1962, pp. 716-25.

Miller, David W., and Starr, Martin K. *Executive Decisions and Operations Research.* Englewood Cliffs, N.J.: Prentice-Hall, Inc., 1960.

Miller, George A. *Mathematics and Psychology.* New York: John Wiley & Sons, Inc., 1964.

Minkin, Jerome M., Brown, James K., and Bailey, Earl L. *Sales Analysis.* New York: National Industrial Conference Board, Inc., 1965.

Miracle, Gordon E. "Product Characteristics and Marketing Strategy," *Journal of Marketing,* Vol. 29 (January, 1965), pp. 18-24.

Mulder, Mark. "Communication Structure, Decison Structure, and Group Performance," *Sociometry* (March, 1960), pp. 1-13.

Myers, Charles A. "Behavioral Sciences for Personnel Managers," *Harvard Business Review,* Vol. 44 (July-August, 1966), pp. 154-62.

National Industrial Conference Board, Inc. *Measuring Salesmen's Performance.* Business Policy Study No. 114. New York: National Industrial Conference Board, 1965.

Nelson, John L. "The Low Prestige of Personal Selling," *Journal of Marketing,* Vol. 29 (October, 1965), pp. 7-10.

Newman, Joseph W. "Put Research into Marketing Decisions," *Harvard Business Review,* Vol. 40 (March-April, 1962), pp. 105-12.

Ogden, C.K., and Richards, I.A. *The Meaning of Meaning.* New York: Harcourt, Brace & World, Inc., 1945.

O'Shaughnessy, J. *Work Study Applied to a Sales Force.* London, England: British Institute of Management, 1965.

Packard, Vance. *The Hidden Persuaders.* New York: Pocket Books, Inc., 1958.

___. *The Waste Makers.* New York: Pocket Books, Inc., 1963.

Palda, Kristian S. "Sales Effects of Advertising: A Review of the Literature," *Journal of Advertising Research,* Vol. 4 (September, 1964).

Papandreou, Andreas G. "Some Basic Problems in the Theory of the Firm," *A Survey of Contemporary Economics.* Edited by Bernard F. Haley. Homewood, Ill.: Richard D. Irwin, Inc., 1952, Vol. II, pp. 183-219.

Parsons, Talcott. *The Structure of Social Action.* New York: McGraw-Hill Book Co., Inc., 1937.

___. *Essays in Sociological Theory.* Rev. ed. New York: The Free Press, 1954.

___. "Present Position and Prospects of Systematic Theory in Sociology," *Essays in Sociological Theory,* Rev. ed. New York: The Free Press, 1954, pp. 212-37.

___. "Pattern Variables Revisited: A Response to Robert Dubin," *American Sociological Review,* Vol. 25 (August, 1960), pp. 467-83.

___, Bales, Robert F., and Shils, Edward A. *Working Papers in the Theory of Action.* New York: The Free Press, 1953.

___, and Shils, Edward A. (eds.). *Toward a General Theory of Action.* Cambridge, Mass.: Harvard University Press, 1952.

___, and Smelser, Neil J. *Economy and Society: A Study in the Integration of Economic and Social Theory.* New York: The Free Press, 1956.

Payne, Donald E. (ed.). *The Obstinate Audience.* Ann Arbor, Mich.: Foundation for Research on Human Behavior, June, 1965.

Phelps, D. Maynard, and Westing, J. Howard. *Marketing Management.* Homewood, Ill.: Richard D. Irwin, Inc., 1960.

"Profiles in Purchasing; How Large Manufacturers Buy." *Sales Management,* Vol. 90 (April 5, 1963), pp. 121-22.

Rapoport, Anatol. *Operational Philosophy: Integrating Knowledge and Action.* New York: Science Editions, John Wiley & Sons, Inc., 1965.

Reichard, Robert. *Practical Techniques of Sales Forecasting.* New York: McGraw-Hill Book Co., Inc., 1966.

Rich, K.A. "An Adaptive Control System for Promotional Spending." Unpublished working paper, Wharton School of Finance and Commerce, University of Pennsylvania, 1966.

Rieser, Carl. "The Salesman Isn't Dead—He's Different," (Distribution Upheaval, 5th Article), *Fortune,* Vol. 66 (November, 1962), p. 124.

Roberts, Alan A. "Applying the Strategy of Market Segmentation," *Business Horizons* (Fall, 1961), pp. 65–72.

Robinson, Patrick J. "R & D in Marketing Management," *The Membership Conference of the Marketing Science Institute.* Proceedings. Philadelphia, Pa.: Marketing Science Institute (May 25, 1965), pp. 1–65.

——, and Faris, Charles W. *Industrial Buying and Creative Marketing.* Boston: Allyn and Bacon, Inc., 1967.

——, and Luck, David J. *Promotional Decision Making: Practice and Theory.* New York: McGraw-Hill Book Co., Inc., 1964.

Roethlisberger, F.J. "Training Supervisors in Human Relations," *Harvard Business Review*, Vol. 29 (September–October, 1951), pp. 47–57.

Rogers, Carl R., and Roethlisberger, F.J. "Barriers and Gateways to Communication," *Harvard Business Review,* Vol. 30 (July–August, 1952), pp. 46–52.

Rogers, E.M. *Diffusion of Innovation.* New York: The Free Press, 1962.

"Salesman's Nemesis: The Computer," *Sales Management,* Vol. 90 (April 5, 1963), pp. 44–46.

"The Salesman's Role at P & G," *Sales Management,* Vol. 89 (October 19, 1962), pp. 71–72.

Sawyer, Howard G. "Can Ads Sell as Well as Salesmen?" *Printer's Ink* (July 16, 1954), pp. 28–30.

Schiff, Michael, and Mellman, Martin. *Financial Management of the Marketing Function.* New York: Financial Executives Research Foundation, 1962.

Schiffman, Leon G. "Programmed Instruction: Its Use in Sales Training," *Industrial Marketing,* Vol. 50 (February, 1965), pp. 82–86.

Schein, Edgar H., and Bennis, Warren G. *Personal and Organizational Change Through Group Methods: The Laboratory Approach.* New York: John Wiley & Sons, Inc., 1965.

Schlain, Bert H. *The Professional Approach to Modern Salesmanship.* New York: McGraw-Hill Book Co., Inc., 1966.

Schramm, Wilbur (ed.). *The Science of Human Communication: New Directions and New Findings in Communication Research.* New York: Basic Books Inc., 1963.

Schwartz, Kenneth. "The Switch to Specialized Sales," *Duns' Review and Modern Industry* (August, 1962), pp. 43–47.

Semlow, W. "How Many Salesmen Do You Need?" *Harvard Business Review,* Vol. 37 (May–June, 1959), pp. 126–32.

Semon, Thomas T. "Assumptions in Measuring Advertising Effectiveness," *Journal of Marketing,* Vol. 28 (July, 1964), pp. 43–44.

Shannon, Claude E., and Weaver, Warren, *The Mathematical Theory of Communication.* Urbana, Ill.: University of Illinois Press, 1949.

Shaw, Michael S. "Are You Communicating?" *The Business Quarterly,* Vol. 31 (Summer, 1966), pp. 63–68.

Shaw, Steven J., and Thompson, Joseph W. *Salesmanship: Modern Viewpoints on Personal Communication.* New York: Holt, Rinehart and Winston, Inc., 1960.

Shepard, Herbert A. "The T-Group as Training in Observant Participation," *The Planning of Change: Readings in the Applied Behavioral Sciences.* Edited by Warren G. Bennis, Kenneth D. Benne, and Robert Chin. New York: Holt, Rinehart and Winston, Inc., 1962, pp. 637–43.

Shockey, Ralph. "Selling Is a Science: The New Consumer," *Department Store Economist* (April, 1965), pp. 24–27.

Simon, Herbert A. *Administrative Behavior.* 2d ed. New York: Macmillan Co., 1957.

Slote, C.T. "Keying Sales Calls to Profits," *Dun's Review and Modern*

Industry, Vol. 76 (November, 1960), pp. 42-44.

Smith, Abbott P. *How To Sell Intangibles.* Englewood Cliffs, N.J.: Prentice-Hall, Inc., 1958.

Smith, Henry Clay. *Sensitivity to People.* New York: McGraw-Hill Book Co., Inc., 1966.

Smith, Wendell R. "Product Differentiation and Market Segmentation as Alternative Marketing Strategies," *Journal of Marketing,* Vol. 21 (July, 1956), pp. 3-8.

Spencer, Robert F. "The Nature and Value of Functionalism in Anthropology," *Functionalism in the Social Sciences.* Edited by Don Martindale. Monograph 5 in a series sponsored by the Academy of Political and Social Science, Philadelphia, February, 1965, pp. 1-17.

Stanton, William J., and Buskirk, Richard H. *Management of the Sales Force.* Homewood, Ill.: Richard D. Irwin, Inc., 1962.

Star, Shirley A., and Hughes, Helen M. "Report on an Educational Campaign: The Cincinnati Plan for the United Nations," *American Journal of Sociology,* Vol. 55 (January, 1950), pp. 389-400.

Stevens, Samuel N. "The Application of Social Science Findings to Selling and the Salesman," *Marketing Management and Administrative Action.* Edited by Steuart Henderson Britt, and Harper W. Boyd, Jr. New York: McGraw-Hill Book Co., Inc., 1963, pp. 601-10.

Stickney, Richard W. "Deploying Multi Line Salesmen," *Harvard Business Review,* Vol. 38 (March, 1960), pp. 110 12.

Tannenbaum, Robert, Weschler, Irving R., and Massarik, Fred. "The Process of Understanding People," *Interpersonal Dynamics: Essays and Readings on Human Interaction.* Edited by Warren G. Bennis, *et al.* Homewood, Ill.: Dorsey Press, Inc., 1964, pp. 725-40.

Taylor, Donald W. "Toward an Information Processing Theory of Motivation," *Nebraska Symposium on Motivation.* Edited by Marshall R. Jones. Lincoln, Neb.: University of Nebraska Press, 1960, pp. 51-79.

Taylor, Frederick W. *The Principles of Scientific Management.* New York: Harper & Row Publishers, 1911.

Thayer, Lee. *Administrative Communication.* Homewood, Ill.: Richard D. Irwin, Inc., 1961.

——. "On Theory Building in Communication: I. Some Conceptual Problems," *Journal of Communication* (December, 1963), pp. 217-35.

——. "Data, Information, Decision: Some Perspectives on Marketing as a Communication System," *Concepts for Advertising Proceedings* from the 8th Annual Meeting of the American Academy of Advertising at Miami Beach, June, 1966.

——. "Communication and Organization," *Human Communication Theory.* Edited by Frank E. X. Dance. New York: Holt, Rinehart and Winston, Inc., 1967.

Thompson, Joseph W. *Selling: A Behavioral Science Approach.* New York: McGraw-Hill Book Co., Inc., 1966.

Thorpe, Merle. *The Greatest Opportunity in the World: Selling.* New York: Hawthorn Books, Inc., 1957.

Torgerson, Warren S. *Theory and Methods of Scaling.* New York: John Wiley & Sons, Inc., 1958.

Tosdal, Harry R. *Principles of Personal Selling.* New York: McGraw-Hill Book Co., Inc., 1925.

——. "How To Design the Salesman's Compensation Plan," *Harvard Business Review,* Vol. 31 (September-October, 1953), pp. 61-70.

Tucker, W.T. *The Social Context of Economic Behavior.* New York: Holt, Rinehart and Winston, Inc., 1964.

——, and Painter, John J. "Personality and Product Use," *Dimensions of Consumer Behavior.* Edited by James U. McNeal. New York: Appleton-Century-Crofts, 1965, pp. 75-82.

Vizza, Robert F. *Improving Salesmen's Use of Time.* New York: Sales
Executives Club of New York, Inc., 1963.
——. *Measuring the Value of the Field Sales Force.* New York: Sales Execu-
tives Club of New York, 1964.
——. *Training and Developing the Field Sales Manager.* New York: Sales
Executives Club of New York, 1965.
Weintraub, Sidney. *Intermediate Price Theory.* Philadelphia, Pa.: Chilton
Books, 1964.
Weiss, Edward B. *The Vanishing Salesman.* New York: McGraw-Hill Book
Co., Inc., 1962.
Weitzenhoffer, A.M. "Mathematical Structures and Psychological Measure-
ments," *Psychometrika,* XVI (December, 1951), pp. 387-406.
"What Are the Best Sales Aids for Industrial Salesmen?" *Industrial Mar-
keting,* Vol. 50 (October, 1965), pp. 96-98.
Wheeler, Elmer. *Tested Ways To Close the Sale.* New York: Harper & Row
Publishers, 1957.
"When Workers Manage Themselves," *Business Week* (March 20, 1965),
pp. 93-95.
White, Robert W. "Motivation Reconsidered: The Concept of Competence,"
Psychological Review, Vol. 46 (September, 1959), pp. 297-333.
Whyte, William F., *et al. Money and Motivation: An Analysis of Incentives
in Industry.* New York: Harper & Row Publishers, 1955.
Whyte, William H. Jr. *The Organization Man.* Garden City, N.Y.: Doubleday
Anchor Books, Doubleday & Co., Inc., 1957.
Wiener, Norbert. *The Human Use of Human Beings: Cybernetics and Society,*
2d ed. rev. Garden City, N.Y.: Doubleday Anchor Books, Doubleday
and Co., Inc., 1954.
Wolfe, H. Deane, and Albaum, Gerald. "Inequality in Products, Orders,
Customers, Salesmen, and Sales Territories," *Journal of Business*
(July, 1962), pp. 298-301.
Zion, Roger H. *Keys to Human Relations in Selling.* Englewood Cliffs, N.J.:
Prentice-Hall, Inc., 1963.

Index